The Financial Programs of Alexander Hamilton

by a Farmer's Daughter

Dianne L. Durante

2021

Copyright, Credits, Acknowledgments

Copyright © 2021 Dianne L. Durante. All rights reserved. For permission to publish lengthy excerpts, contact DuranteDianne@gmail.com.

COVER

Adapted from a series cover design by Allegra Durante (www.allegradurante.com). The cover photo shows a plaster model of Carl Conrads's *Alexander Hamilton*, 1880, at the Museum of American Finance, New York. Supporters' copies of the book have on the spine an image of Augustus Saint Gaudens's "double eagle" gold coin (photo: Jaclyn Nash for the National Numismatic Collection, National Museum of American History / Wikipedia).

ACKNOWLEDGMENTS

Dr. Raymond Niles, Senior Fellow of the American Institute for Economic Research, read a draft with an economist's sharp eye. Michael Newton (http://michaelenewton.com), one of the foremost contemporary scholars on Hamilton, gave valuable comments. John Herzog, Founder and Chairman Emeritus of the Museum of American Finance, graciously allowed me to use images of early American currency and bonds from his collection (pp. 26, 94, and 132). As always, thanks to my sister Jan Robinson for her meticulous proofreading. Any errors that remain are my own responsibility. And to my husband Sal, who aids and abets my need to wrestle with topics such as this one: my thanks to you would fill a Hamilton-size report.

DEDICATION

Dedicated with fond memories to Rand Scholet, Founder of the Alexander Hamilton Awareness Society, for his interest and encouragement over the two years it took to write this book. I wish he could have read the final version. Rand will be missed by all Hamiltonians for his encyclopedic knowledge of Hamilton's life, for his enthusiasm, and for the way he kept the lines of communication open among all the scholars writing on Hamilton today. We miss you already, Rand.

First published 9/11/2021 via Amazon. This version 12/21/2022.

Table of Contents

Copyright, Credits, Acknowledgment 2
Chapter 1: Introduction 4
Chapter 2: The Gordian Knot, Economic Problems in the
  United States in the Late 1780s 12
Chapter 3: Hamilton's Life As It Relates to the Gordian Knot 37
Chapter 4: Policy Paper #1, *First Report on Public Credit* 81
Chapter 5: Policy Paper #2, *Report on a National Bank* 118
Chapter 6: Policy Paper #3, *Report on Manufactures* 133
Chapter 7: Crises of 1790-1795 and Hamilton's Resignation 147
Chapter 8: The Gordian Knot by 1801 171
Chapter 9: Evaluating Hamilton's Programs 184
Appendix 1: *First Report on Public Credit*, with outline headings. 193
Appendix 2: *Report on a National Bank,* with outline headings 235
Appendix 3: *Report on Manufactures,* with outline headings 273
Appendix 4: A Selection of Primary Sources Related to
  the Panic of 1792 355
Appendix 5: A List of Important Writings by Hamilton
  Related to His Financial Programs and to the Threads of the
  Gordian Knot 375
Appendix 6: Select Bibliography 389
About the Author, Dianne L. Durante 392

Many thanks for their support of this publication to John Cerasuolo, Brian Lessing, G.A. Mudge, Godfrey Joseph, Rebecca Wrenn Jones, Carrie Lee-Rickard, Pasquale Giordano, and David W. Sanderson. Special thanks to Adam Reed, E.M. Allison, Jeri Eagan, and Duncan Curry, who have supported my work with substantial recurring payments.
To become a supporter, visit
https://diannedurantewriter.com/sunday-recommendations/

Sculptures of Hamilton outdoors in New York City

Above left: by Carl Conrads, 1880. Central Park, just west of the Metropolitan Museum of Art.

Above center: by William Ordway Partridge, 1892. 287 Convent Ave., near Hamilton Grange National Memorial.

Above right: by William Ordway Partridge, 1908. Columbia University.

Left: by Adolph A. Weinman, ca. 1940. Museum of the City of New York.

For *Alexander Hamilton: A Brief Biography:* https://diannedurantewriter.com/archives/4870. For *Alexander Hamilton: A Friend to America*, in 2 volumes: https://diannedurantewriter.com/archives/4870. For *Alexander Hamilton and the Reynolds Affair:* https://diannedurantewriter.com/archives/9819. The Reynolds book is an expanded version of a talk presented at Fraunces Tavern Museum on 1/10/2019, under the auspices of the Alexander Hamilton Awareness Society.

CHAPTER 1

Introduction

What makes this book on Alexander Hamilton's financial programs unique? Mainly this: we'll be looking at the programs from the perspective of Hamilton's contemporaries, using primary sources. In late 1789, what would the man who cornered Secretary Hamilton in a tavern, or the woman who sat across from him at a dinner party, tell Hamilton he urgently needed to fix? How did Hamilton's programs address those crises? And what made those programs so useful that the programs remained in place long after the crises of the 1780s and 1790s were resolved?

1.1 MY HISTORY WITH HAMILTON

Let me explain why I'm tackling this particular problem in this particular way. Around 2001, when I started writing on sculpture in New York City, I discovered that the city's outdoor spaces included four life-size sculptures of Alexander Hamilton. (See facing page.) Ummm, Alexander who? At the time, Hamilton was little known and less discussed. Apparently he got his face on the $10 bill because he was first secretary of the Treasury: yawn.

But the more I learned about the man, the more I admired him. In 2004, after reading Chernow's *Alexander Hamilton*, I put together a short biography of Hamilton wrapped around a walking tour of sculptures of him in New York. The highlight of the tour was having participants read aloud substantial quotes from Hamilton's works. In 2012 I turned the walking tour into an ebook, *Alexander Hamilton: A Brief Biography*.

When *Hamilton: An American Musical* burst on the scene in 2015, I couldn't afford tickets. I distracted myself by writing some seventy blog posts on Hamilton during 2016 and 2017. At first, I was "illustrating" the lyrics to the musical with letters and essays by Hamilton and his contemporaries. As tends to happen with me, however, the project ballooned. It ended up being a deep dive into primary sources for Hamilton's life and times. Founders Online (https://founders.archives.gov/) made this infinitely easier than it had been in 2004. In 2017, I published the blog posts in two volumes (*Alexander Hamilton: A Friend to America*), along with a revamped version of the brief biography from 2012 that included cross-references to the two-volume set.

Even after all those blog posts, there were a few issues about Hamilton's life that I wanted to study further. One was the Reynolds affair. Given that he loved his wife and family, why did Hamilton choose to have an affair with Maria Reynolds? Why did he publish a pamphlet five years later telling the whole world about it? And (speaking of sexcapades) did he really have a fling with Angelica? After extensive research of primary sources and context, I settled those questions to my satisfaction: see *Alexander Hamilton and the Reynolds Affair*.

1.2 HOW THIS BOOK CAME ABOUT

Another unresolved issue: despite having read all Hamilton's policy papers and a great deal of scholarly commentary on them, I didn't actually understand why Hamilton proposed those particular financial programs, what they accomplished, or how they accomplished it. The people who wrote about them naturally tended to be economists. Being an economic ignoramus, I was constantly struggling to "translate" what they said into terms I could grasp.

It occurred to me that if I went back to the primary sources, I could perhaps get a better grip on Hamilton's programs. Although Hamilton was financially savvy, he was not an economist. Nor were any of his American contemporaries. But 80% or more of Americans in Hamilton's time were farmers, and I am, in fact (as the title says), a farmer's daughter. Learning the farmers' context and then reading Hamilton's explanations of his programs might finally allow me to understand the programs.

This book is written for people like me, who admire Hamilton but don't understand what he accomplished as secretary of the Treasury, or why or how. Why bother? Because Americans in the 1790s were real people with serious problems, many of which remain relevant today. Understanding how they solved their problems can help us understand how to solve ours.

Fair warning: I'm fanatical about reading primary sources. Repeating what other scholars say third- and fourth-hand eventually results in errors and misinterpretations. Furthermore, history, like a novel, is much more gripping if it's told with dialogue rather than third-person exposition. Hamilton loves to explain himself. Whenever possible I let him do the talking, on topics that range from his financial programs to extinguishing the debt and extolling the achievements of Federalist presidents. I've also included many statements by Hamilton's contemporaries, from Jefferson's description of the residence-assumption compromise to a 1796 treaty with Tripoli.

Many of these primary sources appear in double-column footnotes. They comprise about a third of the main text. If you're not already familiar with Hamilton's financial programs, I strongly suggest you focus on the main text, and dip into the footnotes only when a topic particularly interests you.

1.3 STRUCTURE OF THE BOOK

This book falls into four sections. In the first (Chapters 1-2), we look at context: the situation of the United States in 1789, when Hamilton took office as secretary of the Treasury. To discover what the man in the tavern and the woman at the dinner party worried about, I read hundreds of primary sources, including (but not limited to) letters to and from Hamilton. Then I read scholarly works on Hamilton's life and programs, looking especially for primary sources I might have missed, and for facets of his programs that I might not have considered. After that, I went back and reviewed the primary sources, to make sure I could substantiate any generalization I made (or that other scholars made) with contemporary documents. From this reading and rereading, I came up with a list of five interconnected crises that Hamilton and the United States faced in 1789. In Chapter 2, we look at the threads of this "Gordian Knot".

In the next section of the book (Chapter 3), we look at Hamilton's life as it relates to the threads of the Gordian Knot. His knowledge, experience, and premises determine the skills he brought to his position as secretary of the Treasury, the results he wanted to achieve, and the programs he was able to conceive and have implemented.

Hamilton wrote three major policy papers: the *First Report on Public Credit*, January 1790; the *Report on a National Bank*, December 1790; and the *Report on Manufactures,* December 1791. In the third section of the book (Chapters 4-6), we look at how these policy papers addressed the Gordian Knot. The full text of the three papers is printed in Appendixes 1, 2, and 3 (pages 193-354). If you're interested enough to read a book on Hamilton's programs, you should certainly read his policy papers. But since reading eighteenth-century prose can be difficult, I've added outline headings to make it easier to follow Hamilton's line of thought.

The final section of the book covers the aftermath of Hamilton's term as secretary of the Treasury. In Chapter 7, we look at the crises of the 1790s. In Chapter 8, we look at the state of the Gordian Knot in 1801, when Thomas Jefferson (the first non-Federalist president) took office. In Chapter 9, we step back for an overview of how Hamilton's programs alleviated the crises of the 1780s and 1790s, and why the programs lasted after the crises were gone.

I'll be arguing that Hamilton created his financial programs based on his understanding of the Constitution plus his own observations, principles, experience, and knowledge. That included facts and perspectives gained from extensive reading in politics and economics, and from correspondence with some of the foremost figures in the United States. I'll show how his programs were integrated with each other—a major factor in their success. And I'll argue that in proposing

1773	Tea Act; Boston Tea Party
1774	First Continental Congress resolves to boycott British goods
1775	Battles of Lexington and Concord; Washington appointed commander-in-chief
1776	Declaration of Independence
1777	Articles of Confederation drafted; Burgoyne surrenders to Gates at Saratoga, NY
1778	Valley Forge (winter 1777-78); French alliance; Battle of Monmouth
1779	
1780	British capture Charleston, SC; Benedict Arnold defects
1781	Articles of Confederation approved; British surrender at Yorktown
1782	
1783	Treaty signed with Great Britain; British evacuate New York City
1784	
1785	
1786	Annapolis Convention; Shays' Rebellion
1787	Constitutional Convention
1788	Constitution ratified
1789	First Congress convenes; Washington inaugurated

these programs, Hamilton aimed to promote a federal government that was limited, but energetic enough to protect rights; and also, to promote a diverse economy run by individuals pursuing their own interests and happiness.

Aside from Appendixes 1-3, which contain Hamilton's major reports, I've included a selection of primary sources related to the Panic of 1792 (Appendix 4) and a list of Hamilton's most important writings regarding his financial programs and the threads of the Gordian Knot (Appendix 5). Appendix 6 is a bibliography of the scholarly works I found most useful in my research.

1.4 CAVEATS: WHAT WE WON'T COVER IN THIS BOOK

This book is not about how Hamilton moved the United States from the stagnation of the 1780s to the nation that's home to Silicon Valley and Disney World. Looking back with the experience and knowledge gleaned over two hundred years is obviously a valuable exercise. But if we're judging Hamilton as a person, we need to understand his context and the goals he was trying to achieve in his own time. This book is an attempt to get a nitty-gritty understanding of that.

A second caveat: I'm not an economist, so I will not be discussing Hamilton's programs in modern economic terms. If you're looking for a discussion of macroeconomic effects, liquidity problems, information asymmetry, the capital asset pricing model, or whether Hamilton was a *dirigiste* ... this is the wrong book for you.

A third caveat: For the sake of space, I'm focusing on the programs Hamilton proposed during his tenure as secretary of the Treasury. I won't be discussing in detail his proposals before 1789, or his writings on economics after he resigned as secretary in early 1795.

And finally: I'm not discussing Hamilton's economic programs from the point of view of constitutional law. If you're looking for a discussion of the long-term effects of Hamilton's interpretations of implied powers, the general welfare clause, and so on, then again, this is not the book for you. (For that, you might want to read, for starters, Carson Holloway, *Hamilton versus Jefferson in the Washington Administration*.)

1.5 POLITICAL SITUATION OF THE UNITED STATES IN THE 1780S

For the sake of context, we'll begin with a brief overview of the political situation in the United States in late 1789, when Hamilton took office as secretary of the Treasury. As you read this section and Chapters 2-6, try to imagine yourself in the position of a forty-something American in Hamilton's time. That will help you keep the right perspective: that you're in the middle of a crisis and you have no idea what to do, or what's going to happen.

This is what we, as American citizens in late 1789, remember.

The Revolutionary War began in 1775. In 1781, the British under General Cornwallis surrendered at Yorktown. By that point some of us had been in the army for years. Even if we weren't, we all vividly remember six years of death and destruction all around us. About one percent of the American population died, among them some of our family and friends. We won't quickly forget the war, or the tyrannical acts of the British crown that forced us to fight.

In late 1783, the United States signed a peace treaty with Great Britain. We broke free from the nation with the strongest army and navy in the world, and the most productive economy! So far, so good. But within a few years, our new country began to fall apart. General Washington, our commander-in-chief for eight years, lamented in 1786 that the United States was falling into "anarchy and confusion." <u>Many of us agree.</u>

<u>Many of us agree</u>

Hamilton to Washington, 3/24/1783: "The centrifugal is much stronger than the centripetal force in these states; the seeds of disunion much more numerous than those of union."
https://founders.archives.gov/documents/Hamilton/01-03-02-0191

Tench Tilghman of Maryland (former aide-de-camp of Washington) to Matthew Tilghman, 2/5/1786: "We are at this point in time the most contemptible and abject nation on the face of the earth. We have neither reputation abroad nor union at home. We hang together merely because it is not in the interest of any other power to shake us to pieces ..."

Quoted in Charles Rappleye, *Robert Morris: Financier of the American Revolution*, p. 426; see also "Memoir of Lieut. Col. Tench Tilghman," published in Albany, 1876. https://tile.loc.gov/storage-services/service/gdc/lhbcb/22944/22944.pdf

Arthur Lee (physician, lawyer, diplomat and Congressman) to Richard Henry Lee, 4/19/1786: "We have independence without the means of attaining it; and are a nation without one source of national defense .... The Confederation is crumbling to pieces."

Quoted in Rappleye, *Morris*, p. 426.

Washington to Madison, 1/5/1786: "No morn ever dawned more favourable than ours did—and no day was ever more clouded than the present! Without some alteration in our political creed, the superstructure we have been seven years raising at the expence of much blood and treasure, must fall. We are fast verging to anarchy & confusion!"

https://founders.archives.gov/documents/Madison/01-09-02-0070

HAMILTON'S FINANCIAL PROGRAMS

In September 1786, delegates from five states met in Maryland to discuss commercial disputes among the states. The delegates at Annapolis called for a meeting of all thirteen states to discuss revising the Articles of Confederation.

Despite some resistance from individual states, the Constitutional Convention was held from May to September 1787. By June 1788, the Constitution had been ratified by nine states. Elections followed for president of the United States and representatives to the federal legislature. The first Congress under the new Constitution convened in March 1789. Washington was inaugurated as president on April 30, 1789. Hamilton was nominated and confirmed as secretary of the Treasury on September 11, 1789.

So here we are, still in a state of crisis. We all agree that we don't want to fall back under the rule of King George III and the British Parliament. But otherwise, we don't have an agenda. Perhaps the best we can do is work toward the opposite of the grievances set out in the Declaration of Independence. To wit:

- We want to elect our own representatives, and we want them to make laws that fit our situation.
- When we have a dispute, we want a functioning system of courts and judges.
- We want a military that protects us against attacks, but doesn't elevate itself above the civilian authorities.
- We want to keep what we produce, not have it taxed away without our consent.
- We want to trade with whom we please.

In short, we want to make our own living as best we can, without interference from the government or the military. Life, liberty, and the pursuit of happiness: that's what the Declaration of Independence said. That's what we fought for. We are holding our collective breath that the brand-new, untried system of government set out in the Constitution can deliver that.

If we run into Secretary of the Treasury Alexander Hamilton in late 1789 and have a chance to bend his ear, what will we tell him are the problems he urgently needs to deal with?

Andre Castaigne (d. 1930), Alexander the Great cutting the Gordian Knot. Image: Wikipedia

Gordian Knot: After I'd written most of this book, I discovered that Hamilton himself had used "Gordian Knot", but in a different sense, referring to the division of power between state and federal governments. "But though it is admitted that the course pursued by the Convention was the most expedient—yet it is not the less true that the plan involved inherent and great difficulties. It may not unaptly be styled the Gordian Knot of our political situation. To me there appeared but one way of untying or severing it, which was in practice to leave the states under as little necessity as possible of exercising the power of taxation. The narrowness of the limits of its exercise on one side left the field more free and unembarrassed to the other and avoided essentially the interference, and collisions to be apprehended inherent in the plan of concurrent jurisdiction." Hamilton, "Defense of the Funding System," July 1795

https://founders.archives.gov/documents/Hamilton/01-19-02-0001

CHAPTER 2

The Gordian Knot: Economic Problems in the United States in the Late 1780s

Once upon a time, in the kingdom of Phrygia (modern Turkey), an ox-cart was roped to a pole with an intricately complex knot. The rope's ends were worked into the knot so that neither could be seen. An oracle proclaimed that the man who could unravel this perplexing knot would rule all of Asia.

In the late fourth century BC, Alexander the Great heard the prophecy, saw the knot ... and sliced through it with his sword. Ever since, "Gordian Knot" has been used to refer to a problem so complex that it's insoluble, if approached conventionally.

By 1789, America's economic problems are a Gordian Knot. Five major issues are so closely intertwined that none can be solved in isolation. We'll look at these starting with the most personal and immediate—the one we can't ignore, even if we don't give a fig for economics in the abstract or for politics on a national scale.

2.1 FIRST THREAD IN THE GORDIAN KNOT: MAKING A LIVING

Making a living is a matter of simple and immediate self-interest. How do we earn enough to survive and prosper?

Making a living has been difficult for most of us for the past fifteen years or so. Some of us spent years in the army. Even if we didn't,

---

Gordian Knot: see facing page.

Self-interest: On the understanding of self-interest among Americans of the Revolutionary War generation, see C. Bradley Thompson, *America's Revolutionary Mind, A Moral History of the American Revolution and the Declaration That Defined It* (2019), Chapter 6.

beginning in 1775, armies from both sides commandeered our goods, crops, and livestock. The British burned our towns and disrupted our trade. We are short not only of foreign-made luxury items such as silks and wine, but of basics such as plows, gunpowder, woolen cloth, and glass.

Why don't we Americans produce such items for ourselves?

2.1.1 Economic situation of the British colonies in North America

Under British rule, the thirteen American colonies on the Atlantic coast had a symbiotic relationship with the mother country—an arrangement that made sense because of their relative population densities. In Great Britain, all the decent farmland had been claimed for centuries. Many British had immigrated to the American colonies for the sake of owning parcels of the vast, fertile tracts available there. By the time the Revolutionary War broke out, farmers comprised more than 80% of the colonial population. Two and a half million Americans were scattered over 430,000 square miles, resulting in an average population density of barely six people per square mile.

Britain, on the other hand, had a population of about six million in 50,000 square miles, for an average density of about 120 people per square mile. That's far too crowded for farming, but very convenient if you want to hire workers for a factory. By the late eighteenth century, the factories of the Industrial Revolution were springing up across England. Only 40% of British were farmers. Most of the others were involved in trade or manufacturing.

An economy that depends on manufacturers needs a constant supply of raw materials, as well as reliable markets for finished goods. Before the Revolution, the American colonies provided the materials and the market. By inclination and in accordance with British law,

---

Farmers comprised more than 80%: These numbers are estimates because the first United States census, in 1790, did not ask for occupations. In *Financial Founding Fathers* (p. 4), Wright estimated that at the end of the Revolutionary War, at least 9 of 10 Americans worked in agriculture. McDonald stated that around 1789, most American families—possibly 80% of non-slaves—owned their own farms (*Hamilton*, p. 119). According to the tables at Digital History (ID 3837), by 1800, 83% of Americans worked on farms; the number held at that level through 1810, but by 1820 began dropping steadily, to 53% by 1860.

https://www.digitalhistory.uh.edu/disp_textbook.cfm?smtID=11&psid=3837

American colonists sent the mother country raw materials such as cotton, leather, furs, iron, wood, indigo, and tobacco. In Britain, the raw materials were transformed into manufactured goods. Goods that the colonists needed or wanted were then shipped back to America.

Much of the trade was carried on in American ships—a boon for American merchants. On the other hand, owners of large plantations—land rich but cash poor—often fell deeply into debt for luxury imported goods. By 1776, George Washington and Thomas Jefferson both <u>owed substantial sums to British merchants</u>.

2.1.2 Economic situation of the United States during and immediately after the Revolutionary War

The Revolutionary War crippled the symbiotic relationship between America and Great Britain. For the duration, Britain stopped buying American raw materials and stopped sending finished goods. The British navy, the best in the world, blockaded American ports, causing trade with other countries to slow to a trickle.

After the war, Britain did not forgive and forget. She had lost 25,000 to 40,000 men in the fighting and gone deeply into debt for military expenses. The British government imposed severe restrictions on American trade with Britain and British colonies, including those in the West Indies—a major market for American goods. Shipments of American fish, beef, and whale oil were prohibited in British ports. Shipments of grain were permitted, but heavily taxed. Before the war,

---

Owed substantial sums to British merchants: Wright (*Hamilton Unbound*, p. 40) notes that in 1776, colonists in Maryland and points south owed almost 2.5 million pounds sterling to British merchants.

Jefferson to Thomas Adams, 6/1/1771: "I must alter one article in the invoice. I wrote therein for a Clavichord. I have since seen a Forte-piano and am charmed with it. Send me this instrument then instead of the Clavichord. Let the case be of fine mahogany, solid, not vineered. The compass from Double G. to F. in alt. a plenty of spare strings; and the workmanship of the whole very handsome, and worthy the acceptance of a lady for whom I intend it. I must add also ½ doz. pr. India cotton stockings for myself @10/ sterl. per pair. ½doz. pr. best white silk do.; and a large Umbrella with brass ribs covered with green silk, and neatly finished. By this change of the Clavichord into a Forte-piano and addition of the other things I shall be brought in debt to you, to discharge which I will ship you of the first tobaccos I get to the warehouse in the fall." https://founders.archives.gov/documents/Jefferson/01-01-02-0050

British merchants had bought substantial numbers of ships built in the United States, where timber was still plentiful. After the war, those sales also dropped precipitously.

Many Americans still owed British merchants for pre-war purchases, and were refusing to pay. And immediately after the war, British merchants dumped stockpiled British goods on the American market. Since few Americans were selling goods abroad, many went even further into debt. The balance of trade went up and down over the 1780s, but generally it was not in America's favor. By one estimate, per capita income <u>dropped by a horrendous 20%</u> in the 1780s.

2.1.3 Economic situation of the United States in 1789

What does this mean for us, as forty-something Americans in 1789?

A small percentage of Americans are well-to-do merchants. A few others belong to old-money families with huge estates, such as the Schuylers and Rensselaers in New York. Most of us, however, work on our own family-size plots of land. Given the drop in trade during and after the war, we're barely breaking even from year to year.

Suppose we want more than that. Suppose we work very, very hard to increase what we produce, in order to make a better life for ourselves and our families. Where will we sell this excess agricultural produce?

Probably not in the United States: most Americans produce their own food and other necessities. The market here for surplus agricultural products is small, unless your farm is near a sizeable town or city.

Selling produce abroad is not an easy option, either. The Caribbean is close, but the British have cut us off from trade with their colonies there. To ship produce to Europe requires a transatlantic voyage that can last from several weeks to several months. Few agricultural goods can survive such a trip without rotting from moisture or being munched by insects or rodents.

But suppose we get our produce to Europe—let's say to France. It has to be priced rather high compared to similar French goods, since Americans have to cover transatlantic shipping costs. We also have to price it high enough to cover whatever import duties the French king imposes. All European rulers believe wealth is measured by gold and silver in the country's coffers. They slap on import duties so that

---

<u>Dropped by a horrendous 20%</u>: Peter H. Lindert and Jeffrey G. Williamson, "American Incomes 1774-1860," National Bureau of Economic Research Working Paper no. 18396 (Sept. 2012), p. 17; cited in Christopher Parenti, *Radical Hamilton*, p. 82.

sellers will have less profit to carry out of the country. (For more on mercantilism, see §3.3.2.) All in all, selling the produce we've worked so hard to grow, either in America or abroad, is very difficult.

And what if we don't want to spend our lives on a farm? What if we want to start a business such as manufacturing nails? That's no easier. We'd need a substantial sum to buy machinery and pay workers. We'd also need a rudimentary knowledge of how to run a profitable business—not a skillset that subsistence farmers normally develop. A few businessmen in colonial America had that knowledge… but many of them traded with the British, kept their savings in Britain, and sided with the British during the Revolutionary War. At the end of the war those loyalist businessmen fled to Canada or Great Britain, taking with them their capital and their business knowledge.

It looks like many of us, along with all our children, will have to be farmers forever. And that's leading to a significant problem. Disputes are erupting between the wealthy (merchants and landowners) and the poor, between creditors and debtors, between the haves and the have-not-muches. The wealthy sometimes lend farmers like us money, with our land as collateral. What if we can't repay the loan? Then we have neither money nor land.

The 1786 rebellion led by Daniel Shays in Massachusetts was a rebellion of disgruntled farmers who had had to mortgage their farms to get gold and silver to pay their taxes. They aimed to shut down courts so creditors couldn't foreclose on their farms. It was Shays' Rebellion that caused George Washington to cry in despair, "We are fast verging to anarchy and confusion!" (See §1.5.)

In short: the American economy is stagnating. That's not just a boringly flat line on a graph of gross domestic product. It means that all of us have trouble earning money. Providing for ourselves and our families is increasingly difficult. We don't have any options except farming. And there's no relief in sight.

Are we upset? Oh, yes.

1786 Rebellion: See Henry Knox to Washington, 10/23/1786: "Their creed is 'That the property of the United States has been protected from the confiscations of Britain by the joint exertions of all, and therefore ought to be the common property of all. And he that attempts opposition to this creed is an enemy to equity and justice, and ought to be swept from off the face of the earth.' In a word they are determined to annihilate all debts public and private ... by the means of unfunded paper money which shall be a tender in all cases whatever."

https://founders.archives.gov/documents/Washington/04-04-02-0274

2.2 SECOND THREAD IN THE GORDIAN KNOT: THE CENTRIFUGAL TENDENCY OF THE STATES

The Declaration of Independence was issued in 1776 by "the thirteen United States of America." But "united" was not a very accurate description in 1776 or the years that followed. The United States was barely a functioning political entity. Strictly for convenience, I asked you to imagine you're a forty-something American. It would be more accurate for me to ask you to imagine you're a Pennsylvanian, or a New Yorker, or a Georgian, or a Rhode Islander. Most of us think of ourselves as citizens of a particular state rather than the United States.

Alas, even if we don't pay much attention to national politics, the state of the union has profound effects on us.

2.2.1 States vs. federal government

The Articles of Confederation, drafted in 1777 and ratified in 1781, created a weak federal government. When the war ended, many delegates no longer bothered to attend meetings of the Confederation Congress. At that point, in the sense of a body representing all the states, no federal government existed. From 1783 until its dissolution in early 1789, the Confederation Congress passed only two measures of long-term significance: the Land Ordinances of 1784 and 1785, which set out rules for organizing the territory west of the Appalachians.

For some Americans, having a weak federal government seemed right and proper. Thomas Jefferson wrote to James Madison in 1786:

> To make us one nation as to foreign concerns, and keep us distinct in Domestic ones, gives the outline of the proper division of powers between the general and particular governments.

The weakness of the federal government became a serious problem, however, when states flouted promises made by the United States. In New York, for example, some residents who had sided with the British chose to remain in their homes after the British evacuated the city. By the terms of the treaty with Great Britain, such former loyalists were not to be persecuted. But those who had fought for the United States began hauling former loyalists into court in 1783. The federal

---

Thomas Jefferson wrote: Jefferson to Madison, 12/16/1786.
https://founders.archives.gov/documents/Jefferson/01-10-02-0461

Hauling former loyalists into court: See §3.6.2 for Hamilton's role in defending former loyalists.

government had no way to enforce compliance with the treaty. Perhaps the British wouldn't choose to go to war over this issue ... but they had a multitude of other ways of taking revenge, such as attacking American shipping.

Another example of how states fought the federal government: in July 1788, New York's ratification convention proposed an amendment to the Constitution stating that all officials of the United States should swear an oath not to "infringe or violate the Constitutions of the respective states." In effect, the federal government would have been subservient to any particular state.

2.2.2 State vs. state

Throughout the 1780s, the states were at odds with each other as well as the federal government. By 1786, in their desperate attempts to collect money to pay off their Revolutionary War debts, eight states had imposed duties on imports from other states. Virginia imposed duties on ships sailing through the Chesapeake Bay to Maryland. New York imposed duties on goods from New Jersey and Connecticut. In retaliation, Connecticut imposed a year-long embargo on exportation of

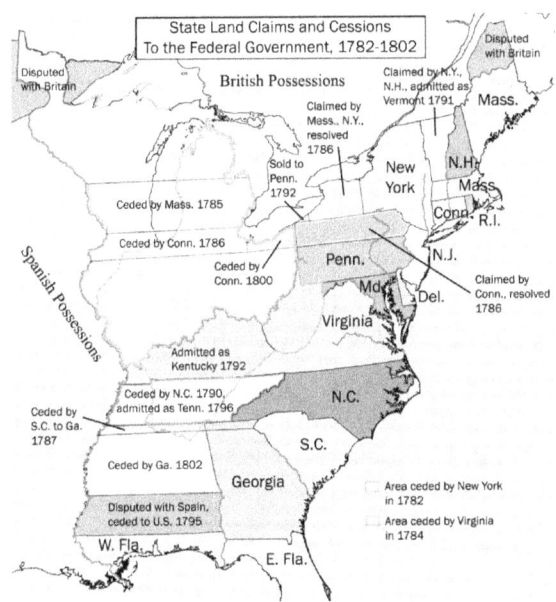

State Land Claims and Cessions to the Federal Government, 1782-1802. Image: Wikipedia

---

Proposed an amendment: New York Ratifying Convention, "Amendments to the Constitution," 7/15/1788.

https://founders.archives.gov/documents/Hamilton/01-05-02-0012-0069

goods to New York, with a substantial fine ($250) for those who broke the embargo. Such competing duties, which Madison called "the anarchy of our commerce," were the primary reason for the Annapolis Convention in 1786.

When the states squabbled with each other, as they often did, there was no referee to settle the disputes. Pennsylvania and Connecticut fought over ownership of the Wyoming Valley, now the site of Wilkes Barre. New York, New Hampshire, and Massachusetts were all claiming territory in the present state of Vermont. (See map on p. 19.)

2.2.3 Federal government vs. foreign powers

Because the federal government under the Articles of Confederation is so weak, it can't negotiate treaties for favorable terms of trade with foreign governments. We'd like to have French import duties decreased, so we'd make more profit on what we sell there. We'd like to be able to sell goods in the British West Indies. But what country will bother to sign a treaty with the United States, if the separate states don't have to abide by the terms of the treaty?

A more immediate danger from the weak federal government is the lack of protection it offers to Americans living along the borders and frontiers. The frontier is where the fertile, unoccupied land is. As the long-settled land along the East Coast becomes exhausted, farmers are moving west. Even if we don't live on the frontier, many of our sons and daughters will move there. That means defense of the American frontier is very important to us.

2.2.3.1 Indians on the frontier

Indians and settlers have been fighting constantly on the frontier. In early 1787, a friend in Kentucky wrote to James Madison:

> The situation of the people of this district, from the war with the Indians, is, really distressing. The expeditions of last fall, tho' carried on at a vast expence, seem not to have been attended, with one single good consequence: on the contrary, there is

---

Madison called: Madison to Jefferson, 3/18/1786.
https://founders.archives.gov/documents/Madison/01-08-02-0268

Wyoming Valley: Blood was shed there in the Pennamite Wars, 1769-1770, 1774, and 1784. The controversy only ended in 1799, with the Wyoming Valley becoming part of Pennsylvania and the Yankee settlers becoming Pennsylvanians with legal claims to their land.

Friend in Kentucky: George Muter to James Madison, 2/20/1787
https://founders.archives.gov/documents/Madison/01-09-02-0144

reason to beleive, the Indians have rather gained a greater degree of confidence than they before possessed, & have been more irritated against us than they were. They seem now to be pushing us on every side; mischief has been done lately, on the frontiers of almost every County in the district ...

Even east of the Appalachians, the frontier and the Indians are not distant. New York is sparsely settled west of the Hudson River. Pennsylvania is heavily settled only in the southeast, Virginia only in the flat eastern section. Georgia is barely settled beyond the coast.

2.2.3.2 British on the frontier

To the north of the United States is the British colony of Canada, with its complement of highly trained troops. By the 1783 treaty, Great Britain recognizes American sovereignty between the Appalachians and the Mississippi River and the right of Americans to navigate the Mississippi River. But British troops still occupy half a dozen frontier posts in American territory, including Oswego, Niagara, Detroit, Michilimackinac, and Miami. The British government refuses to vacate these posts until Americans pay off the debts they owe to British merchants from before the Revolution. While British soldiers seldom skirmish with Americans, they do often encourage Indians to attack American settlers.

2.2.3.3 Spanish on the frontier

The Spanish governor of Florida sometimes encourages Indians to attack Americans across the border in Georgia. Spain also claims all the territory (mostly unexplored) from the Mississippi River west to the Rockies. But most importantly, Spain controls New Orleans, at the mouth of the Mississippi River. Hence it controls the shipment of goods to and from settlements in Kentucky and Tennessee. In 1784, Spain abruptly closes the Mississippi to American commerce. Settlers between the Mississippi and the Appalachians are forced to ship and

---

Beyond the coast: Looking back on this period, Hamilton wrote, "our frontiers have exhibited a state of desolating and expensive hostility." "Defence of the Funding System," in July 1795.
https://founders.archives.gov/documents/Hamilton/01-19-02-0001

Debts they owe: See §2.1.1. The issue of debts to British merchants wasn't settled until the Jay Treaty was signed in 1795. For the list of forts involved, see Rufus King to Hamilton 8/25/1796, n. 2.
https://founders.archives.gov/documents/Hamilton/01-20-02-0195

receive goods via the difficult and dangerous overland route across the mountains.

In 1785-1786, John Jay attempts to hammer out a commercial treaty with Spain that includes the right to transport goods on the Mississippi. America's bargaining position is so weak that Jay ends up suggesting America surrender for the next twenty-five years the right to navigate the Mississippi.

Farmers and merchants in the Northeast, with access to rivers leading to the Atlantic, have no problem with that. But settlers on the frontier in the west and south threaten to raise an army and declare war on Spain. Patrick Henry of Virginia, that eloquent and persuasive orator, says "he would rather part with the confederation than relinquish the navigation of the Mississippi."

In 1787, as the date for the Constitutional Convention approaches, antagonism over this issue between North and South is so severe that there is talk of splitting the nation in two.

2.2.3.4 Military forces

One would expect the federal government to defend American borders against Great Britain, Spain, and the Indians. After all, it should have a budget larger than that of any particular state, as well as a big-picture view of where soldiers were urgently needed. But the national government under the Articles lacks funds to do much of anything, including defend the frontier. (More on that when we discuss the fourth thread of our Gordian Knot, lack of government revenue; see §2.4.)

Relinquish the navigation: quoted by John Marshall to Arthur Lee, 3/5/1787; in Richard Henry Lee, *Life of Arthur Lee* (Boston, 1829), II, 321. Quoted in "The United States, Spain, and the Navigation of the Mississippi River," in *The Documentary History of the Ratification of the Constitution, Digital Edition*, ed. John P. Kaminski, Gaspare J. Saladino, Richard Leffler, Charles H. Schoenleber and Margaret A. Hogan (Charlottesville, 2009).
https://archive.csac.history.wisc.edu/mississippi_essay.pdf

Splitting the nation in two: On the effects of the negotiations with Spain, see "The United States, Spain, and the Navigation of the Mississippi River," in *The Documentary History of the Ratification of the Constitution, Digital Edition*.
https://archive.csac.history.wisc.edu/mississippi_essay.pdf

HAMILTON'S FINANCIAL PROGRAMS

In addition, mounting an effective defense of the frontier and borders would require a standing army. Most of us are vehemently opposed to that. We have vivid memories of British troops being quartered in our homes. As a result, if the borders are protected at all, it's usually by members of a volunteer state militia. That reinforces our inclination to think of ourselves as citizens of a particular state, rather than of the United States.

In sum: under the Articles, we do not benefit much from the existence of a federal government. Many of us don't particularly care if our state remains one of the United States. In 1789, the political force within the new nation remains centrifugal. The states are tending to spin apart.

Do we feel threatened? Do we feel our lives as well as our ability to make a living are in danger? You bet.

2.3 THIRD THREAD IN THE GORDIAN KNOT: INADEQUATE MONEY IN CIRCULATION

"Inadequate money in circulation" sounds more abstract than having a difficult time making a living, or living in a fragmented nation. But shortage of money has serious practical effects. Keeping this discussion to the nitty-gritty level: suppose, as subsistence farmers, we want to decrease the back-breaking labor of planting crops by replacing our hand-held spades with iron plows. It will make us less exhausted and far more productive. We'll be able to cultivate more land, and raise

---

Serious practical effects: Benjamin Franklin, "The Nature and Necessity of a Paper-Currency," 4/3/1729: "First, A great Want of Money in any Trading Country, occasions Interest to be at a very high Rate. ... Now the Interest of Money being high is prejudicial to a Country several Ways: It makes Land bear a low Price, because few Men will lay out their Money in Land, when they can make a much greater Profit by lending it out upon Interest: And much less will Men be inclined to venture their Money at Sea, when they can, without Risque or Hazard, have a great and certain Profit by keeping it at home; thus Trade is discouraged. ... For he that trades with Money he hath borrowed at 8 or 10 per Cent. cannot hold Market with him that borrows his Money at 6 or 4. ... Thirdly, Want of Money in a Country discourages Labouring and Handicrafts Men (which are the chief Strength and Support of a People) from coming to settle in it, and induces many that were settled to leave the Country, and seek Entertainment and Employment in other Places, where they can be better paid. ..." https://founders.archives.gov/documents/Franklin/01-01-02-0041

enough extra produce that we can sell some of it.

But right now, each of us produces and consumes most of our own goods, so we don't see much cash year to year. A plow is a major expense. Iron is costly. It has to be hand-forged into a plow. Blacksmiths near us may not be able to handle a piece of iron that large: it might have to be imported. So to buy a plow, we'll need to save a fair amount of money, or borrow it.

In 1789, that's surprisingly difficult. We have four options.

2.3.1. Barter

We could save up goods and barter for the plow. But how do we calculate how many cows equal a plow? Also, cows cost money to feed, and their value fluctuates depending on the number in our area. And if the cow catches a fatal disease or a wild animal mauls it, poof! goes our asset. A bovine "savings account" is not reliable.

2.3.2 Gold and silver coins

Next option for saving for a plow: collect gold or silver coins. They're lower maintenance than cows, but they're not an easy option, either.

By 1789, the United States still has no coins of its own. We've been using gold and silver from Great Britain, Spain, France, Portugal, and Holland. In 1772, a thief's takings in one of the colonies were listed as "about 190 Half Joes, about 30 Pistoles, 8 Moidores, 4 Guineas, 60 Pieces of Eight, and 48 Pounds in Jersey Six Pound bills." The shapes and weights of these coins are different. The ratio of precious metal to alloy varies from country to country. Many of these coins have been in circulation so long that they are worn down to far less than their original weight. Some have been clipped into pieces to make small change. The only way to determine the value of this multitude of coins is to weigh and assay them. But assaying the content of

---

No coins of its own: The United States Mint was established by the Coinage Act of 1792. By late 1793, it was still only issuing copper cents and half cents. See "The History of U.S. Circulating Coins."
https://www.usmint.gov/learn/history/us-circulating-coins#:~:text=In%20 1792%2C%20during%20construction%20of,%2C%201793%3A%20 11%2C178%20copper%20cents

Thief's takings: Quoted in Wright, *First Wall Street,* p. 51. Half Joes and moidores are Portuguese. Pistoles and pieces of eight are Spanish. Guineas are British. Jersey, in the English Channel, issued its own coinage and bills.

gold pieces is a task that <u>few of us subsistence farmers</u> have the skill to do. Saving and trading coins is challenging.

Another problem: suppose we have a very good year on our farms—so good that we want to put aside money toward our plows. Coins are so scarce in the 1780s that we may not be able to save our profit. Why? Because European rulers accept the theory that wealth is equivalent to actual coins in a nation's coffers. (See §3.3.2.) Rulers do their best to prevent coins from leaving their countries. Hence few coins make it to the United States.

But suppose we manage to make a profit, and we find coins to save. Until we have enough, we put them in a box and bury them under the hearthstone. If a thief hears we're saving for a plow, though, what's to prevent him waiting until we're out in the fields, and then stealing the coins? A hearthstone provides no security.

Furthermore, if the coins remain safe under your hearthstone, then they're out of circulation. That makes it much more difficult for the rest of us to save money to buy plows. Really, how could you?

2.3.3 Government-issued paper money and IOUs

The third option for saving for a plow is to collect the paper money and IOUs issued by the federal government or by the thirteen individual states.

Heaven knows there's enough of that around. Early in the war, the United States government printed millions of "Continental dollars". They rolled off the printing press with no gold and silver to back them or to stabilize their value. In 1780, when a flood of Continentals had drastically reduced their value, Congress decreed the value of a Continental to be one fortieth of its face value. So if the army gave us one

---

<u>Few of us subsistence farmers</u>: Robert Morris to the President of Congress 1/15/1782: "Experience has already told us that the advantage of Gold as a Coin is in this Country very considerably diminished for every distinct Piece must be weighed before it can be safely received. Both Gold and Silver Coins are indeed preferable, in one respect to common Bullion that the Standard is presumed to be just and consequently they are received without the Delays and Expences of assaying. It must however be remembered that they are all foreign Coins and of Course we are not only exposed to the Tricks of Individuals but should it suit the Interest or Convenience of any Sovereign to make base Money for us there is Nothing to prevent it."
https://founders.archives.gov/documents/Jefferson/01-07-02-0151-0002

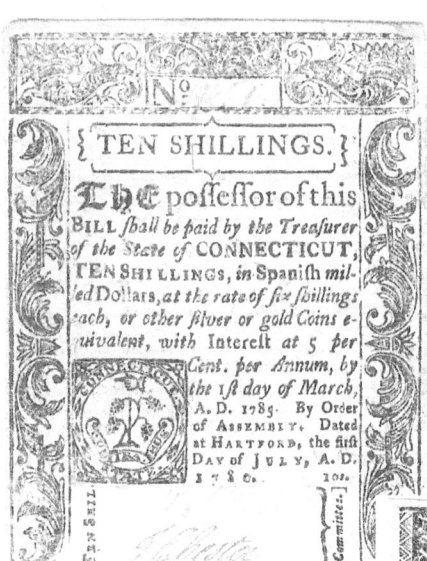

Paper money and IOUs from the 1770s-1780s. All images from the collection of John E. Herzog.

hundred dollars in Continentals in 1778 for a year's worth of crops, and we buried them under the hearthstone, we'd have $2.50 in 1780. By 1781, the value of that hundred Continental dollars had plummeted to seventy cents.

When Continentals became worthless, the federal government began issuing promises of payment instead, with or without interest. Some were bonds with interest (a.k.a. "loan office certificates"), others promissory notes. For interest due, the government issued "indents". Modern sources often refer to these bonds and promissory notes as "government securities" or "public securities". But those terms bring with them a host of associations, including an established market for securities, which did not exist during the Revolutionary War or through the 1780s. Hence I've lumped under the term "IOUs" all the pieces of paper issued by the government when they didn't have money to pay, at the time or in the foreseeable future.

The value of the federal government's IOUs fluctuated wildly from place to place and time to time throughout the 1780s, depending on confidence in the federal government. Most of us saw no hope of receiving payment, so we sold the IOUs for ten cents on the dollar, or whatever someone was willing to pay.

During the Revolutionary War and even after, many state governments also printed paper money whenever they needed it. One estimate puts the total paper money issued by the states at $200 million over a decade or so. That's an enormous sum at a time when most laborers earned less than a dollar a day, and when the population of the United States was less than three million. By 1789, quite a lot of the paper money issued by the states is still in circulation. Like the federal government's IOUs, its value fluctuates wildly, depending on who issued it and when.

$200 million: Gene Pisasale, *Alexander Hamilton, Architect of the American Financial System* (2017), p. 62, says that states issued bills of credit at zero interest (i.e., printed paper money) for $200 million. States often did this as cheap relief for debtors, who used paper money to pay off loans that had been made in gold or silver.

The bottom line is that we can't count on the paper money or IOUs issued by any government to hold their value for a year—or even a month—from now. It's risky to use either paper money or IOUs to save up for a plow.

2.3.4 Banks

The fourth option for getting a plow is the one we'd think of first, if we were living in the twenty-first century: borrow from a bank. We can pay the money back, with interest, when we have the plow, because increased productivity and profit will give us the extra money. If we don't want to borrow the money, we can store our savings in the bank's vaults, which is considerably safer than in a box buried under a hearthstone.

Alas, in 1789, going to a bank is not an option in most of the United States. Britain effectively prohibited the establishment of banks in her colonies. The very first one to open in America is the Bank of North America, established in 1781 to fund purchases of Revolutionary War matériel. The Bank of New York and the Massachusetts Bank are both established in 1784. And that's it for banks by 1789!

All three of these banks are chartered by a specific state, and their activities are generally confined to that state. If you're a farmer looking to buy a plow in Virginia or Rhode Island or South Carolina, tough luck.

There's a further restriction on the few banks that exist. Banks lend based on the amount of gold and silver in their vaults. Because gold and silver coins are so scarce, funds for loans are limited. Because funds are limited, demand is high, and banks can charge a higher interest.

By 1789, the American economy is stagnating. That's partly due to the damage and debts accumulated during the Revolutionary War. It's partly due to the loss of trade with Great Britain. But it's also due to simply having too little money in circulation. That makes trade and savings very difficult. How can we plan long-term for our family, our business, our life, if we don't have a reliable way to save money?

Are we annoyed? Are we frustrated? Yes, indeed.

2.4 FOURTH THREAD IN THE GORDIAN KNOT: LACK OF GOVERNMENT REVENUE

Under the Articles of Confederation, Congress has no power to command revenue. It can only "requisition" money from the states. In 1781 (the year of Cornwallis's surrender at Yorktown), Congress requisitions $3 million from the states. It receives $39,000. From 1781 to 1786, Congress assesses the states $15.7 million. It receives $2.4 million.

We have already seen one result of the federal government's lack of revenue: the United States has no force to defend its borders and frontier. (See §2.2.3.) Since so few delegates attend sessions, by early 1789, the United States also has no effective legislative body. (See §2.2.1.) Under the Articles of Confederation, Congress is responsible for the (very limited) executive and judicial functions of the federal government. Its impotence means there is no head of state, and no courts to settle disputes between squabbling states. The United States cannot long survive without money to pay officers to perform such vital functions.

The federal government needs to be able to fund its operating expenses without relying on the good will of the separate states. Its options are: print more paper money and IOUs; sell assets; or generate revenue from foreign and domestic sources such as taxes or import duties.

2.4.1 Paper money

We have all experienced how much the value of government-issued paper money fluctuates. (See §2.3.3.) Going forward, if we enlist as

---

No power to command revenue: For a good summary of how the United States attempted to deal with expenses during the war, see "Memorandum of the Finances of the Thirteen United States of North America," submitted 4/20/1782 by Francisco Rendon José de Gálvez y Gallardo, a counselor to the King of Spain. Rendon notes: "Because of not being able to remedy the public shortages by means of the taxes, they had been obliged to create each year a new amount of currency which began depreciating as soon as it was issued. On the other hand the enemy inundated America with counterfeit paper. To remedy this disorder, Congress opened a loan office, which even though it did not offer more than the moderate interest of four percent managed to encounter relatively large sums. But this measure without decreasing the depreciation only served to overburden the State with a real debt." Original Spanish with English translation in *Papers of Robert Morris,* v. 4, pp. 595-624.

soldiers, provide the government with goods, or serve as government officials, will we want to accept paper money as payment? Not likely! We've been burned too often to want any more of those worthless bills.

In August 1787, after a vehement debate, the framers of the Constitution decide not to delegate the right of printing paper money to Congress, and to prohibit it to the states.

2.4.2 Revenue from sale of assets

In 1785, the federal government assumes ownership of all the land between the Appalachians and the Mississippi River. Well, why not sell those hundreds of thousands of acres beyond the mountains to support the government? Jefferson, writing in 1787, believed sales of Western land would allow quick repayment of both foreign and domestic debts.

It's not so simple, though. Selling that land means clearing the title to it via treaties with the Indians. It means paying government agents to survey parcels in a wilderness. Usually they require armed escorts

---

Printing paper money: Article I, Section 10 of the Constitution reads in part: "No State shall ... coin Money; emit Bills of Credit; make any Thing but gold and silver Coin a Tender in Payment of Debts." Bills of credit are paper or fiat money—i.e., paper intended to circulate as money, without gold or silver to back it. For quotes from the discussion at the Constitutional Convention, see Clarence Carson, "The Constitution and Paper Money," published 7/1/1983 by the Foundation for Economic Education. https://fee.org/articles/the-constitution-and-paper-money/

Jefferson, writing in 1787: Jefferson to Madison 12/20/1787: "I am much pleased that the sale of Western lands is so successful. I hope they will absorb all the Certificates of our Domestic debt speedily in the first place, and that then offered for cash they will do the same by our foreign one."

https://founders.archives.gov/documents/Jefferson/01-12-02-0454

Armed escorts: On the problems involved in selling land in the west, see, for example, Major-General Arthur St. Clair (governor of the Northwest Territory) to Hamilton, 5/25/1791: "A few days ago Mr. Ludlow presented to me the Instructions he had received from you for compleating the Surveys of certain Tracts of Land in this Territory contracted for with the late Board of Treasury and requested an Escort of Troops to enable him to comply with those Instructions. The situation of Affairs, and the present weakness of this Garrison put it out of my power to furnish him with the necessary Escort; but, on perusing the Instructions, to my astonishment, I found that the purchase made by Judge Symmes did not extend farther up the Ohio than twenty Miles from the ➤

for defense against the Indians, Spanish, or British. It means finding buyers and <u>collecting payment</u>—no small task in our cash-strapped economy.

Possibly the biggest drawback is the physical danger. Which of us will be willing to buy land on the frontier if we can't count on a military force to protect us from attacks by British, Spanish, and Indians? (See §2.2.3.)

2.4.3 Revenue from taxes

As income for the federal government, the only option left is imposing a tax of one sort or another: on imported goods, on commodities within the United States, on real estate, or on citizens (a per capita tax). But ... we Americans don't like paying taxes! We associate taxes with the British. It's one of the reasons we declared our independence from King George: "For imposing Taxes on us without our Consent." For us to agree to such taxes, the federal government would have to do a lot more for us than it's doing now.

Another vivid memory for all of us is that during the 1780s, the government often required payment of taxes in those very scarce gold and silver coins, rather than fluctuating government paper. (Even the government didn't want that paper money!) The most notable tax revolt was Shays' Rebellion in Massachusetts, in 1786 (see §2.1.3), but there were also revolts in Pennsylvania, South Carolina, and Rhode Island.

---

mouth of the Great Miami River. ... I found the Judge here, and a number of People settled already, to whom he had sold Lands far to the eastward of the twenty Miles. It never could have entered into my Head that any person, much less one invested with a respectable public Character, had published a falsehood, was persisting in it, and availing himself of the pecuniary advantages flowing from it. ... It seems to me that all I can do at present, and it may be proper to do it, is to publish a Proclamation warning all Persons against further intrusion, and permitting the occupancy of the present Settlers until the Pleasure of Congress shall be known. To remove those if it could be done, would be ruin to them, and they are innocent not wilful trespassers; and to revoke the Commissions that have been granted would leave them in a State of Anarchy."

https://founders.archives.gov/documents/Hamilton/01-08-02-0335

<u>Collecting payment</u>: As an example of the problems involved in selling land, see the history of the Scioto or Sioto Company, which in 1787 committed to the purchase of almost five million acres north and west of the Ohio River, at $.666 per acre. Unable to sell enough land to meet their payments, they defaulted on their contract in 1792.

Taxes seem somewhat less objectionable when they are less visible. If imports to the United States are taxed, the merchant can simply add the tax onto the selling price. In fact, this option is so appealing that the writers of the Constitution stipulate that the federal government will have the exclusive right to impose taxes on imports. (Article I, Section 10, Clause 2.)

But even an import tax doesn't provide a simple solution to the federal government's revenue problem. Collecting import fees doesn't mean scanning a barcode at the harbor and swiping a credit card. It requires hiring customs agents for seaports scattered over more than a thousand miles of the East Coast. The agents have to be able to identify all the taxed items and estimate their value. Payments have to be collected, stored safely, and transported to the government's coffers. Given lack of money in circulation and difficulties in transportation, that's not easy.

In sum: import duties are the least annoying taxes, but are not easy to collect. So in 1789, the federal government still has no easy and reliable source of income.

Impose taxes on imports: Import duties and tariffs are both taxes paid on good entering the country. However, not all taxes on imported goods are imposed with the same intent. They can be imposed to raise revenue for the government. They can be used as a weapon against foreign governments: lower your taxes on our goods, or we'll raise our taxes on yours. (See Hamilton to the *Daily Advertiser,* 7/21/1787: "They enjoy in our ports unlimited freedom.... while our government is incapable of making those defensive regulations, which would be likely to produce a greater reciprocity of privileges.") And such taxes can be used to raise prices of foreign goods, thereby protecting domestic producers. See Chapter 6, on the *Report on Manufactures.*

https://founders.archives.gov/documents/Hamilton/01-04-02-0114

That's not easy: Otho Williams, a customs agent in Baltimore, wrote despairingly to Hamilton on 10/23/1789: "The difficulties that have occurred in the Execution of the laws respecting the Customs have been infinite, and present themselves daily. The System itself is the most complicated and embarrassing of anything that has employed my attention and the Want of Official forms has produced, every where, an infinite Variety."

https://founders.archives.gov/documents/Hamilton/01-05-02-0252

2.5 FIFTH THREAD IN THE GORDIAN KNOT: MASSIVE GOVERNMENT DEBT

The estimated cost of the Revolutionary War was about $160 million. Since the United States government had no revenue, the war was fought and won with money borrowed from the French and Spanish crowns, Dutch bankers, and American citizens. Once the war was over, we no longer needed to borrow large sums to pay soldiers and purchase war materiel. But that huge debt did not go away.

Because it has no income, the federal government has not been making payments on the principal or interest of that debt. By 1789, when the Constitution takes effect, interest on some of the debt has been accruing for more than a decade.

2.5.1 Foreign debt

In early 1789, no one knows exactly how much the federal government owes to the French, Spanish, and Dutch. It certainly runs to tens of millions of dollars. Congress stopped paying interest on the French loan, in order to pay interest to the Dutch: the Dutch might lend us more money, the French will not. The interest has been steadily accumulating. Payments on the principal will be coming due in the 1790s.

2.5.2 Domestic debt

The debt owed to American citizens is at least four times the size of the foreign debt. During the Revolutionary War, Congress raised money by printing paper money or issuing IOUs. (See §2.3.3 for paper money, and for what I mean by "IOUs".)

Those of us who were soldiers most likely received IOUs instead of pay. Those of us who were farmers or merchants were probably given IOUs for goods or crops commandeered by the army. At the time that was acceptable: we were in a battle for our rights, our future,

---

Estimated cost of the Revolutionary War: Ferguson, *Power of the Purse*, p. 333.

Tens of millions of dollars: On payment of interest to the French and Dutch, see Ferguson, *Power of the Purse*, p. 335. For a list of foreign debts with due dates, see Wright, *One Nation Under Debt*, Table 3.

Debt owed to American citizens: For a simplified description of the types of domestic debt, see McDonald, *Hamilton*, pp. 147. McDonald estimated that when the Revolutionary War ended in 1783, American debts were about twenty times the amount of all the gold and silver in the United States (p. 44).

our lives. But that doesn't mean we don't want to be paid back! We work hard to make a living, and those IOUs represent the cash value of a lot of our effort that we haven't been able to use for our own benefit.

The states are also struggling to repay their Revolutionary War debt. By 1789, Americans were paying taxes three or four times higher than they had in the colonial era.

2.5.3 Repaying the debt and repairing public credit

By the terms printed on the IOUs that it issued to its citizens, the government is to pay 5% or 6% interest to holders of domestic debt. As we know, however, the government has no income. The debts remain. The interest keeps accumulating. By 1789, few of us who hold IOUs expect them to be paid off. (See §2.3.3.)

Hence many of us are willing to sell our IOUs for far less than their face value. In other words: if we have $100 in IOUs for military service (risking our lives!), or for a year's crops, we may be willing to take $10 for those IOUs from anyone who offers ... because we don't think we'll ever see that $100 from the government. But taking $10 means that $90 worth of our time and labor for that period has vanished into thin air.

Since there seems to be no chance of repaying this massive debt, why doesn't the federal government ask its citizens to forgive the debt, thumb its nose at the foreigners far across the sea, and start with a clean slate?

Because the slate would not be clean. Refusing to pay federal debts now means that in the future, the American government would have no credit. "Credit" comes from Latin *credere*, "to believe". If people don't believe you'll pay, they won't lend you money, except perhaps at an exorbitant interest rate. They won't sell to you on credit. They'll insist on cash up front, even in an emergency.

Paying taxes: Parenti, *Radical Hamilton*, p. 88.

No credit: Hamilton, "Continentalist" No. 4, 8/30/1781: "CREDIT supposes specific and permanent funds for the punctual payment of interest, with a moral certainty of a final redemption of the principal." See also Hamilton, "Report on a Plan for the Further Support of Public Credit," 1/16/1795: "Credit is an intire thing. Every part of it has the nicest sympathy with every other part; wound one limb, and the whole tree shrinks and decays."
https://founders.archives.gov/documents/Hamilton/01-02-02-1191 ■
https://founders.archives.gov/documents/Hamilton/01-18-02-0052-0002

HAMILTON'S FINANCIAL PROGRAMS

What if Great Britain declares war again? What if the Indians or the Spaniards attack in force? Even if we desperately need to pay soldiers and buy military supplies, no one will offer a loan to a government that has a record of defaulting on payments. In an emergency, there will be no money for defense. The United States may cease to exist.

At the Constitutional Convention in 1787, the delegates didn't even debate whether America's debt should be paid and American credit restored. Everyone knew it had to be. The only question was how.

2.6 SUMMING UP: WHY THESE PROBLEMS ARE A GORDIAN KNOT

The Gordian Knot has five threads: the difficulty of making a living; the centrifugal impetus of the union; lack of money in circulation; lack of government revenue; and the government's massive debt. Hamilton and his contemporaries are well aware of these threads. President Washington, for example, refers directly or indirectly to each of the five in his address to Congress on January 8, 1790.

If we try to solve these problems one at time, it exacerbates the others. For example:

- If the government imposes import duties, it will have revenue; but then part of the country's gold and silver will always be locked up in government coffers. That means less money in circulation. That in turn means it's more difficult for us as individuals to make a living, especially if we want to save money to buy a plow or some other productivity-enhancing product.

- If the government doesn't have an income, there's more money in circulation, but it can't defend itself. That leaves the American frontier wide open to the British, Spanish, and Indians. Our lives and the lives of our families are at risk.

- If the government doesn't pay the IOUs it owes to its own citizens, its expenses will be far lower. But some of us will have lost years of our lives (as soldiers) or effort (in supplies commandeered by the army). We'll lose money that we could have used to make our lives better, in the present and the future.

In 1789, when the government under the new Constitution comes into effect, most of us are having difficulty making a living, never mind

---

Refers directly or indirectly: see following page for excerpts from Washington's speech.

improving our situation. Money in circulation is so tight that it severely restricts trade and savings. The federal government's debts tie up some of our productive effort from the war years. The federal government doesn't have enough clout to negotiate commercial treaties that allow us to sell our goods abroad at a profit. It can't protect our frontier. What reason do we have to be loyal to it, or to care whether it survives?

Oh, look, there's Alexander Hamilton. Let's go tell him he needs to get moving on these problems!

Washington to the United States Senate and House of Representatives, 1/8/1790

Among the many interesting objects, which will engage your attention, that of providing for the common defence will merit particular regard. To be prepared for war is one of the most effectual means of preserving peace. ...There was reason to hope, that the pacific measures adopted with regard to certain hostile tribes of Indians would have relieved the inhabitants of our Southern and Western frontiers from their depredations. But you will percieve, from the information contained in the papers, which I shall direct to be laid before you ... that we ought to be prepared to afford protection to those parts of the Union; and, if necessary, to punish aggressors. ...

Uniformity in the Currency, Weights and Measures of the United States is an object of great importance, and will, I am persuaded, be duly attended to.

The advancement of Agriculture, commerce and Manufactures, by all proper means, will not, I trust, need recommendation. But I cannot forbear intimating to you the expediency of giving effectual encouragement as well to the introduction of new and useful inventions from abroad, as to the exertions of skill and genius in producing them at home; and of facilitating the intercourse between the distant parts of our Country by a due attention to the Post-Office and Post Roads. ...

I saw with peculiar pleasure, at the close of the last Session, the resolution entered into by you expressive of your opinion, that an adequate provision for the support of the public Credit is a matter of high importance to the national honor and prosperity. In this sentiment, I entirely concur. ... It would be superfluous to specify inducements to a measure in which the character and permanent interests of the United States are so obviously and so deeply concerned ...

The welfare of our Country is the great object to which our cares and efforts ought to be directed. And I shall derive great satisfaction from a co-operation with you, in the pleasing though arduous task of ensuring to our fellow Citizens the blessings, which they have a right to expect, from a free, efficient and equal Government.

https://founders.archives.gov/documents/Washington/05-04-02-0361

CHAPTER 3

Hamilton's Life as It Relates to the Gordian Knot

In this chapter, we look at how Hamilton's experience as a businessman, patriot, soldier, bureaucrat, Congressman, lawyer, and political leader qualified him to deal with various aspects of our Gordian Knot when he was appointed secretary of the Treasury.

3.1 FROM 1767 TO 1772: BUSINESSMAN

Most of the Founding Fathers—like most other Americans—were farmers, on a large or small scale. In addition, most Founders were born either in the American colonies or in England, Scotland, or Ireland. They grew up with British rights, British law, British trade, British finances. Hamilton's background was quite different, and when it came to devising solutions outside the box, quite useful.

Farmers: Pisasale discusses the backgrounds of Washington, Jefferson, Adams, Madison, Franklin, and Morris in *Alexander Hamilton: Architect of the American Financial System,* pp. 15-19. Even when they were not farmers, agriculture played a major role in their thinking. For example, although Benjamin Franklin was a city boy, in his view, national wealth is based on farming. "There seem to be but three Ways for a Nation to acquire Wealth. The first is by War as the Romans did in plundering their conquered Neighbours. This is Robbery. The second by Commerce which is generally Cheating. The third by Agriculture the only honest Way; wherein Man receives a real Increase of the Seed thrown into the Ground, in a kind of continual Miracle wrought by the Hand of God in his Favour, as a Reward for his innocent Life, and virtuous Industry." (See the summary of the Physiocrats in §3.3.2 below.) Franklin, *Positions to Be Examined,* 1769.

https://founders.archives.gov/documents/Franklin/01-16-02-0048

Hamilton's parents were traders and merchants. He grew up on Nevis and St. Kitts, and St. Eustatius. Beginning in 1765 he lived in Christiansted, St. Croix's major port. When Hamilton lived there, Nevis and St. Kitts were under British control, St. Eustatius was Dutch, and St. Croix was Danish. He led a cosmopolitan young life, not firmly attached to any particular place or mother country.

In Christiansted he took his first job, as a clerk for Beekman and Cruger, an import-export firm. Depending on the date one accepts for Hamilton's birth, he was hired somewhere between ages ten and thirteen. Hamilton worked for Nicholas Cruger, and for Cruger's two sometime partners, Beekman and Kortright, for at least five years, from 1767 to 1772.

He did not love the job. To his friend Edward Stevens he wrote, "my Ambition is prevalent that I contemn the grov'ling and condition of a Clerk or the like." But Hamilton apparently performed his duties very competently, because in 1771 he was entrusted with running the St. Croix end of the business while Nicholas Cruger traveled to New York for five months. Young Hamilton sent Cruger detailed reports, six of which have survived.

St. Croix was primarily an agricultural island, where plantation-owners raised sugar for export, using slave labor. Working in a firm involved in international trade, Hamilton glimpsed a wider

---

Hamilton's parents: On Hamilton's father, see Newton, "The Early Business Career of James Hamilton, Alexander Hamilton's Father," and "James Hamilton's Life on St. Croix."
http://discoveringhamilton.com/alexander-hamilton-father-early-business-career/ ■ http://discoveringhamilton.com/james-hamilton-life-st-croix/

Hamilton's birth: Scholars have argued for a date of birth for Hamilton between 1754 and 1757. See the evidence summarized in Michael Newton, *Alexander Hamilton: The Formative Years,* Chapter 2. In *Discovering Hamilton* ("Alexander Hamilton's Birth, Early Biography, and More"), Newton concludes based on recently discovered primary sources that Hamilton was likely born between February 23 and August 5, 1754.

Nicholas Cruger: See the chapter "Alexander Hamilton Working for Nicholas Cruger on St. Croix: More Newly Discovered Records" in Newton's *Discovering Hamilton.*
http://discoveringhamilton.com/oldest-known-alexander-hamilton-documents-implications/

"My ambition is prevalent": Hamilton to Edward Stevens, 11/11/1769.
https://founders.archives.gov/documents/Hamilton/01-01-02-0002

Detailed reports: Hamilton to Nicholas Cruger, letters of 10/31/1771, 11/4/1771, 11/12/1771, 11/27/1771, 1/10/1772, and 2/24/1772, all available on Founders.Archives.gov.

horizon. He saw that trade and agriculture were intricately bound together, dependent on each other for success. He watched patterns of trade: where goods were shipped and why. He saw how the seasons and weather affect such shipments. He saw, as well, the sort of problems that could cause the loss of substantial money and effort. He learned to look ahead and consider the big picture.

Here's teenage Hamilton in 1771, explaining to his employer why he's selling flour at a lower price than anticipated:

> Your Philadelphia flour is realy very bad, being of a most swarthy complexion & withal very untractable; the Bakers complain that they cannot by any means get it to rise. Wherefore & in consideration of the quantity of flour at Market and the little demand for it I have some thought not to refuse 8½ from any good person that will give it, taking 40 or 50 Barrels. Upon opening several barrels I have observ'd a kind of Worm very common in flour about the surface, which is an indication of Age. It could not have been very new when twas shipd and for all these reasons I conceive it highly necessary to lessen the price or probably I may be oblig'd in the end to sell it at a much greater disadvantage. At 8½ you will gain better than 10 rys2 ℔ bbl which is not so bad.

With Cruger, Beekman, and Kortright, Hamilton was introduced to the first thread of our Gordian Knot: making a living. It was a much broader view than he would have developed had he been raised on a plantation or a small farm, or even made a living as a small-town merchant, as his mother had.

On St. Croix, Hamilton also had his first lessons in the risks run by citizens of small, weak countries. Ships in the Caribbean were in constant danger from pirates, especially if they did not fly the flag of a powerful nation such as Britain or Spain. The *guarda costa* (the Spanish coast guard), which patrolled the Caribbean, were often little better than pirates themselves. Hamilton reported to Cruger that he

---

Your Philadelphia flour: Hamilton to Nicholas Cruger, 11/12/1771. In a letter of 2/24/1772, Hamilton explains to Cruger at length his difficulties with a recently arrived batch of mules, how he intends to solve the problem, and how much it will cost.
https://founders.archives.gov/documents/Hamilton/01-01-02-0008 ■

https://founders.archives.gov/documents/Hamilton/01-01-02-0026

NOTE: Throughout this book, I've copied the words of Hamilton and his contemporaries from the Founders Online or elsewhere, without editing their (often erratic) spelling, punctuation, and capitalization. Better to be "quaint" than to edit history.

had asked a ship captain to arm his vessel against such dangers:

> I desird him [the captain] as directed to furnish the Sloop with a few Guns but she went intirely defenceless to the Main; notwithstanding several Vessels had been obligd to put back to get out of the way of the Launches with which the Coast swarms. When Capt Newton urgd him to hire a few Guns for the Sloop He replied to this effect—that I only had mentiond the matter to him but that you had never said a word about it. This last time I mentiond it again & begd the Captain to hire 4 Guns himself if your Brother did not which he has promisd to do. The Expence will not be above 15. or 20 ps., and one escape may not be followd by a second, neither do I see any reason to run the risque of it.

When Hamilton later fought for a stronger, more energetic federal government, it was with the knowledge that a strong government would help protect American merchant ships at sea, as well as settlers on the frontier.

Hamilton's employers received and issued payments in a dozen different currencies. From collecting and dispensing payments, Hamilton saw firsthand how money circulated and how cash flowed. That helps his understanding of the third thread in our Gordian Knot: the need for adequate money in circulation.

He also knew from watching Cruger's cash flow that shipping slowed down to a trickle in the winter. Writing to Cruger in February 1772, Hamilton noted: "The Lumber you contracted for is arrivd & I am a good deal puzzled to fulfil your engagements; it is rather early you know to receivd & Cash is scarce." When he began to plan for collecting revenue income from customs duties (for government revenue, the fourth thread in our Gordian Knot), Hamilton knew payments would not come in steadily year-round, because the shipping season did not last year-round.

Experience in international trade also taught Hamilton to see from the merchant's and the consumer's point of view how government

---

I desir'd him: Hamilton to Cruger, 2/24/1772. On pirates and the *guarda costa*, see Newton, "Alexander Hamilton: Merchant in the West Indies."

https://founders.archives.gov/documents/Hamilton/01-01-02-0026 ∎
http://discoveringhamilton.com/alexander-hamilton-merchant-west-indies

Different currencies: Newton, "Alexander Hamilton: Merchant in the West Indies."

The lumber: Hamilton to Cruger, 2/24/1772.

https://founders.archives.gov/documents/Hamilton/01-01-02-0026

HAMILTON'S FINANCIAL PROGRAMS

laws and decrees (tariffs, duties, restrictions on trade) affected commerce locally and internationally. For example, Hamilton's employer arranged to <u>misrepresent refined sugar</u> as unrefined sugar in order to pay a lower duty. When Hamilton considered supplementary sources of government revenue—the fourth thread in our Gordian Knot—this was valuable knowledge.

In St. Croix, Hamilton learned much more that was relevant to his position as secretary of the Treasury, although it was not directly related to the threads of our Gordian Knot.

For example, Hamilton was exposed to the Lex Mercatoria—the common law that governed trade between nations. <u>Printed versions of the Lex Mercatoria</u> served as handbooks for international business, with information on history, geography, trade goods, and government regulations. When Hamilton was composing his letter to Robert Morris in 1781, he <u>asked a friend</u> to send him an edition of the Lex Mercatoria.

He learned to keep meticulous financial records: that was a large part of his task at Cruger's. When ships arrived, he had to check the quality and quantity of every item in the cargo. If the shipment was owned in partnership, he had to <u>allocate the profits</u> and expenses.

<u>Misrepresent refined sugar</u>: Michael Newton gives examples of Cruger's tax evasion in "Alexander Hamilton: Merchant in the West Indies."

http://discoveringhamilton.com/alexander-hamilton-merchant-west-indies/

<u>Printed versions of the Lex Mercatoria</u>: A sample of the variety of information, from the Dublin, 1773 edition (the sixth) of Wyndham Beawes's *Lex Mercatoria*, p. 569: "This Island [Jamaica], ranked with the largest in America, is of an oval Form, near a hundred and forty Miles in Length ... It is very fertile, and produces several Commodities more than any other of our Plantations do, as Cocoa, Pepper, and wild Cinnamon ... All these Products must give Place to the Sugar Cane, which has brought such immense Riches to the Inhabitants ... It is asserted by some, and not judged by others to exceed the Truth, that a hundred thousand Hogsheads are a Medium communibus annis."

https://catalog.hathitrust.org/Record/009031201

<u>Asked a friend</u>: On 4/20/1781, when he was writing his letter to Robert Morris (see § 3.3.3), Hamilton asked Timothy Pickering, the Army's quartermaster, if he could supply a printed edition of the Lex Mercatoria.

https://founders.archives.gov/documents/Hamilton/01-02-02-1152

<u>Allocate the profits</u>: See Newton, "Alexander Hamilton: Merchant in the West Indies."

http://discoveringhamilton.com/alexander-hamilton-merchant-west-indies

When Hamilton eventually had to hire customs inspectors in the 1790s to collect government revenue, he was under no illusion that it would be a job for an uneducated menial.

As Cruger's deputy, Hamilton became accustomed to dealing with and occasionally giving <u>direction or orders</u> to his elders—not only to other employees at Cruger's, but to merchants, ship captains, and lawyers.

Perhaps most importantly, Hamilton became accustomed to looking not just at the here and now, but at the big picture over time.

These skills are rare in anyone, but they're especially uncommon in people under twenty years old. And this was just the beginning of Hamilton's education.

3.2 FROM 1774 TO 1775: PATRIOT

In 1772, when he was in his late teens, Hamilton left the Caribbean, never to return. He took an intensive academic course in Elizabethtown, New Jersey, then headed to New York. In the fall of 1773, he enrolled at <u>Kings College</u>.

Barely a year later, in December 1774, Hamilton published "<u>A Full Vindication</u> of the Measures of the Congress, from the Calumnies of Their Enemies; in Answer to a Letter, Under the Signature of A.W. Farmer." This reply to Samuel Seabury's "Free Thoughts on the Proceedings of the Continental Congress" was remarkable for several reasons.

First: Hamilton firmly supported the actions of the Continental Congress, the only body that could claim to represent all thirteen American colonies. As an immigrant, Hamilton had no ties to any particular colony. That national viewpoint set him apart from most of the other Founding Fathers. It gave him a unique perspective regarding the second thread of the Gordian Knot: the union of the American colonies, and then the United States.

Direction or orders: For examples, see Newton, "Alexander Hamilton: Merchant in the West Indies."
http://discoveringhamilton.com/alexander-hamilton-merchant-west-indies

Kings College: See Michael Newton, "Timeline of Alexander Hamilton's Attendance at Elizabethtown Academy and King's College."

https://thepathtotyranny.wordpress.com/2015/04/17/timeline-of-alexander-hamiltons-attendance-at-elizabethtown-academy-and-kings-college/

A Full Vindication: Hamilton, "Full Vindication," 12/15/1774.
https://founders.archives.gov/documents/Hamilton/01-01-02-0054

Also notable about "Full Vindication" are the style and tone. Somewhere between his youth in St. Croix and his studies in New York, Hamilton became familiar with John Locke's writings on individual rights. But Locke's name is never mentioned. Even as early as 1774, Hamilton values the flow of the argument over scholarly precision in citing sources. He focuses on setting out facts and composing a logical argument. He strives to explain and educate, to inform and persuade.

> <u>I despise</u> all false pretentions, and mean arts. Let those have recourse to dissimulation and falshood, who can't defend their cause without it. 'Tis my maxim to let the plain naked truth speak for itself; and if men won't listen to it, 'tis their own fault: they must be contented to suffer for it.

Hamilton trusts that those who follow his argument will agree with his plan of action. It's a skill he later exhibits brilliantly in his contributions to the *Federalist Papers*, as well as the *First Report on Public Credit*, the *Report on a National Bank*, and dozens of other essays.

Many other <u>colonists had read Locke</u> and had strong, principled ideas. Hamilton isn't unique in that respect. But he is almost unique in his passion for persuading others to agree with his ideas.

In "Full Vindication" in 1774, Hamilton was already making economic arguments. The Continental Congress had proposed a boycott of British goods. Hamilton didn't ignore the fact that people had to make a living (the first thread of our Gordian Knot), but he did argue that the long-term benefits of the boycott would outweigh the short-term negative effects on everyone's income:

> <u>Is it not better</u>, I ask, to suffer a few present inconveniencies, than to put yourselves in the way of losing every thing that is precious. Your lives, your property, your religion are all at stake. I do my duty. I warn you of your danger. If you should still be so mad, as to bring destruction upon yourselves; if you should still neglect what you owe to God and man, you cannot plead ignorance in your excuse. Your consciences will reproach you for your folly, and your children's children will curse you.

<u>I despise</u> and <u>Is it not better</u>: Hamilton, "Full Vindication," 12/15/1774.
https://founders.archives.gov/documents/Hamilton/01-01-02-0054

<u>Colonists had read Locke</u>: For a detailed discussion of the ideas circulating in the American colonies in the 1760s-1770s, see C. Bradley Thompson, *America's Revolutionary Mind, A Moral History of the American Revolution and the Declaration That Defined It*, 2019.

In 1775, Hamilton published two more substantial essays supporting the patriot cause: "The Farmer Refuted", a reply to Samuel Seabury's response to "Full Vindication," and "Remarks on the Quebec Bill".

3.3 FROM 1776 TO 1781: SOLDIER

3.3.1 Military and aide-de-camp experience

Hamilton was drilling with the militia by spring 1775, and joined the army early in 1776. A glimpse of his business training shows up in the meticulous ledger of payments he made to his troops.

Hamilton fought in several major battles, including Yorktown, the last major conflict in the Revolutionary War. Again and again he put his life on the line for the United States, although he'd been living in the thirteen American colonies for less than three years when the war broke out. For Hamilton, the survival of America as a united nation wasn't an abstract matter. He loved the United States enough to risk dying for it. That's relevant to the second thread of our Gordian Knot: he wants the nation to survive as a unit, not disintegrate into separate states.

As an aide to Commander-in-Chief George Washington from 1777 to 1781, Hamilton had an insider's view of the army's financial situation. He knew how often Washington had to remonstrate with Congress about the army's lack of supplies and money. He knew that the

---

Farmer Refuted: Hamilton, "The Farmer Refuted," 2/23/1775.
https://founders.archives.gov/documents/Hamilton/01-01-02-0057

Remarks: "Remarks on the Quebec Bill," Part 1, 6/15/1775; Part 2, 6/22/1775. These deal with freedom of religion in Canada and with the overweening power of the British government there: "I trust, it will clearly appear, that arbitrary power, and its great engine the Popish Religion, are, to all intents and purposes, established in that province."
https://founders.archives.gov/documents/Hamilton/01-01-02-0058 ■
https://founders.archives.gov/documents/Hamilton/01-01-02-0059

Army's lack: See, for example, Washington to John Hancock (president of the Continental Congress), 12/25/1775: "The Gentlemen by whom you Sent the money are arrived—the Sum they brought—tho Large is not Sufficient to answer the demands of the Army—which at this time are remarkably heavy—there is three months pay due—one months advance—two dollars for each blankett ...." See also Washington's letters to Hancock of 7/3/1776 and 8/7/1776, and many more.
https://founders.archives.gov/documents/Washington/03-02-02-0560-0001

HAMILTON'S FINANCIAL PROGRAMS

thirteen states routinely ignored Congress's requisitions for funds, or sent far less than Congress had requested. In military defeats and in bloody footprints in the snow at Valley Forge, Hamilton saw the concrete effects of the lack of funds and supplies.

Service in the Continental Army demonstrated to Hamilton that to gain and keep political independence, a reliable source of government revenue (the fourth thread in our Gordian Knot) was essential. To many other Americans that was not obvious, or was not a high priority.

But it also demonstrated to him the need for an energetic and well-informed federal government. As early as February 1778, when he had been on Washington's staff for barely a year, he wrote to Governor George Clinton of New York:

> <u>There is a matter</u>, which often obtrudes itself upon my mind, and which requires the attention of every person of sense and influence, among us. I mean a degeneracy of representation in the great council of America. ... Many members of it are no doubt men in every respect, fit for the trust, but this cannot be said of it as a body. Folly, caprice a want of foresight, comprehension and dignity, characterise the general tenor of their actions. Of this I dare say, you are sensible, though you have not perhaps so many opportunities of knowing it as I have. Their conduct with respect to the army especially is feeble indecisive and improvident ...

3.3.2 Early writings on economics, 1779-1780

Late in 1779 or early in 1780, while the Revolutionary War was still in progress, Hamilton wrote his <u>first lengthy piece</u> devoted entirely to an economic matter. (For the economic theories current at the time, see the following two pages.) Addressing an unidentified political figure, Hamilton raised what he saw as the crucial problem facing the United States: a shortage of money in circulation, the third thread of our Gordian Knot. The nation, says Hamilton, has no money with which

---

<u>There is a matter</u>: Hamilton to George Clinton, 2/13/1778.
https://founders.archives.gov/documents/Hamilton/01-01-02-0365

<u>First lengthy piece</u>: Hamilton wrote the "Letter on Currency" between December 1779 and March 1780, when the army was in winter quarters in Morristown, New Jersey. The document as transcribed in Founders Archives has many blanks: either it was never completed, or the version in the Hamilton Papers at the Library of Congress was a draft.
https://founders.archives.gov/documents/Hamilton/01-02-02-0559-0002

Economic Theories Prevalent When Hamilton Begins Writing about Economics

There are three schools of economic thought in the 1780s and 1790s ... or, more precisely, two schools plus one book published in 1776 that will become highly influential, but doesn't yet have a wide following.

Mercantilists

The mercantilist school had been around since the sixteenth century, having become dominant when feudalism was fading and national economies under absolute rulers were on the rise in Europe. Mercantilism thinks in terms of such national economies. It holds that gold and silver are the only source of wealth, and that, therefore, trade is a zero-sum game. If a French merchant sells a case of wine to a Brit, and the Brit pays in gold, then the whole kingdom of France is wealthier, and all of Great Britain is poorer. To avoid this, the government must use its power (tariffs, monopolies, regulation, etc.) to ensure that money flows into the country, but not out. The goal is a positive balance of trade.

Almost by definition, European finance ministers in the eighteenth century are mercantilists. Among them is Jacques Necker, who handled French finances for Louis XVI from 1777-1781 and 1788-1790. In February 1781, Necker became the first finance minister ever to publish an account of the nation's income and expenditures. The report quickly sold some 200,000 copies.

Physiocrats

The Physiocratic school rose in the mid-eighteenth century in France, led by François Quesnay (1694-1774). At the time, the French government was beginning to collect statistical data on production, trade, and population. Based on such information, the Physiocrats argue that wealth comes not from gold and silver gained by trading, but from agriculture. ("Physiocrat" means, roughly, "Nature rules.") Landowners, artisans, and merchants, say the Physiocrats, are all unproductive. They merely subsist on the surpluses produced by farmers.

The Physiocrats also believe that self-interest motivates all the players in the economy. Let people alone to act in their own interest (*laissez-faire*), and they will individually choose what goods they want, as well as the most productive work they can perform to acquire those goods. According to Physiocrats, the trade restrictions advocated by mercantilists distort the market by placing tariffs and other barriers between individuals and their goals. The whole of society suffers due to that distortion.

Americans who favor the Physiocratic school include Benjamin Franklin and Thomas Jefferson. Both believe that a nation's wealth is and should be based on agriculture.

Adam Smith

Adam Smith (1723-1790) met Physiocrats while traveling in France and agreed with them on several points: that the value of a good depends on the amount of labor that goes into it; that capital is most productive when employed in agriculture; and that the economy runs best if individuals pursue their own self-interest in a free market. Smith elaborated his own economic theory in *An Inquiry into the Nature and Causes of the Wealth of Nations,* 1776.

A nation's wealth, says Smith, is not the gold and silver in its coffers, but its production of goods and services. Individuals acting in their self-interest are best qualified to choose what to produce. But the ability to produce depends on an efficient division of labor (specialization) and the accumulation of capital (savings). In order to choose to accumulate money rather than spend it immediately, people must trust the government to protect their savings and other property.

Smith emphasizes that government interference in the form of subsidies, monopolies, tax preferences, and so on, disrupts the working of the free market. The government's role should be restricted to defending the nation, providing a justice system, regulating banks, building major infrastructure to facilitate commerce, and promoting a certain basic level of education. Tariffs can be used to protect industries vital to national defense, but never to protect special interests (particular industries).

Smith is an advocate of free markets, but not a dogmatic advocate of laissez-faire policies. Significant elaborations of his theories include David Ricardo's explanation of the theory of comparative advantage (why free trade benefits everyone), which was not published until 1817.

The Wealth of Nations becomes an extraordinarily influential book, but this being an era before mass communication and transportation, its influence is not immediately felt in America. The first edition is published in Great Britain just as the American Revolution is beginning. It goes through another four British editions by the time Smith dies in 1790, but the first edition in America is not printed until 1789. Demand is not strong enough for a second edition until 1796. So by the time Hamilton becomes secretary of the Treasury in 1789, Smith's theories are known in America, but not nearly as widely as those of the mercantilists or the Physiocrats.

AdamSmith.org has a good summary of the themes of *The Wealth of Nations*, and a link to a useful condensed version of the book by Eamonn Butler.

https://www.adamsmith.org/the-wealth-of-nations/ ◼ https://tinyurl.com/4ejnxxuk

to fight the war. Paper money has been issued freely, but its value soon depreciates. A foreign loan must be sought. Since most Americans are farmers with little cash, they must contribute food, livestock, and so on to support the war effort. A national bank must be established that can lend to the government. Its capital will be subscriptions from wealthy Americans and the proceeds of a foreign loan.

In September 1780, Hamilton writes another essay on America's economic situation. This time it is addressed to Congressman James Duane, and written at Duane's request. Hamilton argues that the federal government should be given more powers: control over waging war and making peace, over raising armies and fleets, and over

---

National bank: Hamilton, "Letter on Currency," late 1779 or early 1780: "The object of principal concern is the state of our currency. ... The war, particularly in the first periods, required exertions beyond our strength; to which neither our population nor riches were equal ... The only plan that can preserve the currency is one that will make it the immediate interest of the monied men to cooperate with government in its support. ... The plan I would propose is that of an American bank, instituted by authority of Congress for ten years under the denomination of The Bank of The United States." NOTE: The first bank to be established in the United States was the Bank of North America, which opened its doors in January 1782. The regulations of the Bank of the United States as proposed in the letter Hamilton wrote at Morristown differ considerably from those of the Bank of the United States established in 1791. For example, as described by Hamilton at Morristown, the Bank of the United States would offer subscriptions for a million pounds, at least a quarter of that in gold and silver; there were to be several branches; and for a limited time, the bank would have the right to coin money. See Chapter 5 and Appendix 2 for more on the Bank of the United States that was established in 1791.
https://founders.archives.gov/documents/Hamilton/01-02-02-0559-0002

Written at Duane's request: Hamilton to James Duane, 9/3/1780: "Agreeably to your request and my promise I sit down to give you my ideas of the defects of our present system, and the changes necessary to save us from ruin. ... The fundamental defect is a want of power in Congress. ... It may however be said that it has originated from three causes—an excess of the spirit of liberty which has made the particular states show a jealousy of all power not in their own hands; and this jealousy has led them to exercise a right of judging in the last resort of the measures recommended by Congress, and of acting according to their own opinions of their propriety or necessity; a diffidence in Congress of their own powers, by which they have been timid and indecisive in their resolutions, constantly making concessions to the states, till they have scarcely left themselves the shadow of power; a want of sufficient means

➢

financial matters such as regulating trade, imposing import and export duties, coining money, and establishing banks. Seven years before the Constitutional Convention, Hamilton calls for a meeting of the states to correct the defects of the Articles of Confederation. He also urges that rather than attempting to run the nation by committee, Congress appoint secretaries of foreign affairs, war, marine, finances, and trade. He recommends General Philip Schuyler for War, General Alexander McDougall for Marine, and Robert Morris for Finance.

In this letter to Duane, Hamilton addresses cementing the union of the states, circulation of money, and government revenue—the second, third and fourth threads of our Gordian Knot. It is surely no coincidence that a few months after Hamilton wrote to Congressman

at their disposal to answer the public exigencies and of vigor to draw forth those means ... [T]he confederation itself is defective and requires to be altered; it is neither fit for war, nor peace. And why can we not have an American bank? Are our monied men less enlightened to their own interest or less enterprising in the persuit?"
https://founders.archives.gov/documents/Hamilton/01-02-02-0838

Regulating trade: Hamilton to Duane, 9/3/1780, re regulating trade: "regulating trade, determining with what countries it shall be carried on, granting indulgencies laying prohibitions on all the articles of export or import, imposing duties granting bounties & premiums for raising exporting importing and applying to their own use the product of these duties, only giving credit to the states on whom they are raised in the general account of revenues and expences, instituting Admiralty courts &c., of coining money, establishing banks on such terms, and with such privileges as they think proper, appropriating funds and doing whatever else relates to the operations of finance, transacting every thing with foreign nations, making alliances offensive and defensive, treaties of commerce, &c. &c."
https://founders.archives.gov/documents/Hamilton/01-02-02-0838

Surely no coincidence: John Sullivan (New Hampshire representative to the Continental Congress) asks Washington on 1/29/1781, "yr opinion with respect to Colo. Hamilton as a Financier." Washington replies on 2/4/1781 that he has never discussed finances with Hamilton, but that "there are few men to be found, of his age, who has a more general knowledge than he possesses—and none whose Soul is more firmly engaged in the cause—or who exceeds him in probity & Sterling virtue. ..." For more on Hamilton's reputation regarding finance during the War, see Forrest McDonald, *Hamilton*, pp. 40-43.
https://founders.archives.gov/documents/Washington/99-01-02-04696
■ https://founders.archives.gov/documents/Washington/99-01-02-04754

Duane, another member of Congress asked Washington about Hamilton's qualifications for the newly created position of superintendent of Finance for the United States. Hamilton's credentials as a businessman and a student of finance and economics were obviously becoming widely known.

Incidentally, although the Revolutionary War was not officially over until the signing of the treaty in September 1783, Hamilton's letter to Duane in 1780 was the last piece on economics that Hamilton wrote from a soldier's point of view:

> Without a speedy change the army must dissolve; it is now a mob, rather than an army, without cloathing, without pay, without provision, without morals, without discipline. We begin to hate the country for its neglect of us; the country begins to hate us for our oppressions of them. Congress have long been jealous of us; we have now lost all confidence in them, and give the worst construction to all they do. Held together by the slenderest ties we are ripening for a dissolution.

3.3.3 Letter to Robert Morris, 1781

In May 1781, Robert Morris, a Philadelphia merchant, took office as superintendent of Finance of the United States. By the end of April, Hamilton has already written a long letter to Morris, his senior by some twenty years. This time Hamilton addresses the union of the nation, money in circulation, government revenue, and government debt: the second, third, fourth, and fifth threads of our Gordian Knot.

Hamilton again emphasizes the importance of finances in winning the war:

> Tis by introducing order into our finances—by restoreing public credit—not by gaining battles, that we are finally to gain our object. Tis by putting ourselves in a condition to continue the war not by temporary, violent and unnatural efforts to bring it to a decisive issue, that we shall in reality bring it to a speedy and successful one.

Without a speedy change: Hamilton to James Duane, 9/3/1780.
https://founders.archives.gov/documents/Hamilton/01-02-02-0838

Letter to Morris and Tis by introducing: Hamilton to Robert Morris, 4/30/1781.
https://founders.archives.gov/documents/Hamilton/01-02-02-1167

He again proposes a convention of the states to revise the Articles of Confederation. To increase money in circulation, he strongly recommends the establishment of a national bank, and lays out how it should be structured. He analyzes the resources available as revenue for the federal government, based on tax revenue in European nations, and estimates the annual expenses of the government. He considers which European nations might lend America money. He suggests that government debt could be funded on the British model, and might be paid off in thirty or thirty-five years, in part because the population will probably double by then, and trade will increase proportionately.

3.3.4 The "Continentalist" essays, 1781-1782

In the summer of 1781—just a few months before the siege of Yorktown—Hamilton went public with his proposals to improve his adopted nation. The very title of these six essays, "The Continentalist", reveals that he opposes the current fragmentation of the United States. In the first essay, published in mid-1781, he writes:

> [T]here is hardly at this time a man of information in America, who will not acknowledge, as a general proposition, that in its

---

National bank: Hamilton spent at least half of his lengthy letter to Morris laying out the structure of the bank. It would sell three million pounds' worth of stock. It would redeem the paper currency issued by the government. For the thirty years of the bank's existence, no other bank would be chartered in the United States. From the letter to Morris: "This [a national bank] I regard, in some shape or other as an expedient essential to our safety and success, unless by a happy turn of European affairs the war should speedily terminate in a manner upon which it would be unwise to reckon. There is no other that can give to government that extensive and systematic credit, which the defect of our revenues makes indispensably necessary to its operations. The longer it is delayed, the more difficult it becomes; our affairs grow every day more relaxed and more involved; public credit hastens to a more irretrievable catastrophe; the means for executing the plan are exhausted in partial and temporary efforts. ... In the present system of things the health of a state particularly a commercial one depends on a due quantity and regular circulation of Cash, as much as the health of an animal body depends upon the due quantity and regular circulation of the blood. There are indisputable indications that we have not a sufficient medium and what we have is in continual fluctuation. The only cure to our public disorders is to fix the value of the currency we now have and increase it to a proper standard in a species that will have the requisite stability. ..."

There is hardly: Hamilton, "Continentalist" No. 1, 7/12/1781. https://founders.archives.gov/documents/Hamilton/01-02-02-1179

present form, it is unequal, either to a vigorous prosecution of the war, or to the preservation of the union in peace.

Hamilton begins by noting that we Americans knew little about governing ourselves when we became independent ... but it's time we learn. The main problem, he argues, is <u>Congress's lack of power</u>. In a monarchy, the danger is that a ruler may gain too much power; but in a federal government, the <u>danger is that the government</u> will not be powerful enough to prevent any of the separate parts from taking control of the whole federation.

The United States, explains Hamilton, is in a <u>dire situation</u>. The federal government has no income, and "<u>power without revenue</u> in political society is a name." It cannot borrow abroad because of its enormous debts: "<u>Credit supposes</u> specific and permanent funds for the punctual payment of interest, with a moral certainty of a final redemption of the principal." The government cannot borrow from its own citizens, because few of them are wealthy, and most of their wealth is in land, not cash. The government needs to borrow, however, and the best way to do that is to establish a <u>national bank</u>—as Robert Morris, the superintendent of Finance, has suggested.

Aside from providing revenue for the federal government and establishing a national bank, the step Hamilton sees as most urgent to the

---

<u>Congress's lack of power</u>: Hamilton, "Continentalist" No. 1, 7/12/1781.
https://founders.archives.gov/documents/Hamilton/01-02-02-1179

<u>Danger is that the government</u>: Hamilton, "Continentalist" No. 2, 7/19/1781. "From the plainest principles of human nature, two inferences are to be drawn, one, that each member of a political confederacy, will be more disposed to advance its own authority upon the ruins of that of the confederacy, than to make any improper concessions in its favour, or support it in unreasonable pretensions; the other, that the subjects of each member, will be more devoted in their attachments and obedience to their own particular governments, than to that of the union."
https://founders.archives.gov/documents/Hamilton/01-02-02-1181

<u>Dire situation</u>: Hamilton, "Continentalist" No. 3, 8/9/1781: "Our whole system is in disorder; our currency depreciated, till in many places it will hardly obtain a circulation at all, public credit at its lowest ebb, our army deficient in numbers, and unprovided with every thing, the government, in its present condition, unable to command the means to pay, clothe, or feed their troops, the enemy making an alarming progress in the southern states ..."
https://founders.archives.gov/documents/Hamilton/01-02-02-1186

<u>Power without revenue</u>; <u>Credit supposes</u>; <u>national bank</u>: Hamilton, "Continentalist" No. 4, 8/30/1781.
https://founders.archives.gov/documents/Hamilton/01-02-02-1191

survival of the United States is to give the federal government <u>power to regulate trade</u>, rather than allowing the states to make whatever laws they please. The best source of revenue for the federal government would be duties on imported goods. As opposed to a tax on land or a per-person (poll) tax, <u>import duties</u> can be passed on from the

---

Power to regulate trade: Hamilton, "Continentalist" No. 4, 8/30/1781: "It may be pronounced with confidence, that nothing short of the following articles can suffice. 1st, THE POWER OF REGULATING TRADE, comprehending a right of granting bounties and premiums by way of encouragement, of imposing duties of every kind, as well for revenue as regulation, of appointing all officers of the customs, and of laying embargoes, in extraordinary emergencies." Here and elsewhere, it's a moot point whether Hamilton is aiming for more government control of trade, or instead wants federal control of trade in order to put an end to the many and varied state regulations of trade. See also §6.4.
https://founders.archives.gov/documents/Hamilton/01-02-02-1191

Import duties: Hamilton, "Continentalist" No. 5 (4/18/1782) is one of the crucial documents regarding Hamilton's attitude toward laissez-faire politics, mercantilism, and pragmatism. "There are some, who maintain, that trade will regulate itself, and is not to be benefitted by the encouragements, or restraints of government. Such persons will imagine, that there is no need of a common directing power. This is one of those wild speculative paradoxes, which have grown into credit among us, contrary to the uniform practice and sense of the most enlightened nations. Contradicted by the numerous institutions and laws, that exist every where for the benefit of trade, by the pains taken to cultivate particular branches and to discourage others, by the known advantages derived from those measures, and by the palpable evils that would attend their discontinuance—it must be rejected by every man acquainted with commercial history. Commerce, like other things, has its fixed principles, according to which it must be regulated; if these are understood and observed, it will be promoted by the attention of government, if unknown, or violated, it will be injured—but it is the same with every other part of administration. To preserve the ballance of trade in favour of a nation ought to be a leading aim of its policy. ... Perhaps it may be thought, that the power of regulation will be left placed in the governments of the several states ... but as they are parts of a whole with a common interest in trade, as in other things, there ought to be a common direction in that as in all other matters. ... General principles in subjects of this nature ought always to be advanced with caution; in an experimental analysis there are found such a number of exceptions as tend to render them very doubtful; and in questions which affect the existence and collective happiness of these states, all nice and abstract distinctions should give way to plainer interests and to more obvious and simple rules of conduct."
https://founders.archives.gov/documents/Hamilton/01-03-02-0015

merchant to the consumer, and being less noticeable, can be imposed "with least exception or disgust."

In the "Continentalist" essays, Hamilton discusses making a living (the concerns of farmers and traders), a stronger federal government, increasing money in circulation via a national bank, and government revenue and debt: all five threads of the Gordian Knot.

One of the remarkable features of the "Continentalist" essays is how completely Hamilton has switched his point of view. He is no longer a soldier speaking to a Congressman (Duane) or a student of finance speaking to a financier (Morris). He is an American speaking to his fellow Americans. He doesn't lecture, pontificate or condescend. He attempts to inform and persuade. The fifth "Continentalist", for example, ends with a call for all Americans to try to look at the big picture:

> It is too much characteristic of our national temper to be ingenious in finding out and magnifying the minutest disadvantages, and to reject measures of evident utility even of necessity to avoid trivial and sometimes imaginary evils. We seem not to reflect, that in human society, there is scarcely any plan, however salutary to the whole and to every part, by the share, each has in the common prosperity, but in one way, or another, and under particular circumstances, will operate more to the benefit of some parts, than of others. Unless we can overcome this narrow disposition and learn to estimate measures, by their general tendency, we shall never be a great or a happy people, if we remain a people at all.

3.3.5 Hamilton as one of the federal government's creditors

The fifth and sixth "Continentalist" essays were published in mid-1782, long after Cornwallis had surrendered and Hamilton had returned to the Schuyler home in Albany. In March 1782, he resigned from the army, renouncing "from this time all claim to the

---

It is too much: Hamilton, "Continentalist" No. 5, 4/18/1782.
https://founders.archives.gov/documents/Hamilton/01-03-02-0015

Renouncing: Hamilton to Washington, two letters of 3/1/1782.
https://founders.archives.gov/documents/Hamilton/01-03-02-0006 ∎
https://founders.archives.gov/documents/Hamilton/01-03-02-0005

compensations attached to my military station during the war or after it." At that point, the government owed him $2,820 for years of service—quite a substantial sum. Having no hopes of receiving it from the federal government, Hamilton submitted a petition to the New York State legislature in February 1784 asking that they pay what he was owed, as they had done for some other officers. There is no record that the legislature did so.

When Hamilton was named secretary of the Treasury and became responsible for settling accounts with all the creditors of the United States, he knew how it felt to be owed substantial sums that one despaired of seeing repaid.

3.4 IN 1782: GOVERNMENT BUREAUCRAT

The federal government needed funds to operate, and under the Articles of Confederation, it could get them only by collecting requisitions from each state. In May 1782, with the peace treaty not yet signed and the British still occupying New York City, Robert Morris asked Hamilton to accept the position of tax receiver for New York State.

While he attempted to gather funds for the federal government, Hamilton observed firsthand the operations of the government of New York. New York was a large and influential state, and the one Hamilton had chosen to reside in. He saw how susceptible its legislature was to being manipulated by a few wealthy or influential individuals. He saw that non-objective tax laws—for instance, giving a tax collector the right to arbitrarily decree a person's taxes—led to corruption. He saw

---

Substantial sum: For comparison, Hamilton's salary as secretary of the Treasury was $3,500 per year. On the money owed to Hamilton, see "Alexander Hamilton's Account with the Government of the United States," 3/7/1789.
https://founders.archives.gov/documents/Hamilton/01-01-02-0078

Petition: Hamilton, "Petition to the New York Legislature" 2/4/1784. See also "Alexander Hamilton's Account with the Government of the United States," 3/7/1789, whose notes in Founders Online describe Eliza's attempts to have the government repay this after Hamilton's death; and Hamilton, "Explanation of His Financial Situation," 7/1/1804, n. 1. Soldiers were also promised land; in 1839, Eliza received a warrant for 450 acres.

https://founders.archives.gov/documents/Hamilton/01-03-02-0321 ∎
https://founders.archives.gov/documents/Hamilton/01-01-02-0078 ∎
https://founders.archives.gov/documents/Hamilton/01-26-02-0001-0244

Tax receiver: Morris to Hamilton, 5/2/1782.
https://founders.archives.gov/documents/Hamilton/01-03-02-0019

the difficulty of collecting gold and silver coins in payment for taxes: everyone preferred to hand over the eternally fluctuating paper money issued by state and federal governments. Writing to Morris, Hamilton decried the government revenue system in New York as "radically vicious, burthensome to the people and unproductive to government."

Having been chosen as a New York delegate to the Confederation Congress, Hamilton resigned as tax receiver after three months. He had badgered New York into providing the federal government with $6,434.10 out of the $54,000 that had been requisitioned. His brief stint as a bureaucrat gave him additional close personal knowledge of several threads in the Gordian Knot: the consequences of having too little money in circulation, the problems of raising government revenue and paying off government debt, and the centrifugal forces operating in the individual states.

3.5 FROM 1782 TO 1783: DELEGATE TO THE CONFEDERATION CONGRESS

In late 1782, Hamilton set off to Philadelphia to serve as New York State's delegate to the Confederation Congress. He was operating again on a national level, as he had while serving as Washington's aide in the Revolutionary War. As a congressman, he saw from an insider's perspective how ineffectual the federal government was, and

---

Radically vicious: Hamilton to Morris, 6/17/1782.
http://founders.archives.gov/documents/Hamilton/01-03-02-0027

Badgered: On the amount requisitioned from each state in 1782-1786, see "Schedule of requisitions on the several states by the United States in Congress assembled: of 10th Sept. 1782 ... and of 2d August, 1786 shewing the quotas assigned to each, the amount paid thereon, and the balances due on the 30th June, 1786." In "Defence of the Funding System," 1795, Hamilton described the system under the Articles of Confederation by which the national government had to request funds from the states as "a system of imbecility and injustice. ... It is against every principle of sound reasoning or constitutional or practical policy to leave the administration in a condition to depend not on legal and obligatory provisions but on such as are gratuitous & voluntary. This is to arbitrate not to govern."
https://www.loc.gov/resource/bdsdcc.19101/?st=gallery ■ https://founders.archives.gov/documents/Hamilton/01-19-02-0001

Ineffectual: Congress seems to have been putting out fires without any overall plan. See Library of Congress, *Journals of the Continental Congress 1774-1789,* vols. 23 (1782, published 1914) and 24 (early 1783, published 1922)
https://archive.org/details/journalscontine04hillgoog ■ https://archive.org/details/journalsofcontin24unit

how difficult it was to pass any legislation.

Hamilton saw that the states were still in danger of splitting apart (the second thread of our Gordian Knot). Writing in 1783 to congratulate Washington on the preliminary peace treaty with Great Britain, he noted:

> It now only remains to make solid establishments within to perpetuate our union to prevent our being a ball in the hands of European powers bandied against each other at their pleasure—in fine to make our independence truly a blessing: This it is to be lamented will be an arduous work, for to borrow a figure from mechanics, the centrifugal is much stronger than the centripetal force in these states—the seeds of disunion much more numerous than those of union.

At the end of his term in Congress, in July 1783, Hamilton drafted a list of twelve defects of the Articles of Confederation, including the fact that the federal government lacks "efficacious authority" to accomplish anything. There is no nationwide judiciary power to rein in states that misbehave, and because Congress has no revenue, it cannot raise troops for the nation's defense, or pay its debts. At the end of the draft, Hamilton noted: "Resolution intended to be submitted to Congress at Princeton in 1783; but abandoned for want of support."

On the positive side, during his tenure in Congress Hamilton corresponded with dozens of prominent Americans, including congressmen, governors, and army officers, among them George Washington, James Madison, Robert Morris, Gouverneur Morris, John Dickinson, John Jay, Henry Laurens, William Duer, George Clinton, and Nathanael Greene. His foreign correspondents included the Marquis de Lafayette, the vicomte de Noailles, and Francisco de Miranda. From this period on, Hamilton carried on a voluminous correspondence with hundreds of people throughout the United States. When he needed data and opinions, he could appeal to a wide range of authoritative sources.

It now only remains: Hamilton to Washington, 3/24/1783.
https://founders.archives.gov/documents/Washington/99-01-02-10908

Twelve defects: Hamilton, "Continental Congress Unsubmitted Resolution Calling for a Convention to Amend the Articles of Confederation," July 1783.
https://founders.archives.gov/documents/Hamilton/01-03-02-0272

3.6 FROM 1782 TO 1789: PRACTICING LAW

3.6.1 In 1782: Becoming a lawyer

In January 1782, Hamilton began studying law. That July, less than a year after Yorktown, he passed the bar. He did not, however, immediately become a practicing lawyer. In the summer of 1782, he was tax collector for Robert Morris. (See §3.4.) In the 1782-1783 term, he served in the Confederation Congress. (See §3.5.) Only after that did he take up the law full time.

With legal training and experience, Hamilton became even more adept at gathering evidence and arguing his case. Given that most Americans didn't know which direction they wanted to go or why, Hamilton's ability to inform and persuade was invaluable. Forrest McDonald pointed out that although Hamilton professed pessimism about human nature, he spent enormous amounts of effort trying to appeal to men's rational side:

> He had come to profess the "pessimistic" view of man, maintaining that people are governed by "passion and prejudice" rather than by "an enlightened sense of their interests"; and yet throughout his career he expended more energy and talent in appeals to the intelligence and virtue of common citizens than did any other American in public life. So much stronger was his natural optimism than his acquired pessimism.

3.6.2 In 1783-1784: Defending former loyalists

In September 1783, the United States signed a treaty with Britain that included an agreement not to prosecute those who had supported

---

Studying law: On Hamilton's studies for the bar, see Durante, "Hamilton Studies Law, 1782 (Hamilton 40)."

https://diannedurantewriter.com/archives/2247

He had come: Forrest McDonald, *Hamilton*, p. 42 and n. 30.

Agreement not to prosecute: Article 6 of the Treaty of Paris, Article 6, signed 9/30/1783: "That there shall be no future confiscations made nor any prosecutions commenced against any person or persons for, or by reason of, the part which he or they may have taken in the present war, and that no person shall on that account suffer any future loss or damage, either in his person, liberty, or property; and that those who may be in confinement on such charges at the time of the ratification of the treaty in America shall be immediately set at liberty, and the prosecutions so commenced be discontinued."

https://avalon.law.yale.edu/18th_century/paris.asp

Britain during the war, but who had chosen to remain in the United States afterwards. Nevertheless, the New York State legislature passed a number of laws that targeted former loyalists. One law prohibited former loyalists from voting or holding office. Another provided that persons of "equivocal and suspected character" could be exiled from the state, and yet another that the state could confiscate their property. The Trespass Act (March 1783) provided that patriots who fled New York City during the British occupation could sue former loyalists who had occupied their property—an <u>ex post facto</u> <u>law</u> declaring that an action that was legal at the time was now illegal.

At the end of the war, some thirty thousand loyalists fled to Canada and Britain. Among the refugees were about a fifth of the population of the state of New York, including many wealthy businessmen. Hamilton noted that by the time the British evacuated New York City in late 1783, dozens of loyalists worth two or three million dollars each (in today's money) had fled:

> <u>The spirit of emigration</u> has greatly increased of late. Some violent papers sent into the city have determined many to depart, who hitherto have intended to remain. Many merchants of second class, characters of no political consequence, each of whom may carry away eight or ten thousand guineas have I am told lately applied for shipping to convey them away. Our state will feel for twenty years at least, the effects of the popular phrenzy.

In 1783 and 1784, more than sixty of Hamilton's cases were <u>defenses</u> of businessmen who had remained in New York City after the British occupied it in 1776.

Ex post facto law: On all these acts of the New York legislature, see Durante, *Hamilton: A Friend to America*, II, Chapter 47 ("Hamilton Defends Former Loyalists in New York"), pp. 5-17. The Trespass Act is reprinted in Mercantile Library Association of the City of New York, *New York City During the American Revolution, Being a Collection of Original Papers (now First Published) from the Manuscripts in the Possession of the Mercantile Library Association, of New York City,* New York, 1861.
https://tinyurl.com/7n3t3d76

The spirit of emigration: Hamilton to Robert R. Livingston, 8/13/1783. A guinea was 1/4 oz. of gold, so at today's prices, each of the "merchants of the second class" were worth $2 or $3 million. Including such merchants, about 30,000 loyalists fled New York in 1783. McDonald, *Hamilton*, p. 74 estimates that one fifth of the population of New York State had fled to Canada and Britain.
https://founders.archives.gov/documents/Hamilton/01-03-02-0277

Defenses: On Hamilton's defense of Tories, see McDonald, *Hamilton*, p. 69.

Hamilton, whose résumé now included being a businessman, a lawyer, a government bureaucrat, and a former Congressman, was very aware that experienced and wealthy businessmen—former loyalists or not—would be crucial for the economic recovery of the United States. They were particularly needed in New York, which had suffered severely under the seven-year British occupation. By defending former loyalists, <u>Hamilton did his best</u> to ensure that such merchants would remain and carry on business.

3.6.3 In 1784: Helping establish the Bank of New York

In February 1784, Hamilton became legal advisor to the newly established <u>Bank of New York</u>, one of only three banks in the United States. (See §2.3.4.) Writing its charter and helping set up its operations gave him a boots-in-the-vault view of how banks operate. From his business experience, he knew that if entrepreneurs could borrow money to establish and grow their businesses, New York would recover much more quickly. The Bank of New York provided capital for such businesses. If the bank was careful to get adequate collateral for loans, it

---

<u>Hamilton did his best</u>: In a pamphlet published under the name "Phocion" in January 1784, Hamilton argued that having wealthy businessmen in the city is good for the economy, even if you are not one of them. "The men who are at the head of the party which contends for, disqualification and expulsion, endeavoured to inlist a number of people on their side by holding out motives of private advantage to them. To the trader they say, you will be overborne by the large capitals of the Tory merchants; to the Mechanic, your business will be less profitable, your wages less considerable by the interference of Tory workmen. A man, the least acquainted with trade, will indeed laugh at such suggestion. He will know, that every merchant or trader has an interest in the aggregate mass of capital or stock in trade; that what he himself wants in capital, he must make up in credit; that unless there are others who possess large capitals, this credit cannot be had, and that in the diminution of the general capital of the State, commerce will decline, and his own prospects of profit will diminish."
https://founders.archives.gov/documents/Hamilton/01-03-02-0314

<u>Bank of New York</u>: The Bank of New York began operations on June 9, 1784, but was not granted a charter by the New York State legislature until 3/21/1791. See "Petition of the President, Directors, and Stockholders of the Bank of New York," 10/8/1784. See also Rufus King to Hamilton, 3/24/1791.
https://founders.archives.gov/documents/Hamilton/01-03-02-0386 ■
https://founders.archives.gov/documents/Hamilton/01-08-02-0150

could lend more money in banknotes than it had gold and silver in its vault. That effectively increased the <u>amount of money</u> in circulation.

3.7 IN 1786: NEW YORK LEGISLATOR AND DELEGATE TO THE ANNAPOLIS CONVENTION

In the 1786-1787 term, Hamilton served in the New York State legislature. He was dispatched by the legislature as a <u>delegate to the Meeting</u> of Commissioners to Remedy Defects of the Federal Government, which has been convened to settle commercial disputes between the states. Only five states bothered to send delegates.

The only significant outcome of the three-day Annapolis Convention was a resolution asking that representatives of the thirteen states gather to revamp the Articles of Confederation. Hamilton, drafting the resolution in September, 1786, wrote that the defects of the Articles rendered the "<u>situation of the US</u> delicate & critical." In particular, the representatives should consider trade: "how far an uniform system in their commercial intercourse and regulations might benecessary to their common interest and permanent harmony." The gathering that the delegates at Annapolis called for convened in Philadelphia in May 1787.

<u>Amount of money</u>: The modern term for this is "fractional banking". See also §5.2 below on how banks work, and of course Hamilton's *Report on a National Bank*, discussed in §5.3; especially Appendix 3, §II.A.1.

<u>Delegate to the Meeting</u>: For more on commercial disputes among the states, see Durante, *Hamilton: A Friend to America,* II, pp. 31-37 ("The Annapolis Convention, 1786").

<u>Situation of the US</u>: Hamilton, "Annapolis Address," 9/14/1786: "Deeply impressed however with the magnitude and importance of the object confided to them on this occasion, your Commissioners cannot forbear to indulge an expression of their earnest and unanimous wish, that speedy measures may be taken, to effect a general meeting, of the States, in a future Convention ... That there are important defects in the system of the Fœderal Government is acknowledged by the Acts of all those States, which have concurred in the present Meeting; That the defects, upon a closer examination, may be found greater and more numerous, than even these acts imply, is at least so far probable, from the embarrassments which characterise the present State of our national affairs—foreign and domestic ... Under this impression, Your Commissioners, with the most respectful deference, beg leave to suggest their unanimous conviction, that it may essentially tend to advance the interests of the union, if the States ... [to meet]at Philadelphia on the second Monday in May next, to take into consideration the situation of the United States, to devise such further provisions as shall appear to them necessary to render the constitution of the Fœderal Government adequate to the exigencies of the Union ..."

https://founders.archives.gov/documents/Hamilton/01-03-02-0556

3.8 IN 1787: DELEGATE TO THE CONSTITUTIONAL CONVENTION

Back in New York, Hamilton was chosen as one of three delegates to Philadelphia, where the Federal Convention (later known as the Constitutional Convention) was held from May to September 1787. His participation there was a chance to exchange ideas with others and to think long-term about the good of the nation. In his speech of June 18, 1787, Hamilton focused on the need for a federal government that could not be overpowered by states' governments. Of the three delegates from New York, Hamilton was the only one to favor a stronger federal government. He was a member of the Committee of Style, which wrote the text of the Constitution, and a signer of the Constitution.

3.9 FROM 1787 TO 1788: AUTHOR OF 51 OF THE 85 FEDERALIST PAPERS

After the Constitution was written, Hamilton campaigned to have it ratified in New York. Governor George Clinton and a majority of the state's residents preferred that power remain at the state rather than the national level. Hamilton spoke frequently at the ratification convention. One of his themes was the need to balance liberty and power:

> There are two objects in forming systems of government—Safety for the people, and energy in the administration. When these objects are united, the certain tendency of the system will be to the public welfare. If the latter object be neglected, the people's security will be as certainly sacrificed, as by disregarding the former. Good constitutions are formed upon a comparison of the liberty of the individual with the strength of government: If the tone of either be too high, the other will be weakened too much. It is the happiest possible mode of conciliating these objects, to institute one branch peculiarly endowed with sensibility, another with knowledge and firmness. Through the opposition and mutual

---

Could not be overpowered: Hamilton, "Speech at the Constitutional Convention," 6/18/1787, as recorded by James Madison. Hamilton's "Plan of Government," of the same date, includes the provision that any laws of the particular states that contradict the United States Constitution should be void, and that no state have any land or naval forces not under control of the federal government.
https://founders.archives.gov/documents/Hamilton/01-04-02-0098-0003
- https://founders.archives.gov/documents/Hamilton/01-04-02-0098-0003

Balance liberty and power: Hamilton, "First Speech to the New York Ratifying Convention, 6/25/1788.
https://founders.archives.gov/documents/Hamilton/01-05-02-0012-0027

HAMILTON'S FINANCIAL PROGRAMS

controul of these bodies, the government will reach, in its regular operations, the perfect balance between liberty and power.

But Hamilton's longest-lasting contribution was the series of essays in support of ratification that was published as the *Federalist Papers*. Hamilton conceived the series and recruited John Jay and James Madison as co-authors. Jay wrote five of the eight-five essays, Madison twenty-nine, and Hamilton the other fifty-one. Together the three elucidated the Constitution's provisions, elaborated on the thinking behind them, and attempted to persuade Americans of the value of this untried form of government.

Because of their eighty essays in the Federalist Papers, Hamilton and Madison were arguably the two Americans most knowledgeable about the Constitution. Certainly none of their contemporaries wrote so extensively on it. Thomas Jefferson described the Federalist Papers in 1788 as "in my opinion, the best commentary on the principles of government which ever was written."

Hamilton's essays went beyond elaborating the wording of the document, to looking at its political and economic implications. His contributions to the *Federalist Papers* include comments on all the threads of the Gordian Knot: making a living, the power of state vs. federal governments, circulation of money, and government revenue and debt. (See following two pages.)

In the state of New York, only residents of New York City were overwhelmingly in favor of ratifying the Constitution. But they were so impressed with Hamilton's actions on its behalf that in their July 1788 parade celebrating the Declaration of Independence, New Yorkers included a twenty-seven foot model of the "Federal Ship Hamilton".

"Hamilton" float in the Grand Federal Procession. The Battery is at the left. This is a nineteenth-century illustration.

Federalist Papers: All 85 appear, with an index, in the Avalon Project. On Founders Online, they're somewhat more difficult to find.
https://avalon.law.yale.edu/subject_menus/fed.asp

Best commentary: Jefferson to Madison, 11/18/1788.
https://founders.archives.gov/documents/Jefferson/01-14-02-0062

Federal Ship Hamilton: On the procession in New York City, see Durante, *Hamilton: A Friend to America*, II, 110-112 and 119.

Excerpts from Hamilton's essays in the Federalist Papers relating to the threads of the Gordian Knot

#1 Making a living

"In a state of disunion ... [t]hat unequaled spirit of enterprise, which signalizes the genius of the American merchants and navigators, and which is in itself an inexhaustible mine of national wealth, would be stifled and lost, and poverty and disgrace would overspread a country which, with wisdom, might make herself the admiration and envy of the world."
Federalist No. 11, 11/24/1787. https://avalon.law.yale.edu/18th_century/fed11.asp

#2 Centrifugal tendency of the United States

"A man must be far gone in Utopian speculations who can seriously doubt that, if these States should either be wholly disunited, or only united in partial confederacies, the subdivisions into which they might be thrown would have frequent and violent contests with each other. To presume a want of motives for such contests as an argument against their existence, would be to forget that men are ambitious, vindictive, and rapacious. To look for a continuation of harmony between a number of independent, unconnected sovereignties in the same neighborhood, would be to disregard the uniform course of human events, and to set at defiance the accumulated experience of ages."
Federalist No. 6, 11/14/1787 https://avalon.law.yale.edu/18th_century/fed06.asp

"We may indeed with propriety be said to have reached almost the last stage of national humiliation. There is scarcely anything that can wound the pride or degrade the character of an independent nation which we do not experience. Are there engagements to the performance of which we are held by every tie respectable among men? These are the subjects of constant and unblushing violation. Do we owe debts to foreigners and to our own citizens contracted in a time of imminent peril for the preservation of our political existence? These remain without any proper or satisfactory provision for their discharge. Have we valuable territories and important posts in the possession of a foreign power which, by express stipulations, ought long since to have been surrendered? These are still retained, to the prejudice of our interests, not less than of our rights. Are we in a condition to resent or to repel the aggression? We have neither troops, nor treasury, nor government. Are we even in a condition to remonstrate with dignity? The just imputations on our own faith, in respect to the same treaty, ought first to be removed. Are we entitled by nature and compact to a free participation in the navigation of the Mississippi? Spain excludes us from it. Is public credit an indispensable resource in time of public danger? We seem to have abandoned its cause as desperate and irretrievable. Is commerce of importance to national wealth? Ours is at the lowest point of declension. Is respectability in the eyes of foreign powers a safeguard against foreign encroachments? The imbecility of our government even forbids them to treat with us. Our ambassadors abroad are the mere pageants of mimic sovereignty.

Federalist No. 15, 12/1/1787. https://avalon.law.yale.edu/18th_century/fed15.asp

#3 Inadequate money in circulation

"Is a violent and unnatural decrease in the value of land a symptom of national distress? The price of improved land in most parts of the country is much lower than can be accounted for by the quantity of waste land at market, and can only be fully explained by that want of private and public confidence, which are so alarmingly prevalent among all ranks, and which have a direct tendency to depreciate property of every kind. Is private credit the friend and patron of industry? That most useful kind which relates to borrowing and lending is reduced within the narrowest limits, and this still more from an opinion of insecurity than from the scarcity of money. To shorten an enumeration of particulars which can afford neither pleasure nor instruction, it may in general be demanded, what indication is there of national disorder, poverty, and insignificance that could befall a community so peculiarly blessed with natural advantages as we are, which does not form a part of the dark catalogue of our public misfortunes?"

Federalist No. 15, 12/1/1787. https://avalon.law.yale.edu/18th_century/fed15.asp

#4 Lack of government revenue

"As revenue is the essential engine by which the means of answering the national exigencies must be procured, the power of procuring that article in its full extent must necessarily be comprehended in that of providing for those exigencies. As theory and practice conspire to prove that the power of procuring revenue is unavailing when exercised over the States in their collective capacities, the federal government must of necessity be invested with an unqualified power of taxation in the ordinary modes."

Federalist No. 31, 1/1/1788. https://avalon.law.yale.edu/18th_century/fed31.asp

#5 Massive government debt

"Who can pretend that commercial imposts are, or would be, alone equal to the present and future exigencies of the Union? Taking into the account the existing debt, foreign and domestic, upon any plan of extinguishment which a man moderately impressed with the importance of public justice and public credit could approve, in addition to the establishments which all parties will acknowledge to be necessary, we could not reasonably flatter ourselves, that this resource alone, upon the most improved scale, would even suffice for its present necessities."

Federalist No. 30, 12/28/1787. https://avalon.law.yale.edu/18th_century/fed30.asp

3.10 SECRETARY OF THE TREASURY: WHO AND WHAT?

In late July 1788, New York State became the eleventh state to ratify the Constitution. Elections for president and Congress were held that winter. Congress convened in March. George Washington was inaugurated as president on April 30, 1789. Over the following months, as Congress laboriously built the machinery of government, Washington considered who to choose for his closest advisors: secretary of War, secretary of State, and secretary of Treasury.

3.10.1 Robert Morris, the other candidate for secretary of the Treasury

In the United States, few men in public office understood business and finance. George Washington understood the importance of a united country, but his business experience was mostly limited to running his plantation. Both Thomas Jefferson and James Madison had a brilliant grasp of the theoretical principles behind the Constitution, but like Washington, they had little experience with business.

In early 1789, the obvious choice for secretary of the Treasury was Robert Morris. Morris had been a successful merchant in Philadelphia since the early 1750s. From 1781 to 1784, he was superintendent of Finance for the United States. In that role, he established the Bank of North America, which helped fund the purchase of supplies for the Continental Army during the Revolutionary War.

Morris was able to make the rapid decisions necessary during war time in part because his financial negotiations were often carried on at a personal level. For example: in the spring of 1783, American soldiers threatened to mutiny if they didn't receive their pay before being

---

James Madison: Madison wrote a long essay on money ca. September 1779-March 1780, which was published in Freneau's *National Gazette* in December 1791, the month the Bank of the United States opened its doors. Its extraordinarily dry tone, geared to those who already know the topic, is a reminder of why Hamilton's essays and his reports as secretary of the Treasury—which included so much background information that almost anyone could follow them—had such strong impact. Madison's essay begins: "It has been taken for an axiom in all our reasonings on the subject of finance, that supposing the quantity and demand of things vendible in a country to remain the same, their price will vary according to the variation in the quantity of the circulating medium; in other words, that the value of money will be regulated by its quantity."

https://founders.archives.gov/documents/Madison/01-01-02-0103

discharged. Morris signed personal IOUs to the soldiers, making himself responsible for their pay. That solved the problem of the mutiny ... but paying the government's bills with personal credit can never be a viable policy in peacetime.

Also: unlike Hamilton, Morris did not have a driving need to explain his position to the American public and attempt to gain a consensus in favor of his programs. Morris was interested in getting the job done, not informing and persuading. Morris's 1782 report on public credit uses language that probably bewildered Congressmen and citizens alike:

> [I]n a Society where the Average Profits of Stock are double to the Interest at which Money can be obtained, every public Loan, for necessary Expenditures, provides a Fund in the Agregate of national Wealth equal to the Discharge of it's own Interest.

And finally: Morris did not enjoy his tenure as superintendent of Finance. On May 1, 1783, he noted in his diary, "I wish for nothing so much as to be relieved from this cursed Scene of Drudgery and Vexation." Little wonder that he declined Washington's offer of the position as secretary of the Treasury in 1789. Washington's adopted grandson reported that Morris, having declined the position, recommended that it be offered to Hamilton.

In a Society: Robert Morris to John Hanson, president of Congress, "Report on Public Credit," 7/29/1782. *Papers of Robert Morris* vol. I (1781-1784), University of Pittsburgh, 1973.

I wish for nothing: Robert Morris's diary for 5/1/1783: "The Honble. Mr. Hamilton, Mr. Fitzsimmons, Mr. Wilson Mr. Carrol Mr. Gorham and Mr. Osgood called to Confer with and Convince me of the Propriety of continuing in this Office untill the Army are disbanded and Peace Arrangements take place &c. To all their Arguments I opposed my Observations on the Conduct of Congress towards me; And I wish for nothing so much as to be relieved from this cursed Scene of Drudgery and Vexation. I determined not to Continue and told them I will immediately write a Letter to that Effect to the President." Cited in n. 3 to "Continental Congress Report on Conference with the Superintendent of Finance," 4/28/1783.
https://founders.archives.gov/documents/Hamilton/01-03-02-0224

Washington's offer: see following page.

Washington's adopted grandson relates Washington's offer to Morris of the post at Treasury

"In 1789, when the first president was on his way to the seat of the new government, he stopped in Philadelphia at the house of Robert Morris, and while consulting with that eminent patriot and benefactor of America, as to the members of the first cabinet, Washington observed, 'The treasury, Morris, will of course be your berth. After your invaluable services as financier of the Revolution, no one can pretend to contest the office of secretary of the treasury with you.' Robert Morris respectfully but firmly declined the appointment, on the ground of his private affairs, and then said, 'But, my dear general, you will be no loser by my declining the secretaryship of the treasury, for I can recommend to you a far cleverer fellow than I am for your minister of finance, in the person of your former aid-de-camp, Colonel Hamilton.' The president was amazed, and continued, 'I always knew Colonel Hamilton to be a man of superior talents, but never supposed that he had any knowledge of finance.' To which Morris replied, 'He knows everything, sir; to a mind like his nothing comes amiss.' Robert Morris, indeed, had had ample proofs of Hamilton's talents in financial matters, the financier having received from the soldier many and important suggestions, plans, and estimates touching the organization and establishment of the bank of North America, in 1780.

"Thus did Alexander Hamilton, from amid the stirring duties of a camp, devote the vast and varied powers of his mind to the organization of a system of finance, as connected with banking operations, that proved of inestimable service to the cause of the Revolution.

"Washington hesitated not a moment in making the appointment of secretary of the treasury agreeably to the recommendation of Morris ... On the very day of the interesting event we have just related, Mr. Dallas met Hamilton in the street and addressed him with, 'Well, colonel, can you tell me who will be the members of the cabinet?'—'Really, my dear sir,' replied the colonel, 'I cannot tell you who will, but I can very readily tell you of one who will not be of the number, and that one is your humble servant.' He had not, at that moment, the remotest idea that Washington had again in peace, as in war, 'marked him for his own.'

"The very best eulogium that can be pronounced upon the fiscal department of the United States, as organized by Alexander Hamilton, is in the remarks of the Hon. Albert Gallatin, a political rival, and the most distinguished financier of the successors of the first secretary of the treasury. Mr. Gallatin has magnanimously declared that all secretaries of the treasury of the United States, since the first, enjoyed a sinecure, the genius and labors of Hamilton having created and arranged everything that was requisite and necessary for the successful operation of the department."

George Washington Parke Custis, *Recollections and Private Memoirs of Washington* (New York, 1860), p. 351. https://ia902804.us.archive.org/11/items/recollectionspr00cust/recollectionspr00cust.pdf

3.10.2 Hamilton as thinker

Within a month after Washington's inauguration, Hamilton probably knew he would be nominated to head the Treasury Department. Madison wrote to Jefferson in late May 1789, regarding the appointment of a secretary of the Treasury, that Hamilton was "perhaps best qualified for that species of business." Madison would know. He had worked closely with Hamilton in the Continental Congress during the 1782-1783 term, and at the Constitutional Convention in 1787. In 1787-1788, the two were allies in getting the Constitution ratified and were co-authors of the *Federalist Papers*.

What made other people believe Hamilton, who was in his early thirties, was qualified to be secretary of the Treasury?

First of all: he was fiercely intelligent. He was able to collect masses of data, integrate it, and plan a course of action. That was clear in "Full Vindication," 1774; in his letter to Robert Morris of 1781; in the "Continentalist" essays; and particularly in his contributions to the *Federalist Papers*. (See §3.2, 3.3.3, 3.3.4, 3.9.)

Equally important: Hamilton was not an ivory-tower philosopher. In 1802, he wrote that Thomas Jefferson and others were "enveloped all their lives in the mists of theory, [and] constantly seeking for an ideal perfection which never was & never will be attainable in reality." Hamilton did not aspire to be an abstract theoretician, deducing from the top down without reference to the facts.

But it's a false alternative to say that if Hamilton wasn't an abstract theoretician, he must have been the other extreme: a pragmatist who

---

Best qualified: Madison to Jefferson, 5/27/1789.

https://founders.archives.gov/documents/Madison/01-12-02-0118

See also Hamilton to Carrington (supervisor of the revenue for the District of Virginia and a long-time friend), 5/26/1792: "When I accepted the Office, I now hold, it was under a full persuasion, that from similarity of thinking, conspiring with personal goodwill, I should have the firm support of Mr. Madison, in the general course of my administration. Aware of the intrinsic difficultties of the situation and of the powers of Mr. Madison, I do not believe I should have accepted under a different supposition."

https://founders.archives.gov/documents/Hamilton/01-11-02-0349

In May, men were already writing to Hamilton asking for government employment: see Jonathan Lawrence, Jr., to Hamilton, 5/4/1789, and and Samuel Loudon to Hamilton, 5/22/1789.

https://founders.archives.gov/documents/Hamilton/01-05-02-0127 ∙ ■
https://founders.archives.gov/documents/Hamilton/01-05-02-0134

Mists of theory: see next page

The mists of theory

Quote in text is from Hamilton, "The Examination" No. 11, 2/3/1802
https://founders.archives.gov/documents/Hamilton/01-25-02-0291

Hamilton to Lafayette 10/6/1789, regarding the French Revolution: "I dread the reveries of your Philosophic politicians who appear in the moment to have great influence and who being mere speculatists may aim at more refinement than suits either with human nature or the composition of your Nation."
https://founders.archives.gov/documents/Hamilton/01-05-02-0202

Hamilton, "The Vindication" No. 1, [May-August 1792], calls Jefferson and his supporters "men of sublimated imaginations and weak judgments pretenders to profound knowlege, yet ignorant of the most useful of all sciences, the science of human nature—men who dignify themselves with the appellation of Philosophers, yet are destitute of the first elements of true philosophy."
https://founders.archives.gov/documents/Hamilton/01-11-02-0376

Hamilton, "Defence of the Funding System," July 1795: "In pursuing too far the idea of absolute perfection in the plan to be proposed unaccommodated to circumstances the chance of an absolutely bad issue was infinitely enhanced, and of the evils connected with it. ...

"Would Time have pronounced a favourable sentence upon a different course? Would it not have said that goodness is often not an absolute but a relative term and that it was culpable refinement to have sacrificed the prospect of accomplishing what was substantially good to the impracticable attainment of what was deemed theoretically perfect?

"I grant that the idea of accommodation was not to be carried so far as to sacrifice to it any essential principle. This is never justifiable. But with the restriction of not sacrificing principle was it not right and adviseable so to shape the course as to secure the best prospect of effecting the greatest possible good?

"To me this appeared the path of policy and duty and I acted under the influence of that impression. ...

"A Government which does not rest on the basis of justice rests on that of force. There is no middle ground. Establish that a Government may decline a provision for its debts, though able to make it, and you overthrow all public morality, you unhinge all the principles that must preserve the limits of free constitutions—you have anarchy, despotism or, what you please, but you have no just or regular Government. ...

"Thus: observing the immense importance of Credit to the strength and security of nations, he will endeavour to obtain it for his own country in its highest perfection by the most efficient means; yet not overlooking the abuses to which like all other good things it is liable he will seek to guard against them, by promoting a spirit of true national œconomy, by pursuing steadily, especially in a country which has no need of external acquisition, the maxims of justice moderation and peace and by endeavouring to establish as far as human inconstancey allows certain

➤

HAMILTON'S FINANCIAL PROGRAMS   71

simply tried one policy after another until he found one that seemed to work. Hamilton despised Aaron Burr for having no principles:

> No mortal can tell what his political principles are. He has talked all around the compass. ... It is probable that if he has any theory 'tis that of a simple despotism.

Hamilton's approach was to gather the facts, and adopt methods that logic and past experience suggested would work, if they accorded with his principles. His extensive correspondence helped him gather those facts. (See §3.5.) In 1788, he told delegates to the New York ratification convention:

> I have found, that Constitutions are more or less excellent, as they are more or less agreeable to the natural operation of things: I am therefore disposed not to dwell long on curious speculations, or pay much attention to modes and forms; but to adopt a system, whose principles have been sanctioned by experience; adapt it to the real state of our country; and depend on probable reasonings for its operation and result.

3.10.3 Hamilton as leader

By 1789 Hamilton was clearly a man able to take charge and give orders or direction. We saw that while he worked for Cruger, Beekman, and Kortright in St. Croix, and when he was in the Continental Army. (See §3.1, 3.3.) We also saw him gathering support for his plans at Annapolis, where he drafted the resolution calling for the Constitutional Convention, and in New York, when he campaigned for ratification of the Constitution. (See §3.7, 3.9.) We saw him recruiting two prominent figures, James Madison and John Jay, to contribute to the *Federalist Papers*. In political, military, and legal circles, Hamilton

---

fixed principles in the administration of the finances calculated to secure efficaciously the extinguishment of debt as fast at least as the probable exigencies of the nation is likely to occasion the contracting of it.

"These, I can truly say, are the principles which have regulated every part of my conduct in my late office."
https://founders.archives.gov/documents/Hamilton/01-19-02-0001

No mortal: Hamilton to John Rutledge, Jr., 1/4/1801.
https://founders.archives.gov/documents/Hamilton/01-25-02-0156-0001

I have found: first speech of 6/21/1788 at the New York ratification convention.
https://founders.archives.gov/documents/Hamilton/01-05-02-0012-0011

had become well known as a man who could take the lead and inspire or persuade others to follow.

Also, Hamilton was adept at presenting his case to others in writing, if he couldn't do it in person. He displayed that ability in applying political theory (see "Full Vindication"), in analyzing masses of economic data (for his position as New York tax receiver), in researching laws and legal precedents (for his defense of former loyalists), and in elucidating constitutional principles (for the *Federalist Papers*). (See §3.2, 3.4, 3.6.2, 3.9.) As a speaker and a writer, he excelled at constructing a logical, principled, persuasive argument backed by facts. Indeed, his ability to inform and persuade was probably one of his qualifications for Washington. After the ferocious battle for ratification of the Constitution, it was entirely likely that the secretary of Treasury would have to be able to persuade Congress and the American public of the value of his proposed programs. No other American had Hamilton's ability to persuade, combined with his knowledge of finance.

Hamilton not only had all this experience and all these abilities: he had a goal. He wanted to make the United States a viable country. He wanted its citizens to prosper. In the final *Federalist* essay, he wrote:

> These judicious reflections contain a lesson of moderation to all the sincere lovers of the Union, and ought to put them upon their guard against hazarding anarchy, civil war, a perpetual alienation of the States from each other, and perhaps the military despotism of a victorious demagogue, in the pursuit of what they are not likely to obtain, but from time and experience. It may be in me a defect of political fortitude, but I acknowledge that I cannot entertain an equal tranquillity with those who affect to treat the dangers of a longer continuance in our present situation as imaginary. A nation, without a national government, is, in my view, an awful spectacle. The establishment of a Constitution, in time of profound peace, by the voluntary consent of a whole people, is a prodigy, to the completion of which I look forward with trembling anxiety.

3.10.4 Hamilton's knowledge of the issues in the Gordian Knot

In addition to his qualifications as a thinker and a leader, Hamilton had extensive experience relevant to all the crises that were plaguing the United States in 1789. In fact, if you met him in a bar or at a party,

---

These judicious: Hamilton, *Federalist* No. 85, 5/28/1788. https://avalon.law.yale.edu/18th_century/fed85.asp

you'd probably find him thoroughly familiar with any problem you wanted to bend his ear about. He had been writing essays on those problems for a decade, and he had been taking actions to ameliorate them when he could.

3.10.4.1 First thread: Making a living

In his teens, Hamilton had years of experience at an international trading company on St. Croix. In the course of business, he had interacted with sea captains, lawyers, businessmen, farmers, government officials, and many others. His service in the army, in Congress, and as a bureaucrat working for Superintendent of Finance Robert Morris had put him in touch with a wide range of Americans: merchants, traders, subsistence farmers, wealthy landowners. Hamilton knew people from many walks of life, and he observed the conditions under which they prospered—or failed to prosper (as for example, in New York City after the Revolutionary War). In "The Farmer Refuted," 1775, he already had the Lockean premise that a proper government should allow men to operate in their own self-interest, allowing them to seek their own happiness and prosperity. In works such as the "Continentalist" and the *Federalist Papers*, he addressed Americans of all occupations and ranks, not just politicians, lawyers, or soldiers.

The Constitution was designed to allow American citizens to have life, liberty, and the pursuit of happiness. Hamilton assumes that men will act in their own self-interest and is adamant about making government plans with that in mind.

Self-interest: from the "Farmer Refuted," 1775: "[T]he supreme being gave existence to man, together with the means of preserving and beatifying that existence. He endowed him with rational faculties, by the help of which, to discern and pursue such things, as were consistent with his duty and interest, and invested him with an inviolable right to personal liberty, and personal safety. ... Hence also, the origin of all civil government, justly established, must be a voluntary compact, between the rulers and the ruled; and must be liable to such limitations, as are necessary for the security of the absolute rights of the latter; for what original title can any man or set of men have, to govern others, except their own consent? To usurp dominion over a people, in their own despite, or to grasp at a more extensive power than they are willing to entrust, is to violate that law of nature, which gives every man a right to his personal liberty; and can, therefore, confer no obligation to obedience."

https://founders.archives.gov/documents/Hamilton/01-01-02-0057

See also See Holloway, *Hamilton versus Jefferson in the Washington Administration,* pp. 16-20: "Good Faith, Self-Interest, and Moral Principle: Hamilton, Machiavelli, and Hobbes."

3.10.4.2 Second thread: Centrifugal tendency of the United States

As an immigrant to the United States, Hamilton did not think of himself as a New Yorker, a Pennsylvanian, or a Virginian. His experience in the army reinforced his inclination to look at the big picture—the national situation.

By 1789 Hamilton had observed, for more than a decade and from many angles, the flaws of the weak federal government created under the Articles of Confederation. As a soldier, he saw that it was unable to provide supplies and funds to the military during the battle for independence. As a lawyer, he saw that the federal government was unable to keep New York State from infringing the American treaty with Britain. As a government tax receiver in New York, he saw that because the federal government depended on voluntary contributions, it had no reliable source of income, and therefore potentially less power than any one state. As a Congressman, Hamilton saw the difficulties of gathering enough support from the separate states to pass any legislation. Like all his fellow citizens, he saw the inability of the federal government to protect its citizens from attacks by Indians, or even disgruntled taxpayers such as those involved in Shays' Rebellion. At national conventions in Annapolis and Philadelphia, he saw the difficulty in reaching a consensus among states. At the ratification convention in New York State for the Constitution, he saw the difficulty of forcing (or even persuading) a powerful state to submit to the federal government.

Hamilton argued early and frequently in favor of an energetic national government. The public saw the "Continentalist" essays and the *Federalist Papers*. Important people in the government saw more in-depth discussion in private letters, such as Hamilton's 1780 letter to Congressman Duane and his 1781 letter to Robert Morris.

It bears repeating that although Hamilton was in favor of an energetic federal government, he did not argue for one that was big for the sake of bigness. He just wanted one that was strong enough to keep the squabbling, diverse states from spinning off on their separate courses.

3.10.4.3 Third thread: Inadequate circulation of money

One of Hamilton's earliest lessons in St. Croix was the need to pay the bills. As Cruger's deputy, he had to be constantly aware of revenue and expenditures, and how to meet payments when money was scarce.

Based on his early experience, Hamilton—unlike most Americans, including most of the other Founding Fathers—believed that a healthy economy depended on a combination of agriculture, business, industry, and trade. Subsistence farmers could make do with a little cash and a lot of barter. Business, trade, and industry required money in circulation.

New York State provided Hamilton another illustration of the problems of having too little money in circulation. Part of the reason he could not collect the money requisitioned by the federal government in 1782 was that there was so little gold and silver in circulation to collect.

In New York City in 1783, Hamilton saw the disastrous effects on the city's economy when wealthy businessmen fled with their savings. He saw that due to lack of money in circulation, it was difficult to rebuild the ruined city, and increasingly difficult even to carry on the most necessary business. Hence Hamilton helped establish the Bank of New York, and defended dozens of former loyalists who wished to continue doing business in New York after the war.

In his earliest writings on economics—letters written in 1780 and 1781, while he was still in the army—Hamilton was already stressing the need for more money in circulation, and recommending the establishment of a national bank. His first mention of such a bank to the general public was in the "Continentalist" essays of 1781-1782.

3.10.4.4 Fourth thread: Lack of government revenue

As Washington's aide-de-camp during the war, Hamilton saw all too often the results of the federal government's lack of revenue. As a tax receiver in New York and later as Congressman, Hamilton saw the difficulties of collecting money requisitioned from the states. Revenue that relied on the good will of the states was not adequate to gain and keep independence. Hamilton had been saying that in print as early as the "Continentalist" essays in 1781-1782, and he was still saying it in the *Federalist Papers* in 1787-1788.

3.10.4.5 Fifth thread: Government debt

Some of Hamilton's own productive effort—his salary for years of serving in the army—was tied up in government IOUs. (See §3.3.5.) He was still in touch with many fellow soldiers in the same situation. He knew merchants and farmers who had supplied goods to the army, and were also owed substantial sums. To Hamilton, the debtors of the United States were not a faceless mob to be ignored if payment of debts was inconvenient.

But Hamilton also saw the other side of the coin. He knew the importance of credit to the nation's survival: Hamilton began discussing repayment of the American debt in print as early as the "Continentalist" essays in 1781-1782. (See §3.3.4.)

3.10.5 Summer 1789: Congress debates the duties of the Treasury secretary

During the summer of 1789, Congress hammered out the duties of the secretaries of the Treasury, State, and War. Congress was particularly worried about the powers that would be given to the secretary of the Treasury. As the man who was in charge of the country's revenue, he would wield enormous power. If the secretary of the Treasury had authority to dispense or withhold money at will, without adequate supervision, who knew what he might do?

As a precaution, Congress arranged that the secretary of the Treasury would never actually handle the government's money. That would be done by the comptroller, auditor, treasurer, and register, with signatures and counter-signatures. The secretary's role would be to deal with the big picture: figuring out how to handle the new country's income, expenditures, and debt.

Duties of the secretaries: See McDonald, *Hamilton*, pp. 129-134, on the Congressional debate regarding the powers to be given to the secretary of the Treasury.

Signatures: These offices were set up by the "Act to Establish the Treasury Department," 9/2/1789, which included the statement that the duty of the secretary of the Treasury is "to digest and prepare plans for the improvement and management of the revenue, and for the support of public credit; to prepare and report estimates of the public revenue, and the public expenditures; to superintend the collection of the revenue; to decide on the forms of keeping and stating accounts and making returns ... to execute such services relative to the sale of the lands belonging to the United States, as may be by law required of him; to make report, and give information to either branch of the legislature, in person or in writing ... respecting all matters referred to him by the Senate or House of Representatives ..."

https://www.treasury.gov/about/history/Pages/act-congress.aspx

For more concrete information on the workings of the Treasury Department, see Hamilton's response of 3/24/1794 to the Congressional investigation mentioned in §7.7.1.

https://founders.archives.gov/documents/Hamilton/01-16-02-0146

3.11 HAMILTON TAKES OFFICE AS SECRETARY OF THE TREASURY

3.11.1 September 11, 1789: Hamilton nominated and confirmed

Washington signed the bill creating the Treasury Department on September 2, 1789. Hamilton was nominated secretary of the Treasury on September 11, and confirmed the same day. He came to office with no precedents to restrict his actions, no laws, no regulations. He had only his own experience and principles, the limitations imposed by the Constitution, and the few restrictions imposed by the new Congress.

In September 1789, the United States faced all the issues in the Gordian Knot that we've discussed above. Strictly speaking, however, Hamilton was only responsible for untangling two of them: government revenue and government debt.

3.11.2 Government debt in September 1789

When Hamilton took office, no one even knew the amount of the United States debt. The total certainly ran into many tens of millions of dollars.

3.11.3 Government revenue: customs duties

The amount of revenue the United States could command was also uncertain. According to the Constitution, the federal government had the sole right to levy import duties. The new Congress passed its first revenue act (and only its second act ever) on July 4, 1789, two months before Hamilton came to office. The act imposed duties on most imported goods. Congress also imposed a duty on ships by their size (tonnage), with the highest duties paid by large ships owned and operated by foreigners.

This is, incidentally, the beginning of what Daniel Webster referred to as the "common and uniform system of commercial regulation". Commercial regulation at this period did not involve imposing new regulations so much as undoing the cut-throat and complicated regulations of the states. For example, during the Confederation, Virginia

---

Act imposed: "An Act for laying a duty on goods, wares, and merchandises imported into the United States," 7/4/1789.
https://en.wikisource.org/wiki/United_States_Statutes_at_Large/Volume_1/1st_Congress/1st_Session/Chapter_2

Commercial regulations: More of Webster's famous 1831 speech in praise of Hamilton is quoted in §9.5 below.

imposed tolls on ships sailing through the Chesapeake to Maryland; Maryland imposed fees if Virginian ships entered her harbors; and those who moved property from Maryland to Virginia or vice versa were forced to pay a tax. (See §2.2.2.)

However, passing the law did not automatically begin to fill the government's coffers. Officers had to be hired to collect the duties. As Hamilton knew from his job in St. Croix, that wasn't a rubber-stamping desk job. The officers had to identify the goods that had duties levied on them. They had to estimate the weight, volume, and/or dimensions of awkward amounts such as barrels. They had to estimate the tonnage of ships and confirm their ownership, at a time when ships often traveled without papers. And the customs officers had to sort out Congress's complicated regulations about all these items.

By the time Hamilton came into office in September, only a few customs officers had been appointed. Many had previously been collecting duties on behalf of their home states, so their loyalties were not necessarily with the federal government.

Aside from customs officers, it would also have been obvious to Hamilton, based on his years at the docks in St. Croix, that the

---

Complicated regulations: Hamilton received so many queries and complaints from his customs officers that nine months after he became head of Treasury, he submitted to Congress a "Report on Defects in the Existing Laws of Revenue," 4/22/1790.
https://founders.archives.gov/documents/Hamilton/01-06-02-0248

Few customs officers: Eventually Hamilton hired some five hundred customs officers. Brookhiser, *Alexander Hamilton, American*, p. 167.

Loyalties: Otho H. Williams (customs officer in Baltimore) to Hamilton, 2/2/1790: "It is to be regretted that the Impost system commenced with an aspect very inauspicious to the respectability of the Officers of the customs. I need not suggest to you sir that the present plan has a tendency to render them despicable, or that men who dispair of respectability will but too commonly stoop to unjust expedients to gratifie a passion yet less patriotic than ambitious."
https://founders.archives.gov/documents/Hamilton/01-06-02-0125-0001

government needed <u>patrol boats</u> to prevent smuggling. Americans had gained years of experience avoiding the British Navy during the war, and before that, avoiding British taxes on imports. Even in 1789, many smugglers would have seen no reason to pay government import duties when they could so easily be avoided.

In the near future, the government would also need to put in place a range of infrastructure so that ships could safely enter any American harbor and pay their fees. That meant installing <u>lighthouses</u>, buoys, piers, and so on. From 1789 to 1795, a remarkable number of letters between President Washington and Secretary Hamilton deal with such mundane matters.

Another problem with raising revenue from customs duties was its seasonal ebb and flow. Customs duties were levied when ships arrived in port. During the late eighteenth century—indeed, until the advent of steamships in the mid-nineteenth century—the sailing season ran from March to October. Hamilton came to office almost at the end of

---

<u>Patrol boats</u>: Hamilton's "Report on Defects in the Existing Laws of Revenue," 4/22/1790, includes a note that Congress had stated that boats should be acquired for "securing the collection of revenue," but Congress had made no provision for them. Hamilton suggests that ten boats be provided. On 8/4/1790, Congress passed "an act to provide more effectually for the collection of the duties imposed by law on goods, wares and merchandise imported into the United States, and on the tonnage of ships or vessels." The Revenue-Marine, now the United States Coast Guard—the oldest permanent armed service in the United States—began with those ten ships.

https://founders.archives.gov/documents/Hamilton/01-06-02-0248

<u>Lighthouses</u>: Hamilton to Washington, 1/3/1790, gives details on lighthouses in eleven states. For example: "New Hampshire. In this State is only one Light house situated on a point of land on the Island of New-Castle, three miles from Portsmouth, without the walls of the Fort which commands the entrance of Piscatqua river. It is under the Superintendance of a Commissary who is Captain of the Fort; and is at present in good repair. The annual expence of maintaining it, is estimated at … Dollars 217.20."

https://founders.archives.gov/documents/Hamilton/01-06-02-0068

the sailing season. He could not expect to see much income for many months. He needed to make a plan to stretch out six or seven months of income over a whole year, in 1789 and every year to come.

And one last quirk about that income: customs duties were not actually paid when a ship arrived. They were paid with bonds due between three months and two years later, when the cargo would presumably have been sold. If the bond wasn't paid, the government had to track down the ship's owner to collect the duties. This added another erratic element to a revenue stream that was already unpredictable.

In his first major report to Congress, Hamilton had to address not just revenue and debt, but (directly or indirectly) all the specific problems raised above: customs officers, seasonality of income, and lagging payment of import duties. Let's see how he did that.

Much income: Hamilton describes this problem on 2/19/1793, when responding to the Giles Resolutions: "It is assumed as an item in the calculation, that a sum of a million of dollars will come into the Treasury by the first of April, on account of the revenue of the current year—while the probability is, that the sum received may not exceed ten thousand dollars. This presumption of a million is evidently founded upon two mistakes. 1st It proceeds on the basis of an annual revenue of four millions of dollars, and supposes this sum equally distributed between the different quarters of the year, a million to each quarter, when in fact there are two seasons of the year incomparably more productive than the other parts of it, viz. Those portions of the spring and fall which are embraced by the second and third quarters, the first and fourth being far less productive. 2d It supposes all the duties which accrue are immediately paid; whereas the cases of prompt payment are confined to those in which the duties on particular articles imported in one vessel, by one person or co-partnership, do not exceed 50 dollars; in all other instances, a credit not less than four months is allowed, which carries the payment on the importations, upon the very first day of the quarter, a month beyond the expiration of it." "Report on the State of the Treasury at the Commencement of Each Quarter During the Years 1791 and 1792," 2/19/1793.

https://founders.archives.gov/documents/Hamilton/01-14-02-0032-0001

CHAPTER 4

Policy Paper #1:
First Report on Public Credit

The *Report Relative to a Provision for the Support of Public Credit* is generally known as the *First Report on Public Credit*. Hamilton completed it by January 9, 1790, and submitted it to Congress on January 14, 1790. Founders Online has a lengthy discussion of writings that influenced the content of this report. The relevant point for us is: Hamilton's *synthesis* of all these ideas was wholly original.

4.1 INTRODUCTORY NOTES

4.1.1 Precedents and perplexities

Lacking the ability to raise revenue directly, the Confederation Congress had instead tried various combinations of paper money and loans. As a result, the debt of the United States steadily increased

---

First Report: *First Report on Public Credit*, 1/9/1790. The full text of this report appears in Appendix 1, with outline headings added. For an excellent walk-through of the First Report, see Carson Holloway, *Hamilton versus Jefferson in the Washington Administration*, Chapter 2. The annotated report is available on Founders Archives.
https://founders.archives.gov/documents/Hamilton/01-06-02-0076-0002-0001

Submitted it to Congress: The debate in the House of Representatives over whether Hamilton should present the report in person or in writing is in the *Annals of Congress, House of Representatives, 1st Congress, 2nd Session*, pp. 1079-1081.
https://memory.loc.gov/cgi-bin/ampage?collId=llac&fileName=001/llac001.db&recNum=540

Founders Online: "Introductory Note: Report Relative to a Provision for the Support of Public Credit"
https://founders.archives.gov/documents/Hamilton/01-06-02-0076-0001

while its creditworthiness decreased. Where can we look for a country that manages its finances in a manner worthy of emulation?

France, America's ally in the Revolutionary War, is hardly a good model. The king out-sources collection of tax revenues, and each collector takes a cut. <u>Less than half</u> the taxes gathered make it into the royal treasury.

Anyone who studies finance in the 1780s knows that the best models are the Dutch and the British. Both governments are able to borrow large sums from their citizens because they guarantee regular payment of interest. The payments come directly from the government's revenues. The Netherlands and Great Britain each have a central bank that works closely with the government.

Even if Britain or the Netherlands is used as a model, many options and questions remain about settling the American debt. Shall we pay the IOUs at full face value, or at a recent price that's lower? Shall we pay original holders of IOUs more than we pay those who bought the IOUs later, at a much lower price? Shall we pay the accumulated interest on the IOUs? Shall we make payments in gold and silver, or bonds, or paper money, or lands in the West? Shall we compensate those who hold the old, depreciated Continental currency? (See §2.4.1.)

4.1.2 Previous reports on United States finances

Two American precedents exist for Hamilton's *First Report*. One is the "<u>Report on Public Credit</u>" issued in July 1782 by Superintendent of Finance Robert Morris. Morris's report was written after Yorktown, but before the peace treaty with Britain had been negotiated. By that time Congress, which had no revenue except the small amounts that the states condescended to send, had stopped all interest payments on its IOUs. Domestic creditors were enraged.

Morris asserted in his report that the United States debt must be paid, and paid in full to current holders of IOUs. He proposed that the government gather revenue using a combination of import duties, taxes on land, excise taxes, and poll (per capita) taxes. Farmers like us can avoid purchasing goods that are imported or that have excise

---

<u>Less than half</u>: Gordon, *Hamilton's Blessing*, p. 4.

<u>Report on Public Credit</u>: See "Other candidates for secretary of the Treasury" (§ 3.10.1). Robert Morris's report on public credit was given to Congress 7/29/1782; for more on the context, see Rappleye, *Robert Morris*, pp. 302-305. For the text, see *Papers of Robert Morris*, vol. 6 (July 22-Oct. 31, 1782), pp. 56-83, with introductory note pp. 36-56.
https://digital.library.pitt.edu/islandora/object/pitt:31735060482019

taxes, but we loathe land and poll taxes: there's no way to avoid them.

Morris's "Report on Public Credit" was not aimed at the general public. He wrote it to persuade Congress to take a particular course of action, and it was dense, full of specialized terminology. (See §3.10.1 for an example.)

The other American precedent for Hamilton's *First Report* is a document submitted in summer 1789 by the Board of Treasury to President Washington. The three-member Board was responsible for the country's finances for five years, from Morris's resignation in 1784 until Hamilton took office as secretary of the Treasury. Its "Report on the General State of the Treasury, with the Official Documents explanatory of the same" consisted mostly of lists of expenses and income, with brief explanations of their sources. Some supplementary material was included, such as a letter of February 1789 from America's bankers in Amsterdam explaining that they had been unable to raise a loan for the United States.

The Board of Treasury report provided little context and made no suggestions for dealing with American's financial problems. Like Morris's report, it would have been difficult for a layman to comprehend.

4.1.3 The stimulus for Hamilton's First Report on Public Credit

In late September 1789, ten days after Hamilton took office, Congress requests a report on the nation's finances, since "an adequate provision for the support of the Public Credit, is a matter of high importance to the honor and prosperity of the United States." Hamilton immediately writes to those among his wide circle of correspondents who are most knowledgeable about business and finance in their respective

---

Board of Treasury: Board of Treasury to George Washington, 7/23/1789.
https://founders.archives.gov/documents/Washington/05-03-02-0157

Immediately writes: A sample of the responses he received came from Stephen Higginson (a Boston merchant), 11/11/1789: "Justice must eventually be done to the public Creditors—the faith of Government must be preserved, as far as possible, & the public credit restored; but those great Objects may be perhaps secured without hazarding the peace of Society, or endangering Government. If the public Creditors were to receive two or three [per] Ct. interest in Specie, & could see funds established equal to the punctual payment of it, & promising an increase; They would in general feel very well satisfied ... They would then be in a situation so much better than they have hitherto enjoyed, or, till very lately, could have sanguinely expected, They would be very easy & contented." For Hamilton's exchange with Madison, see the following page.
https://founders.archives.gov/documents/Hamilton/01-05-02-0303

Tight-lipped

Henry Lee to Hamilton, 11/16/1789: "Your undertaking is truely arduous but I trust as you progress in the work, difficulty will vanish. From your situation you must be able to form with some certainty an opinion concerning the domestic debt. Will it speedily rise, will the interest accruing command specie or any thing nearly as valuable, what will become of the indents already issued? These querys are asked for my private information, perhaps they may be improper, I do not think them so, or I would not propound them—of this you will decide & act accordingly."

Hamilton to Henry Lee, 12/1/1789: "I am sure you are sincere when you say, you would not subject me to an impropriety ... [but] with respect to the Conduct of such men—Suspicion is ever eagle-eyed, and the most innocent things are apt to be misinterpreted."

https://founders.archives.gov/documents/Hamilton/01-05-02-0313 ■
https://founders.archives.gov/documents/Hamilton/01-06-02-0001

Hamilton consults Madison on ways to pay the debt

Hamilton to Madison 10/12/1789: "May I ask of your friendship to put to paper and send me your thoughts on such objects as may have occurred to you for an addition to our revenue; and also as to any modifications of the public debt which could be made consistent with good faith the interest of the Public and of its Creditors? In my opinion, in considering plans for the increase of our revenues, the difficulty lies, not so much in the want of objects as in the prejudices which may be feared with regard to almost every object. The Question is very much What further taxes will be least unpopular? Adieu My Dr Sir"

Madison to Hamilton, 11/19/1789: "The supplemental funds which at present occur to me as on the whole most eligible are 1. an excise on home distilleries ... 2. an augmentation of the duty on spirituous liquors imported. ... 3. a land tax. ... 4. a Stamp tax on proceedings in the federal Courts ... The modification of the public debt is a subject on which I ought perhaps to be silent, having not enough revolved it to form any precise ideas. ... It might be a soothing circumstance ... if by some operation the debt could be lessened by purchases made on public account; and particularly if any impression could be made on it by means of the Western lands. This last is a fund which, tho' overrated by many is I think capable of aiding the redemption of the capital of the debt. ..."

https://founders.archives.gov/documents/Hamilton/01-05-02-0224 and
https://founders.archives.gov/documents/Hamilton/01-05-02-0325

states. He is very tight-lipped about what he is planning, but he actively seeks information and opinions.

When he has been secretary of the Treasury for four months, Hamilton submits the *First Report on Public Credit.* At 16,000 words, it is the length of a novella.

4.1.4 The audience for the First Report

Why is the *First Report* so long? Why does Hamilton not just provide columns of current debts and projected revenue?

Answer: very few Americans—including the members of the First Congress—have experience thinking of finances on a national scale. Hamilton incorporates a great deal of explanatory material into the *First Report* so that his contemporaries can understand why the measures he proposes should be adopted. In this sense, the *First Report* is very much in Hamilton's usual style. He explains the situation and makes logical arguments, with specific proposals for action. He attempts to inform and persuade.

The *Report* is printed for Congress. Excerpts from it are also widely published in newspapers. The Funding Act is widely discussed by the American public, including men in taverns and women at dinner parties.

Back in 1774, in "Full Vindication," Hamilton wrote:

> To render it agreeable to good policy, three things are requisite. First, that the necessity of the times require it: Secondly, that it be not the probable source of greater evils, than those it pretends to remedy: And lastly, that it have a probability of success.

He's still operating by those principles in 1790. In this chapter, we'll see what Hamilton proposes, what Congress passes into law, and how these relate to our Gordian Knot.

Tight-lipped: see facing page.

Discussed: The debate goes on for years. For example, Hamilton summarizes the United States government's actions regarding the debt, beginning in April 1789, in his essay "Civis" (9/5/1792), which was a reply to an attack on Hamilton and the Treasury Department by one "Mercator". The follow-up, which dealt with accumulated interest, was "Civis to Mercator," 9/11/1792.
https://founders.archives.gov/documents/Hamilton/01-12-02-0247 ■
https://founders.archives.gov/documents/Hamilton/01-12-02-0273

To render it: Hamilton, "Full Vindication," 12/15/1774, writing in regard to the Continental Congress's proposed boycott of British goods.
https://founders.archives.gov/documents/Hamilton/01-01-02-0054

Paying debts matters!

Hamilton, "To the Public Creditors of the State of New York," 9/30/1782: "What will be the condition of individuals, if a disregard to the sanctity of public obligations should become the spirit of public councils? We indeed should be the immediate victims; but who can answer when his turn might come? ... What, in short, will be the security of private property, if the powers of government may be employed to take it from us, and no provision be afterwards made to render satisfaction?"
https://founders.archives.gov/documents/Hamilton/01-03-02-0084

Hamilton, *First Report*, 1/9/1790: "And as on the one hand, the necessity for borrowing in particular emergencies cannot be doubted, so on the other, it is equally evident, that to be able to borrow upon good terms, it is essential that the credit of a nation should be well established. For when the credit of a country is in any degree questionable, it never fails to give an extravagant premium, in one shape or another, upon all the loans it has occasion to make."
https://founders.archives.gov/documents/Hamilton/01-06-02-0076-0002-0001

Hamilton, "Defence of the Funding System," July 1795: "What was to be done with the debt? Was it to be wiped off with a sponge or was it to be provided for? The first idea[s] were the extreme of political profligacy and folly. Governments like individuals have burthens which ought to be deemed sacred, else they become mere engines of violence oppression extortion, and misery. Adieu to the security of property adieu to the security of liberty. Nothing is then safe—all our favourite notions of national & constitutional rights vanish. Every thing is brought to a question of power; right is anathematized excommunicated and banished. In the code of moral and political obligations that of paying debts holds a prominent place. Tried by the test of utility there is perhaps none of greater force or extent. Without it, no borrowing nor lending; no selling or purchasing upon time—no credit private or public; consequently a more cramped and less prosperous agriculture, fewer and more imperfect mechanic & other industrial arts less and more embarrassed commerce, an immense contraction of national resource and strength. A most active power in the whole scheme of national happiness would be destroyed. A vast void would be created. Every thing would languish and wither. No one will be hardy enough directly to dispute these positions or advocate the horrid doctrine of applying the sponge, but it was seen to lurk beneath some very insidious suggestions, often reiterated and urged with earnestness and exageration. ...

"A Government which does not rest on the basis of justice rests on that of force. There is no middle ground. Establish that a Government may decline a provision for its debts, though able to make it, and you overthrow all public morality, you unhinge all the principles that must preserve the limits of free constitutions—you have anarchy, despotism

➤

4.1.5 What is the "funding system"?

Hamilton did not anticipate every objection to or misunderstanding of his proposed programs. In this chapter and the following two chapters, I'll occasionally include (as supplementary material) his later explanations. For example ...

Hamilton's contemporaries and modern scholars often refer to the "funding system" set out in his *First Report*. Hamilton explains precisely what that means in an essay of 1801.

> What is the funding system? It is nothing more nor less than the pledging of adequate funds or revenues for paying the interest and for the gradual redemption of the principal, of that very debt which was the sacred price of independence. The country being unable to pay off the principal, what better could have been done?

In other words: the funding system is an arrangement to pay off the debt, both principal (the amount originally borrowed) and interest, in a systematic way and within a limited time.

4.2 CONTENT OF THE FIRST REPORT ON PUBLIC CREDIT

NOTE: If you're interested enough in Hamilton's financial programs to read this book, you should certainly read his *First Report*. The full text of it is in Appendix 1, with outline headings added; these headings are used as section references below. In this chapter, I won't attempt to discuss every point of the *First Report*. I'm giving an overview of sections that relate to the Gordian Knot. I have simplified Hamilton's terminology slightly, using "IOUs" to refer to all debts (see §2.3.3).

4.2.1 Why do we need good credit? [OUTLINE: §II and §III]

Hamilton begins by asking: why worry about credit? Answer: because there's very little money in circulation in the United States (the third thread our Gordian Knot), and we may have to borrow in times of public danger. In order to borrow on good terms—without exorbitantly high interest rates—we must have a reputation for <u>paying our debts</u> promptly.

---

or, what you please, but you have no just or regular Government."
https://founders.archives.gov/documents/Hamilton/01-19-02-0001

<u>What is the funding system</u>: "An Address to the Electors of the State of New-York," 3/21/1801.
https://founders.archives.gov/documents/Hamilton/01-25-02-0197

<u>Paying our debts</u>: see facing page.

Hamilton goes on to relate public credit to two important problems, the first and second threads of our Gordian Knot: making a living and the union of the country.

> In so strong a light nevertheless do they [maxims of public credit] appear to the Secretary, that on their due observance at the present critical juncture, materially depends, in his judgment, the individual and aggregate prosperity of the citizens of the United States; their relief from the embarrassments they now experience; their character as a People; the cause of good government.

And, bringing in the third thread of our Gordian Knot (money in circulation), Hamilton notes that in countries where the national debt is funded (i.e., where revenues are assigned to payment of the principal and interest), a government bond "answers most of the purposes of money. Transfers of stock or public debt are there equivalent to payments in specie." Having more money in circulation also benefits traders, farmers, and manufacturers because it makes it easy to borrow money, lowers interest rates, and increases the value of cultivated land.

Aside from improving American credit, there is an ethical reason for paying the Revolutionary War debt. It rests on "the immutable principles of moral obligation." The debt was the "price of liberty. The faith of America has been repeatedly pledged for it, and with solemnities, that give peculiar force to the obligation." (Appendix 1, §III.A.)

4.2.2 Issues regarding the domestic debt [OUTLINE: §IV]

Everyone agrees that the foreign debt must be paid in full, at the terms on which it was borrowed. But regarding domestic debt, says

---

In so strong: Hamilton, *First Report*, 1/9/1790. Appendix 1, §II.A.

Cultivated land: The reasoning is: Having more money in circulation lowers interest rates. If one can earn 20% from making loans, and only 5% from raising crops, why would anyone buy land? Benjamin Franklin, "The Nature and Necessity of a Paper-Currency," 4/3/1729 (quoted in §2.3): "Now the Interest of Money being high is prejudicial to a Country several Ways: It makes Land bear a low Price, because few Men will lay out their Money in Land, when they can make a much greater Profit by lending it out upon Interest ... On the contrary, A plentiful Currency will occasion Interest to be low: And this will be an Inducement to many to lay out their Money in Lands, rather than put it out to Use, by which means Land will begin to rise in Value and bear a better Price ..."

https://founders.archives.gov/documents/Franklin/01-01-02-0041

Hamilton, there are three major issues: discrimination, assumption, and accumulated interest.

4.2.2.1 Issue 1: Discrimination [OUTLINE: §IV.A]

Discrimination is the question of whether to pay in full all those who currently hold IOUs, or to pay in full only those to whom the IOUs were originally issued. In concrete terms: suppose you were issued an IOU for $100 in 1780, as pay for fighting in the Continental Army. By 1785 you were back on your farm, trying to raise money for a plow. There was no prospect that the government under the Articles of Confederation would ever pay its debts, so you sold the IOU for $20 to Smith. Smith was wealthy enough not to need that $20 in cash, and optimistic enough to hope for payment in the future. By 1790, as many as 75% or 80% of the <u>original holders</u> of IOUs had sold them for ready cash.

James Madison, Thomas Jefferson, and many others <u>feel it's unfair</u> that when the government finally pays that $100 IOU, Smith will be paid the face amount and you (the original holder) won't receive any money at all. They believe that when the government pays the $100 IOU, it should give Smith the current market value of the bond, and give you, the original holder, the rest of the money.

In the *Report*, Hamilton argues that all current holders of IOUs must be paid the full face amount of the IOU. The primary reason: the IOU is a contract, and we must abide by it.

<u>Original holders</u>: Forrest McDonald, *Hamilton*, p. 153; Ferguson, *Power of the Purse*, p. 340, and p. 396, n. 21.

<u>Feel it's unfair</u>: Madison to Jefferson, 2/14/1790: "On the foreign debt the vote has been unanimous. On the domestic, a reduction of the transferred principal has been brought into view by several arguments and propositions. My idea is that there should be no interference of the public in favour of the public either as to principal or interest, but that the highest market price only should be allowed to the purchasers, and the balance be applied to solace the original sufferers, whose claims were not in conscience extinguished by a forced payment in depreciated certificates. The equity of this proposition is not contested. Its impracticability will be urged as an insuperable objection. I am aware of the difficulties of the plan, but believe they might be removed by one-half the exertion that will be used to collect and colour them." Ferguson argues that Madison supported discrimination in order to give Virginia more leverage in the federal government's settlement of war debts (*Power of the Purse*, p. 297ff.)

https://founders.archives.gov/documents/Madison/01-13-02-0033

> The nature of the contract in its origin, is, that the public will pay the sum expressed in the security, to the first holder, or his assignee. The intent, in making the security assignable, is, that the proprietor may be able to make use of this property, by selling it for as much as it may be worth in the market, and that the buyer may be safe in the purchase.

Those who loaned us money, says Hamilton, did so on the understanding that the IOUs could be transferred and that the current holder will receive the full face value. It says so on the IOU.

In addition, the Constitution states that "all debts contracted and engagements entered into before the adoption of that Constitution shall be as valid against the United States under it, as under the confederation." These IOUs are certainly "debts contracted". Hence Hamilton insists that the IOUs must be paid without discrimination, to whoever currently holds them.

Side note from the future: Discrimination in payment of Revolutionary War IOUs may seem like an arcane point that won't matter once the IOUs are paid off. But like so many policies instituted during Washington's presidency, the payment of IOUs sets a precedent. In this case, the precedent applies to property rights regarding financial instruments such as stocks, bonds, and IOUs. It's easy to grasp that the new owner of a piece of real estate, furniture, or clothing, has absolute ownership of it. It isn't so easy to grasp that the same applies to financial instruments. But who would invest in stocks if they had to keep track of all previous transactions, and give part of any profit to the previous owner? Hamilton's determination to pay current holders the face value of their IOUs is, it turns out, essential for the development of the stock market. And the stock market is essential for future

---

The nature: Appendix 1, §IV.A.1.

It says so: Hamilton to Washington, 8/18/1792: "The Dutch were largely adventurers in our domestic debt before the present Government. They did not embark far till they had made inquiries of influential public characters, as to the light in which the Debt was & would be considered in the hands of alienees—and had received assurances that Assignees would be regarded in the same light as original holders. What would have been the state of our Credit with them, if they had been disappointed, or indeed if our conduct had been in any respect inconsistent with the notions entertained in Europe concerning the maxims of public Credit?" NOTE: All the paper illustrated on p. 26 is payable to the "possessor" or the "bearer".

https://founders.archives.gov/documents/Hamilton/01-12-02-0184-0002

growth of the United States, since it allows capital to be gathered that funds innumerable new business enterprises.

Returning to 1790: in the short term, rejecting discrimination is essential to Hamilton's plan to have the IOUs circulate as money. They must be <u>transferable without penalty</u>.

4.2.2.2 Issue 2: Assumption [OUTLINE: §IV.B]

The next major issue regarding the debt is whether the federal government should take over ("assume", as in "assume a burden") the Revolutionary War debts of the separate states. The federal government had so little money during the war that many states paid their own soldiers and furnished them with supplies. By 1789, some states have already paid off their war debts. They have no wish to be burdened with the debts of other states. <u>Almost half</u> the state debts still outstanding are owed by Massachusetts, Connecticut, and South Carolina, which had seen considerable fighting during the war.

Hamilton argues that each state was helping defend the whole. If the states pay separately, those who contributed most and suffered most harm will be paying a <u>disproportionately large</u> sum.

<u>Transferable without penalty</u>: Hamilton explains to Washington, 5/28/1790: "If partial inconveniences and hardships occasion legislative interferences in private contracts, the intercourses of business become uncertain, the security of property is lessened, the confidence in government destroyed or weakened. The constitution of the United States interdicts the States individually from passing any law impairing the obligation of contracts. ... The general rules of property, and all those general rules which form the links of society, frequently involve in their ordinary operation particular hardships and injuries; yet the public order and the general happiness require a steady conformity to them. It is perhaps always better, that partial evils should be submitted to, than that principles should be violated."

https://founders.archives.gov/documents/Jefferson/01-16-02-0267-0002

<u>Almost half</u>: In "Defence of the Funding System," July 1795, Hamilton elaborates on the condition of Rhode Island, Massachusetts, Connecticut, and South. For Madison's views on assumption, see his speech to the House of Representatives, 2/24/1790, and many later speeches. For context and details, see Forrest McDonald, *Hamilton*, pp. 148-150.
https://founders.archives.gov/documents/Hamilton/01-19-02-0001 ■
https://founders.archives.gov/documents/Madison/01-13-02-0042

<u>Disproportionately large</u>: Appendix 1, §IV.B.3. In *Power of the Purse* (p. 308), Ferguson explains the connection between the settling of accounts between the states and the federal government (which was already in progress), and assumption of states' debts.

He also points out that having the federal government pay all the debts will involve less expense, because the separate states won't have to hire their own tax collectors to raise revenue for repayment. Finally, he notes that paying the debt off as a nation rather than as separate states will make the states tend to band together rather than spin apart:

> If all the public creditors receive their dues from one source, distributed with an equal hand, their interest will be the same. And having the same interests, they will unite in the support of the fiscal arrangements of the government.

So yes, says Hamilton, the federal government should assume states' debts.

4.2.2.3 Issue 3: Interest [OUTLINE: §IV.C]

The interest on the federal government's domestic debt—some of it unpaid since 1776—now amounts to about half as much as the principal. The third major issue regarding payment of the debt is whether to make provisions for paying the accumulated interest as well as the principal.

Hamilton says: we promised to pay interest. The fact that it's inconvenient for us to pay it doesn't negate the promise.

> These [accumulated amounts of interest] are now due, and those to whom they are due, have a right to claim immediate payment. To say, that it would be impracticable to comply, would not vary the nature of the right. Nor can this idea of impracticability be honorably carried further, than to justify the proposition of a new contract upon the basis of a commutation of that right for an equivalent.

Having dealt with the issues of discrimination (no), assumption (yes), and payment of accumulated interest (yes), Hamilton moves on to discuss the amount of the government debt.

4.2.3 Amount of the debt [OUTLINE: §V]

When Washington was inaugurated in April 1789, no one knew how much debt the federal government had accumulated during the

---

If all the public and Accumulated amounts: see Appendix 1, §IV.B.1 and §IV.C.3.

HAMILTON'S FINANCIAL PROGRAMS

Revolutionary War and the 1780s. After examining documents and corresponding extensively, Hamilton calculates that the federal government <u>owes to France</u>, Spain, and bankers in the Netherlands about $11.7 million. The interest is 4 or 5%. Payments on the principal for these loans are due in the mid-1790s.

Hamilton calculates that the federal government owes just over $40 million to its own citizens, including accumulated interest, mostly at 6%. The terms of the domestic IOUs are less stringent than those of the foreign loans. The interest is payable indefinitely, and there is no deadline for repayment of the principal.

The total federal debt, foreign and domestic, including interest, is therefore more than $50 million.

Hamilton estimates the Revolutionary War <u>debts of the states</u> at another $25 million. If the federal government assumes the states' debts, as Hamilton urges (see §4.2.2.2), the total owed by the federal government will be nearly $80 million. A third of that is accumulated interest.

Annually, Hamilton calculates that interest payments on the federal debt will be half a million dollars on the foreign debt, plus just over four million dollars for the domestic debt, for a total of $4,587,444. (See §V.B.)

With that number in mind, Hamilton moves on to proposing how to collect revenue that will cover interest payments plus the operating expenses of the government, another $600,000.

<u>Owes to France</u>: On interest rates for the foreign debt, see Board of Treasury to Washington, 7/23/1789, and "Schedule B" of 12/31/1789.

https://founders.archives.gov/documents/Washington/05-03-02-0157 ▪ https://founders.archives.gov/documents/Hamilton/01-06-02-0076-0002-0003

For a table of foreign loans, with amounts and dates of repayment, see Wright, *One Nation under Debt*, p. 286.

NOTE: Over the course of the Revolutionary War, from 1775 to 1783, the French spent 1.3 billion francs aiding the Americans. This was twice the normal annual income of the French government. Rather than figuring out what this would be in 2021 currency, let's just imagine how much deep financial trouble you or I would be in if we suddenly spent twice our annual income, and still had to cover all normal living expenses. Coping with this debt is often cited as one of the reasons for the political and economic instability in France that led in 1789 to the French Revolution.

<u>Debts of the states</u>: The federal government eventually assumed $18.2 million in states' debts. States that were owed money were paid by the federal government. Those that owed money to the government were quietly forgiven: the money was never collected. See Ferguson, *Power of the Purse*, p. 329.

Hamilton's Table of U.S. Debt

	Principal	Interest	Total
Foreign	$10,070,307	$1,640,071	$11,710,378
Domestic*	$27,383,917	$13,030,168	**$40,414,085
Total federal debt			$54,124,464
State debt, estimated ***			$25,000,000
Federal plus state debt			$79,000,000

* Domestic debt owed by the federal government, including debt already paid off by states, which is to be reimbursed. Not included: unliquidated domestic debt (mostly Continental paper money), which Hamilton estimates at $2 million.

** In Appendix 1, §V.A, Hamilton gave this as $40,414,085, but at §VII.A, he gave it as $42,414,085. Hence he calculated the total debt as $79,000,000, when according to the earlier number, it should have been $77,000,000. I've left it as $79,000,000, to prevent confusion. The error might have been introduced in Hamilton's draft (which doesn't survive) or in the edition of the *Report* published in New York, 1790.

*** Hamilton did not separate the states' debts principal from interest.

Receipt for IOUs turned into the Loan Office in Connecticut in 1793. From the collection of John Herzog.

4.2.4 Financing the debt [OUTLINE: §VI]

Hamilton's immediate and urgent goal is not to pay off the whole debt as soon as possible. It is to pay off the debt over time, and, meanwhile, to make regular payments of the interest on the debt. He wants to "fund" the debt by inviolably committing certain revenues to paying interest and principal, until the debt has been extinguished. (See §4.1.5.) Funding the debt will restore American credit, i.e., it will restore trust that the United States government will in future meet its obligations. With its credit restored, the government will be able to borrow in the future at a lower interest rate.

The foreigners to whom the United States owes money—France, Spain, and the Dutch bankers—just want to be repaid. Hamilton proposes paying the interest that's currently owed, and then, when the principal comes due in the mid-1790s, paying it off with a new European loan at a lower interest rate. (See Appendix 1, §VII.B.) The United States will be able to do that if its credit is sound.

Domestically, Hamilton proposes to use a variation on the method used by Great Britain. (See §4.1.1.) To those holding IOUs, the government will issue a new type of security: a bond that can be redeemed by the government at will, but only after a certain time. Until that time, the government will pay the bond-holder a substantial interest.

Hamilton proposes that holders of IOUs be given <u>six or seven options</u> with varying interest rates and terms, including a combination of land in the West, annuities, or specie. Why so many? Because he considers it essential that creditors accept the government's terms voluntarily. He wants them to see that accepting is in their self-interest.

> <u>It is, in his opinion,</u> of the greatest consequence, that the debt should, with the consent of the creditors, be remoulded into such a shape, as will bring the expenditure of the nation to a level with its income. 'Till this shall be accomplished, the finances of the United States will never wear a proper countenance. Arrears of interest, continually accruing, will be as continual a monument, either of inability, or of ill faith; and will not cease to have an evil influence on public credit. In nothing are appearances of greater moment, than in whatever regards credit. Opinion is the soul of it, and this is affected by appearances, as well as realities. By offering an option to the creditors, between a number of plans, the change

---

<u>Six or seven options</u> and <u>It is in his opinion</u>: Appendix 1, §VI.C.1-7 and §VI.D.

meditated will be more likely to be accomplished. Different tempers will be governed by different views of the subject.

Each of Hamilton's options offers a reason that might make self-interested Americans willing to accept it. For example, according to one proposal, holders of IOUs might have two thirds of the debt funded at the current terms, and one third redeemed by a grant of land in the west. Since none of Hamilton's options was adopted by Congress, we won't go into them in detail here. The point is that Hamilton's proposed measures were intended to bring the interest rate on domestic debt from 6% to about 4%. On the government's $79 million debt (estimated, including states' debts), that would be a savings of $1.5 million in interest every year.

4.2.5 Government revenue [OUTLINE: §VII]

After proposing a method to fund the federal debt, Hamilton moves on to the question of how much revenue is needed. The total necessary for government operations (administrative and military expenses, etc.) he calculates at $600,000. Aside from that, the government needs money to pay the interest on its debt, refinanced at a lower rate.

> Thus to pay the interest of the foreign debt, and to pay four per cent on the whole of the domestic debt, principal and interest, forming a new capital, will require a yearly income of $2,239,163 dollars, 9 cents.

How will the government raise that amount? Hamilton calculates that the import and tonnage taxes that Congress signed into law in the summer of 1789 will provide much of the revenue needed: some $1,140,000. To make up the deficit, Hamilton proposes an excise tax on domestic wines and spirits as well as a duty on imported ones. The collectors of import and tonnage duties can also collect the excise tax on the imported wine and spirits: that keeps the number of government officials to a minimum.

$600,000: The Funding Act begins by allotting $600,000 from the government's income for "the support of the government of the United States, and their common defence." First Congress, Session II, Ch. XXXIV, "An Act Making Provision for the Debt of the United States," 8/4/1790.

https://en.wikisource.org/wiki/United_States_Statutes_at_Large/Volume_1/1st_Congress/2nd_Session/Chapter_34

Thus to pay: Appendix 1, §VII.A.

HAMILTON'S FINANCIAL PROGRAMS 97

Hamilton estimates the revenue from the alcohol excise tax at $1,703,400, bringing the <u>total revenue</u> to $2,843,400. That's enough to cover the interest payments and the government's annual operating expenses.

4.2.6 The Sinking Fund [OUTLINE: §VII.E]

Hamilton also proposes that the government establish a sinking fund, into which will be deposited revenue from the postal service, up to one million dollars. If there's money in the sinking fund at a time when government bonds are selling for less than their face value (also known as their "par value"), the government can use money from the sinking fund to purchase its own bonds. By doing so, it can retire some of its debt at less than the expected cost, and help stabilize the price of bonds.

Why would bonds sell for less than their face value? The most obvious reason would be that people didn't trust the government to pay them off, and were willing to take a loss to obviate the risk. Another reason for a drop below face value would be that investors could make more by investing their money elsewhere than by accepting the interest on bonds. (We'll see how that idea plays out during the Panic of 1792; see §7.2.)

In explaining why the sinking fund should be established, Hamilton makes one of his most famous statements about the national debt:

> <u>Persuaded as the Secretary</u> is, that the proper funding of the present debt, will render it a national blessing: Yet he is so far from acceding to the position, in the latitude in which it is sometimes laid down, that "public debts are public benefits," a position inviting to prodigality, and liable to dangerous abuse,— that he ardently wishes to see it incorporated, as a fundamental maxim, in the system of public credit of the United States, that the creation of debt should always be accompanied with the means of extinguishment. This he regards as the true secret for rendering public credit immortal. And he presumes, that it is

---

<u>Total revenue</u>: The revenue estimates are from Schedule K to the *First Report*, 1/9/1790.
https://founders.archives.gov/documents/Hamilton/01-06-02-0076-0002-0011

<u>Persuaded as the Secretary</u>: Appendix 1, §VII.E.2.

difficult to conceive a situation, in which there may not be an adherence to the maxim. At least he feels an unfeigned solicitude, that this may be attempted by the United States, and that they may commence their measures for the establishment of credit, with the observance of it.

4.2.7 Storing the government's revenue [OUTLINE: §VII.E.3]

The government could collect its taxes, then stash them in a locked box until it needs them for interest payments, routine expenses, or emergencies. But doing that would decrease the amount of money in circulation, and Hamilton is well aware that there's already a shortage of that.

He therefore strongly suggests that the government's revenue should be deposited in a trustworthy bank. The bank can then lend against that money to private businesses and citizens. For this purpose, Hamilton proposes the creation of a national bank. The bank's structure is elaborated, at Congress's request, in Hamilton's second major policy paper, the *Report on a National Bank*. (See Chapter 5 and Appendix 2.) In the meantime, the government's revenue is deposited in the three existing banks: the Massachusetts Bank, the Bank of North America, or the Bank of New York.

4.3 SIDE NOTE: HAMILTON'S VIEWS ON EXTINGUISHING THE DEBT (RE OUTLINE: §VII.E.2)

In 1792, Thomas Jefferson told George Washington:

> I would wish the debt paid tomorrow; [Hamilton] wishes it never to be paid, but always to be a thing wherewith to corrupt and manage the legislature.

That's simply not true. In Hamilton's papers in the Founders Online, there are at least two dozen examples from 1781 to 1804 of Hamilton insisting that the government's debt be paid off ("extinguished"), aside

---

I would wish: Jefferson to Washington, 9/9/1792. Jefferson also believed that one generation should not be able to burden the next with debt, for then "the earth would belong to the dead and not the living generation." Jefferson to Madison, 9/6/1789
https://founders.archives.gov/documents/Jefferson/01-24-02-0330 ∎
https://founders.archives.gov/documents/Jefferson/01-15-02-0375-0003

from the one quoted at §4.2.6. For example, in a pamphlet published in August 1792, he wrote:

> As the vicissitudes of nations beget a perpetual tendency to the accumulation of debt, there ought to be in every government a perpetual, anxious and unceasing effort to reduce that, which at any time exists, as fast as shall be practicable, consistently with integrity and good faith. ... Nothing can more interest the national credit and prosperity, than a constant and systematic attention to husband all the means previously possessed for extinguishing the present debt, and to avoid, as much as possible, the incurring of any new debt.

In 1795, just after Hamilton left office as secretary of the Treasury, Congress refused to set aside payments for a portion of the debt. He wrote to his friend Rufus King that such behavior "haunts me every step I take, and afflicts me more than I can express ... To see the character of the Government and the country so sported with, exposed to so indelible a blot puts my heart to the Torture."

Hamilton was equally scrupulous about his personal debts. In his last will and testament, written in July 1804, he begs that if he dies owing people money, his children should, "if they or any of them shall ever be able ... make up the Deficiency." This is a man who takes paying off debts—his own or the government's—very seriously. Because he's still frequently misquoted on this subject, I've included a number of his more important statements on it.

As the vicissitudes: Hamilton, "The Fact" No. 1, 9/11/1792.
https://founders.archives.gov/documents/Hamilton/01-12-02-0274

Haunts me: Hamilton to Rufus King, 2/21/1795.
https://founders.archives.gov/documents/Hamilton/01-18-02-0170

The Deficiency: Hamilton, "Last Will and Testament," 7/9/1804.

When he died, Hamilton owed more than $20,000 to banks in New York, and thousands more to private individuals. See "Statement of My Property and Debts," 7/1/1804.
https://founders.archives.gov/documents/Hamilton/01-26-02-0001-0259
■ https://founders.archives.gov/documents/Hamilton/01-26-02-0001-0243

His more important statements: see following two pages.

Hamilton on Extinguishing Debt: A Chronological Survey of Quotes

To Robert Morris, 4/30/1781: "A national debt if it is not excessive will be to us a national blessing; it will be powerfull cement of our union."
https://founders.archives.gov/documents/Hamilton/01-02-02-1167

"Continentalist" No. 4, 8/30/1781: "It might indeed be a good restraint upon the spirit of running in debt with which governments are too apt to be infected, to make it a condition of the grants to Congress, that they shall be obliged in all their loans to appropriate funds for the payment of principal as well as interest; and such a restriction might be serviceable to public credit."
https://founders.archives.gov/documents/Hamilton/01-02-02-1191

Report on Manufactures, 12/5/1791: "Neither will it follow, that an accumulation of debt is desireable, because a certain degree of it operates as capital. There may be a plethora in the political, as in the Natural body; There may be a state of things in which any such artificial capital is unnecessary. The debt too may be swelled to such a size, as that the greatest part of it may cease to be useful as a Capital, serving only to pamper the dissipation of idle and dissolute individuals: as that the sums required to pay the Interest upon it may become oppressive, and beyond the means, which a government can employ, consistently with its tranquility, to raise them; as that the resources of taxation, to face the debt, may have been strained too far to admit of extensions adequate to exigencies, which regard the public safety. Where this critical point is, cannot be pronounced, but it is impossible to believe, that there is not such a point. And as the vicissitudes of Nations beget a perpetual tendency to the accumulation of debt, there ought to be in every government a perpetual, anxious and unceasing effort to reduce that, which at any time exists, as fast as shall be practicable consistently with integrity and good faith."
See Appendix 3, §II. D. 2. d. iv.

To Washington, 8/18/1792 (re Jefferson's complaints): "Some Gentlemen seem to forget that the faculties of every Country are limited. They talk as if the Government could extend its revenue ad libitum to pay off the debt. Whereas every rational calculation of the abilities of the Country will prove that the power of redemption which has been reserved over the debt is quite equal to those abilities, and that a greater power would be useless."
https://founders.archives.gov/documents/Hamilton/01-12-02-0184-0002

"Second Report on Public Credit," 1/16/1795: "The Revenue set free by these successive redemptions, would be sufficient to redeem the whole of the present foreign Debt in six years, that is within a term of 28 Years from the proposed time; for commencing the Redemption, or the 1st of January 1796, and after extinguishing the foreign debt would more than discharge the whole of the balances to Creditor States and the whole of the unfunded Debt in two years

➢

more. ... With the creation of debt should be incorporated the means of extinguishment; which means are two fold, the establishing at the time of contracting a debt funds for the reimbursement of the Principle, as well as for the payment of Interest within a determinate period—The making it a part of the contract that the funds so established shall be inviolably applied to the object. ... It is believed that it would be happy for the United States, if Congress would adopt this principle as a rule in all future Loans, never to be departed from: And a good evidence of this determination will be to apply it [as far as may be,] to the past."

https://founders.archives.gov/documents/Hamilton/01-18-02-0052-0002

To Theodore Sedgwick, 2/18/1795: "Every moment's reflection increases my chagrin and disgust at the failure of the propositions concerning the unsubscribed Debt. I am tortured by the idea that the Country should be so completely and so unnecessarily dishonored. A day of reckoning must come."

https://founders.archives.gov/documents/Hamilton/01-18-02-0169

"The Examination" No. 2, 12/21/1801: "The past administrations who had so long been calumniated by the imputation of that pernicious design, are of a sudden [under President Jefferson] discovered to have done too much for the speedy discharge of the debt, and its duration is to be prolonged by throwing away a part of the fund destined for its prompt redemption. Wonderful union of consistency and wisdom!"

https://founders.archives.gov/documents/Hamilton/01-25-02-0266

"Last Will and Testament," 7/9/1804: "Though if it shall please God to spare my life I may look for a considerable surplus out of my present property—Yet if he should speedily call me to the eternal wor[l]d, a forced sale as is usual may possibly render it insufficient to satisfy my Debts. I pray God that something may remain for the maintenance and education of my dear Wife and Children. But should it on the contrary happen that there is not enough for the payment of my Debts, I entreat my Dear Children, if they or any of them shall ever be able, to make up the Deficiency."

https://founders.archives.gov/documents/Hamilton/01-26-02-0001-0259

Hamilton, "Statement on Impending Duel with Aaron Burr," written between 6/28 and 7/10/1804 (as a possible reason for avoiding the duel): "I feel a sense of obligation towards my creditors; who in case of accident to me, by the forced sale of my property, may be in some degree sufferers. I did not think my self at liberty, as a man of probity, lightly to expose them to this hazard."

https://founders.archives.gov/documents/Hamilton/01-26-02-0001-0241

"Explanation of His Financial Situation," 7/1/1804: "[M]y lands now in a course of sale & settlement would accelerate the extinguishment of my debt, and in the end leave me a handsome clear property."

https://founders.archives.gov/documents/Hamilton/01-26-02-0001-0244

4.4 PASSAGE OF THE FUNDING BILL

4.4.1 Debate over the funding bill

Hamilton submitted the *First Report* on January 14, 1790. He received much positive response, at home and abroad.

The House of Representatives promptly drafted a funding bill that included all Hamilton's proposals. But several issues were hotly

---

Positive response: Benjamin Lincoln (collector of customs for Boston) to Hamilton, 2/16/1790: "Permit me to say to you sir, and think it not the language of adulation, that notwithstanding the expectations of the people on your appointment, were, from a knowledge of your abilities, raised to a very extraordinary height, yet they suffered no disappointment from seeing your report, saving those who are unfriendly to the great arrangements, necessary to be embraced, for the political salvation of this country. Our best citizens are very desirous of adopting your plan, and their only anxiety now arises from an apprehension lest Congress should so mutilate it, as to destroy its leading and ornamental features, and the necessary and beautiful connexion of its parts, and thereby render it, like all other of our plans of finance, unsystematical imperfect and insecure."
https://founders.archives.gov/documents/Hamilton/01-06-02-0154

Also: William Short (U.S. minister to France, June 1790 to May 1792) to Hamilton, 8/3/1790: "I have recieved your report on finance, which I have communicated to several persons here. They read it as well as myself with infinite pleasure. I am happy to learn that Congress are adopting it, as I am persuaded it will be fixing the credit of the United States on the firmest basis. I know at least that the impression which the report made on those who read it here, was a full persuasion both of the abilities of the author & the competence of the United States to a fulfillment of all their engagements."
https://founders.archives.gov/documents/Hamilton/01-06-02-0423

But see Madison to Henry Lee, 4/13/1790: "I think with you that the Report of the Secretary of the Treasury is faulty in many respects—it departs particularly from that simplicity which ought to be preserved in finance, more than any thing else. The novelty and difficulty of the Task he had to execute form no small apology for his errors, and I am in hopes that in some instances they will be dimi[ni]shed, if not remedied."
https://founders.archives.gov/documents/Madison/01-13-02-0106

debated in the House of Representatives from January to July. In February, Madison spoke strongly in favor of discrimination. His amendment was defeated thirty-six to thirteen. Madison also spoke out against assumption of states' debts, and from February to July 1790, managed to defeat the bill four times.

Assumption was then removed from the funding act that the House was considering. It was not in the act passed by the House of Representatives on June 2, 1790, which did include full payment to current holders of IOUs (i.e., no discrimination) and payment of accumulated interest. The Senate returned the bill to the House with assumption reinstated, and the House took up the issue again on July 22.

Assumption was included in the Funding Act only after Jefferson, Madison, and Hamilton negotiated an exchange. Madison and Jefferson would support assumption; Hamilton and his allies would support a southern location for the United States capital. The Residence Act passed on July 10, 1790. The Funding Act, including assumption, passed on July 26.

Hotly debated: In *Annals of Congress, House of Representatives, 1st Congress, 2nd Session,* the first seven months of 1790 fill about 635 pages. Of those, about 430 deal with discussion of Hamilton's plan for funding the debt. The debates start on January 28.
https://memory.loc.gov/cgi-bin/ampage?collId=llac&fileName=001/llac001.db&recNum=566

In favor of discrimination: Madison spoke several times on discrimination. See, for example, 2/11/1790 and 2/18/1790.
https://founders.archives.gov/documents/Madison/01-13-02-0030 ■
https://founders.archives.gov/documents/Madison/01-13-02-0039

Defeat the bill: One of the most vocal opponents was James Jackson of Georgia, who in the House of Representatives on 7/23/1790 called assumption "a measure which has not only agitated this Legislature, but has more or less convulsed the whole people of the United States. It has elated speculators and State brokers, whilst it has depressed three-fourths of the honest part of the community. It has held out alluring prospects and fortunes to the one, whilst it has blased and withered the just expectations of the other." *Annals of Congress, House of Representatives, 1st Congress, 2nd Session,* p. 1743.
https://memory.loc.gov/cgi-bin/ampage?collId=llac&fileName=002/llac002.db&recNum=235

Negotiated an exchange: see following page for Jefferson's description. On the negotiations regarding the Residence Act and the assumption bill, see also the Founders Online editorial note for Josiah Parker to James Madison, ca. 6/15/1790.
https://founders.archives.gov/documents/Madison/01-13-02-0173

Jefferson's description of the Residence and Assumption Compromise

The only account of the famous dinner meeting between Madison, Hamilton, and Jefferson is written by Jefferson. From my point of view as a fan of primary sources, Jefferson's memoirs, the *Anas* are dicey, because Jefferson edited and re-edited his notes over decades. Usually there is no way to know what he wrote in the 1790s, and what he added many years later.

In this case, though, we have a description written ca. 1792 by Jefferson, as well as an edited version from the *Anas,* 1818. Here's Jefferson's more vivid but less self-justifying version written ca. 1792.

"The assumption of the state debts in 1790. was a supplementary measure in Hamilton's fiscal system. When attempted in the House of Representatives it failed. This threw Hamilton himself and a number of members into deep dismay. Going to the President's one day I met Hamilton as I approached the door. His look was sombre, haggard, and dejected beyond description. Even his dress uncouth and neglected. He asked to speak with me. We stood in the street near the door. He opened the subject of the assumption of the state debts, the necessity of it in the general fiscal arrangement and it's indispensible necessity towards a preservation of the union: and particularly of the New England states, who had made great expenditures during the war, on expeditions which tho' of their own undertaking were for the common cause: that they considered the assumption of these by the Union so just, and it's denial so palpably injurious, that they would make it a sine qua non of a continuance of the Union. That as to his own part, if he had not credit enough to carry such a measure as that, he could be of no use, and was determined to resign. He observed at the same time, that tho' our particular business laid in separate departments, yet the administration and it's success was a common concern, and that we should make common cause in supporting one another. He added his wish that I would interest my friends from the South, who were those most opposed to it. I answered that I had been so long absent from my country that I had lost a familiarity with it's affairs, and being but lately returned had not yet got into the train of them, that the fiscal system being out of my department, I had not yet undertaken to consider and understand it, that the assumption had struck me in an unfavorable light, but still not having considered it sufficiently I had not concerned in it, but that I would revolve what he had urged in my mind. It was a real fact that the Eastern and Southern members (S. Carolina however was with the former) had got into the most extreme ill humor with one another, this broke out on every question with the most alarming heat, the bitterest animosities seemed to be engendered, and tho' they met every day, little or nothing could be done from mutual distrust and antipathy. On considering the situation of things I thought the first step towards some conciliation of views would be to bring Mr. Madison

➢

and Colo. Hamilton to a friendly discussion of the subject. I immediately wrote to each to come and dine with me the next day, mentioning that we should be alone, that the object was to find some temperament for the present fever, and that I was persuaded that men of sound heads and honest views needed nothing more than explanation and mutual understanding to enable them to unite in some measures which might enable us to get along. They came. I opened the subject to them, acknoleged that my situation had not permitted me to understand it sufficiently but encouraged them to consider the thing together. They did so. It ended in Mr. Madison's acquiescence in a proposition that the question should be again brought before the house by way of amendment from the Senate, that tho' he would not vote for it, nor entirely withdraw his opposition, yet he should not be strenuous, but leave it to it's fate. It was observed, I forget by which of them, that as the pill would be a bitter one to the Southern states, something should be done to soothe them; that the removal of the seat of government to the Patowmac was a just measure, and would probably be a popular one with them, and would be a proper one to follow the assumption. It was agreed to speak to Mr. White and Mr. Lee, whose districts lay on the Patowmac and to refer to them to consider how far the interests of their particular districts might be a sufficient inducement to them to yield to the assumption. This was done. Lee came into it without hesitation. Mr. White had some qualms, but finally agreed. The measure came down by way of amendment from the Senate and was finally carried by the change of White's and Lee's votes. But the removal to Patowmac could not be carried unless Pennsylvania could be engaged in it. This Hamilton took on himself, and chiefly, as I understood, through the agency of Robert Morris, obtained the vote of that state, on agreeing to an intermediate residence at Philadelphia. This is the real history of the assumption, about which many erroneous conjectures have been published. It was unjust, in itself oppressive to the states, and was acquiesced in merely from a fear of disunion, while our government was still in it's most infant state. It enabled Hamilton so to strengthen himself by corrupt services to many, that he could afterwards carry his bank scheme, and every measure he proposed in defiance of all opposition: in fact it was a principal ground whereon was reared up that Speculating phalanx, in and out of Congress which has since been able to give laws and to change the political complexion of the government of the US."

Jefferson's revised version of this episode is in Franklin B. Sawvel's 1903 edition of the *Anas*, pp. 32-35. Among the notable changes: Madison's name is deleted, replaced by "another friend or two."

https://archive.org/details/completeanastho00sawvgoog/page/n42/mode/2up?q=hamilton

On the myriad scholarly difficulties with the *Anas*, see "Editorial Note: The 'Anas'."

https://founders.archives.gov/documents/Jefferson/01-22-02-1033-0001

4.4.2 Differences between what Hamilton proposed and what Congress passed

In the *First Report*, Hamilton suggested seven different ways of settling the debt, many of them rather complex. (See §4.2.4 and Appendix 1, §VI.C.1-7.) Congress adopted none of them. Instead, the Funding Act included an elegantly simple plan with three different <u>types of bonds</u>. Hamilton explains the system in his "Address to the Public Creditors," published within a month of the passing of the funding bill. First he warns those of us who are holding IOUs: don't be too eager to sell them!

> <u>It is probable</u> that many of you are not sufficiently apprised of the advantages of your own situation, and that for want of judging rightly of it, and of your future prospects, you may be tempted to part with your securities much below their true value, and considerably below what it is probable they will sell for in eight or nine months from this time.

Then he explains how the payments will work. For two thirds of the

---

<u>Types of bonds</u>: It's not clear who came up with this combination of three types of bonds. They were not among Hamilton's options in the *First Report;* nor are they set out in his other writings of January to July 1790. A Senate committee seems to have started the process of simplification. After the House of Representatives sent "a bill making provision for the debt of the United States" to the Senate on 6/2, the bill went to a committee. On 6/21/1790 the committee proposed an amendment: "The design of this amendment of your committee is to discharge the alternatives proposed in the bill, and to fund the domestic debt of the United States at an interest of four per cent per annum." According to the amendment, which the Senate passed, for any sum subscribed, the bearer will get 4% interest per year, payable quarterly. The government can redeem the certifications at a maximum of six dollars per hundred dollars per year. *Annals of Congress, Senate, 1st Congress, 2nd Session,* p. 1027.

https://memory.loc.gov/cgi-bin/ampage?collId=llac&fileName=001/llac001.db&recNum=514

By 7/27 the bill had gone to the House and back to the Senate, which proposed amendments and refused the House's increase from 3 to 4% for interest on accumulated interest. The Senate also made some changes to the terms of payment for the debt assumed from the states. The specific proposals for the 6%, 6% deferred, and 3% bonds must have been made in committee, where no records were kept.

<u>It is probable</u>: Hamilton, "Address to Public Creditors," 9/1/1790. This essay also explains the three types of bonds in detail, for a lay audience.

https://founders.archives.gov/documents/Hamilton/01-07-02-0001

HAMILTON'S FINANCIAL PROGRAMS

principal owed to us, we'll be given bonds that will pay 6% interest. The interest will begin to accrue immediately and will be payable quarterly. For the other third of the principal, we'll receive bonds that will pay 6% interest beginning in ten years (hence "6% deferred bonds"). The government can redeem either of the 6% bonds by paying off the principal, but the maximum redemption rate is $8 per $100 of bonds, per year.

For the accumulated interest, we'll receive bonds that pay 3%. Interest on the 3% bonds also begins accruing immediately and is payable quarterly. The 3% bonds can be redeemed by the government "whenever provision shall be made by law for that purpose."

Quarterly payment of interest raises the effective interest on the 6% bonds to 6.135%. But the delay in payment on the deferred 6% bonds, combined with the fact that only 3% will be paid on accumulated interest, brings the effective interest rate down to about 4%. The goal of this system, Hamilton explains, is

> to obtain a suspension of the payment of one third of the interest, to which you are entitled, for ten years, in order to avoid the necessity of burthening the community, or carrying taxation to objects which might be displeasing to them. And you cannot wonder that a government, so lately formed, and not without considerable opposition, should be cautious in this respect.

One of the most important features of the Funding Act is that payments on the newly issued bonds are not subject to debate annually. Certain

---

We'll be given bonds: In concrete terms, assume you hold a government IOU for $1,000, on which $200 interest is owed. You'll receive $666.66 worth of bonds at 6%, with the interest payable immediately. You'll receive $333.33 of bonds that will earn 6% interest beginning ten years from now. The government can redeem only $80 of the $1,000 in any given year, which means you have a safe long-term investment. For the interest, you'll receive $200 worth of bonds at 3%, with the interest payable immediately; the government can redeem these bonds at any time.

3% bonds: First Congress, Session II, Ch. XXXIV, "An Act Making Provision for the Debt of the United States," 8/4/1790, Sec. 5.

https://en.wikisource.org/wiki/United_States_Statutes_at_Large/Volume_1/1st_Congress/2nd_Session/Chapter_34

Effective interest: Quarterly interest payments are to be made at the end of March, June, September and December. For Hamilton's calculation of the compound interest, see Appendix 1, §VI.D.

To obtain: "Address to Public Creditors," 9/1/1790.

https://founders.archives.gov/documents/Hamilton/01-07-02-0001

funds are pledged to paying the debt until it has been extinguished.

The Funding Act also states that proceeds of the sales in the western territory will be added to the sinking fund until the debt has been discharged. Hamilton had not proposed that.

4.4.3 Why would we accept lower interest rates and deferred payment?

The Funding Act provides that over the next year, we, the holders of old government IOUs, are to bring them into government offices. There the old IOUs will be cancelled and new bonds issued. Why would we do that, given that we'll be getting a lower interest rate with the new bonds than we would have had with the originals? Hamilton sees two reasons.

First: a 6% interest rate on bonds is quite respectable for a safe investment. In 1790, Dutch bankers, the savviest of the time, are making loans at 5%. Hamilton assumes that people who aren't living day-to-day and are not in dire need of cash will be satisfied with a 6% return on an investment, especially if they can collect that interest indefinitely.

The second major advantage of trading in the old IOUs is that the new ones will be easier to sell, if you find you need cash rather than a safe investment. The old IOUs were issued during the chaos of war, in hundreds of places, in hundreds of denominations, with varying

---

Funds are pledged: First Congress, Session II, Ch. XXXIV, "An Act Making Provision for the Debt of the United States," 8/4/1790, Sec. 20: "The monies arising under the revenue laws ... shall be and are hereby pledged and appropriated for the payment of the interest on the stock [i.e., the new bonds] ... to continue so pledged and appropriated, until the final redemption of the said stock ... [T]he said monies may be inviolably applied in conformity to this act, and may never be diverted to any other purpose ... [T]hat the faith of the United States be, and the same is hereby pledged to provide and appropriate hereafter such additional and permanent funds as may be requisite towards supplying any such deficiency." Congress did not make the same provision for the unsubscribed debt. In February 1795, just after Hamilton left Treasury, it failed to make provision for the unsubscribed debt, which by that time was a very small portion of the government's debt. Hamilton was nevertheless distraught. See §4.3.

https://en.wikisource.org/wiki/United_States_Statutes_at_Large/Volume_1/1st_Congress/2nd_Session/Chapter_34

Old IOUs were issued: On the difficulties of tracking domestic debt during the war, see Oliver Wolcott, Jr. to Hamilton, 8/7/1793, and Hamilton to Washington, 8/9/1793.
https://founders.archives.gov/documents/Hamilton/01-15-02-0151 ∎
https://founders.archives.gov/documents/Hamilton/01-15-02-0159

HAMILTON'S FINANCIAL PROGRAMS

interest rates. Because there was no standardized form to be filled out in quadruplicate and filed somewhere, the IOUs were prone to counterfeiting. The government's records of them did not always survive, so it was difficult to authenticate them. If there was doubt of the authenticity of an old IOU, accepting it as payment was a gamble.

The new bonds, on the other hand, will be easily recognizable. They will be issued from a few government offices, on standard forms. Their authenticity can be confirmed by checking government records. Since Congress has committed funds to paying the interest and principal, the value of the new bonds should be consistent and stable throughout the United States, and even abroad. Therefore it will be easy to sell them or to use them as if they were cash. Coming back to the nitty gritty of making your living: if you want to put aside money for a plow, saving the new bonds will be safe.

A less cold-hard-cash point: most Americans still remember fighting for our new nation. We want it to survive. Over the course of the 1780s, it has become obvious that it will not, unless the government's financial system is put on a sound basis. Hamilton's program has the potential to do that. Hamilton believes people will be willing to "accommodate" the public by helping refinance the debt. (Appendix 1, §VI.A.)

But what if some of us choose not to accept this arrangement? Then our IOUs will be repaid on the original terms. Hamilton considers it crucial not only to settle the debt, but to do so with the consent of the government's many and varying creditors. (See §4.2.4.)

The Funding Act passed by Congress therefore makes provision for those who prefer to keep the old IOUs. These IOUs become the "unsubscribed debt". It is required, however, that old IOUs be brought in and exchanged for new certificates within a certain amount of time, because the old IOUs were "greatly subject to counterfeit." For these

---

Original terms: "Address to Public Creditors," 9/1/1790
https://founders.archives.gov/documents/Hamilton/01-07-02-0001

New certificates: Hamilton, "Address to the Public Creditors," 9/1/1790: "So far is there from being any thing compulsory in the acts of the government in the case, that those of you, who do not choose to subscribe to the new terms, are to receive during the time alotted for determining upon them, exactly as much as those who do subscribe. And the faith of the government remains pledged to you to fulfil its engagements, which must be performed, as fast as its resources can be brought into action for the purpose. ... [Acceptance] is a question of prudent calculation, which you are at liberty to determine as you please."

https://founders.archives.gov/documents/Hamilton/01-07-02-0001

holders, the new certificates will have the same terms as the old IOUs.

Offices for exchanging IOUs for bonds opened in every state by October 1790. By early 1792, almost $32 million old IOUs had been converted to 6%, 6% deferred, and 3% bonds. Much of the $8 million in unsubscribed debt was owed to foreigners, who had not been able to convert their IOUs to bonds before the original deadline of September 1791.

4.4.4 United States borrowing abroad

In late August 1790, in accordance with Congress's instructions, Washington authorizes Hamilton to borrow $14 million from Dutch bankers at 5% interest or less. It is to be used to pay off foreign loans on which the United States is paying 6% interest. Since the United States owes $11 million to foreign countries, cutting interest by a single percentage point can save hundreds of thousands of dollars.

Dutch bankers, seeing that the United States government is serious about paying interest and eventually paying off the debt, raise a loan at 5%.

Unsubscribed debt: The Funding Act of 8/4/1790 provided for payment of interest on the unsubscribed debt, but did not make further provisions for payment. Re the subscribed and unsubscribed debt, see Hamilton's "Report on the Public Debt and Loans," 1/23/1792, where he recommends extending the date for converting IOUs to bonds through 9/30/1792.
https://en.wikisource.org/wiki/United_States_Statutes_at_Large/Volume_1/1st_Congress/2nd_Session/Chapter_34 ∎ https://founders.archives.gov/documents/Hamilton/01-10-02-0124-0001

Borrow $14 million: "An Act making provision for the payment of the debt of the United States," 8/4/1790, Sec. 2.

Raise a loan: Hamilton tells America's Dutch bankers on 11/29/1790 that the fact that the United States has funded the debt should count for something in terms of interest rates. "The nature of our present Government is such, that absolute reliance may be placed on its pecuniary dispositions, once made."

Two years later (4/2/1792), he congratulates William Short (U.S. minister to France, June 1790 to May 1792), on getting a loan at 4%: "The intelligence of it was received with great satisfaction by the President as well as by myself, and has given no small pleasure to the public at large."

Hamilton's "Statement of the Several Sums which Have Been Borrowed for the Use of the United States," 1/3/1793, lists loans taken at Amsterdam from February 1790 to June 1792, at rates of 4.5, 4, 4, 4, 5.5, and 4%.

https://founders.archives.gov/documents/Hamilton/01-07-02-0191 ∎ https://founders.archives.gov/documents/Hamilton/01-11-02-0183 ∎ https://founders.archives.gov/documents/Hamilton/01-13-02-0235-0002

4.4.5 Increase in value of bonds

Hamilton notes in the *First Report* that prices of government IOUs have risen a third from January to November 1789, and from November 1789 to early January 1790, have risen again by half. Even foreigners are beginning to buy American IOUs.

By late 1791, only a year after the offices opened to exchange IOUs for bonds, it is easy to buy and sell bonds throughout the United States. If you want to purchase imported goods such as French wine or English broadcloth, the stable prices of American bonds means they can be sent to Europe in lieu of gold and silver.

For more on the funding system, see Hamilton's "Vindication" essays, written from May to August 1792 in response to criticism by Jefferson, Madison, and the Antifederalists.

4.5 IMMEDIATE EFFECTS OF THE FIRST REPORT ON THE GORDIAN KNOT

How does the passage of the Funding Act affect the threads of our Gordian Knot in 1790 and 1791, before Hamilton's second major policy paper (*Report on a National Bank*) was acted upon?

4.5.1 Making a living

As of summer 1790, the Revolutionary War debt is funded. Provision has been made for paying it off, and it has been done in a way that

---

Risen a third: See the graph in Richard Sambasivam, "What Do Bond Prices Tell Us about the Early Republic?" *Journal of the American Revolution*, 2015.
https://allthingsliberty.com/2016/08/bond-prices-tell-us-early-republic/

Buy and sell bonds: Securities markets (i.e., centralized locations for buying and selling bonds) were opened in Philadelphia in 1790 and in New York City in 1792. See Wright, *Financial Founding Fathers*,

pp. 79 and 171, and Sylla and Cowen, *Alexander Hamilton on Finance, Credit, and Debt*, p. 6.

Vindication: "The Vindication," nos. 1-4.
https://founders.archives.gov/documents/Hamilton/01-11-02-0376 ■
https://founders.archives.gov/documents/Hamilton/01-11-02-0377-0002
■ https://founders.archives.gov/documents/Hamilton/01-11-02-0378
■ https://founders.archives.gov/documents/Hamilton/01-11-02-0379

appeals to our self-interest. If we were issued IOUs for goods and services during the war, and we kept them, we're finally able to spend or save that money. The new bonds are accepted at full value. If we sold our old IOUs years ago, then the current holders will now be able to invest in other goods or enterprises. In either case, productive effort that had been locked up in old IOUs has been translated back into money in circulation.

4.5.2 Centrifugal tendency of the United States

Because the federal government assumed states' debts, many of us are now owed money by the national government. That gives us a reason to want the federal government to survive and prosper. But not everyone is happy about that.

4.5.2.1 States vs. the federal government

Virginia passes a resolution in November 1790 that the assumption of states' debts is "repugnant to the Constitution," and the funding system is "dangerous to the rights and subversive of the interest of the people." John Jay, responding to Hamilton, thinks such arrogant statements will ultimately benefit the federal government:

> The assumption will do its own work—it will justify itself and not want advocates. Every indecent Interference of State assemblies will diminish their Influence. The national Govt has only to do what is right and if possible be silent. If compelled to speak, it shd be in few words strongly evincive of Temper Dignity and self Respect. Conversation and desultory paragraphs will do the rest.

Virginia passes: quoted in Hamilton to John Jay, 11/13/1790, n. 1.
https://founders.archives.gov/documents/Hamilton/01-07-02-0166

The assumption: John Jay to Hamilton, 11/28/1790.
https://founders.archives.gov/documents/Hamilton/01-07-02-0189

Compare Benjamin Lincoln's comments to Hamilton, 12/4/1790: "I hope and trust, that the different States will not ape the doings of the Assembly of Virginia. They may suppose that being dissatisfied with the Acts of Congress they had a right publicly to express that dissatisfaction, in the manner which they have done. I very much doubt their right, I hope it never will become a general practice, for the Assembly of the several States publicly to decide on the doings of Congress. ...[To encourage that would] lead things out from their proper course of system and order, into channels filled with obstructions, and would fast progress to an unfriendly termination."
https://founders.archives.gov/documents/Hamilton/01-07-02-0206

In New York, leading figures who opposed ratification of the Constitution in 1788 are still vigorously opposed to a stronger federal government. They're also opposed to the funding system, which they regard as "a system of public injustice."

In North Carolina, the legislature instructs its senators to oppose certain taxes: "Resolved that they strenuously oppose every excise and direct taxation law should any be attempted in Congress." North Carolina sends copies of their resolution to all the other state legislatures.

4.5.2.2 State vs. state

The states continue to squabble amongst themselves. Timothy Pickering laments to Hamilton in April 1790 that he has been chased off his land in Pennsylvania because he's from Connecticut. Connecticut still claims the Wyoming Valley, even though it does not share a border with Pennsylvania.

The states are frequently at odds with each other and the federal government regarding how to deal with the Indians. Hamilton reports to Washington in 1791 that a party of Virginians crossed into Pennsylvania to murder Indians. Justice for the act would depend not on the federal government apprehending the murderers, but on "the particular

---

Public injustice: James Tillary (physician in New York City) to Hamilton, January 1791: "The Chancellor [Robert R. Livingston] hates, & would destroy you. ... [At a dinner he said] he was not only opposed to your Funding System, but that R. Morris & several other well informed Influential Characters, viewed it as a system of public injustice. ... I have serious fears, that this State will soon appear Conspicuous for its opposition to the Federal Government."
https://founders.archives.gov/documents/Hamilton/01-07-02-0342

North Carolina: Quoted in Benjamin Hawkins to Hamilton, 2/16/1791. Most of the opposition to the excise tax on domestic production of distilled spirits comes from Western Pennsylvania, Kentucky, and North and South Carolina.
https://founders.archives.gov/documents/Hamilton/01-08-02-0043

Wyoming Valley: Timothy Pickering to Hamilton, 4/6/1790: "When I went to Wyoming three years ago, vested with the office of prothonotary & the four other offices usually annexed to it in a new county, I supposed I was fixed for life. But a train of disasters & a ruinous expence have attended my removal ..."
https://founders.archives.gov/documents/Hamilton/01-06-02-0228

policy and energy and good disposition of two state governments."

And of course there is a regional split between the northern and southern states. Southerners complain that their agricultural interests are always being sacrificed to those of the businessmen in the North. They also claim that Southerners owe much of the debt, and that Northerners are the ones collecting on it: hence, they say, Northerners are siphoning money from the South when they collect on debts.

Particular policy: Hamilton to Washington, 4/10/1791: "It is to be lamented that our system is such as still to leave the public peace of the Union at the mercy of each state Government. This is not only the case as it regards direct interferences, but as it regards the inability of the National Government in many particulars to take those direct measures for carrying into execution its views and engagements which exigencies require. For example—A party comes from a County of Virginia into Pennsylvania and wantonly murders some friendly Indians. The National Government instead of having power to apprehend the murderers and bring them to justice, is obliged to make a representation to that of Pennsylvania: That of Pennsylvania again is to make a requisition of that of Virginia. And whether the murderers shall be brought to Justice at all must depend upon the particular policy and energy and good disposition of two state Governments, and the efficacy of the provisions of their respective laws. And the security of other States and the money of all is at the discretion of one [Pennsylvania]. These things require a remedy but when it will come—God knows."

https://founders.archives.gov/documents/Hamilton/01-08-02-0210

Southerners owe: Washington to Hamilton, 7/29/1792 (probably reiterating complaints made by Jefferson): "True wisdom they acknowledge should direct temperate & peaceable measures; but add, the division of sentiment & interest happens unfortunately, to be so geographical, that no mortal can say that what is most wise & temperate, would prevail against what is more easy & obvious; they declare, they can contemplate no evil more incalculable than the breaking of the Union into two, or more parts; yet, ... whenever Northern & Southern prejudices have come into conflict, the latter have been sacraficed and the former soothed. [They also say] That the owers of the debt are in the Southern and the holders of it in the Northern division."

https://founders.archives.gov/documents/Hamilton/01-12-02-0104

Hamilton's reply of 8/18/1792 includes a good summary the 6%, 6% deferred, and 3% bonds, plus (among much else) explanations of why the debt and accumulated interest must be paid, why a national bank is necessary, and the effects of speculation.

https://founders.archives.gov/documents/Hamilton/01-12-02-0184-0002

4.5.2.3 Federal defense of the borders

Now that it has revenue, the federal government begins to play a role in military matters, including the defense of the borders. The United States still has no standing army and no military training program, so many of its soldiers are from state militias. But settlers are already moving into the fertile land beyond the Appalachians, into areas that don't belong to the original thirteen states. Because the federal government's job is to protect them, those settlers tend to be more invested in the federal government's survival.

The first American expedition against the Indians is undertaken in September and October of 1790, in the Northwest Territory (modern Ohio and Indiana). The Indians there are well supplied with arms by the British, who have refused to move out of the area until Americans pay off pre-Revolutionary War debts to British merchants. (See §2.2.3.2.) The American troops, led by General Josiah Harmar, are woefully unprepared and suffer a devastating defeat. A second expedition in 1791, under General Arthur St. Clair, also ends in disaster.

But on the positive side: because the federal government has assumed the states' debts and the national defense, states need less money. A study of tax rates in eight northern states from 1785-1788 and 1792-1795 showed the average tax rate across all those states falling by 77%. Such drastic state tax cuts help fuel an economic boom that begins in the 1790s.

Disaster: The expedition was against the Miami and Shawnee Indians along the Wabash River. Josiah Harmar's page on Wikipedia gives details about the expedition, and is also eye-opening regarding the problems of land sale and ownership in the Northwest Territory, which included parts of modern Ohio, Indiana, Illinois, Michigan, Wisconsin, and Minnesota.

https://en.wikipedia.org/wiki/Josiah_Harmar and https://armyhistory.org/the-battle-of-the-wabash-the-forgotten-disaster-of-the-indian-wars/

Study of tax rates: Max Edling & Mark D. Kaplanoff, "Alexander Hamilton's Fiscal Reform: Transforming the Structure of Taxation in the Early Republic," *William and Mary Quarterly* v. 61, no. 4 (Oct. 2004), pp. 713-44; cited in Parenti, *Radical Hamilton*, p. 173.

Economic boom: Noah Webster (Connecticut merchant, political writer, and future lexicographer) to James Greenleaf, 10/13/1791: "The establishment of funds to maintain public credit has an amazing effect upon the face of business & the country. Commerce revives & the country is full of provision. Manufactures are increasing to a great degree, & in the large towns vast improvements are making in pavements & buildings." Quoted in Wright and Cowen, *Financial Founding Fathers,* p. 24. See also Benjamin Lincoln to Hamilton, 12/4/1790.

https://founders.archives.gov/documents/Hamilton/01-07-02-0206

4.5.3 Inadequate circulation of money

The newly issued government bonds soon begin to <u>circulate as money</u>, because their value is stable and is constant throughout the United States. The difference between these bonds and printed government money ("fiat currency") is this: the bonds represent goods and services that were actually produced. The producers had just been forced to wait before enjoying the fruits of their labor.

Under Hamilton's plan, interest on the bonds is <u>paid in specie</u>, and not annually but quarterly. That means that the government revenue collected to pay the interest doesn't sit in government coffers for a year. Every three months, more than a million dollars is paid out to bond-holders, who can invest it or spend it. This is a tremendous boost to money in circulation.

Another benefit to having stable bonds is that residents of war-torn Europe are investing their money in the United States. In effect, they are saying, "We trust your government more than we trust our own."

4.5.4 Lack of government revenue

Having reliable sources of government revenue means the government itself becomes more reliable. Although defense of American borders is still limited, American citizens can now count on functioning judicial,

---

<u>Circulate as money</u>: Hamilton explains how the issuing of government bonds increased money in circulation in "Defence of the Funding System," July 1795: "The Government borrows of an individual 100 Dollars in specie, for which it gives its funded bonds. These hundred dollars are expended on some branch of the public service. Tis evident they are not annihilated, they only pass from the individual who lent to the individual or individuals to whom the Government has disbursed them. They continue in the hands of their new masters to perform their usual functions, as capital. But besides this the lender has the bonds of the Government for the sum lent. These from their negotiable and easily vendible nature can at any moment be applied by him to any useful or profitable undertaking which occurs; and thus the Credit of the Government produces a new & additional Capital equal to one hundred dollars the equivalent for the interest on that sum temporarily diverted from other employt. while passing into & out of the public coffers, which continues its instrumentality as a Capital while it remains not reimbursed."
https://founders.archives.gov/documents/Hamilton/01-19-02-0001

<u>Paid in specie</u>: see Funding Act of 8/4/1790, Section 8; *Report on a National Bank,* Appendix 2, §II.C.4; and Appendix 4, no. 21.

executive and legislative branches. It's a far cry from the mid-1780s, when delegates often didn't even bother to appear at sessions of Confederation Congress.

4.5.5 Massive government debt

Payment on Revolutionary War debts to the French, the Spanish, and the Dutch bankers is under way by 1791, in part via new loans from the Dutch. The domestic debt is funded: the interest is being paid regularly, and there is a plan to pay off the principal.

4.5.6 Summary of the funding system

The Funding Act is not a magic bullet for the United States. Many unresolved crises remain, and more come in the 1790s. But the improvement from when Hamilton took office in September 1789 to late 1791 is remarkable. Hamilton is enormously popular by the end of 1791.

Let's move on to the second part of Hamilton's financial plan: the national bank.

CHAPTER 5

Policy Paper #2:
Report on a National Bank

5.1 INTRODUCTORY NOTE

On December 13, 1790, eleven months after the *First Report on Public Credit* was issued, Hamilton completed the *Second Report on the Further Provision Necessary for Establishing Public Credit*, usually known as the *Report on a National Bank*. The *Report on a National Bank* is a mere 15,000 words, slightly shorter than the *First Report*. It addresses all the elements of our Gordian Knot: making a living, the centrifugal tendency of the United States, money in circulation, revenue, and debt.

Founders Online has a lengthy discussion of writings that apparently influenced the content of this report. The relevant point for us is, again, that Hamilton's *synthesis* of all these ideas was wholly original.

5.2 HOW BANKS WORK IN THE UNITED STATES IN 1790

In 1790, a bank is not a complicated institution. To become a stockholder, you purchase shares using gold or silver. The gold and silver in the vaults belonging to you and the other stockholders forms the

---

National Bank: Hamilton, *Report on a National Bank*, 12/13/1790; submitted to Congress 12/14/1790. The full text of this report appears in Appendix 2, with outline headings. For an excellent walk-through of the *Report on a National Bank*, see Carson Holloway, *Hamilton versus Jefferson in the Washington Administration*, Chapter 4. The annotated *Report* is at

https://founders.archives.gov/documents/Hamilton/01-07-02-0229-0003

Founders Online: Included in the "Introductory Note: Second Report on the Further Provision Necessary for Establishing Public Credit" are comments on how the Bank of the United States was and was not similar to the Bank of England.

https://founders.archives.gov/documents/Hamilton/01-07-02-0229-0001

HAMILTON'S FINANCIAL PROGRAMS

bank's capital. The bank lends money at interest. If you own stock in the bank, some of the interest is paid to you as a dividend.

If you don't buy stock, you can still earn interest by depositing money you don't need day-to-day in the bank. The bank will lend it out at interest until you need it, and pay you part of the interest. The bank's existence depends on keeping money safe, so your money is at considerably less risk in the bank's vault than if it were buried under your hearthstone.

The gold and silver usually stay in the vault. When making loans, the bank issues banknotes that can be exchanged for gold and silver. If you need to transfer money from one point to another, you can ask for banknotes, which are easier and safer to transport than gold and silver.

However, in order to keep the bank in existence when stockholders like you and I come and go, the bank must be chartered as a corporation. That makes it a legal entity that can continue indefinitely, regardless of who the specific stockholders are. By 1790, only a handful of corporations have been chartered in the United States. All of them have been brought into existence by state legislatures, which means political negotiation at the state level was required.

It's not surprising, then, that by 1790, only three banks exist in the United States. They are exotic creatures that many Americans haven't dealt with and look at askance. Hence the *Report on a National Bank* (like the *First Report on Public Credit*) includes a good deal of explanatory, educational material aimed at Congress and the American public. Hamilton "entreats the indulgence of the House" because the public needs to be informed, being the "ultimate arbiter of every measure of Government." (See Appendix 2, §1.)

Transfer money: Hamilton's customs collectors, who handled substantial amounts of money, were well aware of the dangers of moving gold and silver. Meletiah Jordan (customs collector at Frenchman's Bay, Maine) to Hamilton, 4/1/1790: "There is no possible mode of remitting from hence but in Specie to Boston, by Coasting Vessels. I must confess I would not wish to send such sums on my own risk therefore shall be glad you would point out what I must adopt for such remittance with safety to myself, & satisfaction to the United States...."

Sharp Delany (customs collector at Philadelphia) to Hamilton, 2/23/1790: writes "to solicit your attention to the providing of safe & secure stores. I am confident they will be wanted, as deposits will be made on a large scale. Security therefore is absolutely necessary. I should not trouble you knowing your mind must be taken up on business of the highest nature, if the spring importations were not so near at hand."

https://founders.archives.gov/documents/Hamilton/01-06-02-0218 ■
https://founders.archives.gov/documents/Hamilton/01-06-02-0165

5.3 CONTENT OF THE *REPORT ON A NATIONAL BANK*

NOTE: If you're interested enough in Hamilton's financial programs to read this book, you should certainly read Hamilton's *Report on a National Bank*. The full text of it is in Appendix 2, with outline headings added; these headings are used as section references below. In this chapter, I won't attempt to discuss every point of the Report; I'm just giving an overview of points that relate to the Gordian Knot.

Hamilton states that "a National Bank is an Institution of primary importance to the prosperous administration of the Finances, and would be of the greatest utility in the operations connected with the support of the Public Credit." (See Appendix 2, §1.)

5.3.1 Advantages of banks, especially large banks [OUTLINE: §II.A]

The opening section of the report describes the advantages of a bank. The first advantage is that it will increase money in circulation (the third thread of our Gordian Knot):

> It is evident, for instance, that the money, which a merchant keeps in his chest, waiting for a favourable opportunity to employ it, produces nothing 'till that opportunity arrives. But if instead of locking it up in this manner, he either deposits it in a Bank, or invests it in the Stock of a Bank, it yields a profit, during the interval; in which he partakes, or not, according to the choice he may have made of being a depositor or a proprietor; and when any advantageous speculation offers, in order to be able to embrace it, he has only to withdraw his money, if a depositor, or if a proprietor to obtain a loan from the Bank, or to dispose of his Stock ... (See Appendix 2, §II.A.1)

Hamilton goes on to explain why a bank can lend more money than it has in its vault by issuing banknotes—so long as it's careful about vetting borrowers and getting sufficient collateral. (Appendix 2, §II.A.1.)

Sufficient collateral: Lending out money depended, of course, on having adequate collateral from the borrowers. Adam Smith estimated that banks could safely issue banknotes of up to five times the gold and silver in their vaults. Some of the banks in the United States limited the amount to three times the bank's capital, but others imposed no limits. See Gordon, *An Empire of Wealth*, pp. 114-120. Today this practice is referred to as "fractional banking". See also §3.6.3.

HAMILTON'S FINANCIAL PROGRAMS

The government of the United States derives its income mostly from imports. As Hamilton knew from his years in St. Croix (see §3.1), hardly any imports can be expected to arrive during the harshest part of the winter, when ships don't sail. The second advantage of a large bank is, then, that it can make loans to the government over the winter. Such a bank can also provide funds to the government in an emergency—for example, if the nation is attacked. Obviously the size of the bank is an important factor. The government cannot borrow $100,000 if that's a significant part of the bank's capital.

A third advantage is that having a bank facilitates payment of import and excise taxes by citizens.

> Those who are in a situation to have access to the Bank can have the assistance of loans to answer with punctuality the public calls upon them. ... The other way, in which the effect here contemplated is produced, and in which the benefit is general, is the encreasing of the quantity of circulating medium and the quickening of circulation. (Appendix 2, §II.A.3)

5.3.2 Criticisms of banks [OUTLINE §II.B]

Hamilton moves on to answer the charges against banks. Most notably, some people argue that the existence of banks increases interest rates (i.e., promotes usury). Hamilton points out that having more money in circulation tends to decrease interest rates, and that it is in the interest of the bank to lend to "honest and industrious men." (Appendix 2, §II.B.1.)

Significant part: The Bank of New York did, in fact, refuse the government a loan at least once. Thomas Willing to Hamilton, 3/12/1790, replying to Hamilton's request for a loan to the government of $50,000: "We found it necessary to stop our Discount [i.e., making loans] last Week, & I think we shall not find it convenient to open it again for three or four Weeks to come. If yr. application shou'd be postponed till the Middle of next Month, I have no doubt but we shall be able to furnish Bank paper at 30 or 60 Day's for the Sum you mention. Perhaps it may be done sooner if necessity presses you, & supplies come into the Bank in the usual manner with our Spring Trade—but the Directors must determine at the Moment of application for such large Sums as you require— they can't now say what they will, or may be able to do a Month hence."
https://founders.archives.gov/documents/Hamilton/01-06-02-0190

5.3.3 Why not print paper money? [OUTLINE §II.C.2]

Granted the need for having more money in circulation, Hamilton asks: why not simply have the government print money? On this subject, with memories of Revolutionary War paper money undoubtedly in mind (see §2.3.3), Hamilton is quite firm.

> Paper emissions ... are of a nature so liable to abuse, and it may even be affirmed so certain of being abused, that the wisdom of the Government will be shewn in never trusting itself with the use of so seducing and dangerous an expedient. ... The stamping of paper is an operation so much easier than the laying of taxes, that a government, in the practice of paper emissions, would rarely fail in any such emergency to indulge itself too far, in the employment of that resource, to avoid as much as possible one less auspicious to present popularity. If it should not even be carried so far as to be rendered an absolute bubble, it would at least be likely to be extended to a degree, which would occasion an inflated and artificial state of things incompatible with the regular and prosperous course of the political œconomy. (Appendix 2, §II.C.3)

5.3.4 Why a national bank? [OUTLINE §III]

Hamilton next asks: why do we need a bank chartered by the federal government, rather than one that's chartered by a particular state, as the three existing banks are?

The Massachusetts Bank was chartered in 1784. The Bank of New York was established in 1784, with Hamilton's assistance. (See §3.6.3.) Due to political squabbles at the state level, the Bank of New York had been operating since that time without a charter. The third and oldest bank in the United States was the Bank of North America, in Philadelphia.

The Bank of North America was chartered in 1781 by the state of Pennsylvania and the Confederation Congress, at the urging of Robert Morris, superintendent of Finance. Its purpose was to raise money to buy supplies for the Continental Army.

Hamilton explains in detail why it would not be appropriate simply to designate the Bank of North America as the national bank. The Confederation Congress did not have any authority that could be construed as the right to create a corporation; so the Bank of North

America was also chartered by the state of Pennsylvania. In the mid-1780s, Pennsylvania revoked the bank's charter. When they reinstated it, the Pennsylvania legislature reduced the stock of the Bank from $10 million to $2 million, and set the charter to expire in fourteen years. Some might argue that under those revised terms, the Bank of North America isn't even the same institution that was chartered under Robert Morris.

The Bank's board of directors is also a problem, according to Hamilton. Its directors can serve indefinitely, which may lead them to ignore the best interests of their stockholders and the government. Stockholders have one vote per share, which means a few major stockholders can manipulate bank policy. Also, the Bank of North America does not restrict ownership by foreigners. Foreigners might end up controlling this important tool of America's finances.

Hamilton tactfully doesn't mention another very obvious drawback. The states have different interests from the federal government. To have a state-chartered bank controlling substantial amounts of the federal government's money would allow that state to hold the federal government hostage to local interests. The bank might, for example, refuse to make a loan or demand an excessively high interest rate.

5.3.5 Structure of the national bank [OUTLINE §IV]

The combined capital of the Massachusetts Bank, the Bank of New York, and the Bank of North America is some $4 million. Hamilton

---

Pennsylvania legislature: Hamilton was familiar with the affairs of the Bank of North America because in the 1780s, he was handling his brother-in-law John Church's finances, and Church was a stockholder in that bank. See, among other letters, Hamilton to Jeremiah Wadsworth, 10/29/1785: "to leave so considerable a sum in a Company of this kind not incorporated is dangerous." See also John Chaloner (John B. Church's agent and business associate in Philadelphia) to Hamilton, 12/16/1786.
https://founders.archives.gov/documents/Hamilton/01-03-02-0462 ∎
https://founders.archives.gov/documents/Hamilton/01-03-02-0575

Combined capital: According to the Bank of New York's 1784 charter, its stock was $1 million. The Bank of North America had $2 million in stock by the late 1780s. By 1791, the Massachusetts Bank's capital was $100,000; see Fisher Ames to Hamilton, 8/15/1791. See also Robert E. Wright, "Origins of Commercial Banking in the United States, 1781-1830," *EH.Net Encyclopedia*, ed. Robert Whaples, 3/26/2008.
https://founders.archives.gov/documents/Hamilton/01-09-02-0041 ∎
http://eh.net/encyclopedia/origins-of-commercial-banking-in-the-united-states-1781-1830/

wants the national bank to be much larger. He proposes selling $10 million worth of shares in the national bank, which will be known as the Bank of the United States (BUS). For comparison: the federal government's income in 1791 is just over $4 million.

Those who wish to purchase shares of the BUS will pay $400 per share in four installments over two years. Of the $400, 25% is to be paid with gold and silver, the rest with the newly issued 6% government bonds. This provision encourages Americans to think of the bonds as money. It also prevents a massive amount of gold and silver from sitting in a bank vault when some of it is still needed for trade, especially abroad.

He proposes that the BUS will open with one branch, but will eventually be allowed to open branches anywhere in the United States.

The federal government will buy a maximum of $2 million (one fifth) of the stock, and the secretary of the Treasury will have the right to inspect the books. Otherwise, the bank will operate under a private board of directors, making loans as it sees fit. Hamilton assumes that the self-interest of the directors will be the best guarantee that the bank is properly run:

> The keen, steady, and, as it were, magnetic sense, of their own interest, as proprietors, in the Directors of a Bank, pointing invariably to its true pole, the prosperity of the institution, is the only security, that can always be relied upon, for a careful and prudent administration. (Appendix 2, §IV.A.3)

The structure of the Bank of the United States seems to be Hamilton's attempt at a set of checks and balances. The bank is not subject to political manipulation or control, but it's also not free to be reckless.

Hamilton proposes that the BUS will exist until the public debt is extinguished, and then will cease to operate.

$2 million: According to the bank bill, the government will borrow this amount as part of the $14 million authorized by the Funding Acts of 8/4/1790 or 8/12/1790. The loan will be deposited in the Bank of the United States and then loaned to the government, which will repay it in ten annual payments.

Structure of the bank: In contrast, the Bank of Amsterdam (founded 1609) was wholly owned by the municipality of Amsterdam; the Riksbank (1668) was owned by the Swedish parliament; and the Bank of England (1694) was privately owned.

5.4 OPPOSITION TO THE BANK OF THE UNITED STATES

In 1790, 80% or more of us Americans are farmers … and a farmer's cash flow is unpredictable. One bad harvest and we're in debt to merchants or banks. Not surprisingly, farmers—including Thomas Jefferson, John Adams, many Congressmen, and most of their constituents—detest banks and other money-lenders.

Congress uses Hamilton's proposals to draft a bill chartering the Bank of the United States. Despite strong opposition, the Senate passes the bank bill on January 20, 1791. They do, however, choose to set an expiration date for the bank's charter. It will cease to exist in twenty years (in 1811), rather than when the debt has been extinguished.

The House of Representatives passes the bank bill in early February, despite an impassioned attack on it by James Madison. It is sent to President Washington for his signature. But Washington questions whether the Constitution gives Congress the authority to create

---

Detest banks: Jefferson to John Adams 1/24/1814: "I have ever been the enemy of banks; not of those discounting for cash; but of those foisting their own paper into circulation, and thus banishing our cash. my zeal against those institutions was so warm and open at the establishment of the bank of the US. that I was derided as a Maniac by the tribe of bank-mongers, who were seeking to filch from the public their swindling, and barren gains. but the errors of that day cannot be recalled. the evils they have engendered are now upon us, and the question is how we are to get out of them? shall we build an altar to the old paper money of the revolution, which ruined individuals but saved the republic, and burn on that all the bank charters present and future, and their notes with them? for these are to ruin both republic and individuals. this cannot be done. the Mania is too strong."

John Adams to François Adriaan Van der Kemp, 2/16/1809: "Every dollar of a bank bill that is issued beyond the quantity of gold & silver in the vaults represents nothing, and is therefore a cheat upon somebody."
https://founders.archives.gov/documents/Adams/99-02-02-6238 ■ https://founders.archives.gov/documents/Adams/99-02-02-5302

Expiration date: The BUS went out of existence in 1811, even though the debt hadn't yet been paid off.

Impassioned attack: Madison spoke against the BUS in the House, 2/8/1791. At Washington's request, Madison also drafted a veto for the bank bill, dated 2/21/1791.
https://founders.archives.gov/documents/Madison/01-13-02-0284 ■ https://founders.archives.gov/documents/Madison/01-13-02-0295

a bank. He asks Edmund Randolph, the attorney general, for his opinion. Randolph says the only objection to the bank bill is that it creates a corporation, and the Constitution doesn't give Congress the right to do that.

Washington also asks Jefferson, secretary of State and a lawyer as well as a farmer, for his opinion. Jefferson lists nine ways in which the bank bill violates existing laws. Washington then asks Hamilton to answer Randolph's and Jefferson's objections.

Hamilton responds on February 23, 1791, with *Opinion on the Constitutionality of a National Bank.* The *Opinion* is another educational piece, aiming to explain financial and constitutional principles to Washington, Jefferson, and everyone else. Even though it is not one of Hamilton's major policy papers, the *Opinion* quickly becomes crucial for constitutional interpretation in future court cases.

When explaining in the *Opinion* why Congress can create a corporation, Hamilton makes a point of defining his terms. A bank is "a

---

Randolph: Randolph to Washington 2/12/1791: "It must be acknowledged, that, if any part of the bill does either encounter the Constitution, or is not warranted by it, the clause of incorporation is the only one. ... However, let it be propounded as an eternal question to those, who build new powers on this clause ["necessary and proper"], whether the latitude of construction which they arrogate, will not terminate in an unlimitted power in Congress?"
https://founders.archives.gov/documents/Washington/05-07-02-0200-0002

Jefferson: Jefferson to Washington, 2/15/1791: "It has been much urged that a bank will give great facility, or convenience in the collection of taxes. suppose this were true: yt the constitution allows only the means which are 'necessary' not those which are merely 'convenient' for effecting the enumerated powers. if such a latitude of construction be allowed to this phrase as to gain any non-enumerated power, it will go to every one, for there is no one which ingenuity may not torture into a convenience, in some way or other, to some one of so long a list of enumerated powers. it would swallow up all the delegated powers, and reduce the whole to one phrase as before observed. therefore it was that the constitution restrained them to the necessary means, that is to say, to those means without which the grant of the power would be nugatory."
https://founders.archives.gov/documents/Washington/05-07-02-0207

Opinion: dated 2/23/1791. For an excellent walk-through of Jefferson's comments on the bank and Hamilton's *Opinion*, see Carson Holloway, *Hamilton versus Jefferson in the Washington Administration*, Chapter 5.
https://founders.archives.gov/documents/Hamilton/01-08-02-0060-0003

deposit of coin or other property, as a fund for circulating a credit upon it, which is to answer the purpose of money." A corporation is "a legal person, or person created by act of law, consisting of one or more natural persons authorized to hold property or a franchise in succession in a legal as contradistinguished from a natural capacity."

He argues that the creation of this particular corporation, the Bank of the United States, is a means to an end: collecting taxes and borrowing money in an emergency such as the common defense. The federal government can create a corporation if the corporation is "necessary and proper" to its legitimate role. Creation of a corporation is an implied rather than an express power. Also, Hamilton argues that "necessary and proper" doesn't mean "absolutely necessary." An action is legitimate if it's for the general welfare—for the good of the nation rather than a particular state or locale.

5.5 ESTABLISHMENT OF THE BANK OF THE UNITED STATES AND ITS EFFECTS

Persuaded by Hamilton's arguments, Washington signs the bank bill into law two days later, on February 25, 1791. On July 4, eight million

---

Good of the nation: Hamilton consistently feared that if given too much power, the states would split apart and descend into anarchy. See, for example, his letter to Edward Carrington (supervisor of the revenue for the District of Virginia and a long-time friend), 5/26/1792: "As to State Governments ... I acknowledge that most serious apprehensions that the Government of the U States will not be able to maintain itself against their influence ... Hence a disposition on my part towards a liberal construction of the powers of the National Government and to erect every fence to guard it from depredations, which is, in my opinion, consistent with constitutional propriety."

https://founders.archives.gov/documents/Hamilton/01-11-02-0349

Bank bill: First Congress, Third Session, "An Act to incorporate the subscribers to the Bank of the United States," 2/25/1791, and "An Act supplementary to the act intituled "An act to incorporate the subscribers to the Bank of the United States," 3/8/1791

https://en.wikisource.org/wiki/United_States_Statutes_at_Large/Volume_1/1st_Congress/3rd_Session/Chapter_10 ■ https://en.wikisource.org/wiki/United_States_Statutes_at_Large/Volume_1/1st_Congress/3rd_Session/Chapter_11 dollars' worth of bank stock goes on sale at $400 per share. Within a few hours, the stock sells out. Anyone who has money to spare sees the BUS as a safe and profitable place to put it. Fisher Ames, a congressman from Massachusetts, tells Hamilton:

> The eagerness to subscribe [to the bank] is a proof of the wealth and resources of the country and of the perfect confidence reposed by our opulent men in the Govt. People here are full of exultation and gratitude. They know who merits the praise of it, and they are not loth to bestow it. But with all this good temper, many lament that the Philadelphians have engrossed so much of the stock, & have so divided the shares as to multiply their votes.

The BUS opens its doors in Philadelphia in December 1791. Over the following two decades, it consistently pays 8 to 10% dividends. Such

---

Stock goes on sale: For details on how Congress arranged the sale, see McDonald, *Hamilton*, p. 222. The stock was not issued immediately; for $25, purchasers received a "scrip", which gave them the right to purchase stock. The scrips were in great demand over the next months, selling for as high as $300. See Bob Schoone-Jongen, "William Duer: America's First Wall Street Villain," *Historical Horizons* (Calvin University Historical Studies Department Blog), 5/15/2015.
https://historicalhorizons.org/2015/05/15/william-duer-americas-first-wall-street-villain/

The eagerness: Fisher Ames (member of the House of Representatives from Massachusetts) to Hamilton, 7/31/1791.
https://founders.archives.gov/documents/Hamilton/01-08-02-0533

December 1791: The government does not purchase its $2 million worth of shares until 1792. It uses funds from the $14 million in loans Congress had authorized in the Funding Act of 8/4/1790. Washington at the same time (5/9/1792) authorizes Hamilton to arrange a loan of $2 million from the BUS, reimbursable in ten years by ten equal annual installments, providing the interest is not higher than 6%. The government does not meet its payment schedule for this loan, as Hamilton explains to the House of Representatives, "Report on the Contract Made with the Bank of the United States for a Loan of Two Million Dollars," 4/25/1794.
https://founders.archives.gov/documents/Hamilton/01-11-02-0308 ∎
https://founders.archives.gov/documents/Hamilton/01-16-02-0268

8 to 10% dividends: Wright, *First Wall Street,* p. 69.

is the demand for banks that in 1792, the directors of the Bank of the United States open branches in Charleston, Baltimore, New York, and Boston. By 1800, twenty-eight banks other than the BUS are operating in the United States. Banknotes backed by gold and silver become the nation's principal medium of exchange. Sellers and purchasers no longer need to assay foreign coins or guess the worth of state-issued banknotes or ten-year-old government IOUs. And the government made a profit that it could use to repay debts or cover its operating expenses.

Demand for banks: Many still opposed banks. Jefferson, writing to Madison on 10/1/1792, condemns Governor Henry Lee for suggesting that Virginia counter the Bank of the United States by establishing a state-chartered bank. He calls that a "milk & water measure" because any bank is "a source of poison & corruption." He proposes instead that if the Bank of the United States becomes active in Virginia, anyone who abets it "by signing notes, issuing or passing them, acting as director, cashier or in any other office relating to it shall be adjudged guilty of high treason & suffer death accordingly."

https://founders.archives.gov/documents/Madison/01-14-02-0339

Branches: The BUS also opened branches in Norfolk (1800), Washington, DC (1801), Savannah (1802) and New Orleans (1805).

Government made a profit: In his *Report on a National Bank,* Hamilton pointed out that if the BUS paid more in dividends than the government had to pay in interest on the money borrowed from the BUS to purchase the stock, then revenue would be generated for the government. (Appendix 2, §IV. B. 11 and §IV. C. 5.) Hamilton intended any such revenue to be used to pay off the debt. While it owned $2 million worth of BUS stock, the government received dividends of $1,141,720. But in 1796, Congress voted to sell some bank shares in order to repay short-term loans, and it continued to sell shares to cover immediate expenses, disposing of the last of them by 1802. On the sale of stock, the government made a profit of $671,860. Combining dividends and profit from the sale, the return on the investment in bank stock was 57.5%. See Carl Lane, "For 'A Positive Profit': The Federal Investment in the First Bank of the United States, 1792-1802", *The William and Mary Quarterly,* Vol. 54, No. 3 (Jul., 1997), pp. 601-612.

https://www.jstor.org/stable/2953841

5.6 SIDE NOTE: IS THE BANK OF THE UNITED STATES A CENTRAL BANK?

I have been gnawing away for quite some time at the question of whether the First BUS is a central bank, and frankly, I don't feel qualified to decide. Mostly that's because there's no definition of "central bank" that is accurate for 1791 (when the BUS was created) as well as 2021. Herewith, some points to ponder regarding the powers of a modern central bank, and the BUS's status with respect to them.

- A modern central bank has major government-granted advantages. The Bank of the United States is chartered by the federal government, with the promise that Congress will charter no other bank through 1811—i.e., that no other bank will be allowed to open branches throughout the United States. The BUS therefore has a monopoly at the nationwide level. Hence it can diversify its loans and transfer money without charge among its branches—both great advantages.

- A modern central bank is a government's primary fiscal agent, i.e., handles the government's deposits and loans. This is not always true of the BUS, especially in the early years, when it has few branches. Also, the BUS refuses to accept out-of-town banknotes. When the federal government is paid in such notes, it has to deposit them in a state-chartered bank, even if there is a BUS branch in the same city.

- A modern central bank has a monopoly on issuing banknotes. The BUS doesn't have a monopoly on issuing banknotes. State-chartered banks continue to issue their own notes.

- A modern central bank prints fiat money, i.e., paper that's not backed by gold. The BUS can only lend money against gold and

---

Central bank: I've used the features of central banks as discussed in Raymond Niles, "The Dubious Origins and Purpose of Central Banking," *In Pursuit of Wealth: The Moral Case for Finance*, ed. Brook and Watkins (2017). Many thanks to Dr. Niles for sharing his thoughts on central banking in private correspondence with me. Any errors of interpretation are mine. For more discussion of the BUS as a central bank, see Wright, *Hamilton Unbound*, pp. 99-100 and n. 24; Wright and Cowen, *Financial Founding Fathers*, p. 30; and especially Cowen, *Origins and Economic Impact of the First BUS*, (2000), Chapter IV.

Can only lend money: If I'm reading the Bank Bill correctly, the BUS can only lend twice as much as it has in specie in its vault, and the directors can be prosecuted if they lend more. See section IX of the bill, at

https://en.wikisource.org/wiki/United_States_Statutes_at_Large/Volume_1/1st_Congress/3rd_Session/Chapter_10 silver in its own vaults, by issuing banknotes. Through 1811, when its charter expires, each and every BUS banknote can be redeemed on demand for gold or silver. (But so can notes of the Bank of England, which is certainly a central bank, through the nineteenth century.)

- A modern central bank issues banknotes that are legal tender, i.e., that are mandated as the only acceptable means of payment. The U.S. Constitution, ratified in 1788, explicitly forbids individual states from denoting anything *except* gold and silver as legal tender, because of the shenanigans of some states during the debt-ridden 1780s. The banknotes issued by the BUS beginning in 1791 are *never* designated as the only acceptable form of payment for taxes, or as notes that all individuals and businesses must accept.
- A modern central bank buys bonds to fund the government. The act of 2/25/1791 creating the BUS states that the BUS can sell any bonds that it has as part of its stock, but "shall not be at liberty to purchase *any public debt whatsoever*" (emphasis added).
- A modern central bank regulates interest rates and the money supply. The BUS doesn't regulate the interest rates; each bank sets its own. It doesn't regulate the money supply: state-chartered banks can issue as many banknotes as they think prudent, given the gold and silver in their vaults. But the BUS does have one option to restrain a state-chartered bank that seems to be lending exorbitant amounts. When people pay taxes in notes from that particular bank, the BUS can choose to redeem them from the issuing bank in gold and silver. The prospect of having the BUS collect huge amounts of their gold and silver discourages other banks from issuing too many notes.

The BUS is certainly not a central bank in the sense that the Federal Reserve is today. I'm reluctant to even call it a quasi-central bank, because that seems like viewing it with hindsight—as if Hamilton had the Fed in mind. I'm inclined to call it "semi-public" or "semi-private".

Government institutions being what they are, if the BUS had continued in existence, it would probably have accumulated the powers of a central bank. As it is, the BUS went out of existence in 1811. The Second BUS went out of business in 1837. The Fed wasn't created until 1913. There's a disconnect here: Hamilton's BUS was not, in its structure or function, a predecessor of the Fed. However, its creation did set a legal and constitutional precedent for chartering a bank with government involvement.

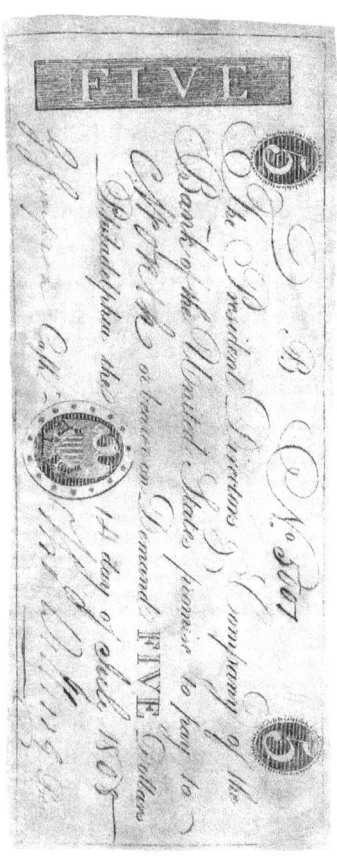
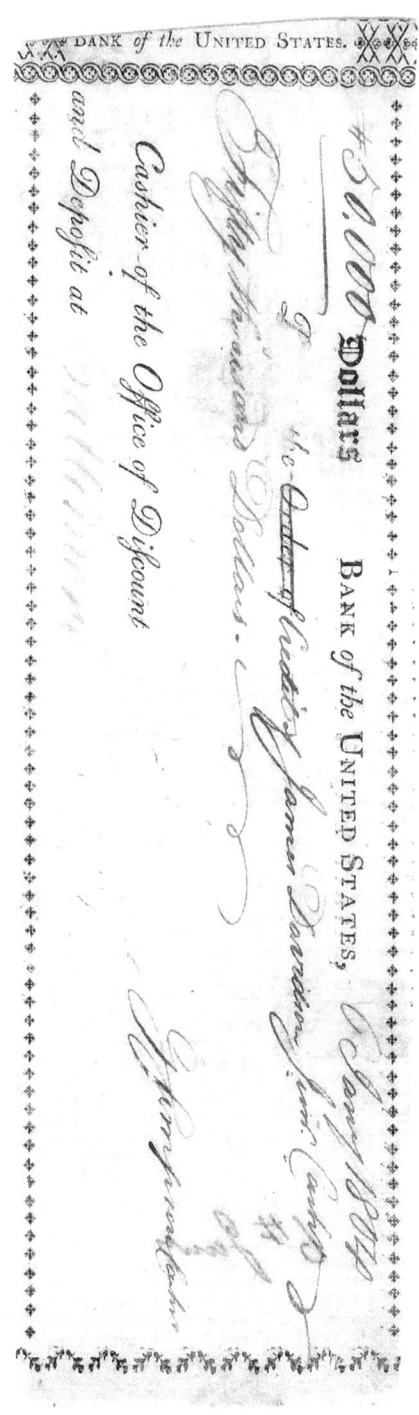

Notes from the Bank of the United States, 1804 and 1808. Collection of John E. Herzog.

CHAPTER 6

Policy Paper #3:
Report on Manufactures

The *Report on the Subject of Manufactures*, completed and submitted to Congress 12/5/1791, is usually called the *Report on Manufactures*. It deals with the first and second threads of our Gordian Knot: making a living and the centrifugal tendency of the United States. At 32,000 words, it's twice the length of the *First Report on Public Credit*.

Scholars of the *Report* have discerned frequent paraphrases of or references to writers on economic theory, including Jacques Necker, France's finance minister, and Adam Smith, author of *The Wealth of Nations*. As usual, Hamilton has synthsized his sources into a wholly original system. We'll circle back to Necker and Smith at the end of the chapter, when we consider what economic school Hamilton belongs to.

6.1 INTRODUCTORY NOTES

Recapping from §2.1.1: the British colonies in North America sent raw materials to the mother country; Great Britain sent manufactured products back. The arrangement made sense, since America had vast

---

Report on Manufactures: The full text appears in Appendix 3, with outline headings added. See also the Founders Online "Introductory Note: Report on Manufactures." For an excellent walk-through of the *Report on Manufactures*, see Holloway, *Hamilton versus Jefferson in the Washington Administration*, Chapter 7.

https://founders.archives.gov/documents/Hamilton/01-10-02-0001-0007

■ https://founders.archives.gov/documents/Hamilton/01-10-02-0001-0001

land and resources but relatively few people, while Britain had a much higher population density and had capital for large industrial enterprises such as textile mills. British policy restricted the movement of raw materials and finished goods. It also prohibited any large-scale manufacturing enterprises in the North American colonies. The colonies had abundant supplies of coal and iron, for example, but according to the Iron Act of 1750, were forbidden to process iron beyond pig iron or bar iron, and were forbidden entirely from making steel. Not surprisingly, by 1776, very little manufacturing was done in the colonies. Eighty percent or more of Americans lived and worked on farms.

Hamilton had seen the potential for American manufacturing as early as 1774, when he explained why the trade embargo with Britain would not necessarily cripple America:

> Those hands, which may be deprived of business by the cessation of commerce, may be occupied in various kinds of manufactures and other internal improvements. If by the necessity of the thing, manufactures should once be established and take root among us, they will pave the way, still more, to the future grandeur and glory of America, and by lessening its need of external commerce, will render it still securer against the encroachments of tyranny.

A few other Americans had also seen the benefits of manufacturing as well as agriculture. But many American farmers still considered manufacturing enterprises to be just as useless or evil as banks. Thomas Jefferson wrote in 1784:

Those hands: "Full Vindication," 12/15/1774.
https://founders.archives.gov/documents/Hamilton/01-01-02-0054

Benefits of manufacturing: For example: Richard Peters (a Pennsylvania farmer) to Hamilton, 8/27/1791: "I find Farming but a bad Trade when Capital is calculated upon. There are few Men of any Talents who cannot employ themselves in any other Business to greater advantage." Also Nathaniel Gorham (supervisor of the revenue for Massachusetts) to Hamilton, 10/13/1791: "It is now worth the observation of the curious traveler through N England to observe (more especially out of the great Roads) the cloathing of the Country Family, & he will find their common cloath almost wholly made by themselves. Let him at night veiw the Bed & beding & he will find it the same from the Bed Tyck to the Pillow case. This has given a most powerful check to the importations, & with other concuring causes has rendered the People of this Country at the present moment the happiest on the face of the Earth & so far as I can recollect historey, does not furnish any instance of a People equally happy. In

➢

HAMILTON'S FINANCIAL PROGRAMS 135

> <u>Those who labour</u> in the earth are the chosen people of God. It is the focus in which he keeps alive that sacred fire, which otherwise might escape from the face of the earth. Corruption of morals in the mass of cultivators is a phaenomenon of which no age nor nation has furnished an example. It is the mark set on those, who not looking up to heaven, to their own soil and industry, as does the husbandman, for their subsistance, depend for it on the casualties and caprice of customers.

Even Robert Morris, an eminent financier and wealthy merchant, assumed the United States would prosper with a combination of <u>agriculture and trade</u>. Given the plentiful land in America, it wasn't an unreasonable assumption.

In January 1790, President Washington tells Congress that the United States should, at the very least, produce the <u>military supplies</u> that it needs: rifles, gunpowder, cannons, and so on. Otherwise, if America goes to war, it will have to hope one of the European powers will be willing to supply such goods. Soon after Washington's speech, Congress asks Hamilton to submit a report on the state of manufacturing in the United States.

To gather data, Hamilton corresponds with dozens of merchants, businessmen, and manufacturers across the nation, and with customs collectors up and down the East Coast. He also has the experience

---

short I believe it is not in the case of Human nature to be exceeded & the People seem sensible of it—all uneasiness and murmuring being at an end & good humour & chearfullness universally privaling."
https://founders.archives.gov/documents/Hamilton/01-09-02-0098-0001
■ https://founders.archives.gov/documents/Hamilton/01-09-02-0272-0001

<u>Those who labour</u>: *Notes on the State of Virginia*, 1784.
https://avalon.law.yale.edu/18th_century/jeffvir.asp

Three decades later, after wars, embargoes, and two terms as president, Jefferson changed his mind. Letter to Benjamin Austin, 1/9/1816: "to be independant for the comforts of life we must fabricate them ourselves. we must now place the manufacturer by the side of the agriculturist."
https://founders.archives.gov/documents/Jefferson/03-09-02-0213

<u>Agriculture and trade</u>: *Robert Morris Papers,* vol. 6 (July 22-Oct. 31, 1782), p. 42 (introductory note).
https://digital.library.pitt.edu/islandora/object/pitt:31735060482019

<u>Military supplies</u>: Washington to Congress, 1/8/1790: "A free people ought not only to be armed but disciplined; to which end a uniform and well digested plan is requisite: And their safety and interest require, that they should promote such manufactories, as tend to render them independent on others for essential, particularly for military supplies."
https://founders.archives.gov/documents/Washington/05-04-02-0361

of working with the Society for Establishing Useful Manufactures, which he helps found in the summer of 1791 in Patterson, New Jersey. Hamilton delivers the report to Congress on December 5, 1791, a year after he submitted the *Report on a National Bank*.

Like Hamilton's first two major policy papers, the *Report on Manufactures* is an educational tour-de-force as well as a proposal for action. In it, he tackles three questions. Why is manufacturing worth doing in America? What are the possible means to encourage it? And what should the government actually do?

6.2 CONTENT OF THE REPORT ON MANUFACTURES

NOTE: If you're interested enough in Hamilton's financial programs to read this book, you should certainly read this report. The full text of it is in Appendix 3, with outline headings added. The headings are used as section references below. In this chapter, I won't attempt to discuss every point of the *Report on Manufactures*. I'm just giving an overview of sections that relate to the Gordian Knot.

6.2.1 Arguments against manufacturing [OUTLINE §II.A.1, II.B.1, II.C.1, II.D.1, II.E.1, and II.F.1]

Hamilton addresses six arguments that government promotion of manufacturing won't work in the United States. One of the arguments he has to address is that private citizens should make all such decisions. This is Hamilton paraphrasing his opponents:

> To endeavor by the extraordinary patronage of Government, to accelerate the growth of manufactures, is in fact, to endeavor, by force and art, to transfer the natural current of industry, from a more, to a less beneficial channel. Whatever has such a tendency must necessarily be unwise. Indeed it can hardly ever be wise in a government, to attempt to give a direction to the industry of its citizens. This under the quick-sighted guidance of private interest, will, if left to itself, infallibly find its own way to the most profitable employment: and 'tis by such employment, that the public prosperity will be most effectually promoted.

Opponents of manufacturing also argue that there's not enough capital

---

Society for Establishing Useful Manufactures: its Prospectus, August 1791, is generally attributed to Hamilton.

https://founders.archives.gov/documents/Hamilton/01-09-02-0114

To endeavor: Appendix 3, §II.A.1.

HAMILTON'S FINANCIAL PROGRAMS

to build factories, and that farming is a more productive use of Americans' time and effort.

Hamilton responds that agriculture and manufacturing are <u>both good</u> and are both necessary. He goes even further: he proposes securing the economic as well as the political <u>independence</u> of the United States. He reminds Americans of our dire situation during the Revolutionary War:

> <u>The extreme</u> embarrassments of the United States during the late War, from an incapacity of supplying themselves, are still matter of keen recollection: A future war might be expected again to exemplify the mischiefs and dangers of a situation, to which that incapacity is still in too great a degree applicable, unless changed by timely and vigorous exertion. To effect this change as fast as shall be prudent, merits all the attention and all the Zeal of our Public Councils; 'tis the next great work to be accomplished.

6.2.2 Benefits of manufacturing over agriculture [OUTLINE §II.A.2, II.B.2, II.C.2, II.D.2, II.E.2, and II.F.2]

Hamilton also lists the benefits that manufacturing can offer, which agriculture alone cannot. These are all closely related to the first thread of our Gordian Knot, making a living. Specifically, Hamilton stresses the advantages of diversifying the economy, not just for the sake of the government, but for the sake of individual American citizens.

- Manufacturing allows division of labor and the use of labor-saving machinery. By performing one job, workers can achieve "greater skill and dexterity," which makes them more productive.
- Manufacturing gives people <u>more options</u> for making a living. Not everyone is physically or temperamentally suited to be a farmer.

<u>Both good</u>: Appendix 3, §II.A.2.b.

<u>Independence</u>: Appendix 3, §III.B.

<u>The extreme</u>: Appendix 3, §III.B.

<u>More options</u>: "It is a just observation, that minds of the strongest and most active powers for their proper objects fall below mediocrity and labour without effect, if confined to uncongenial pursuits. And it is thence to be inferred, that the results of human exertion may be immensely increased by diversifying its objects. When all the different kinds of industry obtain in a community, each individual can find his proper element, and can call into activity the whole vigour of his nature. And the community is benefitted by the services of its respective members, in the manner, in which each can serve it with most effect." Appendix 3, § II.A.2.c.v.

- Manufacturing affords more scope for inventions and enterprise. People can create new labor-saving devices or even whole new businesses.
- Manufacturing helps farmers by creating an increased demand for agricultural products, since those who no longer work on farms still have to eat.

6.2.3 Manufacturing as a way to counter European restrictions on trade [OUTLINE §III.A, III.C]

Hamilton points out that although the United States can easily obtain manufactured goods from abroad, it's very difficult to sell American agricultural products there. If we can manufacture goods here, we

---

Inventions and enterprise: "To cherish and stimulate the activity of the human mind, by multiplying the objects of enterprise, is not among the least considerable of the expedients, by which the wealth of a nation may be promoted. Even things in themselves not positively advantageous, sometimes become so, by their tendency to provoke exertion. Every new scene, which is opened to the busy nature of man to rouse and exert itself, is the addition of a new energy to the general stock of effort. The spirit of enterprise, useful and prolific as it is, must necessarily be contracted or expanded in proportion to the simplicity or variety of the occupations and productions, which are to be found in a Society. It must be less in a nation of mere cultivators, than in a nation of cultivators and merchants; less in a nation of cultivators and merchants, than in a nation of cultivators, artificers and merchants." Appendix 3, § II.A.2.c. vi.

Difficult to sell: Hamilton is not in favor of one-sided laissez-faire trade ... at least in his country's situation.

"If the system of perfect liberty to industry and commerce were the prevailing system of nations—the arguments which dissuade a country in the predicament of the United States, from the zealous pursuits of manufactures would doubtless have great force. ... But the system which has been mentioned, is far from characterising the general policy of Nations. ... The consequence of it is, that the United States are to a certain extent in the situation of a country precluded from foreign Commerce. They can indeed, without difficulty obtain from abroad the manufactured supplies, of which they are in want; but they experience numerous and very injurious impediments to the emission and vent of their own commodities. Nor is this the case in reference to a single foreign nation only. The regulations of several countries, with which we have the most extensive intercourse, throw serious obstructions in the way of the principal staples of the United States. ... Tis for the nations, whose regulations are alluded to, to judge

➤

don't have to purchase them from foreigners, often with hard currency. Our gold and silver can stay in American banks and be the basis for American loans.

6.2.4 Manufacturing in the North vs. the South [OUTLINE §III.C.3]

Hamilton devotes a short section to explaining that North and South do not have contrary interests with respect to manufacturing. Manufacturing can help the United States remain united (the second thread of our Gordian Knot), and anything that makes the United States more stable benefits everyone.

6.2.5 Why the development of manufacturing might be delayed in the United States [OUTLINE § II.C.2.]

Hamilton doesn't disagree that it would ideally be best for the government to allow agriculture and manufacturing to find their own way. But he fears the development of manufacturing in the United States may be delayed for various reasons.

Some people, for example, are afraid of change. Some are daunted by the idea of establishing a manufacturing enterprise. Foreign restrictions make matters even more difficult. In Great Britain, where textile manufacturing is a major source of income, the government forbids the export of any textile machinery and prohibits the emigration of skilled workers from textile factories.

6.2.6 Measures foreign governments have used to stimulate manufacturing [OUTLINE §IV]

Hamilton next surveys eleven means by which foreign countries have promoted manufacturing. Among them are: protective duties (imposed to make foreign goods more expensive than the same items manufactured domestically); prohibiting the export of raw materials; paying bounties for goods that the government wants to promote; offering premiums to reward goods of high quality; encouraging inventions for themselves, whether, by aiming at too much they do not lose more than they gain. 'Tis for the United States to consider by what means they can render themselves least dependent, on the combinations, right or wrong of foreign policy." Appendix 3, § II.B.2.a.

via pecuniary rewards and exclusive privileges; and facilitating transportation.

6.2.7 What measures the United States government should take [OUTLINE §V and VI]

Hamilton urges the government to refrain from certain types of taxes that have deleterious effects on manufacturing. Among them are poll taxes (taxes per capita), taxes on occupations, taxes on business, and taxes imposed in arbitrary amounts at the discretion of the tax collector.

He then offers a short list of sixteen goods whose production he thinks should be <u>encouraged</u>: iron, copper, lead, fossil coal, wood, skins, grain, flax and hemp, cotton, wool, silk, glass, gun powder, paper, printed books, and sugar / chocolate. For each of these, he explains why the United States needs it, what production is already under way, and what means the government might use to encourage more production. For all sixteen categories, he discusses whether current duties should be raised, lowered (usually on the importation of raw materials), or left as they are. In four cases (coal, flax and hemp, cotton, wool), he recommends bounties on a specific product. For two more (wool and silk), he suggests premiums.

Coal, for example, would be very useful in the production of iron and for heating homes. Coal is already mined in Virginia. Bounties could be offered for those who dig it up for use in their homes, and premiums for the opening of new mines.

Another example: wool is in demand in the United States because so much of the country is subject to cold winters. Some households weave wool cloth for their own use, but only the hat-making industry uses wool on a larger scale. The government could promote the raising and improving of sheep, and offer premiums and bounties for production. An additional 2.5% duty on imported carpets and carpeting might encourage production of such items in America.

<u>Encouraged</u>: By Irwin's count, Hamilton recommended tariff increases of 5 to 10% on about twenty products; he recommended tariff reductions on five raw materials; and he recommended bounties to five industries. Douglas A. Irwin, "The Aftermath of Hamilton's 'Report on Manufactures,'" National Bureau of Economic Research, 2003, p. 804.

6.2.8 Conclusion: Why the United States government needs to help manufacturers [OUTLINE §IX]

At the very end of the Report, Hamilton reminds Congress why government support of manufactures is advisable:

> <u>In countries</u> where there is great private wealth much may be effected by the voluntary contributions of patriotic individuals, but in a community situated like that of the United States, the public purse must supply the deficiency of private resource. In what can it be so useful as in prompting and improving the efforts of industry?

6.3 EFFECTS AND INTENT OF THE REPORT ON MANUFACTURES

The *Report on Manufactures* is delivered to the House of Representatives, with a cover letter, on December 5, 1791. The House duly notes that it was written at their request, has the letter read, and then <u>tables the *Report*</u>, returning immediately to their protracted debate over the Post Office and reapportionment of congressional seats. The annals of the House through January 1792 give no indication that the *Report on Manufactures* was ever mentioned again, much less that its recommendations were put into a bill and debated.

Hamilton, too, allows the *Report* to fall into oblivion. In a letter of December 5, he apologizes to John Jay for taking so long to reply to a letter, due to "A <u>temporary absence</u> from this place, some ill health, and much occupation." Otherwise, Hamilton's correspondence through the end of January 1792 makes no mention of the *Report*.

Douglas <u>Irwin points out</u> that most of the duties Hamilton suggested as a way to promote manufacturing were in fact implemented by Congress later in 1792 to raise money for defense of the Western

---

In countries: Appendix 3, §IX.

Tables the Report: the House Annals mentions a cover letter, which might have answered some of the questions that follow. But Founders Online doesn't list the letter.

https://memory.loc.gov/cgi-bin/ampage?collId=llac&fileName=003/llac003.db&recNum=111

Temporary absence: Hamilton to John Jay, 12/5/1791.

https://founders.archives.gov/documents/Hamilton/01-09-02-0421

Irwin points out: Douglas A. Irwin, "The Aftermath of Hamilton's 'Report on Manufactures'," National Bureau of Economic Research, 2003.

https://www.nber.org/papers/w9943

frontier. That is, they were implemented to raise revenue rather than to promote American manufactures. The tariffs Hamilton recommended were so low that in the late 1790s, manufacturers who wanted higher, protective tariffs deserted the Federalists to become Democratic-Republicans.

Enquiring minds want to know: just what was Hamilton hoping to accomplish with the *Report on Manufactures*? He wrote substantial essays in favor of the *First Report* and the Bank of the United States, but nothing in favor of the *Report on Manufactures*. We know he worked on this report for a year, writing dozens of letters for information and producing four surviving drafts. Clearly this topic was important to him, yet he didn't push for action on it. Why?

The short answer is: we don't know. But let's speculate a bit.

1. Perhaps Congress wouldn't budge on this issue. The Federalists were still in the majority in 1792 (by 39 seats to 30), but most Congressmen, like most Americans, were farmers. So perhaps there was enough negative feeling to table the *Report*. But that doesn't explain why Hamilton didn't put more effort into promoting it.

2. Perhaps Hamilton simply wanted to make Congress aware of pro-manufacturing ideas. Wright thinks Hamilton intended the report as an educational tool, rather than as proposals for Congress to implement. He notes that in the *Report on Manufactures,* Hamilton

> did not proffer specific legislation. It was, as David Cowen and Richard Sylla show, more of a primer for clueless Congressmen

---

Tariffs Hamilton recommended: According to Hugo Rabbeno, *The American Commercial Policy, Three Historical Essays* (London, 1895), p. 139 (cited in Parenti, *Radical Hamilton*, p. 197), the average import duty *ad valorem* [i.e., on the price of an item] in 1789 was about 8%; in 1792, it was about 13%. See also John R. Nelson, Jr., *Liberty and Property: Political Economy and Policymaking in the New Nation, 1789-1812*, Chapter 3, especially p. 53: "Genuine support for manufacturing involved more than stirring affirmations of government 'incitement and patronage.' It required the enactment of policies that advanced the development of manufactures. Whatever his rhetorical flourishes, Hamilton was throughout the 1790s an opponent of commercial discrimination and protective tariffs, and an advocate of an unrestricted flow of imports."

39 seats to 30: pro-administration and anti-administration, according to the House's online history.
https://history.house.gov/Institution/Party-Divisions/Party-Divisions/

Did not proffer: Robert E. Wright, "Who Is the Real Alexander Hamilton?"
https://wallstreetwindow.com/2020/01/who-is-the-real-alexander-hamilton-robert-e-wright-01-15-2020/

than a call to action. As John Nelson demonstrated long ago in *Liberty and Property*, protective tariffs or bounties would have blown Hamilton's budget, the former by reducing the federal government's major source of income and the latter by spending it on projects other than Hamilton's prime objectives, servicing the national debt and building an effective system of national defense.

However, I can't think of any other time when Hamilton delivered a lengthy treatise to Congress purely for educational purposes. If he presented a report, it was because he thought Congress needed to take action.

3. Perhaps the year 1792 brought other priorities to the fore. War with the Indians was becoming heated (§7.1): General Arthur St. Clair suffered a devastating defeat at the hands of the Miami and Shawnee in November 1791, just before the *Report on Manufactures* was delivered to Congress. The government urgently needed revenue for the military, so spending money on bounties would not have been a priority. By January, events leading up to the Panic of 1792 (§7.2) required Hamilton's attention; a catastrophic drop in bond prices would threaten the funding system. In 1793, war broke out between France and England. As the French and British began attacking American shipping, Americans were forced to rely more on their own manufactures, without government encouragement. Such shifting priorities seem the most persuasive explanation of why the *Report on Manufactures* languished.

6.4 HAMILTON'S ECONOMIC OUTLOOK

The policies proposed in Hamilton's three major policy reports offer a springboard for the question: whose economic theories did Hamilton support? Mercantilists, Physiocrats, Adam Smith? (See §3.3.2.) Short answer: again, we don't know.

The obvious way to find out would be to see what authors Hamilton quotes with approval in his own writings. But, as I pointed out when discussing the "Full Vindication" of 1774 (§3.2), he is writing to inform and persuade, not for an academic publication. He doesn't interrupt the flow of his argument with footnotes.

It's also quite possible that he deliberately chooses to omit authors' names because he's well aware of long-standing biases among his fellow Americans. In some quarters, a citation of Adam Smith (or any British author) would get you reviled as a traitor or a monarchist. In others, a mention of Jacques Necker, Louis XVI's sometime finance minister, would be equally offensive. Hamilton wants his proposals judged on their merits, not the nationalities of their original proponents. So let's look at what Hamilton says, rather than the names he drops.

6.4.1 Hamilton and mercantilism

One would expect Hamilton to be a thorough-going mercantilist, given that he was America's equivalent of a finance minister. People don't generally volunteer for that position unless they think the government should be playing a role in the economy. Interestingly, the mercantilist thread is much stronger in his early works than his later ones: see his letter to Duane of 1780, and "Continentalist" No. 4 of 1781 (§3.3.2 and 3.3.4). By the time he writes the *Federalist Papers,* Hamilton states that the national government has a role in regulating foreign and domestic commerce, but he no longer gives a laundry list of its duties:

> The principal purposes to be answered by Union are these—The common defence of the members—the preservation of the public peace as well against internal convulsions as external attacks—the regulation of commerce with other nations and between the States—the superintendence of our intercourse, political and commercial, with foreign countries.

Given Hamilton's context, this probably indicates a desire to rein in the multitude of existing state trade regulations (see §3.7), rather than to impose a massive new economic bureaucracy ... but it may also be a mercantilist thread in Hamilton's thinking.

Hamilton sometimes paraphrases and agrees with Jacques Necker, France's finance minister from 1777-1781 and 1788-1790. Both men think a nation attempting to institute free trade will fail, unless other nations reciprocate. (See §6.2.3, the "difficult to sell" footnote.) That argument is, in fact, incorrect, but no one wrote a rebuttal of it until 1817, when David Ricardo published the theory of comparative advantage. Hamilton also agrees with Necker, in opposition to the Physiocrats, that a nation with a diversified economy will have more opportunities to trade, and will have a more favorable balance of trade, than a nation that is purely agricultural.

More specifically, Swanson and Trout point out that Hamilton followed Necker's lead regarding funding only the interest on the debt;

The principal purposes: *Federalist No. 23,* 12/18/1787.
https://founders.archives.gov/documents/Hamilton/01-04-02-0180

Agrees with Jacques Necker: "Introductory Note: Report on Manufactures," citing Necker, *Oeuvres,* III, 260-261 and IV, 32, 34, 89.

Swanson and Trout: following page

converting the debt to a lower interest rate; creating a sinking fund; and assuming that if prices of bonds were stable (offering only moderate returns), then speculators would not be interested in them.

Perhaps most importantly, Necker's memoirs of 1784 gave Hamilton not a specific program, but an image of the benefits a finance minister could achieve. Brookhiser notes that Necker

> paints the job in very glowing terms. He says that finance ministers are the ones who make the happiness of the state and they're really second in importance only to the king. ... Necker's is a personal inspiration rather than a guide to policy or ideology.

That makes sense to me. If Hamilton strongly believes the government must interfere in the economy, then why does he resign his post in 1795, after only five years? (See §7.7.) Nor does his resignation make sense if his ego depends on issuing a continual stream of government rules and regulations. But the resignation does make sense if his aim is primarily to establish a stable financial system that even his enemies would prefer to use rather than destroy. He does what he sets out to do, and then he moves on.

6.4.2 Hamilton and Smith

In the *Report on Manufactures* and his other policy papers, Hamilton agrees with Adam Smith on several important points.

- Wealth is not merely the possession of gold and silver. It's goods and services. Hamilton wrote in 1790, in the *Report on a National Bank*, "The intrinsic wealth of a nation is to be measured, not by the abundance of the precious metals contained in it, but by the quantity of the productions of its labor and industry."

- The best economic outcomes occur when individuals and businesses act in their own self-interest. (See, for example his comments on the BUS at §5.3.5 and Appendix 2, §IV.A.3.)

Swanson and Trout: Donald F. Swanson and Andrew P. Trout, "Alexander Hamilton, 'the Celebrated Mr. Neckar,' and Public Credit," *William and Mary Quarterly*, Vol. 47, No. 3 (Jul. 1990), pp. 422-430. https://www.jstor.org/stable/2938096

Brookhiser notes: "The American Enlightenment's Other Side," 10/22/2010; originally published in June 2000. Cf. Necker, *De l'administration des finances de la France*, 1784, v. 1, pp. vii-x and elsewhere. https://www.atlassociety.org/post/the-american-enlightenments-other-side

Intrinsic wealth: Appendix 2, §II.B.6. See also Hamilton to Robert Morris, 4/30/1781, "true wealth ..." https://founders.archives.gov/documents/Hamilton/01-02-02-1167

- Division of labor is highly beneficial. (See §6.2.2 and Appendix 3, § II.A.2.c.i.)
- Savings (accumulation of capital) are important: hence the Bank of the United States, with its $10 milllion stock offering. (§5.3.1 and Appendix 2, §II.A.)
- The government should build infrastructure to facilitate commerce. (Appendix 3, §IV.K.) That's not a laissez-faire doctrine, but it is advocated in *The Wealth of Nations*.

Against all that, there's the fact that in *The Wealth of Nations,* Smith describes mercantilism in order to refute it. Hamilton <u>paraphrases Smith's descriptions</u> of mercantilism, but ignores Smith's objections to it.

6.4.3 Hamilton's contribution

Based on who Hamilton quotes and the policies he recommends, we can't say Hamilton is wholly in favor of any one economic school. His ideas may well have changed over time. But we can at least summarize what he contributed to the economic development of the United States.

Hamilton was not a strict proponent of laissez faire. Given the national and international context in which he lived, that's somewhat disappointing, but not surprising. In Hamilton's time, laissez-faire was advocated by theoreticians (Adam Smith and the Physiocrats), not by those responsible for government revenue. Finance ministers assumed, as Hamilton did, that one-sided laissez-faire policies would be detrimental to their countries' economies. Only after Ricardo published the theory of comparative advantage in 1817 did those in charge of national finances begin to comprehend that even one-sided laissez-faire would benefit their nations.

Hamilton's writings and policies did, however, promote the growth of laissez-faire capitalism in America. His praise of manufacturing, and of business in general, is unique among the writings of the Founding Fathers. On the national level, his policies are a bridge between the obsessive and erratic control of business and trade by individual states during the 1780s, and a more uniform, less restrictive policy that he helps set at the national level in the 1790s. On the international level, he proposes policies that he hopes will help the American economy despite the mercantilist restrictions imposed by European rulers.

<u>Paraphrases Smith's descriptions:</u> See, for example, Appendix 3, §II.A.1, and Founders Online annotated version, n. 127 regarding Smith's statements.

https://founders.archives.gov/documents/Hamilton/01-10-02-0001-0007

CHAPTER 7

Crises of 1790-1795 and Hamilton's Resignation

As early as spring 1790, when Congress debated the Funding Act, a political faction was developing that opposed Hamilton's programs. Over the following years, Hamilton and his Federalist allies pushed for a limited but energetic national government and a diverse economy. Thomas Jefferson, James Madison, and the Democratic-Republicans preferred that power remain with the separate states and that the United States remain primarily agricultural. In Congress, getting programs passed—whether a national bank or funds to protect the frontier—became a <u>constant battle</u> between these factions.

But during the 1790s, Federalists held the presidency and often had <u>majorities</u> in the House of Representatives, the Senate, or both. The survival of Hamilton's programs would perhaps not have been surprising ... had the decade of the 1790s been a peaceful one. But the 1790s were full of crises at home and abroad that caused the deaths of American citizens, disrupted trade (and hence government revenue), and roused even more factional feeling. In this chapter, we review those crises briefly.

7.1 IN 1790 AND LATER: FRONTIER WARS

In the early 1790s, fighting between Indians and settlers intensified. In the north, British troops in Canada provided the Indians with arms. In the south, the Spanish armed Creeks and Cherokees, encouraging them to attack American settlements. Hamilton estimated in 1795 that

---

<u>Constant battle</u>: see following page.

<u>Majorities</u>: On party divisions in the Senate and in the House of Representatives, see

https://www.senate.gov/history/party-div.htm ■ https://history.house.gov/Institution/Party-Divisions/Party-Divisions/

1789	Washington inaugurated; Hamilton secretary of Treasury
1790	*First Report on Public Credit;* Funding Act; beginning of opposition to Federalists
1791	Bank of the U.S. established; *Report on Manufactures*
1792	Panic of 1792
1793	Louis XVI executed; France declares war on Britain, and both attack American ships; Neutrality Proclamation; Giles Resolutions
1794	Attacks by Indians continue; attacks by Barbary pirates begin
1795	Hamilton resigns; Jay Treaty
1796	Adams elected president
1797	Callender publishes Reynolds affair
1798	Quasi War with France (until 1800)
1801	Jefferson confirmed president in House of Representatives

Hamilton describes his battles with Jefferson and Madison

In a letter to Edward Carrington (supervisor of the revenue for the District of Virginia and a long-time friend) of 5/26/1792, Hamilton summarized his problems so far: "Mr. Jefferson with very little reserve manifests his dislike of the funding system generally; calling in question the expediency of funding a debt at all. Some expressions which he has dropped in my own presence (sometimes without sufficient attention to delicacy) will not permit me to doubt on this point, representations, which I have had from various respectable quarters. I do not mean, that he advocates directly the undoing of what has been done, but he censures the whole on principles, which if they should become general, could not but end in the subversion of the system.

"In various conversations with foreigners as well as citizens, he has thrown censure on my principles of government and on my measures of administration.... When any turn of things in the community has threatened either odium or embarrassment to me, he has not been able to suppress the satisfaction which it gave him. ...

"It was evident from [Madison's] votes & a variety of little movements and appearances, that he was the prompter of Mr. Giles & others, who were the open instruments of opposition. [On Giles, see §7.3.] ...

"In respect to our foreign politics the views of these Gentlemen are in my judgment equally unsound & dangerous. They have a womanish attachment to France and a womanish resentment against Great Britain. They would draw us into the closest embrace of the former & involve us in all the consequences of her politics, & they would risk the peace of the country in their endeavours to keep us at the greatest possible distance from the latter. ... [I]f these Gentlemen were left to pursue their own course there would be in less than six months an open War between the U States & Great Britain."
https://founders.archives.gov/documents/Hamilton/01-11-02-0349

the cost of war with the Indians was running well over a million dollars a year, at a time when the whole government budget was about $7.5 million.

The deaths of American settlers at the hands of Indians led several states to conduct their own foreign policy. Georgia asserted its right to make war or negotiate treaties with the Creek Indians, without consulting the federal government. The Pennsylvania legislature planned to send militia to lay out a town at Presque Isle (near Lake Erie), which would have put them in conflict with Indians and possibly British troops. Kentucky planned to invade the territory held by Spain, whose government cut off their access to the Mississippi River and used the Indians as a buffer between Spanish colonies and the United States.

Cost of war: In the "Report on a Plan for the Further Support of Public Credit," 1/16/1795, "Expenses of Military Land Service" are given as $1,311,975.29.

https://founders.archives.gov/documents/Hamilton/01-18-02-0052-0002

Georgia asserted: For example, see John Habersham (collector of customs in Savannah, Georgia) to Hamilton, 1/16/1794: "Instead of discharging any of the Militia, as was expected, the Governor of the State has lately called out an additional number and those of the most expensive description, namely, Horse. Present appearances do not justify an expectation, that any part of the force will be immediately discharged; for although the Agent of the United States is now in the Creek country, and has lately communicated very agreable information respecting his prospects there, yet I am sorry to inform you that authentic accounts have been just received of two Creek Indians being killed on the western frontier of this State...."

https://founders.archives.gov/documents/Hamilton/01-15-02-0467 (especially n.5)

Pennsylvania legislature: see "Cabinet Meeting. Opinion on Drafting of Militia by Governor Thomas Mifflin," 5/24/1794.

https://founders.archives.gov/documents/Hamilton/01-16-02-0371

Kentucky planned: see "Cabinet Meeting. Opinion on Expeditions Being Planned in Kentucky for the Invasion of the Spanish Dominions," 3/10/1794. See also Edmund Randolph to Hamilton, William Bradford, and Henry Knox, 7/11/1794.

https://founders.archives.gov/documents/Hamilton/01-16-02-0108 ■
https://founders.archives.gov/documents/Hamilton/01-16-02-0588

Territory held by Spain: see following page and §2.2.3.3.

Spain and the United States

Tench Coxe (commissioner of the revenue) to Hamilton, 11/8/1792: "In the Course of the Conversation Mr. Jaudines [commissioner of Spain to the United States] took occasion to observe, that the U. S., in all their treaties with the indians, had introduced clauses by which the tribes had been made to submit themselves to the U. S and that a consequent protection of them had been held up and promised on our part—that similar engagements had subsisted between Spain and the Southern Indians ... [T]hat he would not say the Governor of New Orleans had supplied them with Arms and stores, but that it would be best that the U. S. should not attempt to run the line contemplated in the Treaty of New York, for, that if they did, Spain would support the Indians in preventing it."
https://founders.archives.gov/documents/Hamilton/01-13-02-0026

Report by George Hammond (British Minister Plenipotentiary to the United States), 12/3/1792: "In a recent conversation which I have had with Mr Hamilton, that Gentleman informed me that this government has in its possession the most indisputable proofs of an active interference on the part of the Spanish government in exciting the Creeks and Cherokees to war against the United States. He added that Baron Corrondolet, Governor of West Florida, had furnished the Indians with considerable supplies and ammunition for carrying into effect their hostile purposes."
https://founders.archives.gov/documents/Hamilton/01-13-02-0038

Medad Mitchell (surveyor) to Hamilton, 8/27/1793: "[I] Shall draw this inference from the conduct of the Spanish Government, which has come to my knowledge, partly from experience, and partly from information.

"1st. that they intend to Monopolize the Indian Trade upon the Mississippi, and to Aleniate the affections of the Savages from the Citizens of the United States, and to fix them as a Barrier between us and them, to present as much as possible the rapid population of our frontiers, while they gain time to fortify the River, so that nothing but a successful war can ever wrest it from their hands.

"2nd. That they intended to fortify the Chicasaw Bluffs, this Summer, from their strengthening all their out posts ...

"And lastly, By their holding a Treaty with the Savages inhabiting the Southern Teritories of the United States, it appears highly probable to me, that they have already purchased the Chicasaw Bluffs. The same right existed, to purchase those Bluffs, as there did, to purchase the Walnut Hills. They treat with those Savages, as sovereighn independent states, who have a right to dispose of Their Teritories, as they think proper.

"The Chicasaw Bluffs being the only high land, between the Iron Banks and walnut Hills, makes them of consequence to the Spanish Government, to command the River, And being well acquainted with the Value of the Indian Trade, most certainly will not omit securing them, whenever it lies in their power so to do."
https://founders.archives.gov/documents/Hamilton/01-15-02-0224

7.2 IN 1792: THE PANIC OF 1792

Stock in the Bank of the United States had to be purchased with one payment in gold and silver, three in United States bonds. (See §5.5.) One of the four stock payments was due in mid-1792. Several months before that, a group of New York speculators led by William Duer (who had been on Hamilton's staff at Treasury in late 1789 and early 1790) set out to buy up most of the available government bonds. They hoped stockholders in Bank of the United States would be forced to buy bonds at <u>exorbitant prices</u> in order to make the stock payment.

Duer purchased bonds by borrowing money from "<u>widows, orphans</u>, merchants mechanicks &c.," offering 5 or 6% interest monthly. He had no collateral to back those loans, and no money to repay them. Keeping his game going required that the prices of bonds rise and keep on rising, so that people would continue lending him money, rather than call for payment.

In late January, bond prices began to fall. Duer, who owed about half a million dollars, <u>defaulted on his loans</u> in early March 1792. All Duer's bonds suddenly came back on the market. The price of bonds plummeted. Panic spread throughout New York City as the merchants, widows, and mechanics realized their money had vanished.

Due to the instability of bond prices, bonds could no longer function as money. The amount of money in circulation <u>suddenly shrunk</u>,

---

Exorbitant prices: Hamilton was extremely worried about this sharp rise in stocks. To Rufus King, 8/17/1791 (regarding scrip for purchase of stock in the Bank of the United States): "[A] bubble connected with my operations is of all the enemies I have to fear, in my judgment, the most formidable—and not only not to promote, but as far as depends on me, to counteract delusions, appears to me to be the only secure foundation on which to stand."
https://founders.archives.gov/documents/Hamilton/01-09-02-0056

Widows, orphans: Robert Troup (New York City lawyer and longtime friend) to Hamilton, 3/19/1792.
https://founders.archives.gov/documents/Hamilton/01-11-02-0123

Defaulted on his loans: For more on Duer, see the notes to William Duer to Hamilton, 3/12/1792.
https://founders.archives.gov/documents/Hamilton/01-11-02-0099

Suddenly shrunk: Governor George Clinton of New York, an ally of Thomas Jefferson, used the financial situation as a political bludgeon against Hamilton and the Federalists. Clinton and his allies sold short all the stock they could to Duer. When the city's banks began to restrict the amount they were willing to lend, Clinton and allies began to withdraw large amounts of money to exacerbate the credit shortage.
https://globalfinancialdata.com/the-panic-of-1792

with all the problems we saw in §2.3. Not surprisingly, opponents of Hamilton's plans crowed that Duer's speculation proved the whole funding system was corrupt.

In March and April, at Hamilton's urging, $250,000 from the Sinking Fund was used to purchase, on the open market, bonds that were selling below their face value. This paid off some of the government's debt at a lower price than expected, and demonstrated that the government was still backing its bonds. To restore confidence in bonds, Hamilton also urged the Bank of New York to accept bonds as collateral for loans, at their face value. By late April 1792, bonds were again selling at their normal value, and the Panic was over.

7.3 IN 1793: THE GILES RESOLUTIONS

In January 1793, William Branch Giles, a Democratic-Republican, attacked Hamilton in Congress. The resolutions he presented were drafted by Jefferson and supported in Congress by Madison. Giles

---

Bonds as collateral: Hamilton to Williams Seton (Bank of New York), 3/19/1792: "I am far from wishing to encourage an imprudent extension of accommodation at such a crisis. Perhaps however it may be worth considering how much more can be done in favour of parties who can pledge public Stock as collateral security. This foundation of Credit you are sure is a good one."
https://founders.archives.gov/documents/Hamilton/01-11-02-0122

Normal value: "Report of the Sinking Fund," 3/26/1792. The members of the Sinking Fund (Vice President John Adams, Chief Justice John Jay, Secretary of State Thomas Jefferson, Secretary of the Treasury Alexander Hamilton, and Attorney General Edmund Randolph) noted in their "Report of the Commissioners of the Sinking Fund," 11/17/1792, that by purchasing bonds that were priced at less than face value, the government had redeemed bonds worth $1,495,457.89 with payments of only $967,821.65.
https://founders.archives.gov/documents/Hamilton/01-11-02-0155 ■
https://founders.archives.gov/documents/Hamilton/01-13-02-0046

Panic was over: Appendix 4 includes contemporary accounts of the Panic of 1792. Especially enlightening are those of Hamilton to William Short (U.S. minister to France, June 1790 to May 1792), 4/16/1792, and Henry Remsen to Thomas Jefferson, 4/23/1792.

Attacked Hamilton: On the Giles Resolutions, see McDonald, *Hamilton,* pp. 138, 260-261, 286.

Drafted by Jefferson: Jefferson, "Resolutions on the Secretary of the Treasury," [before 2/27/1793]. Among the ten resolutions drafted by Jefferson are: "4. Resolved, That the Secretary of the Treasury has deviated from the instructions given by

➤

HAMILTON'S FINANCIAL PROGRAMS

and his allies demanded a full account of transactions in the Treasury Department during the past three and a half years. They accused Hamilton of juggling foreign loans and debts in an improper (and, it was implied, nefarious) manner. In short, they cast aspersions on the integrity of Hamilton and the funding system.

Giles and his allies assumed that Hamilton would not be able to answer the charges before Congress adjourned in early March. Even if Hamilton successfully refuted the accusations later, they hoped the memory of it would tarnish his reputation.

Hamilton replied to the Giles Resolutions in four weeks, with a

---

the President of the United States, in exceeding the authorities for making loans under the acts of the 4th and 12th of August, 1790.

"9. Resolved, That at the next meeting of Congress, the act of Sep 2d, 1789, establishing a Department of Treasury should be so amended as to constitute the office of the Treasurer of the United States a separate department, independent of the Secretary of the Treasury.

"10. Resolved, That the Secretary of the Treasury has been guilty of maladministration in the duties of his office, and should, in the opinion of Congress, be removed from his office by the President of the United States."

https://founders.archives.gov/documents/Jefferson/01-25-02-0259-0002.

The versions presented to the House by Giles are printed in "Introductory Note: Report on the Balance of All Unapplied Revenues at the End of the Year 1792 and on All Unapplied Monies Which May Have Been Obtained by the Several Loans Authorized by Law" [2/4/1793]. They include: "Resolved, That the President of the United States be requested to cause to be laid before this House copies of the authorities under which loans have been negotiated, pursuant to the acts of the fourth and twelfth of August, one thousand seven hundred and ninety, together with copies of the authorities directing the application of the moneys borrowed. ...

"Resolved, That the Secretary of the Treasury be directed to lay before this House an account exhibiting, half-monthly, the balances between the United States and the Bank of the United States, including the several Branch Banks, from the commencement of those Institutions, to the end of the year one thousand seven hundred and ninety-two.

"Resolved, That the Secretary of the Treasury be directed to report to this House the balance of all unapplied revenues at the end of the year one thousand seven hundred and ninety-two, specifying whether in money or bonds, and noting where the money is deposited; that he also make report of all unapplied moneys which may have been obtained by the several loans authorized by law, and where such moneys are now deposited."

https://founders.archives.gov/documents/Hamilton/01-13-02-0299-0001

document of <u>60,000 words</u> plus multiple appendixes. He demonstrated that the perceived "irregularities" in the Treasury Department's accounts arose from the failure of Giles and his allies to understand the basics of income and expenditure, and from their failure to gather all the relevant facts. For example: the law states that payment of import duties may be postponed for up to twenty-four months. At the end of 1791, some $1.8 million in bonds for import duties were outstanding. That money was not in the Treasury, and could not be considered an <u>unaccounted-for surplus</u>.

<u>60,000 words</u>: Hamilton, "Report on the Balance of All Unapplied Revenues," 2/4/1793, with supplementary material. See also "Report Relative to the Loans Negotiated Under the Acts of the Fourth and Twelfth of August, 1790," 2/13-14/1793, in which Hamilton discusses why payments for the foreign and domestic debt were not kept separate, problems with making payments in Europe, funding the war with the Indians, the need for a cash buffer, and the application of the Sinking Fund.
https://founders.archives.gov/documents/Hamilton/01-13-02-0299-0002
■ Supplementary: https://founders.archives.gov/ancestor/ARHN-01-13-02-0299 ■ https://founders.archives.gov/documents/Hamilton/01-14-02-0013-0001

<u>Unaccounted-for surplus</u>: Hamilton, "Report on the Balance of All Unapplied Revenues," 2/4/1793: "But among the misconceptions, which have obtained, what relates to the surplus of revenue of the year 1792, is not the least striking. The laws inform, (and consequently, no information on that point from this department could have been necessary) that credits are allowed upon the duties on imports, of four, six, nine, twelve months, and in some cases, of two years. Reason dictates, that a surplus in such case must be considered as postponed in the collection or receipt, 'till all the appropriations upon the fund have been first satisfied. The account of receipts and expenditures to the end of 1791, in possession of the House, shews, that at that time, no less a sum than one million eight hundred and twenty eight thousand two hundred and eighty nine dollars and twenty eight cents, of the antecedent duties, were outstanding in bonds. How, then, could it have happened, that the surplus of 1792 was sought for in the Treasury, at the very instant of the expiration of the year? I forbear to attempt to trace the source of a mistake so extraordinary. ...

"Is it not truly matter of regret, that so formal an explanation on such a point should have been made requisite? Could no personal enquiry of either of the Officers concerned, have superseded the necessity of publicly calling the attention of the House of Representatives, to an appearance in truth, so little significant? Was it seriously supposable, that there could be any real difficulty in explaining that appearance, when the very disclosure of it proceeded from a voluntary act of the head of this department?"
https://founders.archives.gov/documents/Hamilton/01-13-02-0299-0002

Congress considered Hamilton's report and quickly cleared him of any wrongdoing. When Giles proposed a new set of resolutions attacking Hamilton, Congress voted overwhelmingly to take no action on them. The reputation of Hamilton and the funding system remained unblemished.

7.4 IN 1793 AND LATER: EFFECTS OF THE WAR BETWEEN FRANCE AND GREAT BRITAIN

Following the execution of King Louis XVI in 1793, France went to war with Great Britain. The war lasted off and on—mostly on—until 1815. It had wide-ranging effects on American trade, government revenue, and government expenditures, all of which put stress on Hamilton's programs.

Much of America's import and export trade was carried on American ships. After the war began, the French and the British both began to prey on those ships. It was an easy way to capture supplies for their own use, and to keep them out of the hands of opponents. French and British privateers sometimes operated within American territorial waters, just outside New York City. In 1794, British ships captured almost three hundred American merchant ships in the West Indies.

Lacking an army or navy, the United States government had no means to protect its shipping. Shipowners and merchants had to insure their ships and cargos (often at high premiums), or accept the losses. American sailors were often stranded abroad, or forced to serve in

---

Privateers: See, for example, "Cabinet Opinion on the *Polly* (Republican) and the *Catherine*," 6/12/1793: "The President having also required the same opinions on the Memorial of the British minister of the 11st inst. on the subject of the British brigantine *Catherine* captured by the French frigate the *Embuscade* within the limits of the protection of the U.S. as is said, and carried into the harbour of New York, they are of the opinion unanimously, that the Governor of N. York be desired to seize the said vessel in the first instance, and then deliver her over to the civil power ..."
https://founders.archives.gov/documents/Washington/05-13-02-0042

American sailors: For example, see Edmund Randolph to William Bradford, Alexander Hamilton, and Henry Knox, 3/15/1794.
https://founders.archives.gov/documents/Hamilton/01-16-02-0123

foreign navies. The American government had to fortify the ports of cities along the eastern seaboard and stock up on military stores—both expensive propositions.

Washington issued the Neutrality Proclamation on April 22, 1793. But as Hamilton predicted in 1787 in the *Federalist Papers*, "The rights of neutrality will only be respected when they are defended by an adequate power. A nation, despicable by its weakness, forfeits even the privilege of being neutral." France and Britain simply ignored the Neutrality Proclamation.

The United States could not simply wait out the war. Trade was vital to a country that still imported most manufactured goods. Also, by 1793, 90% of the federal government's revenue came from customs duties. Cutting off trade would mean eviscerating the United States government's revenue, hence its ability to operate—including to defend its borders and its merchant fleet.

The European war had other financial repercussions as well. In 1793, the French government began demanding early repayment of its Revolutionary War loan to America. The French and British and their

---

Fortify the ports: Washington to Hamilton, Jefferson, Knox, and Randolph 7/29/1793: "It will not be amiss, I conceive, at the meeting you are about to have to day, to consider the expediency of directing the Customhouse Officers to be attentive to the arming or equipping Vessels, either for offensive or defensive war, in the several ports to which they belong; and make report thereof to the Governor or some other proper Officer. Unless this, or some other effectual mode is adopted to check this evil in the first stage of it's growth, the Executive of the UStates will be incessantly harrassed with complaints on this head, & probably when it may be difficult to afford a remedy." Hamilton sent out notices to his customs officers on fortifications: see, for example, "Treasury Department Circular to the Collectors of the Customs," 4/3-6/4/1794. On the expense of gunpowder and the difficulty of acquiring it, see for example Tench Coxe to Hamilton, 7/8/1794.

https://founders.archives.gov/documents/Hamilton/01-16-02-0183
■ https://founders.archives.gov/documents/Hamilton/01-15-02-0118
■ https://founders.archives.gov/documents/Hamilton/01-16-02-0565

Rights of neutrality: *Federalist Papers* No. 11, 11/24/1787.
http://avalon.law.yale.edu/18th_century/fed11.asp

Early repayment: see following page.

HAMILTON'S FINANCIAL PROGRAMS 157

allies were borrowing so heavily from the Dutch that interest rates rose sharply. It became much more expensive for the United States to borrow in Europe—for example, to pay off its debt to the French.

And of course, many Americans had strong opinions on whether their country should support France or Britain. France had, after all, been America's ally during the Revolutionary War; but our language,

---

Early repayment: French envoy Edmond Charles Genet tried to raise troops in the United States among French sympathizers (usually Democratic-Republicans), and to commission privateers. But Genet was also instructed by his government to request early payment on the American debt to France. Indeed, Genet began purchasing goods in the United States and telling the sellers that the American government would reimburse them. Re payments on the French debt, see, for example, Hamilton to Edmond Charles Genet, 7/24/1793. Hamilton explained the situation in detail to Washington, 1/4/1794. On 3/11/1794, Washington's cabinet advised unanimously that the French be told that debt payments would be made on schedule, not before.
https://founders.archives.gov/documents/Hamilton/01-15-02-0102
■ https://founders.archives.gov/documents/Hamilton/01-15-02-0441
■ https://founders.archives.gov/documents/Hamilton/01-16-02-0110

France had: We can get a sense of the opposition to the Neutrality Proclamation from Hamilton's essays signed "Pacificus". The Founders Online version of "Pacificus" No. 1 (6/29/1793) has links to the other issues. See also Hamilton's "Americanus" essays, beginning 1/31/1794, in which he lays out the political and philosophical differences between the British and French.
https://founders.archives.gov/documents/Hamilton/01-15-02-0038 ■
https://founders.archives.gov/documents/Hamilton/01-15-02-0510

See also Rufus King to Hamilton, 8/3/1793: "These Gentlemen will not be stopped by Trifles, they already affirm that the Cause of France is that of america, that it is time to distinguish its friends from its Enemies, that in respect to the rumour of Mr. Genest's appeal to the People from the Decision of the Executive the people are competent Judges of their own Interest & obligations, that there can be no Danger to them from the free exercise of their Judgment on so great & interesting an Occasion."
https://founders.archives.gov/documents/Hamilton/01-15-02-0138

And of course, Jefferson to Madison, 7/7/1793 (regarding the Pacificus essays): "Nobody answers him, & his doctrine will therefore be taken for confessed. For god's sake, my dear Sir, take up your pen, select the most striking heresies, and cut him to peices in the face of the public. There is nobody else who can & will enter the lists with him."
https://founders.archives.gov/documents/Madison/01-15-02-0037

Excerpts from the Treaty with Tripoli, 11/4/1796

"The money and presents demanded by the Bey of Tripoli as a full and satisfactory consideration on his part and on the part of his subjects for this treaty of perpetual peace and friendship are acknowledged to have been recieved by him previous to his signing the same, according to a reciept which is hereto annexed ...

[Receipt:] The present writing done by our hand and delivered to the American Captain OBrien makes known that he has delivered to us forty thousand Spanish dollars,-thirteen watches of gold, silver & pinsbach,-five rings, of which three of diamonds, one of saphire and one with a watch in it, One hundred & forty piques of cloth, and four caftans of brocade,-and these on account of the peace concluded with the Americans.

"Note: On the arrival of a consul of the United States in Tripoli he is to deliver to Jussuf Bashaw Bey: twelve thousand Spanish dollars, five hawsers-8 Inch, three cables-10 Inch, twenty five barrels tar, twenty five ditto pitch, ten ditto rosin, five hundred pine boards, five hundred oak ditto, ten masts (without any measure mentioned, suppose for vessels from 2 to 300 ton), twelve yards, fifty bolts canvas, four anchors

"And these when delivered are to be in full of all demands on his part or on that of his successors from the United States according as it is expressed in the tenth article of the following treaty. And no farther demand of tributes, presents or payments shall ever be made."

https://avalon.law.yale.edu/18th_century/bar1796t.asp

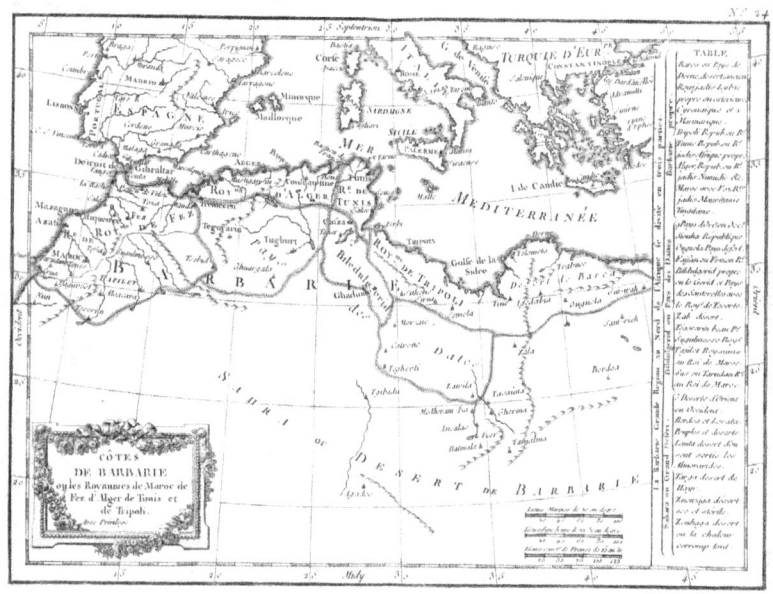

Delamarche & Lattre, Cotes de Barbarie, Paris, 1800.
Image: David Rumsey Map Collection

HAMILTON'S FINANCIAL PROGRAMS

our heritage, and most of our trade was still British. The conflicting opinions exacerbated the factions that already existed. Federalists tended to favor the British, Democratic-Republicans the French.

7.5 IN 1794 AND LATER: PIRACY IN THE MEDITERRANEAN

For centuries, pirates and privateers from the Barbary coast of Africa—Algiers, Tunis, Tripoli, and Morocco—raided coastal towns around the Mediterranean and attacked merchant ships. Sometimes the pirates demanded ransom for those captured. Sometimes they simply sold the captives into slavery. The European nations who traded in the Mediterranean never managed to eliminate the pirates, but they usually managed to curb their activities.

Until 1775, the American colonies were under the rule of Great Britain, which had the best navy in the world. The Barbary pirates left American ships alone. After America became independent, however, her ships became the targets of pirates lurking at the Strait of Gibraltar. The situation was exacerbated by the ongoing war between France and Britain. Allies of the French and British throughout Europe were drawn into the war. No country had manpower to spare for policing the pirates.

In 1794, Congress commissioned six frigates to protect American shipping. It was three years before the first three were launched. Meanwhile, Americans (like most Europeans) bribed the pirates to leave them alone. In a 1795 treaty with Algiers, for example, the United States agreed to pay $21,600 annually. The Bey of Tripoli demanded money, jewelry, and naval stores. By 1800, 20% of United States government revenue was being sent to the Barbary pirates.

Six frigates: On Algiers and the building of frigates, see notes on Hamilton to Wolcott, 6/16/1796.

https://founders.archives.gov/documents/Hamilton/01-20-02-0140

Algiers: The Treaty of Peace and Amity was signed with Algiers 9/5/1795.

https://avalon.law.yale.edu/18th_century/bar1795t.asp#1

Bey of Tripoli: Excerpts on the facing page.

Barbary Pirates: For treaties with the pirates, see Avalon Project, "The Barbary Treaties 1786-1836."

https://avalon.law.yale.edu/subject_menus/barmenu.asp

On payments to the pirates, see Gregory Fremont-Barnes, *The Wars of the Barbary Pirates*, 2006, pp. 36-37.

On the lead-up to Jefferson's war on the Barbary pirates, see Christopher Hitchens, "Jefferson Versus the Muslim Pirates," 2007.

https://www.city-journal.org/html/jefferson-versus-muslim-pirates-13013.html

7.6 IN 1794: WHISKEY REBELLION

By September 1792, Hamilton knew that the excise tax on distilled liquor, which had been imposed to pay for defense of the frontier, was being vehemently opposed by the frontiersmen in western Pennsylvania—even though they were among those who most needed defending from Indians.

Hamilton gathered information regarding which western counties had violent activity and which were relatively peaceful. He argued that such behavior could not be tolerated:

> <u>Such persevering</u> and violent opposition to the Law gives the business a still more serious aspect than it has hitherto worn, and seems to call for vigorous & decisive measures on the part of the Government. ... My present clear conviction is, that it is indispensable, if competent evidence can be obtained, to exert the full force of the Law against the Offenders, with every circumstance that can manifest the determination of the Government to enforce it's execution .... If this is not done, the spirit of disobedience will naturally extend and the authority of the Government will be prostrate.

For Washington's use, he <u>compiled a narrative</u> of events in Pennsylvania through July 1794 that included specifics of attacks on government agents and properties burned. The account was disseminated widely in the press.

In early August 1794, Henry Knox decided to visit Maine to take care of some business interests there. <u>Knox didn't return</u> until October 5. During that period, Hamilton did the work of the secretary of War as well as secretary of the Treasury.

<u>Such persevering</u>: Hamilton to Washington, 9/1/1792. There was also unrest, although not so violent, in Maryland, Virginia, North Carolina, Kentucky, and what became Ohio.
https://founders.archives.gov/documents/Hamilton/01-12-02-0239

<u>Compiled a narrative</u>: Hamilton to Washington, 8/5/1794. This detailed narrative became the basis for most historians' accounts of the Whiskey Rebellion.

https://founders.archives.gov/documents/Hamilton/01-17-02-0017

<u>Knox didn't return</u>: See Washington to Hamilton, 8/12/1794. Hamilton acted unofficially as secretary of State from September 1789 until March 1790, when Jefferson returned from Paris. That makes Hamilton the only person in history to have held all three of those major cabinet positions.

https://founders.archives.gov/documents/Hamilton/01-17-02-0046

HAMILTON'S FINANCIAL PROGRAMS

By late September, more than 12,000 militiamen were called up from Pennsylvania and three other states, led by Washington, Major-General Henry ("Lighthorse Harry") Lee III from Virginia, and Hamilton. The rebels dispersed without a major confrontation. Washington returned to Philadelphia. Hamilton remained in western Pennsylvania until late November, to help complete the mopping-up operations.

The expedition against the rebels in western Pennsylvania was the first time the United States government flexed its military muscle effectively. Had it not, doubtless other rebellions would have followed. As it was, revenue from excise taxes continued to arrive in the government's coffers, and continued to be used to repay the debt and defend the frontier, among other things.

7.7 HAMILTON'S RESIGNATION, 1795

7.7.1 Contemplating resignation

Hamilton mentioned resigning from Treasury as early as November 1791. In early 1793, he faced a Congressional investigation spear-headed by William Branch Giles. (See §7.3.) Having been

---

Mopping-up operations: Hamilton reported lightly to Angelica Church (10/23/1794), "A large army has cooled the courage of those madmen & the only question seems now to be how to guard best against the return of the phrenzy." More seriously, he wrote to his ally Rufus King, 10/30/1794: "This business must not be skinned over. The political putrefaction of Pensylvania is greater than I had any idea of. Without vigour every where our tranquillity is likely to be of very short duration & the next storm will be infinitely worse than the present one."

https://founders.archives.gov/documents/Hamilton/01-17-02-0324 ■
https://founders.archives.gov/documents/Hamilton/01-17-02-0334

Mentioned resigning: Hamilton to Angelica Church, November 1791: "Things are tending fast to a point, which will enable me honorably to retreat from a situation in which I make the greatest possible sacrifices to a little empty praise, or if you like the turn better, to a disposition to make others happy. But this disposition must have its limits."

https://founders.archives.gov/documents/Hamilton/01-09-02-0407

cleared of all charges, he <u>mentioned to Washington</u> a few months later his intention to resign after giving Congress another chance to investigate his conduct.

In early 1794, Congress <u>again investigated</u> the Treasury Department, this time at the request of Hamilton, who wanted them to acknowledge that his records were in order before he left office. This time the major issue was how funds had been disbursed. By June, Congress had again found nothing to criticize about Hamilton's conduct. But with violence in western Pennsylvania ratcheting up,

---

<u>Mentioned to Washington</u>: Hamilton to Washington, 6/21/1793, noting that he has a few propositions for Congress "necessary to the full developement of my original plan, and, as I supposed, of some consequence to my reputation," and because he wants to give Congress another opportunity to investigate his running of the Treasury Department, while still in office.

https://founders.archives.gov/documents/Hamilton/01-15-02-0012

<u>Again investigated</u>: Congress asked Hamilton to provide written authorizations from Washington for raising European loans. Hamilton replied that sometimes the authorizations were verbal. Washington stated that he did not recall every time that Hamilton had asked for authorization verbally. See "Introductory note on Hamilton to Frederick A.C. Muhlenberg," 12/16/1793, and Hamilton to Muhlenberg, 12/16/1793. For the progress of the investigation, see Hamilton to the Select Committee Appointed to Examine the Treasury Department, 3/24/1794.

https://founders.archives.gov/documents/Hamilton/01-15-02-0387-0001
- https://founders.archives.gov/documents/Hamilton/01-15-02-0387-0002
- https://founders.archives.gov/documents/Hamilton/01-16-02-0146

Hamilton's request to Washington for clarification on written authorizations was dated 4/8/1794.

https://founders.archives.gov/documents/Hamilton/01-16-02-0195

The Congressional investigation was finally wrapped up in June 1794. Stephen Higginson to Hamilton, 6/17/1794, n. 5.

https://founders.archives.gov/documents/Hamilton/01-16-02-0453

William Heth (customs collector for the Bermuda Hundred, Virginia) to Hamilton, 7/6/1794: "It was a cruel thing in Congress ... to oblige your persecutors, & prosecutors, to sit as your Judges, and ... to convict you, of purity of conduct, & unshaken integrity, and a constant watchfulness over the public interest."

https://founders.archives.gov/documents/Hamilton/01-16-02-0557

HAMILTON'S FINANCIAL PROGRAMS

Hamilton postponed his resignation yet again in May 1794.

But on December 1, 1794, just after he returned from helping to deal with the Whiskey Rebellion, Hamilton tendered his resignation to Washington, effective January 31, 1795. On the same day, he notified Frederick A. C. Muhlenberg, speaker of the House of Representatives, of his impending resignation, "in order that an opportunity may be given previous to that event, to institute any further proceeding which may be contemplated." A week later he wrote reassuringly to Angelica Church:

> Don't let Mr. Church be alarmed at my retreat—all is well with the public. Our insurrection is most happily terminated. Government has gained by it reputation and strength, and our finances are in a most flourishing condition. Having contributed to place those of the Nation on a good footing, I go to take a little care of my own; which need my care not a little.

7.7.2 Hamilton's last major report to Congress

The report Hamilton submitted to Congress in mid-January 1795 revealed just how much United States finances had improved. The

---

Postponed his resignation: Hamilton to Washington, 5/27/1794: "Events, which have lately accumulated, [are] of a nature to render the prospect of the continuance of our peace in a considerable degree precarious. I do not perceive, that I could voluntarily quit my post at such as juncture, consistently with considerations either of duty or character."
https://founders.archives.gov/documents/Hamilton/01-16-02-0380

Hamilton tendered: Hamilton to Washington, 12/1/1794.
https://founders.archives.gov/documents/Hamilton/01-17-02-0392

In order that: Hamilton to Frederick A.C. Muhlenberg, 12/1/1794.
https://founders.archives.gov/documents/Hamilton/01-17-02-0385

Don't let Mr. Church: Hamilton to Angelica Church, 12/8/1794.
https://founders.archives.gov/documents/Hamilton/01-17-02-0407

Report Hamilton submitted: "Report on a Plan for the Further Support of Public Credit," 1/16/1795, includes a summary of each of the bills that Congress passed for government revenue from 1789 to 1795, with the duration of each source and what it is allocated for, if anything; a summary of all United States debts outstanding; and the provisions that have been made for paying the interest on the debt and for extinguishing it.
https://founders.archives.gov/documents/Hamilton/01-18-02-0052-0002

credit of the United States had never been better, Hamilton said, because payments on the foreign and domestic debts had been made promptly and consistently. Hamilton estimated that the debt would be paid off in thirty years at most—somewhat less if additional revenue was raised by sale of land in the West.

Hamilton told Congress that he did have concerns going forward about extinguishing the debt. He wanted temporary duties to be continued until the principal had been paid off, so that they would not be subject to annual debates over renewal. He also wanted Congress to authorize a domestic loan (i.e., issue more government bonds) in order to pay off the foreign debt. Experience over the past few years showed that arranging to pay France in France, to pay Spain in Spain, and to pay Dutch bankers in The Netherlands often involved delay and extra expense. And because European monarchs were borrowing heavily for the war between France and Great Britain, it was becoming difficult to raise loans in Europe, and interest rates were high.

Hamilton left office on January 31, 1795. He was succeeded by Oliver Wolcott, Jr., who had been his comptroller at Treasury.

Debt would be paid: Hamilton, "Enclosure E: View of Sinking Fund According to Plan Proposed," January 1795.

https://founders.archives.gov/documents/Hamilton/01-18-02-0052-0007

Annual debates: Hamilton realized that undoing a commitment for funding sometime down the road would be difficult; but refusing to fund it if it came up annually would be easier. And indeed, the month after Hamilton resigned, Congress failed to make provision for payment on the "unsubscribed debt" (see § 4.4.3). By this time, the unsubscribed debt amounted to only about $1.5 million of the total debt (foreign and domestic) of $76 million—a relatively small amount—but Hamilton was distraught at the news. See §4.3, quoting his letter to Theodore Sedgwick of 2/18/1795.

Pay off the foreign debt: The foreign debts from the Revolutionary War were paid off in 1795. See United States Department of State, Office of the Historian, "U.S. Debt and Foreign Loans, 1775–1795."

https://history.state.gov/milestones/1784-1800/loans

When word spread that Hamilton was resigning, there was an outpouring of thanks and support from his allies and even his customs collectors. The one that probably meant the most came from Washington:

> Dear Sir,
>
> After so long an experience of your public services, I am naturally led, at this moment of your departure from office—which it has always been my wish to prevent—to review them.
>
> In every relation, which you have borne to me, I have found that my confidence in your talents, exertions and integrity, has been well placed. I the more freely render this testimony of my approbation, because I speak from opportunities of information which cannot deceive me, and which furnish satisfactory proof of your title to public regard.
>
> My most earnest wishes for your happiness will attend you in your retirement, and you may assure yourself of the sincere esteem, regard and friendship of
>
> Dear Sir, Your affectionate
>
> Go: Washington

7.7.3 Hamilton's career, 1795-1801

In June 1795, Hamilton moved back to New York City with the aim of improving his own financial situation. To Angelica he wrote:

> My Dear Sister, I tell you without regret what I hope you anticipate, that I am poorer than when I went into office. I allot myself full five or six years of more work than will be pleasant though much less than I have had for the last five years.

Thanks and support: See following page.

Dear Sir: Washington to Hamilton, 2/2/1795.
https://founders.archives.gov/documents/Hamilton/01-18-02-0148

My Dear Sister: Hamilton to Angelica Church, 3/6/1795. Hamilton's friends also considered him as far from wealthy. Robert Troup wrote to Hamilton, 5/11/1795: "I sincerely hope that … you may by some fortunate & unexpected event acquire the means of perfect independence in spite of all your efforts to be poor. … I have often said that your friends would be obliged to bury you at their own expence."
https://founders.archives.gov/documents/Hamilton/01-18-02-0181 ∎
https://founders.archives.gov/documents/Hamilton/01-18-02-0234

Thanks and support as Hamilton leaves office

Sharp Delany, William MacPherson, and Walter Stewart (customs collectors) to Hamilton, 1/12/1795: "Among that Class of your Fellow Citizens, who truly lament your intended Resignation, We also as Officers of The Revenue of this District, beg leave to assure you, We feel it in the most sensible Degree. And if the warmest heartfelt Sentiments of your Conduct, as a Statesman and in your Official Duties, can be pleasing or Usefull to your Feelings, We in the most explicit sense now offer them."

https://founders.archives.gov/documents/Hamilton/01-18-02-0037

Thomas Willing (president of the Philadelphia branch of the Bank of the United States) to Hamilton, 2/3/1795: "The President & Directors of the Bank of the United States acknowledge the receipt of your letter of the 31st. Ulto. & feel with peculiar sensibility the notification of your Resignation; With sincerity they offer their best wishes, that you may be as happy in private, as your administration has rendered you useful, in public life. ... It must be to you a source of the most pleasing sensations to reflect on the extensive utility of an Institution, which you had such an essential agency in organizing; which has been strikingly evident, as well in the aid it has afforded to the fiscal Administration as in the important support, it has given to public & private Credit."

 https://founders.archives.gov/documents/Hamilton/01-18-02-0151

James McHenry (former aide-de-camp of Washington who had served in Congress under the Articles and the Constitution) to Hamilton, 2/17/1795: "The tempest weathered and landed on the same shore I may now congratulate you upon having established a system of credit and having conducted the affairs of our country upon principles and reasoning which ought to insure its immortality as it undoubtedly will your fame. Few public men have been so eminently fortunate as voluntarily to leave so high a station with so unsullied a character and so well-assured a reputation, and still fewer have so well deserved the gratitude of their country and the elogiums of history."

https://founders.archives.gov/documents/Hamilton/01-18-02-0166

Bird, Savage & Bird (South Carolina merchant and banking firm operating in London) to Hamilton, 2/23/1795: "In your retreat from the Office of Secretary of the Treasury of the United States, it can be of little moment to you to have any addition to the public & private testimonies you have receiv'd of the high opinion your Country entertains of your distinguish'd integrity & abilities, which have been so successfully employ'd in restoring her public credit, & placing it on the most favorable footing to her future prosperity. We cannot however refuse ourselves the gratification of communicating to you the applause that the wisdom of your financial measures has procur'd from all persons in this Country where the subject is so well known, & understood."

https://founders.archives.gov/documents/Hamilton/01-18-02-0172

HAMILTON'S FINANCIAL PROGRAMS

Over the next decade he ran a thriving law practice and remained the leading spokesman (in person and in writing) of the Federalists. While Washington was in office, Hamilton continued to answer questions from the president and the new secretary of the Treasury. Until mid-1800, Hamilton also advised several cabinet members under President Adams.

During the 1790s, France and Great Britain continued to attack American ships, seizing goods and imprisoning crews. (See §7.4.) In 1794, Washington dispatched John Jay to London to negotiate a treaty. Jay's goals: persuade the British to stop their attacks on American ships, and to vacate seven fortified posts on the northern and western frontier, from which they were arming and abetting the Indians.

When the Jay Treaty was announced in March 1795, the pro-French faction was furious. Hamilton defended the treaty in a series of thirty-eight essays published over six months, entitled "The Defence." After extensive debate in Congress, the treaty was ratified by

---

Answer questions: See, for example, his response to Oliver Wolcott, Jr. (secretary of the Treasury) on 4/10/1795, regarding the debt; and Washington's request for Hamilton's thoughts on the Jay Treaty, 7/3/1795.
https://founders.archives.gov/documents/Hamilton/01-18-02-0216-0002
■ https://founders.archives.gov/documents/Hamilton/01-18-02-0275

Negotiate a treaty: Hamilton drafted the instructions to John Jay; see "Enclosure: Points to be Considered in the Instructions to Mr. Jay, Envoy Extraordinary to G B," 4/23/1794. The Jay Treaty was signed on November 19, 1794, and a copy reached the United States on 3/7/1795; see Hamilton to Washington, 2/25/1795, n. 3.
https://founders.archives.gov/documents/Hamilton/01-16-02-0252-0002
■ https://founders.archives.gov/documents/Hamilton/01-18-02-0174

Furious: On the riots following publication of the Jay Treaty, see, for example, Oliver Wolcott, Jr. (secretary of the Treasury, writing from Philadelphia) to Hamilton, 7/30/1795: "The true state of things in this city is, that the Treaty was at first unpopular, the expectations of vain sanguine men, who considered this Country as all powerful & intittled to dictate, were not satisfied—every engine of faction was successfully set at work; at present there is more temper & moderation—the truth begins to prevail. I think we shall have no dangerous riots—but one month will determine the fate of our Country, so far as depends on ourselves—the extreme hazards of foreign war I do not take into account."
https://founders.archives.gov/documents/Hamilton/01-18-02-0320

The Defence: Hamilton, writing under the pseudonym "Camillus," published thirty-eight essays under the title "The Defence" from 7/22/1795-1/9/1796. First in the series:
https://founders.archives.gov/documents/Hamilton/01-18-02-0305-0002

the Senate and signed by the president in August 1795. It took effect in early 1796.

In a letter of May 1797 to William Hamilton, his uncle in Scotland, Hamilton wrote:

> It is impossible to be happier than I am in a wife and I have five Children, four sons and a daughter, the eldest a son somewhat passed fifteen, who all promise well, as far as their years permit and yield me much satisfaction. Though I have been too much in public life to be wealthy, my situation is extremely comfortable and leaves me nothing to wish but a continuance of health. With this blessing, the profits of my profession and other prospects authorise an expectation of such addition to my resources as will render the eve of life, easy and agreeable; so far as may depend on this consideration.

Shortly after Hamilton wrote that letter, in summer 1797, James Callender broadcast Hamilton's affair with Maria Reynolds. His enemies gloated, even as Hamilton published his own version of events.

Meanwhile, once the Jay Treaty was in place with Great Britain, France became America's major problem, attacking hundreds of her

---

It is impossible: Hamilton to William Hamilton, 5/2/1797.

https://founders.archives.gov/documents/Hamilton/01-21-02-0037

His own version: Its full title: *Observations on Certain Documents Contained in No. V & VI of "The History of the United States for the Year 1796," In Which the Charge of Speculation against Alexander Hamilton, Late Secretary of the Treasury, is Fully Refuted,* 1797.

https://founders.archives.gov/documents/Hamilton/01-21-02-0138-0002

See also Durante, *Alexander Hamilton and the Reynolds Affair,* 2019.

Major problem: Hamilton to Washington, 1/19/1797: "Our Merchants here are becoming very uneasy on the subject of the French captures and seizures. They are certainly very perplexing and alarming—and present an evil of a magnitude to be intolerable if not shortly remedied. My anxiety to present Peace with France is known to you... Yet there are bounds to all things. This Country cannot see its Trade an absolute prey to France without resistance. We seem to be where we were with G Britain when Mr Jay was sent there—and I cannot discern but that the Spirit of the Policy then pursued with regard to England will be the proper one now in respect to France ➤

ships. In 1798, when war with France seemed inevitable, Washington agreed once again to be commander in chief—but only if Hamilton was appointed his <u>right-hand man</u>. A year after the *Reynolds Pamphlet* appeared, Hamilton was named inspector general of the United States army for the Quasi War with France, with the rank of major-general. He was also <u>expected to do the work</u> of the secretary of War. James McHenry, the incumbent, was generally agreed to be ill-suited to fulfill his duties. Hamilton was preoccupied with military business until the summer of 1800. The army was disbanded after commissioners dispatched by President Adams negotiated the Convention of 1800 with France.

Let's see how Hamilton's programs affected the Gordian Knot by 1801, when Thomas Jefferson took office as president.

(viz) a solemn and final appeal to the Justice and interest of France & if this will not do, measures of self defence. Any thing is better than absolute humiliation. France has already gone much further than Great Britain ever did."

https://founders.archives.gov/documents/Hamilton/01-20-02-0304

<u>Right-hand man</u>: See following page.

<u>Expected to do the work</u>: Philip Schuyler to Hamilton, 8/6/1798: "I am not surprised My Dear Sir that you found much had not been done in the execution of the important Objects, for I have some time since perceived that Mr McHenry had not a mind sufficiently extensive & energetic to embrace & execute all the Objects incident to the war department, and I foresee that you will be under the necessity to direct the principle operations of that department, to avoid those embarrassments which must otherwise inevitably result from incompetency in the Officer."

https://founders.archives.gov/documents/Hamilton/01-22-02-0035

Also: Oliver Wolcott, Jr., to Hamilton, 8/9/1798: "You must my friend come on with the expectation of being Secy of War in fact. Mr. McH's good sense, industry & virtues, are of no avail, without a certain address & skill in business which he has not & cannot acquire."

https://founders.archives.gov/documents/Hamilton/01-22-02-0043

In addition, Hamilton took on the task of reorganizing the army: see introductory note of Hamilton to James Gunn, 12/22/1798.

https://founders.archives.gov/documents/Hamilton/01-22-02-0205-0001

Washington and Hamilton brace for war with France

Hamilton to Washington, 6/2/1798: "It is a great satisfaction to me to ascertain what I had anticipated in hope, that you are not determined in an adequate emergency against affording once more your Military services. There is no one but yourself that could unite the public confidence in such an emergency, independent of other considerations—and it is of the last importance that this confidence should be full and complete. As to the wish of the Country it is certain that it will be ardent and universal. You intimate a desire to be informed what would be my part in such an event as to entering into military service. I have no scruple about opening myself to you on this point. If I am invited to a station in which the service I may render may be proportioned to the sacrifice I am to make—I shall be willing to go into the army. If you command, the place in which I should hope to be most useful is that of Inspector General with a command in the line. This I would accept. The public must judge for itself as to whom it will employ; but every individual must judge for himself as to the terms on which he will serve and consequently must estimate himself his own pretensions."
https://founders.archives.gov/documents/Hamilton/01-21-02-0264

Washington to Hamilton, 7/14/1798: "I have consented to embark once more on a boundless field of responsibility & trouble, with two reservations—first, that the principal Officers in the line, and of the Staff, shall be such as I can place confidence in; and, that I shall not be called into the field until the Army is in a situation to require my presence, or it becomes indispensible by the urgency of circumstances. ... It will be needless after giving you this information, and having indelibly engraved on my mind, the assurance contained in your letter of the 2d. of June, to add, that I rely upon you as a Coadjutor, and assistant in the turmoils I have consented to encounter."
https://founders.archives.gov/documents/Hamilton/01-22-02-0002-0002

CHAPTER 8

The Gordian Knot by 1801

In 1801, a Democratic-Republican was elected to the presidency for the first time. In his first annual message to Congress, Thomas Jefferson congratulated his fellow Americans on the progress of the United States. In military affairs, he said, there was a "spirit of peace and friendship" among the Indians, although there were still problems with the Barbary pirates. He recommended reducing the size of the army and navy, and relying instead on state militia. Population had increased and land was being settled: he recommended revising naturalization laws so that immigrants could become citizens more quickly. Federal revenue had increased so much due to America's growing population that Jefferson recommended abolishing all internal taxes (excise taxes), and relying only on import duties. Even with this change in revenue, Jefferson estimated that the Revolutionary War debt would be paid off in fifteen years.

Hamilton was infuriated that Jefferson praised the state of the union without crediting the Federalists, during whose administrations all those improvements had happened. He responded to Jefferson's inaugural message with a series of eighteen essays: "The Examination".

Jefferson congratulated: Jefferson, "First Annual Message to Congress," 12/8/1801.
https://founders.archives.gov/documents/Jefferson/01-36-02-0034-0003

The Examination: Hamilton had supported Jefferson rather than Adams in part so that he could be critical of the new administration; see his letter to Theodore Sedgwick of 5/10/1800. He attacked Jefferson in "An Address to the Electors of New York State," 3/21/1801, and in the "Examination" series (12/17/1801 to 4/8/1802).
https://founders.archives.gov/documents/Hamilton/01-24-02-0387
■ https://founders.archives.gov/documents/Hamilton/01-25-02-0197 ■
https://founders.archives.gov/ancestor/ARHN-01-25-02-0264

In them he defended his actions as secretary of the Treasury and the actions of President Washington.

Hamilton's lengthy summing-up in 1801 makes this a perfect point to review what has happened to our Gordian Knot over the decade of the 1790s. This time, we'll work our way from broad issues such as the national debt back to the nitty-gritty of making a living. We'll also see how the solutions Hamilton proposed were integrated. Each one improved the state of the other threads in the Gordian Knot as well.

8.1 MASSIVE GOVERNMENT DEBT

In 1790, Hamilton calculated the United States debt (foreign and domestic, including states' debts) at $79 million. Beginning that year, the government faithfully paid the interest and began paying off the principal as well. Americans and foreigners began to trust the government to make good on its debts. For the first time in its existence, the United States government had good credit. It could borrow at low interest rates to pay off higher-interest debts. If emergencies arose, it could borrow for military expenses.

In January 1795, in <u>one of his final reports</u> as secretary of the Treasury, Hamilton estimated the debt (including foreign debt, 6% bonds, 6% deferred bonds, 3% bonds, and the unsubscribed debt) at $76 million. That's a $3 million decrease, despite spending unanticipated millions of dollars to fight the Indians, the British, the French, the Spanish, the Barbary pirates, and the Whiskey Rebellion.

Guaranteeing payment of the debt meant that soldiers, traders, farmers, businessmen, and others recovered "lost" income from the war years. They could use it to expand their businesses or enjoy their leisure. If a speculator had purchased the old IOUs, then he could invest in private businesses or corporations that created goods people needed and wanted. Everyone's lives became better.

The results of Hamilton's restructuring of the debt were described by America's Dutch bankers in June 1795:

<u>One of his final reports</u>: "Report on a Plan for the Further Support of Public Credit," 1/16/1795.

https://founders.archives.gov/documents/Hamilton/01-18-02-0052-0002

> The success of those efforts you have been pleased to deem meritorious in us, have been greatly facilitated, by the unlimited Confidence, We have had in your abilities, probity, and Zeal for the support of the honor of your Country, and the credit of its Government: which have enabled us most boldly and conscientiously, as well to our dearest Relations and nearest Friends, as to the most indifferent Money lenders, to recommend the Investment of their Capitals in Bonds of the United States preferently to those of any European Power whatever.

In a speech to Congress in December 1795, Washington was able to relegate provisions for the American debt to a two-sentence paragraph.

The best indication of the status of American credit came two years after Jefferson took office. In 1803, Jefferson sent commissioners to France to purchase New Orleans from Napoleon. Napoleon offered instead to sell the whole of the Louisiana Territory for $15 million. A few million of that was to be paid to American merchants and ship-owners, to reimburse them for losses of ships captured by the French in the 1790s. (See §7.4.) The other $11.25 million had to be paid to Napoleon.

The United States Treasury didn't have spare millions: the country was still in debt from the Revolutionary War twenty years earlier. But because the United States now had a track record of paying its debts, it was able to issue $11.25 million in bonds to Napoleon. Napoleon sold the bonds via Dutch bankers to the British. Napoleon got the money. The British got marketable investments with reliable

---

The success: Wilhem and Jan Willink, Nicholaas and Jacob Van Staphorst, and Nicholas Hubbard to Hamilton, 6/1/1795.
https://founders.archives.gov/documents/Hamilton/01-18-02-0246

Relegate provisions: Washington to the United States Senate and House of Representatives, 12/8/1795: "Congress have demonstrated their sense to be, and it were superfluous to repeat mine, that whatsoever will tend to accelerate the honorable extinction of our public debt, accords as much with the true interest of our Country, as with the general sense of our constituents."

https://founders.archives.gov/documents/Washington/05-19-02-0174.

Michael Newton notes in *Angry Mobs and Founding Fathers* (2011), p. 141: "As the American population and economy grew, the relatively stable debt level became less burdensome. Although federal government debt rose 9.9 percent in the 1790s, debt per person fell from $18.54 in 1791 to $15.62 in 1800, a 15.7 percent decrease. Relative to the overall economy, debt fell from 35 percent of gross domestic product in 1792 to 17 percent by 1800, a greater than 50 percent reduction."

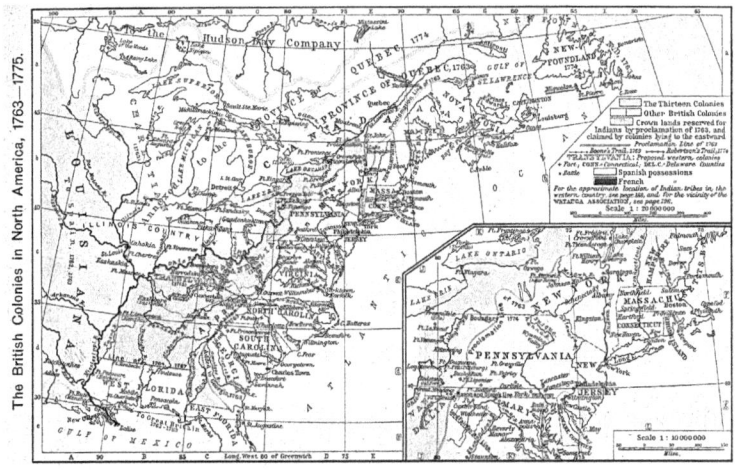

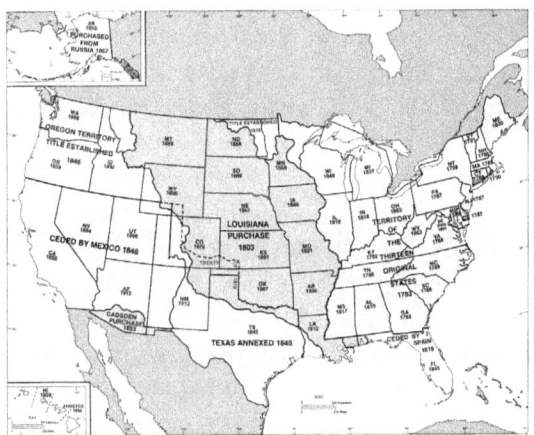

*Above: Map of the British colonies, 1763-1776.
Below: Territorial acquisitions of the United States
through 1867. Both images: Wikipedia*

Nearly doubled: On the sale of the "Louisiana Sixes", see Wright, *One Nation Under Debt*, p. 171. A side note: because it had good credit, the United States was able to expand its territory during the nineteenth century by purchase rather than military conquest. In 1848, the Mexican-American War ended with the United States paying Mexico $15 million for half Mexico's territory (now the southwestern United States). In 1853, the United States paid Mexico another $10 million for southern Arizona and New Mexico. In 1867, just after the Civil War, the United States paid Russia $7.2 million for Alaska. From 1801 to 1867, America increased its original territory more than fourfold by employing the public credit that Hamilton had established. Sylla and Cowen, *Alexander Hamilton on Finance, Credit, and Debt*, p. 320.

interest. The United States nearly doubled its size, gaining control of the Mississippi River and eliminating a major European power from its western frontier.

In short, when Jefferson took office, the payment of the Revolutionary War debt was well in hand. As a result, the government had good credit. This thread in the Gordian Knot was not a major source of concern any more.

8.2 LACK OF GOVERNMENT REVENUE

Hamilton calculated in the *First Report* that the government needed about $2.8 million annually to pay government expenses plus interest on the refinanced debt. (See §4.2.4.) He proposed revenue that would bring in that amount: import and tonnage duties plus a handful of excise taxes. Congress passed laws accordingly.

When Hamilton left office in 1795, federal revenues were $6.1 million. In 1800, they were $10.85 million. That was mostly due to a higher population and the increased international trade that came with it. The government now had adequate income for all normal expenses. When a crisis arose, such as the Whiskey Rebellion or the Quasi War with France, Congress passed taxes on items such as distilled beverages, carriages, and auction sales.

Looked at another way: adequate income allowed the federal government to fulfill its proper functions, including defending its citizens and borders. This helped decrease the centrifugal tendency of the states.

By 1801, the United States government had a reliable source of income. This thread of the Gordian Knot was also no longer a serious concern.

8.3 INADEQUATE CIRCULATION OF MONEY

Unlike the fluctuating IOUs and paper money issued during the Revolutionary War, the government's bonds (6%, 6% deferred, and 3% bonds), issued beginning in 1790, had stable values. They could be

---

Nearly doubled: see facing page.

Federal revenues: The federal budgets for 1792-1996 (revenues, outlays, surplus, debt as percentage of GNP, and accumulated debt) are printed in Gordon, *Hamilton's*

Blessing, pp. 200-204. The government ran deficits in 1792, 1794, 1795, and 1799. When Jefferson took office, the accumulated national debt was just over $80 million.

bought, sold, or transferred throughout the United States and internationally. In effect, they could function as currency. By the time Jefferson took office, banknotes from the Bank of the United States and a couple dozen state-chartered banks were also circulating widely, further increasing money in circulation.

In 1801, if you wanted to send money from New York to a child in South Carolina, you wouldn't have to send gold or silver. You could send banknotes, or have one bank transfer the sum to another. If you wanted to borrow money for a plow—or a merchant ship, or a textile factory—you didn't have to hope one of three banks in the country would lend you money. You had your choice of a couple dozen.

The increased money in circulation allowed more farmers, traders, and businessmen to save money, or to borrow it at lower interest rates. They could expand their productivity and eventually improve their standard of living ... or just save money for a rainy day.

The increased money in circulation also made it easier for the government to collect its revenue. Back in 1786, Daniel Shays led a rebellion in Massachusetts of disgruntled farmers who owed money, often because they could not collect the gold and silver coins required to pay their taxes or their debts. Those Massachusetts farmers aimed to shut down courts so their creditors couldn't foreclose on their farms. (See §2.1.3.) From the 1790s on, there was no repetition of Shays' Rebellion.

So by 1801, there was a more-than-adequate supply of money in circulation, including gold and silver, government bonds, and banknotes. That's another thread of the Gordian Knot that wasn't a major concern any more.

8.4 CENTRIFUGAL TENDENCY OF THE UNITED STATES

In Chapter 2, we looked at the fragmentation of the United States under the Articles of Confederation. Let's see where we are with disagreements between the federal government and the states, the states

---

No repetition: Fries's Rebellion in 1799-1800 was a reaction to taxes on houses and land imposed during the Quasi War with France. The Pennsylvania farmers didn't owe money; they were objecting to the possibility that they might owe it.

HAMILTON'S FINANCIAL PROGRAMS

and each other, and the federal government and foreign powers.

By the time Jefferson took office, the United States had fully functional executive, legislative and judicial branches. Because foreign powers now trusted America to act as a nation, not a collection of squabbling states, America had been able to sign treaties with Great Britain, France, and Spain, and with the Indians in the Northwest Territory and Georgia. In this way, the federal government reduced the pressure on its frontier.

American citizens were beginning to see that the federal government under the Constitution (as opposed to under the Articles of Confederation) was a useful entity. States at the frontier became less inclined to conduct their own foreign policy once the federal government began to negotiate treaties. The government's ability to pay soldiers made it somewhat less hazardous to live in frontier settlements.

But the federal government's presence, activity, and energy were noticeable even if you lived in long-settled areas. By 1801, many Americans were saving money by buying government bonds and/or stock in the Bank of the United States. Some paid customs duties and excise taxes directly to the United States. State tax payments had decreased because the federal government had assumed the burden of paying off states' Revolutionary War debts. That money was now available for citizens to use to improve their own lives.

All these factors helped people across the United States begin to think of themselves as part of the United States, rather than just citizens of their home states.

Sign treaties: Washington to the United States Senate and House of Representatives, 12/8/1795.
https://founders.archives.gov/documents/Washington/05-19-02-0174

States at the frontier: In 1799, the military outposts on the frontier included Oswego and Niagara in New York, Detroit (now in Michigan), Fort Wayne (now in Indiana), and Chicasaw Bluffs (now in Tennessee). See James McHenry to Hamilton, 2/4/1799, and Hamilton to Washington, 9/9/1799.
https://founders.archives.gov/documents/Hamilton/01-22-02-0269 ∎
https://founders.archives.gov/documents/Hamilton/01-23-02-0390

But disagreements still existed. In his Farewell Address in 1796, Washington thought it worthwhile to remind Americans that they were not divided into North and South or East and West.

The even more divisive split since 1790 was between the Federalists and the Democratic-Republicans. They disagreed on the best way to make a living, with the Democratic-Republicans tending to favor agriculture over trade and manufacturing. They disagreed on foreign policy: whether the United States should support France or Great Britain. They disagreed on the distribution of power between the federal and state governments.

The centrifugal force thread of our Gordian Knot was still a concern in 1801, although less so than in 1790. Hamilton's programs played a large role in making that happen.

8.5 MAKING A LIVING

Hamilton's programs directly allowed individual Americans to improve their situations in at least four immediate and obvious ways.

8.5.1 Easier ways to borrow and save

Hamilton's plan for paying off the debt and making regular interest payments increased money in circulation. So did the banknotes of the Bank of the United States, and of the multitude of state-chartered banks incorporated during the 1790s. Suddenly there were more options for an inventor with an idea, a trader who wanted to sell new goods on new routes, or a farmer who wanted to buy machinery to improve his productivity. If individuals were showing a profit, they had more options for saving their money safely (in a bank) or investing it so that it earned interest (in a bank or a corporation).

North and South: Washington, "Farewell Address" 9/19/1796: "In contemplating the causes which may disturb our Union, it occurs as matter of serious concern, that any ground should have been furnished for characterising parties by Geographical discriminations—Northern and Southern—Atlantic and Western; whence designing men may endeavour to excite a belief that there is a real difference of local interests and views. One of the expedients of party to acquire influence, within particular districts, is to misrepresent the opinions and aims of other districts. You cannot shield yourselves too much against the jealousies and heart burnings which spring from these misrepresentations."

https://founders.archives.gov/documents/Washington/99-01-02-00963

8.5.2 Uniform trade regulation

In the 1780s, states had imposed a patchwork of trade regulations, making it difficult and complex to trade across state lines. (See §3.7 and 3.11.3.) Under the Constitution, Congress instituted coherent rules and regulations for trade. It became easier to trade between states. In the process, it became easier to think of oneself as belonging to a nation as well as a state.

8.5.3 Corporations

The creation of the Bank of the United States in 1791 was the catalyst that induced states to charter <u>many other corporations</u>. Through 1780, only seven corporations had been chartered. During the 1780s, the states chartered twenty-eight more. By 1795, 114 more corporations were chartered; by 1801, another 181. When Jefferson took office, 330 corporations existed in the United States.

What did those corporations do? They allowed people of moderate means to invest in large projects, by consolidating a lot of small amounts. One frequent aim was to improve transportation by building roads, canals, and bridges. In 1792, the Philadelphia and Lancaster Turnpike became the first American company chartered to create a road. The sixty-mile turnpike opened in 1795. The <u>company prospered</u>, collecting most of its tolls from November to April, when rain and snow made the badly maintained government roads impassable.

Another common purpose of early American corporations was to offer marine insurance. Such insurance was paid by merchants and ship-owners against loss of ships and cargo to storms, attacks by warring European nations, or pirates. In peacetime, the rate was sometimes as low as 2%. In times of war, it could be 35% or more. Until such insurance companies were established in the United States, American shipowners had to pay whatever premiums companies such as Lloyd's of London asked ... or else they had to shoulder the risk of losing ship and cargo without recompense.

Once these corporations were created, someone had to staff the offices and build those roads, bridges, and canals. This gave Americans options for making a living that had never been available to them before.

Many other corporations: The numbers are from Sylla and Cowen, *Alexander Hamilton on Finance, Credit, and Debt*, pp. 318-9.

Company prospered: Wright, *First Wall Street*, p. 119. The route of the Philadelphia and Lancaster Turnpike is now U.S. Route 30.

8.5.4 A diverse economy with more options for making a living

No matter where they lived or what faction they favored, in the 1790s and later, Americans had options for making a living that few had conceived of before Hamilton's programs were legislated into place. And that wasn't a side-effect. Hamilton explained in the *Report on Manufactures* why a diverse economy benefited individual citizens:

> It is a just observation, that minds of the strongest and most active powers for their proper objects fall below mediocrity and labour without effect, if confined to uncongenial pursuits. And it is thence to be inferred, that the results of human exertion may be immensely increased by diversifying its objects. When all the different kinds of industry obtain in a community, each individual can find his proper element, and can call into activity the whole vigour of his nature. And the community is benefitted by the services of its respective members, in the manner, in which each can serve it with most effect.

And again:

> Every new scene, which is opened to the busy nature of man to rouse and exert itself, is the addition of a new energy to the general stock of effort. The spirit of enterprise, useful and prolific as it is, must necessarily be contracted or expanded in proportion to the simplicity or variety of the occupations and productions, which are to be found in a Society.

Americans had more choices for their life's work: more ways than ever to pursue wealth and happiness. This was the most significant change in making a living from 1790 to 1801, and the one with the broadest effect, short-term and long-term.

8.5.5 Washington and Hamilton on the state of the nation

Hearing of Shays' Rebellion in 1786, Washington had written: "We are fast verging to anarchy & confusion!" (See § 2.1.3.) In his address to Congress in December 1795, Washington found cause for "contentment and satisfaction" in the internal situation of America:

It is a just: Appendix 3, §II.A.2.c.v.
Every new scene: Appendix 3, §II.A.2.c.v.

Anarchy & confusion: Washington to Madison, 11/5/1786.
https://founders.archives.gov/documents/Madison/01-09-02-0070

> Our agriculture, commerce and manufactures prosper beyond former example; the molestations of our trade (to prevent a continuance of which, however, very pointed remonstrances have been made) being over-balanced by the aggregate benefits which it derives from a neutral position. Our population advances with a celerity, which, exceeding the most sanguine calculations, proportionally augments our strength and resources, and guarantees our future security. Every part of the Union displays indications of rapid and various improvement, and with burthens so light as scarcely to be perceived; with resources fully adequate to our present exigencies; with Governments founded on the genuine principles of rational liberty, and with mild and wholesome Laws; is it too much to say, that our Country exhibits a spectacle of national happiness never surpassed, if ever before equalled?

In 1801, responding to Jefferson, Hamilton pointed out that during the 1780s, industrious work and the blessings of Providence were not enough to bring prosperity. A stable federal government was necessary, and that's what the Constitution created.

> What have been the effects of this system?—An extension of commerce and manufactures, the rapid growth of our cities and towns, the consequent prosperity of agriculture and the advancement of the farming interest.

Our agriculture: Washington to the United States Senate and House of Representatives, 12/8/1795. A year later (12/12/1796), John Adams told Washington on behalf of the Senate: "We cordially acquiesce in the reflection, that the United States, under the operation of the Federal Government, have experienced a most rapid aggrandizement and prosperity, as well political as commercial."

https://founders.archives.gov/documents/Washington/05-19-02-0174
https://founders.archives.gov/documents/Adams/99-02-02-1807

What have been: Hamilton, "An Address to the Electors of the State of New-York," 3/21/1801. Further excerpt on following pages.
https://founders.archives.gov/documents/Hamilton/01-25-02-0197

Hamilton on the state of the nation, 1801

"An Address to the Electors of the State of New-York," 3/21/1801: "What have been the effects of this system?—An extension of commerce and manufactures, the rapid growth of our cities and towns, the consequent prosperity of agriculture and the advancement of the farming interest. All this was effected, by giving life and activity to a capital in the public obligations, which was before dead, and by converting it into a powerful instrument of mercantile and other industrious enterprize. ... [Y]ou have eminently prospered under the system of public measures pursued and supported by the Federalists.

"In vain are you told that you owe your prosperity to your own industry and to the blessings of Providence. To the latter doubtless you are primarily indebted. You owe to it among other benefits the constitution you enjoy and the wise administration of it, by virtuous men as its instruments. You are likewise indebted to your own industry. But has not your industry found aliment and incitement in the salutary operation of your government—in the preservation of order at home—in the cultivation of peace abroad—in the invigoration of confidence in pecuniary dealings—in the increased energies of credit and commerce—in the extension of enterprize ever incident to a good government well administered. Remember what your situation was immediately before the establishment of the present constitution. Were you then deficient in industry more than now? If not, why were you not equally prosperous? Plainly because your industry had not at that time the vivifying influences of an efficient, and well conducted government."

https://founders.archives.gov/documents/Hamilton/01-25-02-0197

"The Examination," No. 18, 4/8/1802: "In the view given of the very flourishing state of our finances, the worst of the calumnies against those men is refuted, and it is admitted, that in this article of vital importance to the public welfare, their measures have been provident and effectual beyond example. To the charge of a design to saddle the nation with a perpetual debt, a plain contradiction is given by the concession, that the provisions which have been made for it are so ample, as even to justify the relinquishment of a part no less considerable than the whole of the internal revenue. The same proposal testifies the brilliant success of our fiscal system generally; and that it is more than equal to all that has been undertaken, to all that has been promised to the nation.

"The report of the Secretary of the Treasury, as published, confirms this high commendation of the conduct of the former administrations. After relieving each state from the burden of its particular debt, by assuming the payment of it on account of the United States, in addition to the general debt of the nation; after settling the accounts between the states rela-

➢

tively to their exertions for the common defence in our revolutionary war, and providing for the balances found due to such of them as were creditors; after maintaining with complete success, an obstinate and expensive war with the Indian tribes; after making large disbursements for the suppression of two insurrections against the Government; after liberal contributions to the Barbary powers to induce them to open to our merchants the trade of the Mediterranean; after incurring a responsibility for indemnities to a large amount, due to British merchants, in consequence of infractions of the Treaty of peace by some of the states; after heavy expenditures for creating and supporting a navy and for other preparations, to guard our independence and territory against the hostilities of a foreign nation; after the accomplishment of all these very important objects, it is now declared to the United States by the present head of the Treasury, by the confidential minister of the present Chief Magistrate, the most subtil and implacable of the enemies of the former administrations, 'That the actual revenues of the Union are sufficient, to defray all the expences civil and military of Government, to the extent authorised by existing laws, to meet all the engagements of the united states; and to discharge in fifteen years and a half, the whole of our public debt'—foreign as well as domestic, new as well as old. Let it be understood, that the revenues spoken of were all provided under the two first administrations; and that the 'existing laws' alluded to, were all passed under the same administrations; consequently, that the revenues had not been increased, nor the expences diminished by the men who now hold the reins: and then let it be asked, whether so splendid a result does not reflect the highest credit on those, who in times past, have managed the affairs of the Nation? Does not the picture furnish matter not only for consolation, but even for exultation to every true friend of his country? And amidst the joy which he must feel in the contemplation, can he be so unjust as to refuse the tribute of commendation to those, by whose labors his country has been placed on so fair an eminence? Will he endure to see any part of the fruits of those labors blasted or hazarded, by a voluntary surrender of any portion of the means which are to insure the advantages of so bright a prospect?

"In vain will envy or malevolence reply, 'The happy situation in which we are placed is to be attributed not to the labors of those who have heretofore conducted our affairs, but to an unforeseen and unexpected progress of our country.' Candor and truth will answer—Praise is always due to public men who take their measures in such a manner as to derive to the nation the benefit of favorable circumstances which are possible, as well as of those which are foreseen."

https://founders.archives.gov/documents/Hamilton/01-25-02-0316

CHAPTER 9

Evaluation of Hamilton's programs

Back in Chapter 1, I said I would argue that Hamilton created his financial programs based on his understanding of the Constitution, plus his own observations, principles, experience, and knowledge. I set out to show how his programs were integrated with each other—a major factor in their success. And I promised to demonstrate that Hamilton's aim in proposing these programs was first, to promote a federal government that was limited, but energetic enough to protect rights; and second, to promote a diverse economy run by individuals pursuing their own interests and happiness.

Let's circle back and see where we are with those promises.

9.1 THE BASIS OF HAMILTON'S PROGRAMS

By the time he was nominated for secretary of the Treasury in 1789, Hamilton's background included being a businessman, soldier, government bureaucrat, and political leader. Not only did he perform those jobs, but he was also eager to think about how to perform them in the best possible way. He delved into books on economics, finance, and politics. He formulated his own ideas. Then he shared his knowledge with others, in a flood of publications and correspondence, ranging from "Full Vindication" in 1774, to his 1781 letter to Robert Morris, to the *Federalist Papers* in 1787-1788.

In years of poring over writings by the Founding Fathers, I've never seen anyone else who had this type of knowledge combined with such a drive to communicate it. In this respect, he was unique among the Founding Fathers.

9.2. INTEGRATION OF HAMILTON'S PROGRAMS

Hamilton's assignment as secretary of the Treasury was to deal with inadequate government revenue and massive government debt—the fourth and fifth threads of our Gordian Knot. But he had been thinking for years about the other three threads as well: making a living, the centrifugal force of the states, and money in circulation. From long study, he knew these issues were so intertwined that solving only two of them would have been impossible.

And contrariwise, he knew the right programs could help solve several issues at once. Arranging payment of government debt gave "lost" money back to American citizens, who could use it to help make a living. The citizens produced more and traded more. That brought the government more revenue from import duties and excise taxes. More revenue allowed the federal government consistently to perform duties such as protecting the frontier. The protection of the frontier by the military made it more obvious to citizens that the federal government was deserving of their support. With the cooperation of its citizens, the federal government was in a position to negotiate treaties with foreign powers, which gave its citizens better terms for trading abroad, and protected American shipping. Trading abroad brought more gold and silver into the country, increasing money in circulation. And so on, and so on, and so on.

To use a modern catch-phrase, Hamilton's programs created a "virtuous cycle". Integration wasn't an add-on feature of Hamilton's programs. It was essential, designed into them.

9.3. BROAD AIMS OF HAMILTON'S PROGRAMS

9.3.1 A federal government strong enough to protect rights

To anyone who lived through the 1780s in the United States, the close connection between government revenue and protection of the rights of American citizens was obvious. The Confederation government was weak. Rather than commanding revenue, it had to request that the states give it money. Chronically short of funds, it had no funds to pay an army. Hence its citizens were subject to attack by Indians, who were often given arms and encouragement by Great Britain and Spain. Foreign powers saw that the federal government under the Confederation was too weak to rein in the separate states. During the 1780s, no treaties were signed with foreign powers, except the one ending the Revolutionary War.

As I noted in Chapter 1, Americans in the 1780s had no party platform listing what they expected their government to achieve. The closest we can come is listing the opposite of the complaints made in the Declaration of Independence.

1. They wanted to elect their own representatives, and they wanted them to make laws that fit the situation of Americans.

2. When they had a dispute, they wanted a functioning system of courts and judges.

3. They wanted a military that protected them against attacks, but didn't elevate itself above the civilian authorities.

4. They wanted to keep what they produced, not have it taxed away without their consent.

5. They wanted to trade with whomever they pleased.

By the end of the 1790s, all those desires were being fulfilled. In part that was, of course, because the Constitution was in operation, with fully functional executive, legislative, and judicial branches, and a system of checks and balances between the branches. But the government was functional and <u>more energetic</u> in part because the Constitution gave it the power to collect its own revenue. This was the balance of liberty and power that Hamilton spoke of at the New York Ratifying Convention in

---

<u>More energetic</u>: Hamilton uses the term "energetic" of the federal government in the first Federalist essay: "I propose in a series of papers to discuss the following interesting particulars—The utility of the UNION to your political prosperity—The insufficiency of the present Confederation to preserve that Union—The necessity of a government at least equally energetic with the one proposed to the attainment of this object—The conformity of the proposed constitution to the true principles of republican government—Its analogy to your own state constitution—and lastly, The additional security, which its adoption will afford to the preservation of that species of government, to liberty and to property." For more on Hamilton as a proponent of an energetic government, see Carson Calloway, "The Myth of Hamiltonian Big Government": "The aim of the Constitution, then, is to create a government that is both energetic but also limited. And Hamilton's career reminds us that this is what we should want: a government that energetically executes its proper functions but does not go beyond them."
https://founders.archives.gov/documents/Hamilton/01-04-02-0152 and https://www.dailysignal.com/2015/04/23/the-myth-of-hamiltonian-big-government/

1788. (See §3.9.) Hamilton's programs ensured that the government's revenue was collected and used efficiently. They also allowed the new government to survive long enough to be tried and tested.

That was an enormous achievement. No other Founding Father had the practical knowledge, the economic knowledge, and the inclination to do it better.

9.3.2 A diverse economy run by individual choices

When Hamilton came to office, more than 80% of Americans were farmers. The programs he instituted were certainly beneficial to them. For example: treaties with Great Britain and Spain clarified where Americans could settle. The farmers who were pushing the frontier west now had a government with adequate revenue to provide some military garrisons that helped prevent skirmishes with the Indians. Increased money in circulation meant that if farmers needed to borrow money, interest rates were lower. Uniform commercial regulations meant that trading produce with other states or with foreign countries was considerably less complicated.

But Hamilton believed—and persuaded others to agree—that for the United States to thrive, it needed an economy that included manufacturing and trade as well as agriculture. A diverse economy did not only benefit individuals (see §8.5.4). It led to economic independence, which was closely related to political independence:

> Not only the wealth; but the independence and security of a Country, appear to be materially connected with the prosperity of manufactures. Every nation, with a view to those great objects, ought to endeavour to possess within itself all the essentials of national supply. These comprise the means of Subsistence habitation clothing and defence. The possession of these is necessary to the perfection of the body politic, to the safety as well as to the welfare of the society; the want of either, is the want of an important organ of political life and Motion; and in the various crises which await a state, it must severely feel the effects of any such deficiency.

In 1800, 83% of Americans worked on farms. The number held at that level through 1810, but by 1820 began dropping steadily, down to 53% by 1860. No one was forcing those people to move off the farm

---

Not only the wealth: *Report on Manufactures,* 12/6/1791; see Appendix 3, §III.B.

83% of Americans: "Agriculture." Digital History ID 3837.
https://www.digitalhistory.uh.edu/disp_textbook.cfm?smtID=11&psid=3837

and take up other jobs. They were freely choosing to do so.

Hamilton was the only Founding Father who constantly and vocally advocated a diversified economy, and was in a position influential enough to make his advocacy count. His programs as secretary of the Treasury played an essential role in the expansion of the United States from an agricultural economy to an economy that included industry and manufacturing. More money in circulation and greater prosperity led to an increase in savings, which meant more capital for investment in such enterprises. And on that subject ...

9.3.3 Protection of rights plus individual economic choices leads to accumulation of wealth

In *Hamilton Unbound*, Robert E. Wright has a brilliant discussion of how protection of rights leads to wealth. (Adam Smith said it earlier, but Wright's formulation really struck home with me.) The two requirements for the accumulation of wealth are that the government not be predatory (does not confiscate wealth), and that it protects its citizens' rights to property. If those two requirements are fulfilled, citizens expect that what they earn or create will be theirs to keep. They will invent and invest. How the individual citizens create wealth doesn't matter: it could be anything from plows to iPhones.

The government established under the Constitution protected individual rights. The financial programs established by Hamilton—efficient in collection and in spending—guaranteed that the government took limited amounts from its citizens. The creation of wealth soon followed. An eminent scholar of American economic history describes the progress:

> During the Revolutionary War, productivity fell off and remained relatively low during the Confederation period. Then it appears to have risen rapidly during the 1790's, so that by the first five or six years of the new century the average level of living was about where it had been in the early 1770's. Conditions continued good to 1807; but thereafter embargoes, non-intercourse acts, and the War of 1812 definitely depressed living standards.

Protection of rights: Wright, *Hamilton Unbound*, pp. 123-124.

During the Revolutionary War: George Rogers Taylor, "American Economic Growth Before 1840: An Exploratory Essay," *Journal of Economic History*, XXIV:4 (1964), p. 437.

9.4. WHY HAMILTON'S PROGRAMS LASTED

To their intense exasperation, Hamilton's opponents, including President Jefferson, soon realized that they couldn't eliminate any element of Hamilton's system without upsetting the balance of the others. The programs were too well integrated. And overall, the system worked too well for people to want it dismantled. Hamilton's programs remained in place after the Federalists were out of power because they allowed people who cared nothing about politics to make a living and even prosper.

In 1795, a few months after he left office, Hamilton summarized the effects of his funding system on trade, agriculture, manufacturing, transportation, insurance, and settlement of the frontier:

> Whoever will impartially look around will see that the great body of the new Capital created by the Stock has been employed in extending commerce, agriculture, manufactures, and other improvements. Our own real navigation has been much increased. Our external commerce is carried on much more upon our own capitals than it was—our marine insurances in a much greater proportion are made by ourselves. Our manufactures are increased in number and carried on upon a larger scale. Settlements of our waste land are progressing with more vigour than at any former period. Our Cities and Towns are increasing rapidly by the addition of new and better houses. Canals are opening, bridges are building with more spirit & effect than was ever known at a former period. The value of lands has risen every where.
>
> These circumstances (though other causes may have cooperated) it cannot be doubted by a well informed or candid man are imputable in a great degree to the increase of Capital in public Debt and they prove that the predictions of its dissipation in luxurious extravagances have not been verified.

9.5 NOT A MIRACLE

You've probably read Daniel Webster's comment that Hamilton "smote the rock of the national resources, and abundant streams of revenue gushed forth. He touched the dead corpse of the public credit, and it sprang upon its feet." It's a vivid metaphor ... but I never got a

---

Whoever will: Hamilton, "Defence of the Funding System," July 1795

https://founders.archives.gov/documents/Hamilton/01-19-02-0001

sense from it of what Hamilton had actually done. While researching this book, I happened to come across Webster's whole speech. In context, Webster's words make much more sense. Speaking in 1831 to a group of New Yorkers, he said:

> All these local advantages, and all this enlightened state policy, could never have made your city what it now is, without the aid and protection of a general government, extending over all the States, and establishing for all a common and uniform system of commercial regulation. Without national character, without public credit, without systematic finance, without uniformity of commercial laws, all other advantages possessed by this city would have decayed and perished, like unripe fruit. ...
>
> The discerning eye of Washington immediately called [Hamilton] to that post, which was far the most important in the administration of the new system. He was made Secretary of the Treasury; and how he fulfilled the duties of such a place, at such a time, the whole country perceived with delight and the whole world saw with admiration. He smote the rock of the national resources, and abundant streams of revenue gushed forth. He touched the dead corpse of the public credit, and it sprang upon its feet. The fabled birth of Minerva from the brain of Jove was hardly more sudden or more perfect than the financial system of the United States, as it burst forth from the conceptions of Alexander Hamilton.

The only part of this I disagree with is the suggestion that Alexander Hamilton performed a miracle or had a sudden inspiration about what to do. What he accomplished was the result of a lifetime of working,

---

All these local: Webster, Speech at a public dinner at New York, 3/10/1831, from *The Writings and Speeches of Daniel Webster*, vol. 2 (1903), pp. 48-50.

https://babel.hathitrust.org/cgi/pt?id=umn.31951d00641433p&view=1up&seq=74&q1=smote

of reading, of observing, of discussing, of writing, of persuading. So, while Webster's description is thrilling, I prefer that of John Marshall, written four years after Hamilton's death:

> To talents of the highest grade, he united a patient industry, not always the companion of genius, which fitted him in a peculiar manner for the difficulties to be encountered by the man who should be placed at the head of the American finances.

To talents: John Marshall, *Life of Washington*, 1808, pp. 339-340.
https://tinyurl.com/6ebmcbbf

APPENDIX 1

First Report on Public Credit

Full title:
Report Relative to a Provision for the Support of Public Credit

https://founders.archives.gov/documents/Hamilton/01-06-02-0076-0002-0001
(modern editorial notes not included)

Treasury Department, January 9, 1790.
Communicated on January 14, 1790]
[To the Speaker of the House of Representatives]

I. INTRODUCTION TO THE *First Report*

The Secretary of the Treasury, in obedience to the resolution of the House of Representatives, of the twenty-first day of September last, has, during the recess of Congress, applied himself to the consideration of a proper plan for the support of the Public Credit, with all the attention which was due to the authority of the House, and to the magnitude of the object.

In the discharge of this duty, he has felt, in no small degree, the anxieties which naturally flow from a just estimate of the difficulty of the task, from a well-founded diffidence of his own qualifications for executing it with success, and from a deep and solemn conviction of the momentous nature of the truth contained in the resolution under which his investigations have been conducted, "That an *adequate* provision for the support of the Public Credit, is a matter of high importance to the honor and prosperity of the United States."

With an ardent desire that his well-meant endeavors may be conducive to the real advantage of the nation, and with the utmost deference to the superior judgment of the House, he now respectfully submits the result of his enquiries and reflections, to their indulgent construction.

In the opinion of the Secretary, the wisdom of the House, in giving their explicit sanction to the proposition which has been stated, cannot but be applauded by all, who will seriously consider, and trace through their obvious consequences, these plain and undeniable truths.

II. MAINTAINING GOOD CREDIT

II. A. The U.S. might need to borrow in the future.

That exigencies are to be expected to occur, in the affairs of nations, in which there will be a necessity for borrowing.

That loans in times of public danger, especially from foreign war, are found an indispensable resource, even to the wealthiest of them.

And that in a country, which, like this, is possessed of little active wealth, or in other words, little monied capital, the necessity for that resource, must, in such emergencies, be proportionably urgent.

And as on the one hand, the necessity for borrowing in particular emergencies cannot be doubted, so on the other, it is equally evident, that to be able to borrow upon *good terms*, it is essential that the credit of a nation should be well established.

For when the credit of a country is in any degree questionable, it never fails to give an extravagant premium, in one shape or another, upon all the loans it has occasion to make. Nor does the evil end here; the same disadvantage must be sustained upon whatever is to be bought on terms of future payment.

From this constant necessity of *borrowing* and *buying dear*, it is easy to conceive how immensely the expences of a nation, in a course of time, will be augmented by an unsound state of the public credit.

To attempt to enumerate the complicated variety of mischiefs in the whole system of the social œconomy, which proceed from a neglect of the maxims that uphold public credit, and justify the solicitude manifested by the House on this point, would be an improper intrusion on their time and patience.

In so strong a light nevertheless do they appear to the Secretary, that on their due observance at the present critical juncture, materially depends, in his judgment, the individual and aggregate prosperity of the citizens of the United States; their relief from the embarrassments they now experience; their character as a People; the cause of good government.

II. B. How does one maintain credit so one can borrow on good terms?

If the maintenance of public credit, then, be truly so important, the next enquiry which suggests itself is, by what means it is to be effected? The ready answer to which question is, by good faith, by a punctual performance of contracts. States, like individuals, who observe their engagements, are respected and trusted: while the reverse is the fate of those, who pursue an opposite conduct.

Every breach of the public engagements, whether from choice or necessity, is in different degrees hurtful to public credit. When such a necessity does truly exist, the evils of it are only to be palliated by a scrupulous attention, on the part of the government, to carry the violation no farther than the necessity absolutely requires, and to manifest, if the nature of the case admits of it, a sincere disposition to make reparation, whenever circumstances shall permit. But with every possible mitigation, credit must suffer, and numerous mischiefs ensue. It is therefore highly important, when an appearance of necessity seems to press upon the public councils, that they should examine well its reality, and be perfectly assured, that there is no method of escaping from it, before they yield to its suggestions. For though it cannot safely be affirmed, that occasions have never existed, or may not exist, in which violations of the public faith, in this respect, are inevitable; yet there is great reason to believe, that they exist far less frequently than precedents indicate; and are oftenest either pretended through levity, or want of firmness, or supposed through want of knowledge. Expedients might often have been devised to effect, consistently with good faith, what has been done in contravention of it. Those who are most commonly creditors of a nation, are, generally speaking, enlightened men; and there are signal examples to warrant a conclusion, that when a candid and fair appeal is made to them, they will understand their true interest too well to refuse their concurrence in such modifications of their claims, as any real necessity may demand.

III. WHY SHOULD WE FUND THE DEBT?

III. A. Good faith in paying debts is a moral obligation, especially for the U.S.

While the observance of that good faith, which is the basis of public credit, is recommended by the strongest inducements of political expediency, it is enforced by considerations of still greater authority. There are arguments for it, which rest on the immutable principles of moral obligation. And in proportion as the mind is disposed to contemplate, in the order of Providence, an intimate connection between public virtue and public happiness, will be its repugnancy to a violation of those principles.

This reflection derives additional strength from the nature of the debt of the United States. It was the price of liberty. The faith of America has been repeatedly pledged for it, and with solemnities, that give peculiar force to the obligation. There is indeed reason to regret that it has not hitherto been kept; that the necessities of the war, conspiring with inexperience in the subjects of finance, produced direct infractions; and that the subsequent period has been a continued scene of negative violation, or non-compliance. But a diminution of this regret arises from the reflection, that the last seven years have exhibited an earnest and uniform effort, on the part of the government of the union, to retrieve the national credit, by doing justice to the creditors of the nation; and that the embarrassments of a defective constitution, which defeated this laudable effort, have ceased.

From this evidence of a favorable disposition, given by the former government, the institution of a new one, cloathed with powers competent to calling forth the resources of the community, has excited correspondent expectations. A general belief, accordingly, prevails, that the credit of the United States will quickly be established on the firm foundation of an effectual provision for the existing debt. The influence, which this has had at home, is witnessed by the rapid increase, that has taken place in the market value of the public securities. From January to November, they rose thirty-three and a third per cent, and from that period to this time, they have risen fifty per cent more. And the intelligence from abroad announces effects proportionably favourable to our national credit and consequence.

It cannot but merit particular attention, that among ourselves the most enlightened friends of good government are those, whose expectations are the highest.

III. B. Obvious benefits of funding the debt

To justify and preserve their confidence; to promote the encreasing respectability of the American name; to answer the calls of justice; to restore landed property to its due value; to furnish new resources both to agriculture and commerce; to cement more closely the union of the states; to add to their security against foreign attack; to establish public order on the basis of an upright and liberal policy. These are the great and invaluable ends to be secured, by a proper and adequate provision, at the present period, for the support of public credit.

To this provision we are invited, not only by the general considerations, which have been noticed, but by others of a more particular nature. It will procure to every class of the community some important advantages, and remove some no less important disadvantages.

The advantage to the public creditors from the increased value of that part of their property which constitutes the public debt, needs no explanation.

III. C. Less obvious benefits of funding the debt: use of IOUs as money, supplementing gold and silver

But there is a consequence of this, less obvious, though not less true, in which every other citizen is interested. It is a well known fact, that in countries in which the national debt is properly funded, and an object of established confidence, it answers most of the purposes of money. Transfers of stock or public debt are there equivalent to payments in specie; or in other words, stock, in the principal transactions of business, passes current as specie. The same thing would, in all probability happen here, under the like circumstances.

The benefits of this are various and obvious.

First. Trade is extended by it; because there is a larger capital to carry it on, and the merchant can at the same time, afford to trade for smaller profits; as his stock, which, when unemployed, brings him in an interest from the government, serves him also as money, when he has a call for it in his commercial operations.

Secondly. Agriculture and manufactures are also promoted by it: For the like reason, that more capital can be commanded to be employed in both; and because the merchant, whose enterprize in foreign trade, gives to them activity and extension, has greater means for enterprize.

Thirdly. The interest of money will be lowered by it; for this is always in a ratio, to the quantity of money, and to the quickness of circulation. This circumstance will enable both the public and individuals to borrow on easier and cheaper terms.

And from the combination of these effects, additional aids will be furnished to labour, to industry, and to arts of every kind.

But these good effects of a public debt are only to be looked for, when, by being well funded, it has acquired an *adequate* and *stable* value. Till then, it has rather a contrary tendency. The fluctuation and insecurity incident to it in an unfunded state, render it a mere commodity, and a precarious one. As such, being only an object of occasional and particular speculation, all the money applied to it is so much diverted from the more useful channels of circulation, for which the thing itself affords no substitute: So that, in fact, one serious inconvenience of an unfunded debt is, that it contributes to the scarcity of money.

This distinction which has been little if at all attended to, is of the greatest moment. It involves a question immediately interesting to every part of the community; which is no other than this—Whether the public debt, by a provision for it on true principles, shall be rendered a *substitute* for money; or whether, by being left as it is, or by being provided for in such a manner as will wound those principles, and destroy confidence, it shall be suffered to continue, as it is, a pernicious drain of our cash from the channels of productive industry.

III. D. Less obvious benefits of funding the debt: Increasing the value of land

The effect, which the funding of the public debt, on right principles, would have upon landed property, is one of the circumstances attending such an arrangement, which has been least adverted to, though it deserves the most particular attention. The present depreciated state of that species of property is a serious calamity. The value of cultivated lands, in most of the states, has fallen since the revolution from 25 to 50 per cent. In those farthest south, the decrease is still more considerable. Indeed, if the representations, continually received from that quarter, may be credited, lands there will command no price, which may not be deemed an almost total sacrifice.

This decrease, in the value of lands, ought, in a great measure, to be attributed to the scarcity of money. Consequently whatever produces an augmentation of the monied capital of the country, must have a proportional effect in raising that value. The beneficial tendency of a funded debt, in this respect, has been manifested by the most decisive experience in Great-Britain.

The proprietors of lands would not only feel the benefit of this increase in the value of their property, and of a more prompt and better sale, when they had occasion to sell; but the necessity of selling would be, itself, greatly diminished. As the same cause would contribute to the facility of loans, there is reason to believe, that such of them as are indebted, would be able through that resource, to satisfy their more urgent creditors.

III.E. When will the benefits of funding the debt happen?

It ought not however to be expected, that the advantages, described as likely to result from funding the public debt, would be instantaneous. It might require some time to bring the value of stock to its natural level, and to attach to it that fixed confidence, which is necessary to its quality as money. Yet the late rapid rise of the public securities encourages an expectation, that the progress of stock to the desireable point, will be much more expeditious than could have been foreseen. And as in the mean time it will be increasing in value, there is room to conclude, that it will, from the outset, answer many of the purposes in contemplation. Particularly it seems to be probable, that from creditors, who are not themselves necessitous, it will early meet with a ready reception in payment of debts, at its current price.

IV. PRELIMINARY ISSUES REGARDING FUNDING THE DEBT

Having now taken a concise view of the inducements to a proper provision for the public debt, the next enquiry which presents itself is, what ought to be the nature of such a provision? This requires some preliminary discussions.

It is agreed on all hands, that that part of the debt which has been contracted abroad, and is denominated the foreign debt, ought to be provided for, according to the precise terms of the contracts relating to it. The discussions, which can arise, therefore, will have reference essentially to the domestic part of it, or to that which has been contracted at home. It is to be regretted, that there is not the same unanimity of sentiment on this part, as on the other.

IV. A. Preliminary issues re funding the debt: Discrimination

The Secretary has too much deference for the opinions of every part of the community, not to have observed one, which has, more than once, made its appearance in the public prints, and which is occasionally to be met with in conversation. It involves this question, whether a discrimination ought not to be made between original holders of the public securities, and present possessors, by purchase. Those who advocate a discrimination are for making a full provision for the securities of the former, at their nominal value; but contend, that the latter ought to receive no more than the cost to them, and the interest: And the idea is sometimes suggested of making good the difference to the primitive possessor.

In favor of this scheme, it is alledged, that it would be unreasonable to pay twenty shillings in the pound, to one who had not given more for it than three or four. And it is added, that it would be hard to aggravate the misfortune of the first owner, who, probably through necessity, parted with his property at so great a loss, by obliging him to contribute to the profit of the person, who had speculated on his distresses.

IV. A. 1. First argument against discrimination: Breach of contract

The Secretary, after the most mature reflection on the force of this argument, is induced to reject the doctrine it contains, as equally unjust and impolitic, as highly injurious, even to the original holders of public securities; as ruinous to public credit.

It is inconsistent with justice, because in the first place, it is a breach of contract; in violation of the rights of a fair purchaser.

The nature of the contract in its origin, is, that the public will pay the sum expressed in the security, to the first holder, or his *assignee*. The *intent*, in making the security assignable, is, that the proprietor may be able to make use of his property, by selling it for as much as it *may be worth in the market*, and that the buyer may be *safe* in the purchase.

Every buyer therefore stands exactly in the place of the seller, has the same right with him to the identical sum expressed in the security, and having acquired that right, by fair purchase, and in conformity to the original *agreement* and *intention* of the government, his claim cannot be disputed, without manifest injustice.

That he is to be considered as a fair purchaser, results from this: Whatever necessity the seller may have been under, was occasioned by the government, in not making a proper provision for its debts. The buyer had no agency in it, and therefore ought not to suffer. He is not even chargeable with having taken an undue advantage. He paid what the commodity was worth in the market, and took the risks of reimbursement upon himself. He of course gave a fair equivalent, and ought to reap the benefit of his hazard; a hazard which was far from inconsiderable, and which, perhaps, turned on little less than a revolution in government.

That the case of those, who parted with their securities from necessity, is a hard one, cannot be denied. But whatever complaint of injury, or claim of redress, they may have, respects the government solely.

They have not only nothing to object to the persons who relieved their necessities, by giving them the current price of their property, but they are even under an implied condition to contribute to the reimbursement of those persons. They knew, that by the terms of the contract with themselves, the public were bound to pay to those, to whom they should convey their title, the sums stipulated to be paid to them; and, that as citizens of the United States, they were to bear their proportion of the contribution for that purpose. This, by the act of assignment, they tacitly engage to do; and if they had an option, they could not, with integrity or good faith, refuse to do it, without the consent of those to whom they sold.

But though many of the original holders sold from necessity, it does not follow, that this was the case with all of them. It may well be supposed, that some of them did it either through want of confidence in an eventual provision, or from the allurements of some profitable speculation. How shall these different classes be discriminated from each other? How shall it be ascertained, in any case, that the money, which the original holder obtained for his security, was not more beneficial to him, than if he had held it to the pressent time, to avail himself of the provision which shall be made? How shall it be known, whether if the purchaser had employed his money in some other way, he would not be in a better situation, than by having applied it in the purchase of securities, though he should now receive their full amount? And if neither of these things can be known, how shall it be determined whether a discrimination, independent of the breach of contract, would not do a real injury to purchasers; and if it included a compensation to the primitive proprietors, would not give them an advantage, to which they had no equitable pretension.

It may well be imagined, also, that there are not wanting instances, in which individuals, urged by a present necessity, parted with the securities received by them from the public, and shortly after replaced them with others, as an indemnity for their first loss. Shall they be deprived of the indemnity which they have endeavoured to secure by so provident an arrangement?

Questions of this sort, on a close inspection, multiply themselves without end, and demonstrate the injustice of a discrimination, even on the most subtile calculations of equity, abstracted from the obligation of contract.

IV. A. 2. Second argument against discrimination: Difficulties of settling accounts

The difficulties too of regulating the details of a plan for that purpose, which would have even the semblance of equity, would be found immense. It may well be doubted whether they would not be insurmountable, and replete with such absurd, as well as inequitable consequences, as to disgust even the proposers of the measure.

As a specimen of its capricious operation, it will be sufficient to notice the effect it would have upon two persons, who may be supposed two years ago to have purchased, each, securities at three shillings in the pound, and one of them to retain those bought by him, till the discrimination should take place; the other to have parted with those bought by him, within a month past, at nine shillings. The former, who had had most confidence in the government, would in this case only receive at the rate of three shillings and the interest; while the latter, who had had less confidence would receive *for what cost him the same money* at the rate of nine shillings, and his representative, *standing in his place*, would be entitled to a like rate.

IV. A. 3. Third argument against discrimination: Bonds will not be able to circulate as money

The impolicy of a discrimination results from two considerations; one, that it proceeds upon a principle destructive of that *quality* of the public debt, or the stock of the nation, which is essential to its capacity for answering the purposes of money—that is the *security* of *transfer;* the other, that as well on this account, as because it includes a breach of faith, it renders property in the funds less valuable; consequently induces lenders to demand a higher premium for what they lend, and produces every other inconvenience of a bad state of public credit.

It will be perceived at first sight, that the transferable quality of stock is essential to its operation as money, and that this depends on the idea of complete security to the transferree, and a firm persuasion, that no distinction can in any circumstances be made between him and the original proprietor.

The precedent of an invasion of this fundamental principle, would of course tend to deprive the community of an advantage, with which no temporary saving could bear the least comparison.

IV. A. 4. Fourth argument against discrimination: The value of all bonds will be diminished.

And it will as readily be perceived, that the same cause would operate a diminution of the value of stock in the hands of the first, as well as of every other holder. The price, which any man, who should incline to purchase, would be willing to give for it, would be in a compound ratio to the immediate profit it afforded, and to the chance of the continuance of his profit. If there was supposed to be any hazard of the latter, the risk would be taken into the calculation, and either there would be no purchase at all, or it would be at a proportionably less price.

For this diminution of the value of stock, every person, who should be about to lend to the government, would demand a compensation; and would add to the actual difference, between the nominal and the market value, and equivalent for the chance of greater decrease; which, in a precarious state of public credit, is always to be taken into the account.

Every compensation of this sort, it is evident, would be an absolute loss to the government.

In the preceding discussion of the impolicy of a discrimination, the injurious tendency of it to those, who continue to be the holders of the securities, they received from the government, has been explained. Nothing need be added, on this head, except that this is an additional and interesting light, in which the injustice of the measure may be seen. It would not only divest present proprietors by purchase, of the rights they had acquired under the sanction of public faith, but it would depreciate the property of the remaining original holders.

It is equally unnecessary to add any thing to what has been already said to demonstrate the fatal influence, which the principle of discrimination would have on the public credit.

IV. A. 5. Fifth argument against discrimination: The Constitution forbids it.

But there is still a point in view in which it will appear perhaps even more exceptionable, than in either of the former. It would be repugnant to an express provision of the Constitution of the United States. This provision is, that "all debts contracted and engagements entered into before the adoption of that Constitution shall be as valid against the United States under it, as under the confederation." which amounts to a constitutional ratification of the contracts respecting the debt, in the state in which they existed under the confederation. And resorting to that standard, there can be no doubt, that the rights of assignees and original holders, must be considered as equal.

In exploding thus fully the principle of discrimination, the Secretary is happy in reflecting, that he is the only advocate of what has been already sanctioned by the formal and express authority of the government of the Union, in these emphatic terms—"The remaining class of creditors (say Congress in their circular address to the states, of the 26th of April 1783) is composed, partly of such of our fellow-citizens as originally lent to the public the use of their funds, or have since manifested *most confidence* in their country, by receiving transfers from the lenders; and partly of those, whose property has been either advanced or assumed for the public service. To *discriminate* the merits of these several descriptions of creditors, would be a task equally unnecessary and invidious. If the voice of humanity plead more loudly in favor of some than of others, the voice of policy, no less than of justice, pleads in favor of all. A WISE NATION will never permit those who relieve the wants of their country, or who *rely most* on its *faith*, its *firmness*, and its *resources*, when either of them is distrusted, to suffer by the event."

The Secretary concluding, that a discrimination, between the different classes of creditors of the United States, cannot with propriety be *made*, proceeds to examine whether a difference ought to be permitted to *remain* between them, and another description of public creditors—Those of the states individually.

IV. B. Preliminary issues re funding the debt: Assumption

The Secretary, after mature reflection on this point, entertains a full conviction, that an assumption of the debts of the particular states by the union, and a like provision for them, as for those of the union, will be a measure of sound policy and substantial justice.

IV. B. 1. First argument in favor of assumption: The states will not have to compete with the federal government for revenue.

It would, in the opinion of the Secretary, contribute, in an eminent degree, to an orderly, stable and satisfactory arrangement of the national finances.

Admitting, as ought to be the case, that a provision must be made in some way or other, for the entire debt; it will follow, that no greater revenues will be required, whether that provision be made wholly by the United States, or partly by them, and partly by the states separately.

The principal question then must be, whether such a provision cannot be more conveniently and effectually made, by one general plan issuing from one authority, than by different plans originating in different authorities.

In the first case there can be no competition for resources; in the last, there must be such a competition. The consequences of this, without the greatest caution on both sides, might be interfering regulations, and thence collision and confusion. Particular branches of industry might also be oppressed by it. The most productive objects of revenue are not numerous. Either these must be wholly engrossed by one side, which might lessen the efficacy of the provisions by the other; or both must have recourse to the same objects in different modes, which might occasion an accumulation upon them, beyond what they could properly bear. If this should not happen, the caution requisite to avoiding it, would prevent the revenue's deriving the full benefit of each object. The danger of interference and of excess would be apt to impose restraints very unfriendly to the complete command of those resources, which are the most convenient; and to compel the having recourse to others, less eligible in themselves, and less agreeable to the community.

The difficulty of an effectual command of the public resources, in case of separate provisions for the debt, may be seen in another, and perhaps more striking light. It would naturally happen that different states, from local considerations, would in some instances have recourse to different objects, in others, to the same objects, in different degrees, for procuring the funds of which they stood in need. It is easy to conceive how this diversity would affect the aggregate revenue of the country. By the supposition, articles which yielded a full supply in some states, would yield nothing, or an insufficient product, in others. And hence the public revenue would not derive the full benefit of those articles, from state regulations. Neither could the deficiencies be made good by those of the union. It is a provision of the national constitution, that "all duties, imposts and excises, shall be uniform throughout the United States." And as the general government would be under a necessity from motives of policy, of paying regard to the duty, which may have been previously imposed upon any article, though but in a single state, it would be constrained, either to refrain wholly from any further imposition, upon such article, where it had been already rated as high as was proper, or to confine itself to the difference between the existing rate, and what the article would reasonably bear. Thus the pre-occupancy of an article by a single state, would tend to arrest or abridge the impositions of the union on that article. And as it is supposeable, that a great variety of articles might be placed in this situation, by dissimilar arrangements of the particular states, it is evident, that the aggregate revenue of the country would be likely to be very materially contracted by the plan of separate provisions.

If all the public creditors receive their dues from one source, distributed with an equal hand, their interest will be the same. And having the same interests, they will unite in the support of the fiscal arrangements of the government: As these, too, can be made with more convenience, where there is no competition: These circumstances combined will insure to the revenue laws a more ready and more satisfactory execution.

If on the contrary there are distinct provisions, there will be distinct interests, drawing different ways. That union and concert of views, among the creditors, which in every government is of great importance to their security, and to that of public credit, will not only not exist, but will be likely to give place to mutual jealousy and opposition. And from this cause, the operation of the systems which may be adopted, both by the particular states, and by the union, with relation to their respective debts, will be in danger of being counteracted.

IV. B. 2. Second argument in favor of assumption: It's more fair to state creditors.

There are several reasons, which render it probable, that the situation of the state creditors would be worse, than that of the creditors of the union, if there be not a national assumption of the state debts. Of these it will be sufficient to mention two; one, that a principal branch of revenue is exclusively vested in the union; the other, that a state must always be checked in the imposition of taxes on articles of consumption, from the want of power to extend the same regulation to the other states, and from the tendency of partial duties to injure its industry and commerce. Should the state creditors stand upon a less eligible footing than the others, it is unnatural to expect they would see with pleasure a provision for them. The influence which their dissatisfaction might have, could not but operate injuriously, both for the creditors, and the credit, of the United States.

Hence it is even the interest of the creditors of the union, that those of the individual states should be comprehended in a general provision. Any attempt to secure to the former either exclusive or peculiar advantages, would materially hazard their interests.

Neither would it be just, that one class of the public creditors should be more favoured than the other. The objects for which both descriptions of the debt were contracted, are in the main the same.

Indeed a great part of the particular debts of the States has arisen from assumptions by them on account of the union. And it is most equitable, that there should be the same measure of retribution for all.

IV. B. 3. Third argument in favor of assumption: The states' debts can be equitably settled with the federal government.

There is an objection, however, to an assumption of the state debts, which deserves particular notice. It may be supposed, that it would increase the difficulty of an equitable settlement between them and the United States.

The principles of that settlement, whenever they shall be discussed, will require all the moderation and wisdom of the government. In the opinion of the Secretary, that discussion, till further lights are obtained, would be premature.

All therefore which he would now think adviseable on the point in question, would be, that the amount of the debts assumed and provided for, should be charged to the respective states, to abide an eventual arrangement. This, the United States, as assignees to the creditors, would have an indisputable right to do.

But as it might be a satisfaction to the House to have before them some plan for the liquidation of accounts between the union and its members, which, including the assumption of the state debts, would consist with equity: The Secretary will submit in this place such thoughts on the subject, as have occurred to his own mind, or been suggested to him, most compatible, in his judgment, with the end proposed.

Let each state be charged with all the money advanced to it out of the treasury of the United States, liquidated according to the specie value, at the time of each advance, with interest at six per cent.

Let it also be charged with the amount, in specie value, of all its securities which shall be assumed, with the interest upon them to the time, when interest shall become payable by the United States.

Let it be credited for all monies paid and articles furnished to the United States, and for all other expenditures during the war, either towards general or particular defence, whether authorized or unauthorized by the United States; the whole liquidated to specie value, and bearing an interest of six per cent. from the several times at which the several payments, advances and expenditures accrued.

And let all sums of continental money now in the treasuries of the respective states, which shall be paid into the treasury of the United States, be credited at specie value.

Upon a statement of the accounts according to these principles, there can be little doubt, that balances would appear in favor of all the states, against the United States.

To equalize the contributions of the states, let each be then charged with its proportion of the aggregate of those balances, according to some equitable ratio, to be devised for that purpose.

If the contributions should be found disproportionate, the result of this adjustment would be, that some states would be creditors, some debtors to the union.

Should this be the case, as it will be attended with less inconvenience for the United States, to have to pay balances to, than to receive them from the particular states, it may perhaps, be practicable to effect the former by a second process, in the nature of a transfer of the amount of the debts of debtor states, to the credit of creditor states, observing the ratio by which the first apportionment shall have been made. This, whilst it would destroy the balances due from the former, would increase those due to the latter. These to be provided for by the United States, at a reasonable interest, but not to be transferable.

The expediency of this second process must depend on a knowledge of the result of the first. If the inequalities should be too great, the arrangement may be impracticable, without unduly increasing the debt of the United States. But it is not likely, that this would be the case. It is also to be remarked, that though this second process might not, upon the principle of apportionment, bring the thing to the point aimed at, yet it may approach so nearly to it, as to avoid essentially the embarrassment, of having considerable balances to collect from any of the states.

The whole of this arrangment to be under the superintendence of commissioners, vested with equitable discretion, and final authority.

The operation of the plan is exemplified in the schedule A.

The general principle of it seems to be equitable, for it appears difficult to conceive a good reason, why the expences for the particular defence of a part in a common war, should not be a common charge, as well as those incurred professedly for the general defence. The defence of each part is that of the whole; and unless all the expenditures are brought into a common mass, the tendency must be, to add, to the calamities suffered, by being the most exposed to the ravages of war, an increase of burthens.

This plan seems to be susceptible of no objection, which does not belong to every other, that proceeds on the idea of a final adjustment of accounts. The difficulty of settling a ratio, is common to all. This must, probably, either be sought for in the proportions of the requisitions, during the war, or in the decision of commissioners appointed with plenary power. The rule prescribed in the Constitution, with regard to representation and direct taxes, would evidently not be applicable to the situation of parties, during the period in question.

The existing debt of the United States is excluded from the computation, as it ought to be, because it will be provided for out of a general fund.

IV. C. Preliminary issues re funding the debt: Paying principal vs. paying principal plus interest

The only discussion of a preliminary kind, which remains, relates to the distinctions of the debt into principal and interest. It is well known, that the arrears of the latter bear a large proportion to the amount of the former. The immediate payment of these arrears is evidently impracticable, and a question arises, what ought to be done with them?

There is good reason to conclude, that the impressions of many are more favorable to the claim of the principal than to that of the interest; at least so far, as to produce an opinion, that an inferior provision might suffice for the latter.

But to the Secretary, this opinion does not appear to be well founded. His investigations of the subject, have led him to a conclusion, that the arrears of interest have pretensions, at least equal to the principal.

IV. C. 1. Sources of the debt: Loans and IOUs for services and goods

The liquidated debt, traced to its origin, falls under two principal discriminations. One, relating to loans; the other to services performed and articles supplied.

The part arising from loans, was at first made payable at fixed periods, which have long since elapsed, with an early option to lenders, either to receive back their money at the expiration of those periods, or to continue it at interest, 'till the whole amount of continental bills circulating should not exceed the sum in circulation at the time of each loan. This contingency, in the sense of the contract, never happened; and the presumption is, that the creditors preferred continuing their money indefinitely at interest, to receiving it in a depreciated and depreciating state.

The other parts of it were chiefly for objects, which ought to have been paid for at the time, that is, when the services were performed or the supplies furnished; and were not accompanied with any contract for interest.

IV. C. 2. Debt without payment date can be considered as an annuity at 6%

But by different acts of government and administration, concurred in by the creditors, these parts of the debt have been converted into a capital, bearing an interest of six per cent. per annum, but without any definite period of redemption. A portion of the loan-office debt has been exchanged for new securities of that import. And the whole of it seems to have acquired that character, after the expiration of the periods prefixed for re-payment.

If this view of the subject be a just one, the capital of the debt of the United States, may be considered in the light of an annuity at the rate of six per cent. per annum, redeemable at the pleasure of the government, by payment of the principal. For it seems to be a clear position, that when a public contracts a debt payable with interest, without any precise time being stipulated or understood for payment of the capital, that time is a matter of pure discretion with the government, which is at liberty to consult its own convenience respecting it, taking care to pay the interest with punctuality.

Wherefore, as long as the United States should pay the interest of their debt, as it accrued, their creditors would have no right to demand the principal.

IV. C. 3. Arrears in interest are due *now*.

But with regard to the arrears of interest, the case is different. These are now due, and those to whom they are due, have a right to claim immediate payment. To say, that it would be impracticable to comply, would not vary the nature of the right. Nor can this idea of impracticability be honorably carried further, than to justify the proposition of a new contract upon the basis of a commutation of that right for an equivalent. This equivalent too ought to be a real and fair one. And what other fair equivalent can be imagined for the detention of money, but a reasonable interest? Or what can be the standard of that interest, but the market rate, or the rate which the government pays in ordinary cases?

From this view of the matter, which appears to be the accurate and true one, it will follow, that the arrears of interest are entitled to an equal provision with the principal of the debt.

The result of the foregoing discussions is this—That there ought to be no discrimination between the original holders of the debt, and present possessors by purchase—That it is expedient, there should be an assumption of the state debts by the Union, and that the arrears of interest should be provided for on an equal footing with the principal.

V. WHAT WE OWE

The next enquiry, in order, towards determining the nature of a proper provision, respects the quantum of the debt, and the present rates of interest.

V. A. What the federal government owes

The debt of the union is distinguishable into foreign and domestic.

	Dollars	*Cents*
The foreign debt as stated in the schedule B, amounts to principal bearing an interest of four, and partly an interest of five per cent.	10,070,307	
Arrears of interest to the last of December, 1789	1,640,071	62
Making together, dollars	11,710,378	62
The domestic debt may be sub-divided into liquidated and unliquidated; principal and interest.		
The principal of the liquidated part, as stated in schedule C, amounts to bearing an interest of six per cent.	27,383,917	74
The arrears of interst as stated in the schedule D. to the end of 1790, amount to	13,030,168	20
Making altogether, dollars	40,414,085	94

This includes all that has been paid in indents (except what has come into the treasury of the United States) which, in the opinion of the Secretary, can be considered in no other light, than as interest due.

The unliquidated part of the domestic debt, which consists chiefly of the continental bills of credit, is not ascertained, but may be estimated at 2,000,000 dollars.

These several sums constitute the whole of the debt of the United States, amounting together to 54,124,464 dollars, and 56 cents.

V. B. What the state governments owe

That of the individual states is not equally well ascertained. The schedule E. shews the extent to which it has been ascertained by returns pursuant to the order of the House of the 21st September last; but this not comprehending all the states, the residue must be estimated from less authentic information. The Secretary, however, presumes, that the total amount may be safely stated at 25 millions of dollars, principal and interest. The present rate of interest of the state debts is in general, the same with that of the domestic debt of the union.

On the supposition, that the arrears of interest ought to be provided for, on the same terms with the principal, the annual amount of the interest, which, at the existing rates, would be payable on the entire mass of the public debt, would be,

	Dollars	*Cents*
On the foreign debt, computing the interest on the principal, as it stands, and allowing four per cent on the arrears of interest,	542,599	66
On the domestic debt, including that of the states,	4,044,845	15
Making together, dollars	4,587,444	81

VI. CONSIDERATIONS RE RESTRUCTURING THE DEBT

VI. A. Why not pay off the whole debt now?

The interesting problem now occurs. Is it in the power of the United States, consistently with those prudential considerations, which ought not to be overlooked, to make a provision equal to the purpose of funding the whole debt, at the rates of interest which it now bears, in addition to the sum which will be necessary for the current service of the government?

The Secretary will not say that such provision would exceed the abilities of the country; but he is clearly of opinion, that to make it, would require the extension of taxation to a degree, and to objects, which the true interest of the public creditors forbids. It is therefore to be hoped, and even to be expected, that they will chearfully concur in such modifications of their claims, on fair and equitable principles, as will facilitate to the government an arrangement substantial, durable and satisfactory to the community. The importance of the last characteristic will strike every discerning mind. No plan, however flattering in appearance, to which it did not belong, could be truly entitled to confidence.

It will not be forgotten, that exigencies may, ere long, arise, which would call for resources greatly beyond what is now deemed sufficient for the current service; and that, should the faculties of the country be exhausted or even *strained* to provide for the public debt, there could be less reliance on the sacredness of the provision.

But while the Secretary yields to the force of these considerations, he does not lose sight of those fundamental principles of good faith, which dictate, that every practicable exertion ought to be made, scrupulously to fulfil the engagements of the government; that no change in the rights of its creditors ought to be attempted without their voluntary consent; and that this consent ought to be voluntary in fact, as well as in name. Consequently, that every proposal of a change ought to be in the shape of an appeal to their reason and to their interest; not to their necessities. To this end it is requisite, that a fair equivalent should be offered for what may be asked to be given up, and unquestionable security for the remainder. Without this, an alteration, consistently with the credit and honor of the nation, would be impracticable.

It remains to see, what can be proposed in conformity to these views.

VI. B. Debt as an annuity at 6%

It has been remarked, that the capital of the debt of the union is to be viewed in the light of an annuity at the rate of six per cent. per annum, redeemable at the pleasure of the government, by payment of the principal. And it will not be required, that the arrears of interest should be considered in a more favourable light. The same character, in general, may be applied to the debts of the individual states.

This view of the subject admits, that the United States would have it in their power to avail themselves of any fall in the market rate of interest, for reducing that of the debt.

This property of the debt is favourable to the public; unfavourable to the creditor. And may facilitate an arrangement for the reduction of interest, upon the basis of a fair equivalent.

Probabilities are always a rational ground of contract. The Secretary conceives, that there is good reason to believe, if effectual measures are taken to establish public credit, that the government rate of interest in the United States, will, in a very short time, fall at least as low as five per cent. and that in a period not exceeding twenty years, it will sink still lower, probably to four.

There are two principal causes which will be likely to produce this effect; one, the low rate of interest in Europe; the other, the increase of the monied capital of the nation, by the funding of the public debt.

From three to four per cent. is deemed good interest in several parts of Europe. Even less is deemed so, in some places. And it is on the decline; the increasing plenty of money continually tending to lower it. It is presumable, that no country will be able to borrow of foreigners upon better terms, than the United States, because none can, perhaps, afford so good security. Our situation exposes us less, than that of any other nation, to those casualties, which are the chief causes of expence; our incumbrances, in proportion to our real means, are less, though these cannot immediately be brought so readily into action, and our progress in resources from the early state of the country, and the immense tracts of unsettled territory, must necessarily exceed that of any other. The advantages of this situation have already engaged the attention of the European moneylenders, particularly among the Dutch. And as they become better understood, they will have the greater influence. Hence as large a proportion of the cash of Europe as may be wanted, will be, in a certain sense, in our market, for the use of government. And this will naturally have the effect of a reduction of the rate of interest, not indeed to the level of the places, which send their money to market, but to something much nearer to it, than our present rate.

The influence which the funding of the debt is calculated to have, in lowering interest, has been already remarked and explained. It is hardly possible, that it should not be materially affected by such an increase of the monied capital of the nation, as would result from the proper funding of seventy millions of dollars. But the probability of a decrease in the rate of interest, acquires confirmation from facts, which existed prior to the revolution. It is well known, that in some of the states, money might with facility be borrowed, on good security, at five per cent. and, not unfrequently, even at less.

The most enlightened of the public creditors will be most sensible of the justness of this view of the subject, and of the propriety of the use which will be made of it.

The Secretary, in pursuance of it, will assume, as a probability, sufficiently great to be a ground of calculation, both on the part of the government and of its creditors—That the interest of money in the United States will, in five years, fall to five per cent. and, in twenty, to four. The probability, in the mind of the Secretary, is rather that the fall may be more rapid and more considerable; but he prefers a mean, as most likely to engage the assent of the creditors, and more equitable in itself; because it is predicated on probabilities, which may err on one side, as well as on the other.

VI. C. Proposed methods for restructuring the debt

Premising these things, the Secretary submits to the House, the expediency of proposing a loan to the full amount of the debt, as well of the particular states, as of the union, upon the following terms.

First—That for every hundred dollars subscribed, payable in the debt (as well interest as principal) the subscribed be entitled, at his option, either

To have two thirds funded at an annuity, or yearly interest of six per cent, redeemable at the pleasure of the government, by payment of the principal; and to receive the other third in lands in the Western Territory, at the rate of twenty cents per acre. Or,

To have the whole sum funded at an annuity or yearly interest of four per cent. irredeemable by any payment exceeding five dollars per annum on account both of principal and interest; and to receive, as a compensation for the reduction of interest, fifteen dollars and eighty cents, payable in lands, as in the preceding case. Or

To have sixty-six dollars and two thirds of a dollar funded immediately at an annuity or yearly interest of six per cent. irredeemable by any payment exceeding four dollars and two thirds of a dollar per annum, on account both of principal and interest; and to have, at the end of ten years, twenty-six dollars and eighty-eight cents, funded at the like interest and rate of redemption. Or

To have an annuity for the remainder of life, upon the contingency of living to a given age, not less distant than ten years, computing interest at four per cent. Or

To have an annuity for the remainder of life, upon the contingency of the survivorship of the youngest of two persons, computing interest, in this case also, at four per cent.

In addition to the foregoing loan, payable wholly in the debt, the Secretary would propose, that one should be opened for ten millions of dollars, on the following plan.

That for every hundred dollars subscribed, payable one half in specie, and the other half in debt (as well principal as interest) the subscriber be entitled to an annuity or yearly interest of five per cent. irredeemable by any payment exceeding six dollars per annum, on account both of principal and interest.

The principles and operation of these different plans may now require explanation.

VI. C. 1. First proposed method for funding the debt: Land plus bonds

The first is simply a proposition for paying one third of the debt in land, and funding the other two thirds, at the existing rate of interest, and upon the same terms of redemption, to which it is at present subject.

Here is no conjecture, no calculation of probabilities. The creditor is offered the advantage of making his interest principal, and he is asked to facilitate to the government an effectual provision for his demands, by accepting a third part of them in land, at a fair valuation.

The general price, at which the western lands have been, heretofore, sold, has been a dollar per acre in public securities; but at the time the principal purchases were made, these securities were worth, in the market, less than three shillings in the pound. The nominal price, therefore, would not be the proper standard, under present circumstances, nor would the precise specie value then given, be a just rule. Because, as the payments were to be made by instalments, and the securities were, at the times of the purchases, extremely low, the probability of a moderate rise must be presumed to have been taken into the account. Twenty cents, therefore, seem to bear an equitable proportion to the two considerations of value at the time, and likelihood of increase.

It will be understood, that upon this plan, the public retains the advantage of availing itself of any fall in the market rate of interest, for reducing that upon the debt, which is perfectly just, as no present sacrifice, either in the quantum of the principal, or in the rate of interest, is required from the creditor.

The inductment to the measure is, the payment of one third of the debt in land.

VI. C. 2. Second proposed method for restructuring the debt: Bonds with 4% interest, supplemented by another 2% for 5 years, then 1% for 15 years after that.

The second plan is grounded upon the supposition, that interest, in five years, will fall to five per cent. in fifteen more, to four. As the capital remains entire, but bearing an interest of four per cent. only, compensation is to be made to the creditor, for the interest of two per cent. per annum for five years, and of one per cent. per annum, for fifteen years, to commence at the distance of five years. The present value of these two sums or annuities, computed according to the terms of the supposition, is, by strict calculation, fifteen dollars and seven hundred and ninety-two thousandth parts of a dollar; a fraction less than the sum proposed.

The inducement to the measure here is, the reduction of interest to a rate, more within the compass of a convenient provision; and the payment of the compensation in lands.

The inducements to the individual are—the accommodation afforded to the public, the high probability of a complete equivalent—the chance even of gain, should the rate of interest fall, either more speedily or in a greater degree, than the calculation supposes. Should it fall to five per cent. sooner than five years; should it fall lower than five before the additional fifteen were expired; or should it fall below four, previous to the payment of the debt, there would be, in each case, an absolute profit to the creditor. As his capital will remain entire, the value of it will increase, with every decrease of the rate of interest.

VI. C. 3. Third proposed method for restructuring the debt: Bonds with 6% for 5 years, then 5% for 15 years, then 4%.

The third plan proceeds upon the like supposition of a successive fall in the rate of interest. And upon that supposition offers an equivalent to the creditor. One hundred dollars, bearing an interest of six per cent. for five years; of five per cent. for fifteen years, and thenceforth of four per cent. (these being the successive rates of interest in the market) is

Equal to a capital of	122 dollars 410725 parts
bearing an interest of four per cent. which, converted into a capital, bearing a fixed rate of interest of six per cent, is equal to	81 dollars, 6738166 parts.
The difference between sixty-six dollars and two thirds of a dollar (the sum to be funded immediately) and this last sum is	15 dollars, 0172 parts,
which at six per cent. per annum, amounts at the end of ten years, to the sum to be funded at the expiration of that period.	26 dollars, 8755 parts.
It ought, however, to be acknowledged, that this calculation does not make allowance for the principle of redemption, which the plan itself includes; upon which principle the equivalent in a capital of six per cent. would be by strict calculation,	87 dollars, 50766 parts.

But there are two considerations which induce the Secretary to think, that the one proposed would operate more equitably than this: One is, that it may not be very early in the power of the United States to avail themselves of the right of redemption reserved in the plan: The other is, that with regard to the part to be funded at the end of ten years, the principal of redemption is suspended during that time, and the full interest at six per cent. goes on *improving* at the *same rate;* which for the *last five years* will exceed the market rate of interest, according to the supposition.

The equivalent is regulated in this plan, by the circumstance of fixing the rate of interest higher, than it is supposed it will continue to be in the market; permitting only a gradual discharge of the debt, in an established proportion, and consequently preventing advantage being taken of any decrease of interest below the stipulated rate.

Thus the true value of eighty-one dollars and sixty-seven cents, the capital proposed, considered as a perpetuity, and bearing six per cent. interest, when the market rate of interest was five per cent. would be a small fraction more than ninety-eight dollars, when it was four per cent. would be one hundred and twenty-two dollars and fifty-one cents. But the proposed capital being subject to gradual redemption, it is evident, that its value, in each case, would be somewhat less. Yet from this may be perceived, the manner in which a less capital at a fixed rate of interest, becomes an equivalent for a greater capital, at a rate liable to variation and diminution.

It is presumable, that those creditors, who do not entertain a favorable opinion of property in western lands, will give a preference to this last mode of modelling the debt. The Secretary is sincere in affirming, that, in his opinion, it will be likely to prove, *to the full* as beneficial to the creditors, as a provision for his debt upon its present terms.

It is not intended, in either case to oblige the government to redeem, in the proportion specified, but to secure to it, the right of doing so, to avoid the inconvenience of a perpetuity.

VI. C. 4-5. Fourth and fifth proposed methods for restructuring the debt: 4% interest, compounded, as an annuity, with survivorship

The fourth and fifth plans abandon the supposition which is the basis of the two preceding ones, and offer only four per cent. throughout.

The reason of this is, that the payment being deferred, there will be an accumulation of compound interest, in the intermediate period against the public, which, without a very provident administration, would turn to its detriment. And the suspension of the burthen would be too apt to beget a relaxation of efforts in the mean time. The measure therefore, its object being temporary accommodation, could only be adviseable upon a moderate rate of interest.

With regard to individuals, the inducement will be sufficient at four per cent. There is no disposition of money, in private loans, making allowance for the usual delays and casualties, which would be equally beneficial as a future provision.

A hundred dollars advanced upon the life of a person of eleven years old, would produce an annuity

	Dollars	*Parts*
If commencing at twenty-one, of	10	346
If commencing at thirty-one, of	18	803
If commencing at forty-one, of	37	286
If commencing at fifty-one, of	78	580

The same sum advanced upon the chance of the survivorship of the youngest of two lives, one of the persons being twenty-five, the other, thirty years old, would produce, if the youngest of the two, should survive, an annuity† for the remainder of life of

23 dollars, 556 parts.

From these instances may readily be discerned, the advantages, which these deferred annuities afford, for securing a comfortable provision for the evening of life, or for wives, who survive their husbands.

VI. C. 6. Sixth proposed method for restructuring the debt: Repayment of half of amount in specie

The sixth plan also relinquishes the supposition, which is the foundation of the second, and third, and offers a higher rate of interest upon similar terms of redemption, for the consideration of the payment of one half of the loan in specie. This is a plan highly advantageous to the creditors, who may be able to make that payment; while the specie itself could be applied in purchases of the debt, upon terms, which would fully indemnify the public for the increased interest.

It is not improbable, that foreign holders of the domestic debt, may embrace this as a desireable arrangement.

VI. C. 7. Seventh proposed method for restructuring the debt: tontine.

As an auxiliary expedient, and by way of experiment, the Secretary would propose a loan upon the principles of a tontine.

To consist of six classes, composed respectively of persons of the following ages:

First class, of those 20 years and under.
Second class, of those above 20, and not exceeding 30.
Third class, of those above 30, and not exceeding 40.
Fourth class, of those above 40 and not exceeding 50.
Fifth class, of those above 50, and not exceeding 60.
Sixth class, of those above 60.

Each share to be two hundred dollars. The number of shares in each class, to be indefinite. Persons to be at liberty to subscribe on their own lives, or on those of others, nominated by them.

		Dollars	Cents
The annuity	upon a share in the first class to be	8	40
	upon a share in the second class to be	8	65
	upon a share in the third class to be	9	0
	upon a share in the fourth class to be	9	65
	upon a share in the fifth class to be	10	70
	upon a share in the sixth class to be	12	80

The annuities of those who die, to be equally divided among the survivors, until four-fifths shall be dead, when the principle of survivorship shall cease, and each annuitant thenceforth enjoy his dividend as a several annuity during the life, upon which it shall depend.

These annuities are calculated upon the best life in each class, and at a rate of interest of four per cent. with some deductions in favor of the public. To the advantages which these circumstances present, the cessation of the right of survivorship on the death of four-fifths of the annuitants, will be no inconsiderable addition.

The inducements to individuals are, a competent interest for their money from the outset, secured for life, and the prospect of continual encrease, and even of large profit to those, whose fortune it is, to survive their associates.

It will have appeared, that in all the proposed loans, the Secretary has contemplated the putting the interest upon the same footing with the principal: *That* on the debt of the United States, he would have computed to the last of the present year: *That* on the debt of the particular states, to the last of the year 1791; the reason for which distinction will be seen hereafter.

VI. D. Quarterly interest payments

In order to keep up a due circulation of money, it will be expedient, that the interest of the debt should be paid quarter-yearly. This regulation will, at the same time, conduce to the advantage of the public creditors, giving them, in fact, by the anticipation of payment, a higher rate of interest; which may, with propriety, be taken into the estimate of the compensation to be made to them. Six per cent. per annum, paid in this mode, will truly be worth six dollars, and one hundred and thirty-five thousandth parts of a dollar, computing the market interest at the same rate.

The Secretary thinks it advisable, to hold out various propositions, all of them compatible with the public interest, because it is, in his opinion, of the greatest consequence, that the debt should, with the consent of the creditors, be remoulded into such a shape, as will bring the expenditure of the nation to a level with its income. 'Till this shall be accomplished, the finances of the United States will never wear a proper countenance. Arrears of interest, continually accruing, will be as continual a monument, either of inability, or of ill faith; and will not cease to have an evil influence on public credit. In nothing are appearances of greater moment, than in whatever regards credit. Opinion is the soul of it, and this is affected by appearances, as well as realities. By offering an option to the creditors, between a number of plans, the change meditated will be more likely to be accomplished. Different tempers will be governed by different views of the subject.

But while the Secretary would endeavour to effect a change in the form of the debt, by new loans, in order to render it more susceptible of an adequate provision; he would not think it proper to aim at procuring the concurrence of the creditors by operating upon their necessities.

Hence whatever surplus of revenue might remain, after satisfying the interest of the new loans, and the demand for the current service, ought to be divided among those creditors, if any, who may not think fit to subscribe to them. But for this purpose, under the circumstance of depending propositions, a temporary appropriation will be most adviseable, and the sum must be limited to four per cent. as the revenues will only be calculated to produce, in that proportion, to the entire debt.

The Secretary confides for the success of the propositions, to be made, on the goodness of the reasons upon which they rest; on the fairness of the equivalent to be offered in each case; on the discernment of the creditors of their true interest; and on their disposition to facilitate the arrangements of the government, and to render them satisfactory to the community.

VII. WHERE WILL THE MONEY COME FROM TO FUND THE DEBT?

The remaining part of the task to be performed is, to take a view of the means of providing for the debt, according to the modification of it, which is proposed.

On this point the Secretary premises, that, in his opinion, the funds to be established, ought, for the present, to be confined to the existing debt of the United States; as well, because a progressive augmentation of the revenue will be most convenient, as because the consent of the state creditors is necessary, to the assumption contemplated; and though the obtaining of that consent may be inferred with great assurance, from their obvious interest to give it; yet 'till it shall be obtained, an actual provision for the debt, would be premature. Taxes could not, with propriety, be laid for an object, which depended on such a contingency.

All that ought now to be done, respecting it, is, to put the matter in an effectual train for a future provision. For which purpose, the Secretary will, in the course of this report, submit such propositions, as appear to him adviseable.

The Secretary now proceeds to a consideration of the necessary funds.

VII. A. Total needed

It has been stated that the debt of the United States consists of

	Dollars	*Cents*
The foreign debt, amounting, with arrears of interest, to	11,710,378	62
And the domestic debt amounting, with like arrears, computed to the end of the year 1790, to	42,414,085	94
Making together, Dollars	54,124,464	56

The interest on the domestic debt is computed to the end of this year, because the details of carrying any plan into execution, will exhaust the year.

	Dollars	*Cents*
The annual interest of the foreign debt has been stated at	542,599	66
And the interest on the domestic debt at four percent. would amount to	1,696,563	43
Making together, dollars	2,239,163	09

Thus to pay the interest of the foreign debt, and to pay four per cent on the whole of the domestic debt, principal and interest, forming a new capital,

| will require a yearly income of | 2,239,163 dollars, 9 cents. |

The sum which, in the opinion of the Secretary, ought now to be provided in addition to what the current service will require.

For, though the rate of interest, proposed by the third plan, exceeds four per cent. on the whole debt, and the annuities on the tontine will also exceed four per cent. on the sums which may be subscribed; yet, as the actual provision for a part is, in the former case, suspended; as measures for reducing the debt, by purchases, may be advantageously pursued, and as the payment of the deferred annuities will of course be postponed, four per cent. on the whole, will be a sufficient provision.

VII. B. Payments on the foreign debt via loans

With regard to the instalments of the foreign debt, these, in the opinion of the Secretary, ought to be paid by new loans abroad. Could funds be conveniently spared, from other exigencies, for paying them, the United States could ill bear the drain of cash, at the present juncture, which the measure would be likely to occasion.

VII. C. Payments the domestic debt via duties on imports and tonnage fees, and on alcohol

But to the sum which has been stated for payment of the interest, must be added a provision for the current service. This the Secretary estimates at six hundred thousand dollars; making, with the amount of the interest, two millions, eight hundred and thirty-nine thousand, one hundred and sixty-three dollars, and nine cents.

VII. C. 1 Why impose duties on these items?

This sum may, in the opinion of the Secretary, be obtained from the present duties on imports and tonnage, with the additions, which, without any possible disadvantage either to trade, or agriculture, may be made on wines, spirits, including those distilled within the United States, teas and coffee.

The Secretary conceives, that it will be sound policy, to carry the duties upon articles of this kind, as high as will be consistent with the practicability of a safe collection. This will lessen the necessity, both of having recourse to direct taxation, and of accumulating duties where they would be more inconvenient to trade, and upon objects, which are more to be regarded as necessaries of life.

That the articles which have been enumerated, will, better than most others, bear high duties, can hardly be a question. They are all of them, in reality—luxuries—the greatest part of them foreign luxuries; some of them, in the excess in which they are used, pernicious luxuries. And there is, perhaps, none of them, which is not consumed in so great abundance, as may, justly, denominate it, a source of national extravagance and impoverishment. The consumption of ardent spirits particularly, no doubt very much on account of their cheapness, is carried to an extreme, which is truly to be regretted, as well in regard to the health and the morals, as to the œconomy of the community.

Should the increase of duties tend to a decrease of the consumption of those articles, the effect would be, in every respect desirable. The saving which it would occasion, would leave individuals more at their ease, and promote a more favourable balance of trade. As far as this decrease might be applicable to distilled spirits, it would encourage the substitution of cyder and malt liquors, benefit agriculture, and open a new and productive source of revenue.

It is not however, probable, that this decrease would be in a degree, which would frustrate the expected benefit to the revenue from raising the duties. Experience has shewn, that luxuries of every kind, lay the strongest hold on the attachments of mankind, which, especially when confirmed by habit, are not easily alienated from them.

VII. C. 2. Accomodating merchants

The same fact affords a security to the merchant, that he is not likely to be prejudiced by considerable duties on such articles. They will usually command a proportional price. The chief things in this view to be attended to, are, that the terms of payment be so regulated, as not to require inconvenient advances, and that the mode of collection be secure.

To other reasons, which plead for carrying the duties upon the articles which have been mentioned, to as great an extent as they will bear, may be added these; that they are of a nature, from their extensive consumption, to be very productive, and are amongst the most difficult objects of illicit introduction.

VII. C. 3. Collection and evasion of duties

Invited by so many motives to make the best use of the resource, which these articles afford, the essential enquiry is—in what mode can the duties upon them be most effectually collected?

With regard to such of them, as will be brought from abroad, a duty on importation recommends itself by two leading considerations;

one is, that meeting the object at its first entrance into the country, the collection is drawn to a point, and so far simplified; the other is, that it avoids the possibility of interference between the regulations of the United States, and those of the particular states.

But a duty, the precautions for the collection of which should terminate with the landing of the goods, as is essentially the case in the existing system, could not, with safety, be carried to the extent, which is contemplated.

In that system, the evasion of the duties, depends as it were, on a single risk. To land the goods in defiance of the vigilance of the officers of the customs, is almost, the sole difficulty. No future pursuit, is materially, to be apprehended. And where the inducement is equivalent to the risk, there will be found too many, who are willing to run it. Consequently there will be extensive frauds of the revenue, against which the utmost rigor of the penal laws, has proved, as often as it has been tried, an ineffectual guard.

The only expedient which has been discovered, for conciliating high duties with a safe collection, is, the establishment of a *second*, or interior scrutiny.

By pursuing the article, from its importation, into the hands of the dealers in it, the risk of detection is so greatly inhanced, that few, in comparison, will venture to incur it. Indeed every dealer, who is not himself the fraudulent importer, then becomes, in some sort, a centinel upon him.

The introduction of a system, founded on this principle, in some shape or other, is, in the opinion of the Secretary, essential to the efficacy of every attempt, to render the revenues of the United States equal to their exigencies, their safety, their prosperity, their honor.

Nor is it less essential to the interest of the honest and fair trader. It might even be added, that every individual citizen, besides his share in the general weal, has a particular interest in it. The practice of smuggling never fails to have one of two effects, and sometimes unites them both. Either the smuggler undersells the fair trader, as, by saving the *duty*, he can afford to do, and makes *it* a charge upon him; or he sells at the increased price occasioned by the duty, and defrauds every man, who buys of him, of his share of what the public ought to receive. For it is evident, that the loss falls ultimately upon the citizens, who must be charged with other taxes to make good the deficiency, and supply the wants of the state.

The Secretary will not presume, that the plan, which he shall submit to the consideration of the house, is the best that could be devised.

But it is the one, which has appeared to him freest from objections of any, that has occurred of equal efficacy. He acknowledges too, that it is susceptible of improvement, by other precautions in favor of the revenue, which he did not think it expedient to add. The chief outlines of the plan are not original, but it is no ill recommendation of it, that it has been tried with success.

VII. C. 4. Specific duties to impose to raise revenue

The Secretary accordingly proposes,

That the duties heretofore laid upon wines, distilled spirits, teas and coffee, should, after the last day of May next, cease, and that instead of them, the following duties be laid.

Upon every gallon of Madeira Wine, of the quality of London particular, thirty-five cents.

Upon every gallon of other Madeira Wine, thirty cents.

Upon every gallon of Sherry, twenty-five cents.

Upon every gallon of other Wine, twenty cents.

Upon every gallon of distilled Spirits, more than ten per cent. below proof, according to Dicas's hydrometer, twenty cents.

Upon every gallon of those Spirits under five, and not more than ten per cent. below proof, according to the same hydrometer, twenty-one cents.

Upon every gallon of those Spirits of proof, and not more than five per cent. below proof, according to the same hydrometer, twenty-two cents.

Upon every gallon of those Spirits above proof, but not exceeding twenty per cent. according to the same hydrometer, twenty-five cents.

Upon every gallon of those spirits more than twenty, and not more than forty per cent. above proof, according to the same hydrometer, thirty cents.

Upon every gallon of those spirits more than forty per cent. above proof, according to the same hydrometer, forty cents.

Upon every pound of Hyson Tea, forty cents.

Upon every pound of other Green Tea, twenty-four cents.

Upon every pound of Souchong and other black Teas, except Bohea, twenty cents.

Upon every pound of Bohea Tea, twelve cents.

Upon every pound of Coffee, five cents.

That upon Spirits distilled within the United States, from Molasses, Sugar, or other foreign materials, there be paid—

Upon every gallon of those Spirits, more than ten per cent below proof, according to Dicas's hydrometer, eleven cents.

Upon every gallon of those spirits under five, and not more than ten per cent. below proof, according to the same hydrometer, twelve cents.

Upon every gallon of those Spirits of proof, and not more than five per cent. below proof, according to the same hydrometer, thirteen cents.

Upon every gallon of those Spirits, above proof, but not exceeding twenty per cent. according to the same hydrometer, fifteen cents.

Upon every gallon of those Spirits, more than twenty, and not more than forty per cent. above proof, according to the same hydrometer, twenty cents.

Upon every gallon of those Spirits more than forty per cent. above proof, according to the same hydrometer, thirty cents.

That upon Spirits distilled within the United States, in any city, town or village, from materials of the growth or production of the United States, there be paid—

Upon every gallon of those Spirits more than ten per cent. below proof, according to Dicas's hydrometer, nine cents.

Upon every gallon of those Spirits under five, and not more than ten per cent. below proof, according to the same hydrometer, ten cents.

Upon every gallon of those Spirits of proof, and not more than five per cent. below proof, according to the same hydrometer, eleven cents.

Upon every gallon of those Spirits above proof, but not exceeding twenty per cent. according to the same hydrometer, thirteen cents.

Upon every gallon of those Spirits more than twenty, and not more than forty per cent. above proof, according to the same hydrometer, seventeen cents.

Upon every gallon of those Spirits, more than forty per cent. above proof, according to the same hydrometer, twenty-five cents.

That upon all Stills employed in distilling Spirits from materials of the growth or production of the United States, in any other place, than a city, town or village, there be paid the yearly sum of sixty cents, for every gallon, English wine measure, of the capacity of each Still, including its head.

The Secretary does not distribute the duties on Teas into different classes, as has been done in the impost act of the last session; because this distribution depends on considerations of commercial policy, not of revenue. It is sufficient, therefore, for him to remark, that the rates, above specified, are proposed with reference to the lowest class.

The Secretary conceiving, that he could not convey an accurate idea of the plan contemplated by him, for the collection of these duties, in any mode so effectual as by the draft of a bill for the purpose, begs leave respectfully to refer the House to that, which will be found annexed to this report, relatively to the article of distilled spirits; and which, for the better explanation of some of its parts, is accompanied with marginal remarks.

It would be the intention of the Secretary, that the duty on wines should be collected upon precisely the same plan with that on imported spirits.

But with regard to teas and coffee, the Secretary is inclined to think, that it will be expedient, till experience shall evince the propriety of going further, to exclude the *ordinary* right of the officers to visit and inspect the places in which those articles may be kept. The other precautions, without this, will afford, though not complete, considerable security.

It will not escape the observation of the House, that the Secretary, in the plan submitted, has taken the most scrupulous care, that those citizens upon whom it is immediately to operate, be secured from every species of injury by the misconduct of the officers to be employed. There are not only strong guards against their being guilty of abuses of authority; they are not only punishable, criminally, for any they may commit, and made answerable in damages, to individuals, for whatever prejudice these may sustain by their acts or neglects: But even where seizures are made with probable cause, if there be an acquittal of the article seized, a compensation to the proprietors for the injury their property may suffer, and even for its detention, is to be made out of the public treasury.

So solicitous indeed has the Secretary been, to obviate every appearance of hardship, that he has even included a compensation to the dealers, for their agency in aid of the revenue.

With all these precautions to manifest a spirit of moderation and justice on the part of government: And when it is considered, that the object of the proposed system is the firm establishment of public credit; that on this depends the character, security and prosperity of the nation; that advantages in every light important, may be expected to result from it; that the immediate operation of it will be upon an enlightened class of citizens, zealously devoted to good government, and to a liberal and enlarged policy, and that it is peculiarly the interest of the virtuous part of them to co-operate in whatever will restrain the spirit of illicit traffic; there will be perceived to exist, the justest ground of confidence, that the plan, if eligible in itself, will experience the chearful and prompt acquiescence of the community.

VII. C. 5. Estimated revenue from the sources above

The Secretary computes the nett product of the duties proposed in this report at about one million seven hundred and three thousand four hundred dollars, according to the estimate in schedule K, which if near the truth, will, together with the probable product of the duties on imports and tonnage, complete the sum required. But it will readily occur, that in so unexplored a field there must be a considerable degree of uncertainty in the data. And that, on this account, it will be prudent to have an auxiliary resource for the first year, in which the interest will become payable, that there may be no possibility of disappointment to the public creditors, ere there may be an opportunity of providing for any deficiency, which the experiment may discover. This will accordingly be attended to.

VII. D. Which revenue goes to which debts?

The proper appropriation of the funds provided, and to be provided, seems next to offer itself to consideration.

On this head, the Secretary would propose, that the duties on distilled spirits, should be applied in the first instance, to the payment of the interest of the foreign debt.

That reserving out of the residue of those duties an annual sum of six hundred thousand dollars, for the current service of the United States; the surplus, together with the product of the other duties, be applied to the payment of the interest on the new loan, by an appropriation, co-extensive with the duration of the debt.

And that if any part of the debt should remain unsubscribed, the excess of the revenue be divided among the creditors of the unsubscribed part, by a temporary disposition; with a limitation, however, to four per cent.

VII.E Extinguishing the debt

VII. E. 1. Additional revenue: the Sinking Fund

It will hardly have been unnoticed, that the Secretary had been thus far silent on the subject of the post-office. The reason is, that he has had in view the application of the revenue arising from that source, to the purposes of a sinking fund. The post-master-general gives it as his opinion, that the immediate product of it, upon a proper arrangement, would probably be, not less than one hundred thousand dollars. And from its nature, with good management, it must be a growing, and will be likely to become a considerable fund. The post-master-general is now engaged in preparing a plan, which will be the foundation of a proposition for a new arrangement of the establishment. This, and some other points relative to the subject referred to the Secretary, he begs leave to reserve for a future report.

VII. E. 2. Extinguishing the debt

Persuaded as the Secretary is, that the proper funding of the present debt, will render it a national blessing: Yet he is so far from acceding to the position, in the latitude in which it is sometimes laid down, that "public debts are public benefits," a position inviting to prodigality, and liable to dangerous abuse,—that he ardently wishes to see it incorporated, as a fundamental maxim, in the system of public credit of the United States, that the creation of debt should always be accompanied with the means of extinguishment. This he regards as the true secret for rendering public credit immortal. And he presumes, that it is difficult to conceive a situation, in which there may not be an adherence to the maxim. At least he feels an unfeigned solicitude, that this may be attempted by the United States, and that they may commence their measures for the establishment of credit, with the observance of it.

VII. E. 3 The Sinking Fund, continued

Under this impression, the Secretary proposes, that the nett product of the post-office, to a sum not exceeding one million of dollars, be vested in commissioners, to consist of the Vice-President of the United States or President of the Senate, the Speaker of the House of Representatives, the Chief Justice, Secretary of the Treasury and Attorney-General of the United States, for the time being, in trust, to be applied, by them, or any three of them, to the discharge of the existing public debt, either by purchases of stock in the market, or by payments on account of the principal, as shall appear to them most adviseable, in conformity to the public engagements; to continue so vested, until the whole of the debt shall be discharged.

As an additional expedient for effecting a reduction of the debt, and for other purposes which will be mentioned, the Secretary would further propose that the same commissioners be authorised, with the approbation of the President of the United States, to borrow, on their credit, a sum, not exceeding twelve millions of dollars, to be applied,

First. To the payment of the interest and instalments of the foreign debt, to the end of the present year, which will require 3,491,923 dollars, and 46 cents.

Secondly. To the payment of any deficiency which may happen in the product of the funds provided for paying the interest of the domestic debt.

Thirdly. To the effecting a change in the form of such part of the foreign debt, as bears an interest of five per cent. It is conceived, that, for this purpose, a new loan, at a lower interest, may be combined with other expedients. The remainder of this part of the debt, after paying the instalments, which will accrue in the course of 1790, will be 3,888,888 dollars, and 81 cents.

Fourthly. To the purchase of the public debt at the price it shall bear in the market, while it continues below its true value. This measure, which would be, in the opinion of the Secretary, highly dishonorable to the government, if it were to precede a provision for funding the debt, would become altogether unexceptionable, after that had been made. Its effect would be in favor of the public creditors, as it would tend to raise the value of stock. And all the difference, between its true value, and the actual price, would be so much clear gain to the public. The payment of foreign interest on the capital to be borrowed for this purpose, should that be a necessary consequence, would not, in the judgment of the Secretary, be a good objection to the measure. The saving by the operation would be itself, a sufficient indemnity; and the employment of that capital, in a country situated like this, would much more than compensate for it. Besides, if the government does not undertake this operation, the same inconvenience, which the objection in question supposes, would happen in another way, with a circumstance of aggravation. As long, at least, as the debt shall continue below its proper value, it will be an object of speculation to foreigners, who will not only receive the interest, upon what they purchase, and remit it abroad, as in the case of the loan, but will reap the additional profit of the difference in value. By the government's entering into competition with them, it will not only reap a part of this profit itself, but will contract the extent, and lessen the extra profit of foreign purchases. That competition will accelerate the rise of stock; and whatever greater rate this obliges foreigners to pay, for what they purchase, is so much clear saving to the nation. In the opinion of the Secretary, and contrary to an idea which is not without patrons, it ought to be the policy of the government, to raise the value of stock to its true standard as fast as possible. When it arrives to that point, foreign speculations (which, till then, must be deemed pernicious, further than as they serve to bring it to that point) will become beneficial. Their money laid out in this country, upon our agriculture, commerce and manufactures, will produce much more to us, than the income they will receive from it.

The Secretary contemplates the application of this money, through the medium of a national bank, for which, with the permission of the House, he will submit a plan in the course of the session.

VIII. STEPS TOWARD THE ASSUMPTION OF STATES' DEBTS

The Secretary now proceeds, in the last place, to offer to the consideration of the House, his ideas, of the steps, which ought at the present session, to be taken, towards the assumption of the state debts.

These are briefly, that concurrent resolutions of the two Houses, with the approbation of the President, be entered into, declaring in substance,

That the United States do assume, and will at the first session in the year 1791, provide, on the same terms with the present debt of the United States, for all such part of the debts of the respective states, or any of them, as shall, prior to the first day of January in the said year 1791, be subscribed towards a loan to the United States, upon the principles of either of the plans, which shall have been adopted by them, for obtaining a re-loan of their present debt.

Provided that the provision to be made as aforesaid, shall be suspended, with respect to the debt, of any state, which may have exchanged the securities of the United States for others issued by itself, until the whole of the said securities shall, either be re-ex-changed, or surrendered to the United States.

And provided also, that the interest upon the debt assumed, be computed to the end of the year 1791; and that the interest to be paid by the United States, commence on the first day of January, 1792.

That the amount of the debt of each state so assumed and provided for, be charged to such state in account with the United States, upon the same principles, upon which it shall be lent to the United States.

That subscriptions be opened for receiving loans of the said debts at the same times and places, and under the like regulations, as shall have been prescribed in relation to the debt of the United States.

IX. CONCLUSION

The Secretary has now completed the objects, which he proposed to himself, to comprise in the present report. He has, for the most part, omitted details, as well to avoid fatiguing the attention of the House, as because more time would have been desirable even to digest the general principles of the plan. If these should be found right, the particular modifications will readily suggest themselves in the progress of the work.

The Secretary, in the views which have directed his pursuit of the subject, has been influenced, in the first place, by the consideration, that his duty from the very terms of the resolution of the House, obliged him to propose what appeared to him an adequate provision for the support of the public credit, adapted at the same time to the real circumstances of the United States; and in the next, by the reflection, that measures which will not bear the test of future unbiassed examination, can neither be productive of individual reputation, nor (which is of much greater consequence) public honor, or advantage.

Deeply impressed, as the Secretary is, with a full and deliberate conviction, that the establishment of public credit, upon the basis of a satisfactory provision, for the public debt, is, under the present circumstances of this country, the true desideratum towards relief from individual and national embarrassments; that without it, these embarrassments will be likely to press still more severely upon the community—He cannot but indulge an anxious wish, that an effectual plan for that purpose may, during the present session, be the result of the united wisdom of the legislature.

He is fully convinced, that it is of the greatest importance, that no further delay should attend the making of the requisite provision; not only, because it will give a better impression of the good faith of the country, and will bring earlier relief to the creditors; both which circumstances are of great moment to public credit: but, because the advantages to the community, from raising stock, as speedily as possible, to its natural value, will be incomparably greater, than any that can result from its continuance below that standard. No profit, which could be derived from purchases in the market, on account of the government, to any practicable extent, would be an equivalent for the loss, which would be sustained by the purchases of foreigners, at a low value. Not to repeat, that governmental purchases, to be honorable, ought to be preceded by a provision. Delay, by disseminating doubt, would sink the price of stock; and as the temptation to foreign speculations, from the lowness of the price, would be too great to be neglected, millions would probably be lost to the United States.

All which is humbly submitted.

Alexander Hamilton, *Secretary of the Treasury.*

APPENDIX 2

Report on a National Bank

Full title: *The Second Report on the Further Provision Necessary for Establishing Public Credit*

https://founders.archives.gov/documents/Hamilton/01-07-02-0229-0003
(modern editorial notes not included)

Treasury Department
December 13th, 1790
[Communicated on December 14, 1790]

[To the Speaker of the House of Representatives]

I. INTRODUCTION

In obedience to the order of the House of Representatives of the ninth day of August last, requiring the Secretary of the Treasury to prepare and report on this day such further provision as may, in his opinion, be necessary for establishing the public Credit

The said Secretary further respectfully reports

That from a conviction (as suggested in his report No. 1 herewith presented) That a National Bank is an Institution of primary importance to the prosperous administration of the Finances, and would be of the greatest utility in the operations connected with the support of the Public Credit, his attention has been drawn to devising the plan of such an institution, upon a scale, which will intitle it to the confidence, and be likely to render it equal to the exigencies of the Public.

Previously to entering upon the detail of this plan, he entreats the indulgence of the House, towards some preliminary reflections naturally arising out of the subject, which he hopes will be deemed, neither useless, nor out of place. Public opinion being the ultimate arbiter of every measure of Government, it can scarcely appear improper, in deference to that, to accompany the origination of any new proposition with explanations, which the superior information of those, to whom it is immediately addressed, would render superfluous.

II. PRELIMINARIES: ADVANTAGES AND DISADVANTAGES OF BANKS

It is a fact well understood, that public Banks have found admission and patronage among the principal and most enlightened commercial nations. They have successively obtained in Italy, Germany, Holland, England and France, as well as in the United States. And it is a circumstance, which cannot but have considerable weight, in a candid estimate of their tendency, that after an experience of centuries, there exists not a question about their utility in the countries in which they have been so long established. Theorists and men of business unite in the acknowlegment of it.

Trade and industry, wherever they have been tried, have been indebted to them for important aid. And Government has been repeatedly under the greatest obligations to them, in dangerous and distressing emergencies. That of the United States, as well in some of the most critical conjunctures of the late war, as since the peace, has received assistance from those established among us, with which it could not have dispensed.

With this two fold evidence before us, it might be expected, that there would be a perfect union of opinions in their favour. Yet doubts have been entertained; jealousies and prejudices have circulated: and though the experiment is every day dissipating them, within the spheres in which effects are best known; yet there are still persons by whom they have not been intirely renounced. To give a full and accurate view of the subject would be to make a Treatise of a report; but there are certain aspects in which it may be cursorily exhibited, which may perhaps conduce to a just impression of its merits. These will involve a comparison of the advantages, with the disadvantages, real or supposed, of such institutions.

II. A. Advantages of a bank

The following are among the principal advantages of a Bank.

II. A. 1. First advantage: Banks increase the amount of money in circulation.

First. The augmentation of the active or productive capital of a country.

Gold and Silver, when they are employed merely as the instruments of exchange and alienation, have been not improperly denominated dead Stock; but when deposited in Banks, to become the basis of a paper circulation, which takes their character and place, as the signs or representatives of value, they then acquire life, or, in other words, an active and productive quality. This idea, which appears rather subtil and abstract, in a general form, may be made obvious and palpable, by entering into a few particulars. It is evident, for instance, that the money, which a merchant keeps in his chest, waiting for a favourable opportunity to employ it, produces nothing 'till that opportunity arrives. But if instead of locking it up in this manner, he either deposits it in a Bank, or invests it in the Stock of a Bank, it yields a profit, during the interval; in which he partakes, or not, according to the choice he may have made of being a depositor or a proprietor; and when any advantageous speculation offers, in order to be able to embrace it, he has only to withdraw his money, if a depositor, or if a proprietor to obtain a loan from the Bank, or to dispose of his Stock; an alternative seldom or never attended with difficulty, when the affairs of the institution are in a prosperous train. His money thus deposited or invested, is a fund, upon which himself and others can borrow to a much larger amount. It is a well established fact, that Banks in good credit can circulate a far greater sum than the actual quantum of their capital in Gold & Silver. The extent of the possible excess seems indeterminate; though it has been conjecturally stated at the proportions of two and three to one. This faculty is produced in various ways. First. A great proportion of the notes, which are issued and pass current as Cash, are indefinitely suspended in circulation, from the confidence which each holder has, that he can at any moment turn them into gold and silver. Secondly, Every loan, which a Bank makes is, in its first shape, a credit given to the borrower on its books, the amount of which it stands ready to pay, either in its own notes, or in gold or silver, at his option. But, in a great number of cases, no actual payment is made in either. The Borrower frequently, by a check or order, transfers his credit to some other person, to whom he has a payment to make; who, in his turn, is as often content with a similar credit, because he is satisfied, that he can, whenever he pleases, either convert it into cash, or pass it to some other hand, as an equivalent for it. And in this manner the credit keeps circulating, performing in every stage the office of money, till it is extinguished by a discount with some person, who has a payment to make to the Bank, to an equal or greater amount. Thus large sums are lent and paid, frequently through a variety of hands, without the intervention of a single piece of coin. Thirdly, There is always a large quantity of gold and silver in the repositories of the Bank, besides its own Stock, which is placed there, with a view partly to its safe keeping and partly to the accommodation of an institution, which is itself a source of general accommodation. These deposits are of immense consequence in the operations of a Bank. Though liable to be redrawn at any moment, experience proves, that the money so much oftener changes proprietors than place, and that what is drawn out is generally so speedily replaced, as to authorise the counting upon the sums deposited, as an effective fund; which, concurring with the Stock of the Bank, enables it to extend its loans, and to answer all the demands for coin, whether in consequence of those loans, or arising from the occasional return of its notes.

These different circumstances explain the manner, in which the ability of a bank to circulate a greater sum, than its actual capital in coin, is acquired. This however must be gradual; and must be preceded by a firm establishment of confidence; a confidence which may be bestowed on the most rational grounds; since the excess in question will always be bottomed on good security of one kind or another. This, every well conducted Bank carefully requires, before it will consent to advance either its money or its credit; and where there is an auxiliary capital (as will be the case in the plan hereafter submitted) which, together with the capital in coin, define the boundary, that shall not be exceeded by the engagements of the Bank, the security may, consistently with all the maxims of a reasonable circumspection be regarded as complete.

The same circumstances illustrate the truth of the position, that it is one of the properties of Banks to increase the active capital of a country. This, in other words is the sum of them. The money of one individual, while he is waiting for an opportunity to employ it, by being either deposited in the Bank for safe keeping, or invested in its Stock, is in a condition to administer to the wants of others, without being put out of his own reach, when occasion presents. This yields an extra profit, arising from what is paid for the use of his money by others, when he could not himself make use of it; and keeps the money itself in a state of incessant activity. In the almost infinite vicissitudes and competitions of mercantile enterprise, there never can be danger of an intermission of demand, or that the money will remain for a moment idle in the vaults of the Bank. This additional employment given to money, and the faculty of a bank to lend and circulate a greater sum than the amount of its stock in coin are to all the purposes of trade and industry an absolute increase of capital. Purchases and undertakings, in general, can be carried on by any given sum of bank paper or credit, as effectually as by an equal sum of gold and silver. And thus by contributing to enlarge the mass of industrious and commercial enterprise, banks become nurseries of national wealth: a consequence, as satisfactorily verified by experience, as it is clearly deducible in theory.

II. A. 2. Second advantage: In an emergency, the government can seek financial aid from a bank.

Secondly. Greater facility to the Government in obtaining pecuniary aids, especially in sudden emergencies. This is another and an undisputed advantage of public banks: one, which as already remarked, has been realised in signal instances, among ourselves. The reason is obvious: The capitals of a great number of individuals are, by this operation, collected to a point, and placed under one direction. The mass, formed by this union, is in a certain sense magnified by the credit attached to it: And while this mass is always ready, and can at once be put in motion, in aid of the Government, the interest of the bank to afford that aid, independent of regard to the public safety and welfare, is a sure pledge for its disposition to go as far in its compliances, as can in prudence be desired. There is in the nature of things, as will be more particularly noticed in another place, an intimate connection of interest between the government and the Bank of a Nation.

II. A. 3. Third advantage: A bank can facilitate payment of taxes.

Thirdly. The facilitating of the payment of taxes. This advantage is produced in two ways. Those who are in a situation to have access to the Bank can have the assistance of loans to answer with punctuality the public calls upon them. This accommodation has been sensibly felt in the payment of the duties heretofore laid, by those who reside where establishments of this nature exist. This however, though an extensive, is not an universal benefit. The other way, in which the effect here contemplated is produced, and in which the benefit is general, is the encreasing of the quantity of circulating medium and the quickening of circulation. The manner in which the first happens has already been traced. The last may require some illustration. When payments are to be made between different places, having an intercourse of business with each other, if there happen to be no private bills, at market, and there are no Bank notes, which have a currency in both, the consequence is, that coin must be remitted. This is attended with trouble, delay, expence and risk. If on the contrary, there are bank notes current in both places, the transmission of these by the post, or any other speedy, or convenient conveyance answers the purpose; and these again, in the alternations of demand, are frequently returned, very soon after, to the place from whence they were first sent: Whence the transportation and retransportation of the metals are obviated; and a more convenient and more expeditious medium of payment is substituted. Nor is this all. The metals, instead of being suspended from their usual functions, during this process of vibration from place to place, continue in activity, and administer still to the ordinary circulation; which of course is prevented from suffering either diminution or stagnation. These circumstances are additional causes of what, in a practical sense, or to the purposes of business, may be called greater plenty of money. And it is evident, that whatever enhances the quantity of circulating money adds to the ease, with which every industrious member of the community may acquire that portion of it, of which he stands in need; and enables him the better to pay his taxes, as well as to supply his other wants. Even where the circulation of the bank paper is not general, it must still have the same effect, though in a less degree. For whatever furnishes additional supplies to the channels of circulation, in one quarter, naturally contributes to keep the streams fuller elsewhere. This last view of the subject serves both to illustrate the position, that Banks tend to facilitate the payment of taxes; and to exemplify their utility to business of every kind, in which money is an agent.

II. B. Criticisms of banks

It would be to intrude too much on the patience of the house, to prolong the details of the advantages of Banks; especially as all those, which might still be particularized are readily to be inferred as consequences from those, which have been enumerated. Their disadvantages, real or supposed, are now to be reviewed. The most serious of the charges which have been brought against them are—

That they serve to increase usury:

That they tend to prevent other kinds of lending:

That they furnish temptations to overtrading:

That they afford aid to ignorant adventurers who disturb the natural and beneficial course of trade:

That they give to bankrupt and fraudulent traders a fictitious credit, which enables them to maintain false appearances and to extend their impositions: And lastly

That they have a tendency to banish gold and silver from the country.

There is great reason to believe, that on a close and candid survey, it will be discovered, that these charges are either destitute of foundation; or that, as far as the evils, they suggest, have been found to exist, they have proceeded from other, or partial, or temporary causes, are not inherent in the nature and permanent tendency of such institutions; or are more than counterbalanced by opposite advantages. This survey shall be had, in the order in which the charges have been stated.

II. B. 1. Criticisms of banks: They increase usury, i.e., lending at high rates of interest.

The first of them is, that Banks serve to increase usury.

It is a truth, which ought not to be denied, that the method of conducting business, which is essential to bank operations, has among us, in particular instances, given occasion to usurious transactions. The punctuality, in payments, which they necessarily exact has sometimes obliged those, who have adventured beyond both their capital and their credit to procure money, at any price, and consequently to resort to usurers for aid.

But experience and practice gradually bring a cure to this evil. A general habit of punctuality among traders is the natural consequence of the necessity of observing it with the Bank; a circumstance which itself more than compensates for any occasional ill, which may have sprung from that necessity, in the particular, under consideration. As far therefore as Traders depend on each other for pecuniary supplies, they can calculate their expectations with greater certainty; and are in proportionably less danger of disappointments, which might compel them to have recourse to so pernicious an expedient, as that of borrowing at usury; the mischiefs of which, after a few examples, naturally inspire great care, in all but men of desperate circumstances, to avoid the possibility of being subjected to them. One, and not the least of the evils incident to the use of that expedient, if the fact be known or even strongly suspected, is loss of credit with the bank itself.

The Directors of a bank too, though in order to extend its business and its popularity, in the infancy of an institution, they may be tempted to go further in accommodations, than the strict rules of prudence will warrant, grow more circumspect of course, as its affairs become better established, and as the evils of too great facility are experimentally demonstrated. They become more attentive to the situation and conduct of those, with whom they deal; they observe more narrowly their operations and pursuits; they œconomise the credit, they give to those of suspicious solidity; they refuse it to those whose career is more manifestly hazardous. In a word, in the course of practice, from the very nature of things, the interest will make it the policy of a Bank, to succour the wary and industrious; to discredit the rash and unthrifty; to discountenance both usurious lenders and usurious borrowers.

There is a leading view, in which the tendency of banks will be seen to be, to abrige rather than to promote usury. This relates to their property of increasing the quantity and quickening the circulation of money. If it be evident, that usury will prevail or diminish, according to the proportion which the demand for borrowing bears to the quantity of money at market to be lent; whatever has the property just mentioned, whether it be in the shape of paper or of coin, by contributing to render the supply more equal to the demand, must tend to counteract the progress of usury.

II. B. 2. Criticisms of banks: They discourage lending by anyone except banks.

But bank-lending, it is pretended, is an impediment to other kinds of lending; which, by confining the resource of borrowing to a particular class, leaves the rest of the community more destitute, and therefore more exposed to the extortions of usurers. As the profits of bank stock exceed the legal rate of interest, the possessors of money, it is argued, prefer investing it in that article to lending it at this rate; to which there are the additional motives of a more prompt command of the capital, and of more frequent and exact returns, without trouble or perplexity in the collection. This constitutes the second charge, which has been enumerated.

The fact on which this charge rests is not to be admitted without several qualifications; particularly in reference to the state of things in this country. First. The great bulk of the Stock of a bank will consist of the funds of men in trade, among ourselves, and monied foreigners; the former of whom could not spare their capitals out of their reach, to be invested in loans, for long periods, on mortgages, or personal security; and the latter of whom would not be willing to be subjected to the casualties, delays and embarassments of such a disposition of their money in a distant country. Secondly. There will always be a considerable proportion of those, who are properly the money lenders of a Country, who from that spirit of caution, which usually characterises this description of men will incline rather to vest their funds in mortgages on real estate, than in the Stock of a Bank, which they are apt to consider as a more precarious security.

These considerations serve in a material degree to narrow the foundation of the objection, as to the point of fact. But there is a more satisfactory answer to it. The effect supposed, as far as it has existence, is temporary. The reverse of it takes place, in the general and permanent operation of the thing.

The capital of every public bank will of course be restricted within a certain defined limit. It is the province of legislative prudence so to adjust this limit, that while it will not be too contracted for the demand, which the course of business may create, and for the security, which the public ought to have for the solidity of the paper, which may be issued by the bank, it will still be within the compass of the pecuniary resources of the community; so that there may be an easy practicability of completing the subscriptions to it. When this is once done, the supposed effect of necessity ceases. There is then no longer room for the investment of any additional capital. Stock may indeed change hands by one person selling and another buying; but the money, which the buyer takes out of the common mass to purchase the stock, the seller receives, and restores to it. Hence the future surplusses, which may accumulate, must take their natural course, and lending at interest must go on, as if there were no such institution.

It must indeed flow in a more copious stream. The Bank furnishes an extraordinary supply for borrowers, within its immediate sphere. A larger supply consequently remains for borrowers elsewhere. In proportion, as the circulation of the Bank is extended, there is an augmentation of the aggregate mass of money, for answering the aggregate mass of demand. Hence a greater facility in obtaining it for every purpose.

It ought not to escape without a remark, that as far as the citizens of other countries become adventurers in the Bank, there is a positive increase of the gold and silver of the Country. It is true, that from this a half yearly rent is drawn back, accruing from the dividends upon the Stock. But as this rent arises from the employment of the capital, by our own citizens, it is probable, that it is more than replaced by the profits of that employment. It is also likely, that a part of it is, in the course of trade, converted into the products of our Country: And it may even prove an incentive, in some cases, to emigration to a country, in which the character of citizen is as easy to be acquired, as it is estimable and important. This view of the subject furnishes an answer to an objection, which has been deduced from the circumstance here taken notice of, namely the income resulting to foreigners from the part of the Stock, owned by them, which has been represented as tending to drain the country of its specie. In this objection, the original investment of the capital, and the constant use of it afterwards seem both to have been overlooked.

II. B. 3. Criticisms of banks: Banks encourage people to risk more money than they otherwise would.

That Banks furnish temptations to overtrading is the third of the enumerated objections. This must mean, that by affording additional aids to mercantile enterprise, they induce the merchant sometimes to adventure beyond the prudent or salutary point. But the very statement of the thing shews, that the subject of the charge is an occasional ill, incident to a general good. Credit of every kind (as a species of which only can bank lending have the effect supposed) must be in different degrees, chargeable with the same inconvenience. It is even applicable to gold and silver, when they abound in circulation. But would it be wise on this account to decry the precious metals, to root out credit; or to proscribe the means of that enterprise, which is the main spring of trade and a principal source of national wealth, because it now and then runs into excesses, of which overtrading is one?

If the abuses of a beneficial thing are to determine its condemnation, there is scarcely a source of public prosperity, which will not speedily be closed. In every case, the evil is to be compared with the good; and in the present case such a comparison will issue in this, that the new and increased energies derived to commercial enterprise, from the aid of banks, are a source of general profit and advantage; which greatly outweigh the partial ills of the overtrading of a few individuals, at particular times, or of numbers in particular conjunctures.

II. B. 4-5. Criticisms of banks: Money borrowed from banks makes fraudulent people appear trustworthy.

The fourth and fifth charges may be considered together. These relate to the aid, which is sometimes afforded by banks to unskilful adventurers and fraudulent traders. These charges also have some degree of foundation; though far less than has been pretended, and they add to the instances of partial ills, connected with more extensive and overbalancing benefits.

The practice of giving fictitious credit to improper persons is one of those evils, which experience guided by interest speedily corrects. The bank itself is in so much jeopardy of being a sufferer by it, that it has the strongest of all inducements to be on its guard. It may not only be injured immediately by the delinquencies of the persons, to whom such credit is given; but eventually, by the incapacities of others, whom their impositions, or failures may have ruined.

Nor is there much danger of a bank's being betrayed into this error, from want of information. The Directors, themselves, being, for the most part, selected from the class of Traders are to be expected to possess individually an accurate knowlege of the characters and situations of those, who come within that description. And they have, in addition to this, the course of dealing of the persons themselves with the bank to assist their judgment, which is in most cases a good index of the state, in which those persons are. The artifices and shifts, which those in desperate or declining circumstances are obliged to employ, to keep up the countenance, which the rules of the Bank require, and the train of their connections, are so many prognostics, not difficult to be interpreted, of the fate which awaits them. Hence it not unfrequently happens, that Banks are the first to discover the unsoundness of such characters, and, by withholding credit, to announce to the public, that they are not intitled to it.

If banks, in spite of every precaution, are sometimes betrayed into giving a false credit to the persons described; they more frequently enable honest and industrious men, of small or perhaps of no capital to undertake and prosecute business, with advantage to themselves and to the community; and assist merchants of both capital and credit, who meet with fortuitous and unforeseen shocks, which might without such helps prove fatal to them and to others; to make head against their misfortunes, and finally to retrieve their affairs: Circumstances, which form no inconsiderable encomium on the utility of Banks.

II. B. 6. Criticisms of banks: Banks tend to make gold and silver disappear from a country.

But the last and heaviest charge is still to be examined. This is, that Banks tend to banish the gold and silver of the Country.

The force of this objection rests upon their being an engine of paper credit, which by furnishing a substitute for the metals, is supposed to promote their exportation. It is an objection, which if it has any foundation, lies not against Banks, peculiarly, but against every species of paper credit.

The most common answer given to it is, that the thing supposed is of little, or no consequence; that it is immaterial what serves the purpose of money, whether paper or gold and silver; that the effect of both upon industry is the same; and that the intrinsic wealth of a nation is to be measured, not by the abundance of the precious metals, contained in it, but by the quantity of the productions of its labor and industry.

This answer is not destitute of solidity, though not intirely satisfactory. It is certain, that the vivification of industry, by a full circulation, with the aid of a proper and well regulated paper credit, may more than compensate for the loss of a part of the gold and silver of a Nation; if the consequence of avoiding that loss should be a scanty or defective circulation.

But the positive and permanent increase or decrease of the precious metals, in a Country, can hardly ever be a matter of indifference. As the commodity taken in lieu of every other, it is a species of the most effective wealth; and as the money of the world, it is of great concern to the state, that it possess a sufficiency of it to face any demands, which the protection of its external interests may create.

The objection seems to admit of another and a more conclusive answer, which controverts the fact itself. A nation, that has no mines of its own, must derive the precious metals from others; generally speaking, in exchange for the products of its labor and industry. The quantity, it will possess, will therefore, in the ordinary course of things, be regulated by the favourable, or unfavourable balance of its trade; that is, by the proportion between its abilities to supply foreigners, and its wants of them; between the amount of its exportations and that of its importations. Hence the state of its agriculture and manufactures, the quantity and quality of its labor and industry must, in the main, influence and determine the increase or decrease of its gold and silver.

If this be true, the inference seems to be, that well constituted Banks favour the increase of the precious metals. It has been shewn, that they augment in different ways, the active capital of the country. This, it is, which generates employment; which animates and expands labor and industry. Every addition, which is made to it, by contributing to put in motion a greater quantity of both, tends to create a greater quantity of the products of both: And, by furnishing more materials for exportation, conduces to a favourable balance of trade and consequently to the introduction and increase of gold and silver.

This conclusion appears to be drawn from solid premises. There are however objections to be made to it.

It may be said, that as Bank paper affords a substitute for specie, it serves to counteract that rigorous necessity for the metals, as a medium of circulation, which in the case of a wrong balance, might restrain in some degree their exportation; and it may be added, that from the same cause, in the same case, it would retard those œconomical and parsimonious reforms, in the manner of living, which the scarcity of money is calculated to produce, and which might be necessary to rectify such wrong balance.

There is perhaps some truth in both these observations; but they appear to be of a nature rather to form exceptions to the generality of the conclusion, than to overthrow it. The state of things, in which the absolute exigencies of circulation can be supposed to resist with any effect the urgent demands for specie, which a wrong balance of trade may occasion, presents an extreme case. And a situation in which a too expensive manner of living of a community, compared with its means, can stand in need of a corrective, from distress or necessity, is one, which perhaps rarely results, but from extraordinary and adventitious causes: such for example, as a national revolution, which unsettles all the established habits of a people, and inflames the appetite for extravagance, by the illusions of an ideal wealth, engendered by the continual multiplication of a depreciating currency or some similar cause. There is good reason to believe, that where the laws are wise and well executed, and the inviolability of property and contracts maintained, the œconomy of a people will, in the general course of things, correspond with its means.

The support of industry is probably in every case, of more consequence towards correcting a wrong balance of trade, than any practicable retrenchments, in the expences of families, or individuals: And the stagnation of it would be likely to have more effect, in prolonging, than any such savings in shortening its continuance. That stagnation is a natural consequence of an inadequate medium, which, without the aid of Bank circulation, would in the cases supposed, be severely felt.

It also deserves notice, that as the circulation is always in a compound ratio to the fund, upon which it depends, and to the demand for it, and as that fund is itself affected by the exportation of the metals, there is no danger of its being overstocked, as in the case of paper issued at the pleasure of the Government; or of its preventing the consequences of any unfavourable balance from being sufficiently felt, to produce the reforms alluded to, as far as circumstances may require and admit.

Nothing can be more fallible, than the comparisons, which have been made between different countries, to illustrate the truth of the position under consideration. The comparative quantity of gold and silver, in different countries, depends upon an infinite variety of facts and combinations, all of which ought to be known, in order to judge, whether the existence or non existence of paper currencies has any share in the relative proportions they contain. The mass and value of the productions of the labor and industry of each, compared with its wants; the nature of its establishments abroad; the kind of wars in which it is usually engaged; the relations it bears to the countries, which are the original possessors of those metals; the privileges it enjoys in their trade; these and a number of other circumstances are all to be taken into the account, and render the investigation too complex to justify any reliance on the vague and general surmises, which have been hitherto hazarded on the point.

In the foregoing discussion, the objection has been considered as applying to the permanent expulsion and diminution of the metals. Their temporary exportation, for particular purposes, has not been contemplated. This, it must be confessed is facilitated by Banks, from the faculty they possess of supplying their place. But their utility is in nothing more conspicuous, than in these very cases. They enable the Government to pay its foreign debts, and to answer any exigencies, which the external concerns of the community may have produced. They enable the Merchant to support his credit, (on which the prosperity of trade depends) when special circumstances prevent remittances in other modes. They enable him also to prosecute enterprises, which ultimately tend to an augmentation of the species of wealth in question. It is evident, that gold and silver may often be employed in procuring commodities abroad; which, in a circuitous commerce, replace the original fund, with considerable addition. But it is not to be inferred from this facility given to temporary exportation, that Banks, which are so friendly to trade and industry, are in their general tendency, inimical to the increase of the precious metals.

II. C. Summing up: banks are very useful to the government.

These several views of the subject appear sufficient to impress a full conviction, of the utility of Banks, and to demonstrate that they are of great importance, not only in relation to the administration of the finances, but in the general system of the political œconomy.

II. C. 1. Shortage of money in circulation after the war caused many problems.

The judgment of many concerning them has no doubt been perplexed, by the misinterpretation of appearances, which were to be ascribed to other causes. The general devastation of personal property, occasioned by the late war, naturally produced, on the one hand, a great demand for money, and on the other a great deficiency of it to answer the demand. Some injudicious laws, which grew out of the public distresses, by impairing confidence and causing a part of the inadequate sum in the country to be locked up, aggravated the evil: The dissipated habits, contracted by many individuals, during the war, which after the peace plunged them into expences beyond their incomes: The number of adventurers without capital and in many instances, without information, who at that epoch rushed into trade, and were obliged to make any sacrifices to support a transient credit; the employment of considerable sums in speculations upon the public debt, which from its unsettled state was incapable of becoming itself a substitute: All these circumstances concurring necessarily led to usurious borrowing, produced most of the inconveniencies, and were the true causes of most of the appearances; which, where the Banks were established, have been by some erroneously placed to their account: a mistake, which they might easily have avoided, by turning their eyes towards places, where there were none, and where, nevertheless, the same evils would have been perceived to exist, even in a greater degree, than where those institutions had obtained.

These evils have either ceased, or been greatly mitigated. Their more complete extinction may be looked for, from that additional security to property, which the constitution of the United States happily gives (a circumstance of prodigious moment in the scale both of public and private prosperity) from the attraction of foreign capital, under the auspices of that security, to be employed upon objects & in enterprises, for which the state of this country opens a wide and inviting field, from the consistency and stability, which the public debt is fast acquiring, as well in the public opinion, at home and abroad, as in fact; from the augmentation of capital, which that circumstance and the quarter yearly payment of interest will afford; and from the more copious circulation, which will be likely to be created by a well constituted National Bank.

II. C. 2. Why issuing paper money is a problem.

The establishment of Banks in this country seems to be recommended by reasons of a peculiar nature. Previously to the revolution circulation was in a great measure carried on by paper emitted by the several local governments. In Pennsylvania alone the quantity of it was near a million and a half of dollars. This auxiliary may be said to be now at an end. And it is generally supposed, that there has been for some time past, a deficiency of circulating medium. How far that deficiency is to be considered as real or imaginary is not susceptible of demonstration, but there are circumstances and appearances, which, in relation to the country at large, countenance the supposition of its reality.

The circumstances are, besides the fact just mentioned respecting paper emissions the vast tracts of waste land, and the little advanced state of manufactures. The progressive settlement of the former, while it promises ample retribution, in the generation of future resources, diminishes or obstructs, in the mean time, the active wealth of the country. It not only draws off a part of the circulating money, and places it in a more passive state, but it diverts into its own channels a portion of that species of labor and industry, which would otherwise be employed, in furnishing materials for foreign trade, and which by contributing to a favourable balance, would assist the introduction of specie. In the early periods of new settlements, the settlers not only furnish no surplus for exportation, but they consume a part of that which is produced by the labour of others. The same thing is a cause, that manufactures do not advance or advance slowly. And notwithstanding some hypotheses to the contrary, there are many things to induce a suspicion, that the precious metals will not abound, in any country, which has not mines or variety of manufactures. They have been sometimes acquired by the sword, but the modern system of war has expelled this resource, and it is one upon which it is to be hoped the United States will never be inclined to rely.

The appearances, alluded to, are, greater prevalency of direct barter, in the more interior districts of the country, which however has been for some time past gradually lessening; and greater difficulty, generally, in the advantageous alienation of improved real estate; which, also, has, of late, diminished, but is still seriously felt in different parts of the Union. The difficulty of getting money, which has been a general complaint, is not added to the number; because it is the complaint of all times, and one, in which imagination must ever have too great scope, to permit an appeal to it.

If the supposition of such a deficiency be in any degree founded, and some aid to circulation be desireable, it remains to inquire what ought to be the nature of that aid.

The emitting of paper money by the authority of Government is wisely prohibited to the individual States, by the National Constitution. And the spirit of that prohibition ought not to be disregarded, by the Government of the United States. Though paper emissions, under a general authority, might have some advantages, not applicable, and be free from some disadvantages, which are applicable, to the like emissions by the States separately; yet they are of a nature so liable to abuse, and it may even be affirmed so certain of being abused, that the wisdom of the Government will be shewn in never trusting itself with the use of so seducing and dangerous an expedient. In times of tranquillity, it might have no ill consequence, it might even perhaps be managed in a way to be productive of good; but in great and trying emergencies, there is almost a moral certainty of its becoming mischievous. The stamping of paper is an operation so much easier than the laying of taxes, that a government, in the practice of paper emissions, would rarely fail in any such emergency to indulge itself too far, in the employment of that resource, to avoid as much as possible one less auspicious to present popularity. If it should not even be carried so far as to be rendered an absolute bubble, it would at least be likely to be extended to a degree, which would occasion an inflated and artificial state of things incompatible with the regular and prosperous course of the political œconomy.

II. C. 3. How paper money differs from bank notes.

Among other material differences between a paper currency, issued by the mere authority of Government, and one issued by a Bank, payable in coin, is this—That in the first case, there is no standard to which an appeal can be made, as to the quantity which will only satisfy, or which will surcharge the circulation; in the last, that standard results from the demand. If more should be issued, than is necessary, it will return upon the bank. Its emissions, as elsewhere intimated, must always be in a compound ratio to the fund and to the demand: Whence it is evident, that there is a limitation in the nature of the thing: While the discretion of the government is the only measure of the extent of the emissions, by its own authority.

This consideration further illustrates the danger of emissions of that sort, and the preference, which is due to Bank paper.

II. C. 4. Why it would be better to use bank notes rather than specie for paying the interest on the U.S. debt.

The payment of the interest of the public debt, at thirteen different places, is a weighty reason, peculiar to our immediate situation, for desiring a Bank circulation. Without a paper, in general currency, equivalent to gold and silver, a considerable proportion of the specie of the country must always be suspended from circulation and left to accumulate, preparatorily to each day of payment; and as often as one approaches, there must in several cases be an actual transportation of the metals at both expence and risk, from their natural and proper reservoirs to distant places. This necessity will be felt very injuriously to the trade of some of the States; and will embarrass not a little the operations of the Treasury in those States. It will also obstruct those negociations, between different parts of the Union, by the instrumentality of Treasury bills, which have already afforded valuable accommodations to Trade in general.

III. Given that we need a national bank, what are its requirements?

Assuming it then as a consequence, from what has been said, that a national bank is a desireable institution; two inquiries emerge. Is there no such institution, already in being, which has a claim to that character, and which supersedes the propriety, or necessity of another? If there be none, what are the principles upon which one ought to be established.

III. A. Problems with the Bank of North America

There are at present three banks in the United States. That of North America, established in the city of Philadelphia; that of New York, established in the city of New York; that of Massachusetts, established in the city of Boston. Of these three, the first is the only one, which has at any time had a direct relation to the Government of the United States.

The Bank of North America originated in a resolution of Congress of the 26th of May 1781, founded upon a proposition of the Superintendant of finance, which was afterwards carried into execution, by an ordinance of the 31st of december following, entitled, "An Ordinance to incorporate the Subscribers to the Bank of North America."

The aid afforded to the United States, by this institution, during the remaining period of the war, was of essential consequence, and its conduct towards them since the peace, has not weakened its title to their patronage and favour. So far its pretensions to the character in question are respectable; but there are circumstances, which militate against them; and considerations, which indicate the propriety of an establishment on different principles.

The Directors of this Bank, on behalf of their constituents, have since accepted and acted under a new charter from the State of Pennsylvania, materially variant from their original one; and which so narrows the foundation of the institution, as to render it an incompetent basis for the extensive purposes of a National Bank.

III. A. 1. The Bank of North America does not have enough capital to serve as the government's banker.

The limit assigned by the ordinance of Congress to the Stock of the Bank is ten millions of Dollars. The last charter of Pennsylvania confines it to two millions. Questions naturally arise, whether there be not a direct repugnancy between two charters so differently circumstanced; and whether the acceptance of the one is not to be deemed a virtual surrender of the other. But perhaps it is neither adviseable nor necessary to attempt a solution of them.

III. A. 1. a. By the way: The Bank of North America was not given an exclusive charter.

There is nothing in the Acts of Congress, which imply an exclusive right in the institution, to which they relate, except during the term of the war. There is therefore nothing, if the public good require it, which prevents the establishment of another. It may however be incidentally remarked, that in the general opinion of the citizens of the United States, the Bank of North America has taken the station of a bank of Pennsylvania only. This is a strong argument for a new institution, or for a renovation of the old, to restore it to the situation in which it originally stood, in the view of the United States.

But though the ordinance of Congress contains no grant of exclusive privileges, there may be room to allege, that the Government of the United States ought not, in point of candour and equity, to establish any rival or interfering institution, in prejudice of the one already established; especially as this has, from services rendered, well founded claims to protection and regard.

The justice of such an observation ought within proper bounds to be admitted. A new establishment of the sort ought not to be made, without cogent and sincere reasons of public good. And in the manner of doing it every facility should be given to a consolidation of the old with the new, upon terms not injurious to the parties concerned. But there is no ground to maintain, that in a case, in which the Government has made no condition restricting its authority, it ought voluntarily to restrict it, through regard to the interests of a particular institution, when those of the state dictate a different course; especially too after such circumstances have intervened, as characterise the actual situation of the Bank of North America.

III. A. 2. The Bank of North America's charter expires in 14 years.

The inducements, to a new disposition of the thing are now to be considered. The first of them which occurs is, the, at least ambiguous, situation, in which the Bank of North America has placed itself, by the acceptance of its last charter. If this has rendered it the mere Bank of a particular State, liable to dissolution at the expiration of fourteen years, to which term the act of that state has restricted its duration, it would be neither fit nor expedient to accept it, as an equivalent for a Bank of the United States.

III. A. 3. The Bank of North America's directors can serve indefinitely, which may lead them to conspire against the best interests of the stockholders and the government.

The restriction of its capital also, which according to the same supposition, cannot be extended beyond two millions of dollars, is a conclusive reason for a different establishment. So small a capital promises neither the requisite aid to government, nor the requisite security to the community. It may answer very well the purposes of local accommodation, but is an inadequate foundation for a circulation coextensive with the United States, embracing the whole of their revenues, and affecting every individual, into whose hands the paper may come.

And inadequate as such a capital would be to the essential ends of a National Bank, it is liable to being rendered still more so, by that principle of the constitution of the Bank of North America, contained equally in its old and in its new charter, which leaves the increase of the actual capital at any time (now far short of the allowed extent) to the discretion of the Directors, or Stockholders. It is naturally to be expected, that the allurements of an advanced price of Stock and of large dividends may disincline those, who are interested, to an extension of capital; from which they will be apt to fear a diminution of profits. And from this circumstance, the interest and accommodation of the public (as well individually as collectively) are made more subordinate to the interest, real or imagined, of the Stockholders, than they ought to be. It is true, that unless the latter be consulted, there can be no bank (in the sense at least in which institutions of this kind, worthy of confidence, can be established in this Country) but it does not follow, that this is alone to be consulted, or that it even ought to be paramount. Public utility is more truly the object of public Banks, than private profit. And it is the business of Government, to constitute them on such principles, that while the latter will result, in a sufficient degree, to afford competent motives to engage in them, the former be not made subservient to it. To effect this, a principal object of attention ought to be to give free scope to the creation of an ample capital; and with this view, fixing the bounds, which are deemed safe and convenient, to leave no discretion either to stop short of them or to overpass them. The want of this precaution, in the establishment of the Bank of North America, is a further and an important reason for desiring one differently constituted.

There may be room, at first sight, for a supposition, that as the profits of a Bank will bear a proportion to the extent of its operations, and as, for this reason, the interest of the Stockholders will not be disadvantageously affected, by any necessary augmentations of capital, there is no cause to apprehend, that they will be indisposed to such augmentations. But most men in matters of this nature, prefer the certainties, they enjoy, to probabilities depending on untried experiments; especially when these promise rather, that they will not be injured, than that they will be benefited.

From the influence of this principle, and a desire of enhancing its profits, the Directors of a Bank will be more apt to overstrain its faculties, in the attempt to face the additional demands, which the course of business may create, than to set on foot new subscriptions, which may hazard a diminution of the profits, and even a temporary reduction of the price of Stock.

Banks are among the best expedients for lowering the rate of interest, in a country; but to have this effect, their capitals must be completely equal to all the demands of business, and such as will tend to remove the idea, that the accommodations they afford, are in any degree favours; an idea very apt to accompany the parsimonious dispensation of contracted funds. In this, as in every other case, the plenty of the commodity ought to beget a moderation of the price.

The want of a principle of rotation, in the constitution of the Bank of North America, is another argument for a variation of the establishment. Scarcely one of the reasons, which militate against this principle in the constitution of a country, is applicable to that of a Bank; while there are strong reasons in favour of it, in relation to the one, which do not apply to the other. The knowlege, to be derived from experience, is the only circumstance common to both, which pleads against rotation in the directing officers of a Bank.

But the objects of the Government of a nation, and those of the government of a bank are so widely different, as greatly to weaken the force of that consideration, in reference to the latter. Almost every important case of legislation requires, towards a right decision, a general and an accurate acquaintance with the affairs of the state; and habits of thinking seldom acquired, but from a familiarity with public concerns. The administration of a bank, on the contrary, is regulated, by a few simple fixed maxims, the application of which is not difficult to any man of judgment, especially if instructed in the principles of trade. It is in general a constant succession of the same details.

But though this be the case, the idea of the advantages of experience is not to be slighted. Room ought to be left for the regular transmission of official information: And for this purpose the head of the direction ought to be excepted from the principle of rotation. With this exception, and with the aid of the information of the subordinate officers, there can be no danger of any ill effects from want of experience, or knowlege; especially as the periodical exclusion ought not to reach the whole of the Directors at one time.

The argument in favour of the principle of rotation is this, that by lessening the danger of combinations among the Directors, to make the institution subservient to party views, or to the accommodation, preferably, of any particular set of men, it will render the public confidence more firm, stable and unqualified.

When it is considered, that the Directors of a Bank are not elected by the great body of the community, in which a diversity of views will naturally prevail, at different conjunctures, but by a small and select class of men, among whom it is far more easy to cultivate a steady adherence to the same persons and objects; and that those Directors have it in their power so immediately to conciliate, by obliging the most influential of this class, it is easy to perceive, that without the principle of rotation, changes in that body can rarely happen, but as a concession which they may themselves think it expedient to make to public opinion.

The continual administration of an institution of this kind, by the same persons, will never fail, with, or without, cause, from their conduct, to excite distrust and discontent. The necessary secrecy of their transactions gives unlimited scope to imagination to infer that something is, or may be wrong. And this inevitable mystery is a solid reason, for inserting in the constitution of a Bank the necessity of a change of men. As neither the mass of the parties interested nor the public in general can be permitted to be witnesses of the interior management of the Directors, it is reasonable, that both should have that check upon their conduct, and that security against the prevalency of a partial or pernicious system, which will be produced by the certainty of periodical changes. Such too is the delicacy of the credit of a Bank, that every thing, which can fortify confidence and repel suspicion, without injuring its operations, ought carefully to be sought after in its formation.

III. A. 4. Voting of Bank of North America stock is one vote per share, which would allow the principal stockholders to do whatever they wish.

A further consideration in favour of a change, is the improper rule, by which the right of voting for Directors is regulated in the plan, upon which the Bank of North America was originally constituted, namely a vote for each share, and the want of a rule in the last charter; unless the silence of it, on that point, may signify that every Stockholder is to have an equal and a single vote, which would be a rule in a different extreme not less erroneous. It is of importance that a rule should be established, on this head, as it is one of those things, which ought not to be left to discretion; and it is consequently, of equal importance, that the rule should be a proper one.

A vote for each share renders a combination, between a few principal Stockholders, to monopolise the power and benefits of the Bank too easy. An equal vote to each Stockholder, however great or small his interest in the institution, allows not that degree of weight to large stockholders, which it is reasonable they should have, and which perhaps their security and that of the bank require. A prudent mean is to be preferred. A conviction of this has produced a bye-law of the corporation of the bank of North America, which evidently aims at such a mean. But a reflexion arises here, that a like majority with that which enacted this law, may at any moment repeal it.

III. A. 5. The Bank of North America has no restrictions on foreign ownership of stock.

The last inducement, which shall be mentioned, is the want of precautions to guard against a foreign influence insinuating itself into the Direction of the Bank. It seems scarcely reconcileable with a due caution to permit, that any but citizens should be eligible as Directors of a National Bank, or that non-resident foreigners should be able to influence the appointment of Directors by the votes of their proxies. In the event however of an incorporation of the Bank of North America in the plan, it may be necessary to qualify this principle, so as to leave the right of foreigners, who now hold shares of its stock unimpaired; but without the power of transmitting the privilege in question to foreign alienees.

It is to be considered, that such a Bank is not a mere matter of private property, but a political machine of the greatest importance to the State.

There are other variations from the Constitution of the Bank of North America, not of inconsiderable moment, which appear desireable, but which are not of magnitude enough to claim a prliminary discussion. These will be seen in the plan, which will be submitted in the sequel.

If the objections, which have been stated to the constitution of the Bank of North America, are admitted to be well founded, they will nevertheless not derogate from the merit of the main design, or of the services which that bank has rendered, or of the benefits which it has produced. The creation of such an institution, at the time it took place, was a measure dictated by wisdom. Its utility has been amply evinced by its fruits. American Independence owes much to it. And it [is] very conceivable, that reasons of the moment may have rendered those features in it inexpedient which a revision, with a permanent view, suggests as desireable.

IV. PROPOSED RULES FOR A NATIONAL BANK

The order of the subject leads next to an inquiry into the principles, upon which a national Bank, ought to be organised.

IV. A. What a national bank should not be allowed to do

IV. A. 1. A national bank should not open many branches, at least at first.

The situation of the United States naturally inspires a wish, that the form of the institution could admit of a plurality of branches. But various considerations discourage from pursuing this idea. The complexity of such a plan would be apt to inspire doubts, which might deter from adventuring in it. And the practicability of a safe and orderly administration, though not to be abandoned as desparate cannot be made so manifest in perspective, as to promise the removal of those doubts, or to justify the Government in adopting the idea as an original experiment. The most that would seem adviseable, on this point, is to insert a provision, which may lead to it hereafter; if experience shall more clearly demonstrate its utility, and satisfy those, who may have the Direction, that it may be adopted with safety. It is certain, that it would have some advantages both peculiar and important. Besides more general accommodation, it would lessen the danger of a run upon the bank.

The argument, against it, is, that each branch must be under a distinct, though subordinate direction; to which a considerable latitude of discretion must of necessity be entrusted. And as the property of the whole institution would be liable for the engagements of each part, that and its credit would be at stake, upon the prudence of the Directors of every part. The mismanagement of either branch, miight hazard serious disorder in the whole.

IV. A. 2. A national bank should not be allowed to lend money with land as collateral, at least at first.

Another wish, dictated by the particular situation of the country, is, that the Bank could be so constituted as to be made an immediate instrument of loans to the proprietors of land; but this wish also yields to the difficulty of accomplishing it. Land is alone an unfit fund for a bank circulation. If the notes issued upon it were not to be payable in coin, on demand, or at a short date; this would amount to nothing more than a repetition of the paper emissions, which are now exploded by the general voice. If the notes are to be payable in coin, the land must first be converted into it by sale, or mortgage. The difficulty of effecting the latter is the very thing, which begets the desire of finding another resource, and the former would not be practicable on a sudden emergency, but with sacrifices which would make the cure worse than the disease. Neither is the idea of constituting the fund partly of coin and partly of land free from impediments. These two species of property do not for the most part unite in the same hands. Will the monied man consent to enter into a partnership with the landholder by which the latter will share in the profits which will be made by the money of the former? The money it is evident will be the agent or efficient cause of the profits. The land can only be regarded as an additional security. It is not difficult to foresee, that an union, on such terms, will not readily be formed. If the landholders are to procure the money by sale or mortgage of a part of their lands, this they can as well do, when the Stock consists wholly of money, as if it were to be compounded of money and land.

To procure for the landholders the assistance of loans is the great desideratum. Supposing other difficulties surmounted, and a fund created, composed partly of coin and partly of land, yet the benefit contemplated could only then be obtained, by the banks advancing them its notes for the whole or part of the value of the lands, they had subscribed to the Stock. If this advance was small, the relief aimed at would not be given; if it was large, the quantity of notes issued would be a cause of distrust, and, if received at all, they would be likely to return speedily upon the Bank for payment; which, after exhausting its coin, might be under a necessity of turning its lands into money, at any price, that could be obtained for them, to the irreparable prejudice of the proprietors.

IV. A. 3. A national bank should not be wholly government owned.

Considerations of public advantage suggest a further wish, which is, that the Bank could be established upon principles, that would cause the profits of it to redound to the immediate benefit of the State. This is contemplated by many, who speak of a National Bank, but the idea seems liable to insuperable objections. To attach full confidence to an institution of this nature, it appears to be an essential ingredient in its structure, that it shall be under a private not a public Direction, under the guidance of individual interest, not of public policy; which would be supposed to be, and in certain emergencies, under a feeble or too sanguine administration would, really, be, liable to being too much influenced by public necessity. The suspicion of this would most probably be a canker, that would continually corrode the vitals of the credit of the Bank, and would be most likely to prove fatal in those situations, in which the public good would require, that they should be most sound and vigorous. It would indeed be little less, than a miracle, should the credit of the Bank be at the disposal of the Government, if in a long series of time, there was not experienced a calamitous abuse of it. It is true, that it would be the real interest of the Government not to abuse it; its genuine policy to husband and cherish it with the most guarded circumspection as an inestimable treasure. But what Government ever uniformly consulted its true interest, in opposition to the temptations of momentary exigencies? What nation was ever blessed with a constant succession of upright and wise Administrators?

The keen, steady, and, as it were, magnetic sense, of their own interest, as proprietors, in the Directors of a Bank, pointing invariably to its true pole, the prosperity of the institution, is the only security, that can always be relied upon, for a careful and prudent administration. It is therefore the only basis on which an enlightened, unqualified and permanent confidence can be expected to be erected and maintained.

The precedents of the Banks established in several cities of Europe, Amsterdam, Hamburgh and others, may seem to militate against this position. Without a precise knowlege of all the peculiarities of their respective constitutions, it is difficult to pronounce how far this may be the case. That of Amsterdam, however, which we best know, is rather under a municipal than a governmental direction. Particular magistrates of the city, not officers of the republic, have the management of it. It is also a Bank of deposit, not of loan, or circulation; consequently less liable to abuse, as well as less useful. Its general business consists in receiving money for safekeeping; which if not called for within a certain time becomes a part of its Stock and irreclaimable: But a Credit is given for it on the books of the Bank, which being transferable, answers all the purposes of money.

The Directors being Magistrates of the city, and the Stockholders in general, its most influential citizens, it is evident, that the principle of private interest must be prevalent in the management of the Bank. And it is equally evident, that from the nature of its operations, that principle is less essential to it, than to an Institution, constituted with a view to the accommodation of the Public and Individuals by direct loans and a paper circulation.

As far as may concern the aid of the Bank, within the proper limits, a good government has nothing more to wish for, than it will always possess; though the management be in the hands of private individuals. As the institution, if rightly constituted, must depend for its renovation from time to time on the pleasure of the Government, it will not be likely to feel a disposition to render itself, by its conduct, unworthy of public patronage. The Government too in the administration of its finances, has it in its power to reciprocate benefits to the Bank, of not less importance, than those which the bank affords to the Government, and which besides are never unattended with an immediate and adequate compensation. Independent of these more particular considerations, the natural weight and influence of a good Government will always go far towards procuring a compliance with its desires; and as the Directors will usually be composed of some of the most discreet, respectable and well informed citizens, it can hardly ever be difficult to make them sensible of the force of the inducements, which ought to stimulate their exertions.

It will not follow, from what has been said, that the State may not be the holder of a part of the Stock of a Bank, and consequently a sharer in the profits of it. It will only follow, that it ought not to desire any participation in the Direction of it, and therefore ought not to own the whole or a principal part of the Stock; for if the mass of the property should belong to the public, and if the direction of it should be in private hands, this would be to commit the interests of the State to persons, not interested, or not enough interested in their proper management.

IV. A. 4. The government should be able to look at the books of the national bank.

There is one thing, however, which the Government owes to itself and to the community; at least to all that part of it, who are not Stockholders; which is to reserve to itself a right of ascertaining, as often as may be necessary, the state of the Bank, excluding however all pretension to controul. This right forms an article in the primitive constitution of the Bank of North America. And its propriety stands upon the clearest reasons. If the paper of a Bank is to be permitted to insinuate itself into all the revenues and receipts of a country; if it is even to be tolerated as the substitute for gold and silver, in all the transactions of business, it becomes in either view a national concern of the first magnitude. As such the ordinary rules of prudence require, that the Government should possess the means of ascertaining, whenever it thinks fit, that so delicate a trust is executed with fidelity and care. A right of this nature is not only desireable, as it respects the Government; but it ought to be equally so to all those, concerned in the institution; as an additional title to public and private confidence; and as a thing which can only be formidable to practices, that imply mismanagement. The presumption must always be, that the characters who would be entrusted with the exercise of this right, on behalf of the Government, will not be deficient in the discretion, which it may require; at least the admitting of this presumption cannot be deemed too great a return of confidence for that very large portion of it, which the Government is required to place in the Bank.

IV. B. Proposed rules for a national bank

Abandoning, therefore, ideas, which however agreeable or desireable, are neither practicable nor safe, the following plan for the constitution of a National Bank is respectfully submitted to the consideration of the House.

IV. B. 1. Capital of $10 million; and terms of stock purchase

I. The capital Stock of the Bank shall not exceed ten Millions of Dollars, divided into Twenty five thousand shares, each share being four hundred Dollars; to raise which sum, subscriptions shall be opened on the first monday of april next, and shall continue open, until the whole shall be subscribed. Bodies politic as well as individuals may subscribe.

II. The amount of each share shall be payable, one fourth in gold and silver coin, and three fourths in that part of the public debt, which according to the loan proposed by the Act making provision for the debt of the United States, shall bear an accruing interest at the time of payment of six per centum per annum.

III. The respective sums subscribed shall be payable in four equal parts, as well specie as debt, in succession, and at the distance of six calendar months from each other; the first payment to be made at the time of subscription. If there shall be a failure in any subsequent payment, the party failing shall lose the benefit of any dividend which may have accrued, prior to the time for making such payment, and during the delay of the same.

IV. B. 2. The bank's charter will expire when the national debt is paid off.

IV. The Subscribers to the Bank and their successors shall be incorporated, and shall so continue until the final redemption of that part of its stock, which shall consist of the public debt.

IV. B. 3. Restrictions on assets and loans.

V. The capacity of the corporation to hold real and personal estate shall be limited to fifteen millions of Dollars, including the amount of its capital, or original stock. The lands and tenements, which it shall be permitted to hold, shall be only such as shall be requisite for the immediate accommodation of the institution; and such as shall have been bona fide mortgaged to it by way of security, or conveyed to it in satisfaction of debts previously contracted, in the usual course of its dealings, or purchased at sales upon judgments which shall have been obtained for such debts.

VI. The totality of the debts of the company, whether by bond, bill, note, or other contract, (credits for deposits excepted) shall never exceed the amount of its capital stock. In case of excess, the Directors, under whose administration it shall happen, shall be liable for it in their private or separate capacities. Those who may have dissented may excuse themselves from this responsibility by immediately giving notice of the fact and their dissent to the President of the United States, and to the Stockholders, at a general meeting to be called by the President of the Bank at their request.

VII. The Company may sell or demise its lands and tenements, or may sell the whole, or any part of the public Debt, whereof its Stock shall consist; but shall trade in nothing, except bills of exchange, gold and silver bullion, or in the sale of goods pledged for money lent: nor shall take more than at the rate of six per centum, per annum, upon its loans or discounts.

IV. B. 4. Limitations on lending to the U.S. government and to foreign governments.

VIII. No loan shall be made by the bank, for the use or on account of the Government of the United States, or of either of them to an amount exceeding fifty thousand Dollars, or of any foreign prince or State; unless previously authorised by a law of the United States.

IV. B. 5. Bank stock is transferable.

IX. The Stock of the Bank shall be transferable according to such rules as shall be instituted by the Company in that behalf.

IV. B. 6. Directors, voting, staff

X. The affairs of the Bank shall be under the management of Twenty five Directors, one of whom shall be the President. And there shall be on the first monday of January, in each year, a choice of Directors, by plurality of suffrages of the Stockholders, to serve for a year. The Directors at their first meeting, after each election, shall choose one of their number as President.

XI. The number of votes, to which each Stockholder shall be entitled, shall be according to the number of shares he shall hold in the proportions following, that is to say, for one share and not more than two shares one vote; for every two shares, above two and not exceeding ten, one vote; for every four shares above ten and not exceeding thirty, one vote; for every six shares above thirty and not exceeding sixty, one vote; for every eight shares above sixty and not exceeding one hundred, one vote; and for every ten shares above one hundred, one vote; but no person, copartnership, or body politic, shall be entitled to a greater number than thirty votes. And after the first election, no share or shares shall confer a right of suffrage, which shall not have been holden three calendar months previous to the day of election. Stockholders actually resident within the United States and none other may vote in elections by proxy.

XII. Not more than three fourths of the Directors in office, exclusive of the President, shall be eligible for the next succeeding year. But the Director who shall be President at the time of an election may always be reelected.

XIII. None but a Stockholder being a citizen of the United States, shall be eligible as a Director.

XIV. Any number of Stockholders not less than sixty, who together shall be proprietors of two hundred shares, or upwards, shall have power at any time to call a general meeting of the Stockholders, for purposes relative to the Institution; giving at least six weeks notice in two public gazettes of the place where the Bank is kept, and specifying in such notice the object of the meeting.

XV. In case of the death, resignation, absence from the United States, or removal of a Director by the Stockholders, his place may be filled by a new choice for the remainder of the year.

XVI. No Director shall be entitled to any emolument, unless the same shall have been allowed by the Stockholders at a General meeting. The Stockholders shall make such compensation to the President, for his extraordinary attendance at the Bank, as shall appear to them reasonable.

XVII. Not less than seven Directors shall constitute a Board for the transaction of business.

XVIII. Every Cashier, or Treasurer, before he enters on the duties of his office shall be required to give bond, with two or more sureties, to the satisfaction of the Directors, in a sum not less than twenty thousand Dollars, with condition for his good behaviour.

IV. B. 7. Payment of bank dividends, and redemption of bank bills and bank notes

XIX. Half yearly dividends shall be made of so much of the profits of the Bank as shall appear to the Directors adviseable: And once in every three years the Directors shall lay before the Stockholders, at a General Meeting, for their information, an exact and particular statement of the debts, which shall have remained unpaid, after the expiration of the original credit, for a period of treble the term of that credit; and of the surplus of profit, if any, after deducting losses and dividends.

XX. The bills and notes of the Bank originally made payable, or which shall have become payable on demand, in gold and silver coin, shall be receivable in all payments to the United States.

IV. B. 8. The secretary of the Treasury may examine the bank's books.

XXI. The Officer at the head of the Treasury Department of the United States, shall be furnished from time to time, as often as he may require, not exceeding once a week, with statements of the amount of the capital Stock of the Bank and of the debts due to the same; of the monies deposited therein; of the notes in circulation, and of the Cash in hand; and shall have a right to inspect such general account in the books of the bank as shall relate to the said statements; provided, that this shall not be construed to imply a right of inspecting this account of any private individual or individuals with the Bank.

IV. B. 9. No other national bank shall be established while this one still exists.

XXII. No similar institution shall be established by any future act of the United States, during the continuance of the one hereby proposed to be established.

IV. B. 10. The directors of the bank may establish branches.

XXIII. It shall be lawful for the Directors of the Bank to establish offices, wheresoever they shall think fit, within the United States, for the purposes of discount and deposit only, and upon the same terms, and in the same manner, as shall be practiced at the Bank; and to commit the management of the said offices, and the making of the said discounts, either to Agents specially appointed by them, or to such persons as may be chosen by the Stockholders residing at the place where any such office shall be, under such agreements and subject to such regulations as they shall deem proper; not being contrary to law or to the Constitution of the Bank.

IV. B. 11. The U.S. government may purchase up to $2 million of the bank's stock.

XXIV. And lastly. The President of the United States shall be authorised to cause a subscription to be made to the Stock of the said Company, on behalf of the United States, to an amount not exceeding two Millions of Dollars, to be paid out of the monies which shall be borrowed by virtue of either of the Acts, the one entitled "an Act making provision for the debt of the United States," and the other entitled "An Act making provision for the reduction of the Public Debt"; borrowing of the bank an equal sum, to be applied to the purposes for which the said monies shall have been procured, reimbursable in ten years by equal annual instalments; or at any time sooner, or in any greater proportions, that the Government may think fit.

The reasons for the several provisions contained in the foregoing plan, have been so far anticipated, and will, for the most part, be so readily suggested, by the nature of those provisions, that any comments, which need further be made, will be both few and concise.

IV. C. Explanations of various provisions above

IV. C. 1. Why should U.S. bonds be used in the purchase of bank stock?

The combination of a portion of the public Debt in the formation of the Capital, is the principal thing, of which an explanation is requisite. The chief object of this is, to enable the creation of a capital sufficiently large to be the basis of an extensive circulation, and an adequate security for it. As has been elsewhere remarked, the original plan of the Bank of North America contemplated a capital of ten millions of Dollars, which is certainly not too broad a foundation for the extensive operations, to which a National Bank is destined. But to collect such a sum in this country, in gold and silver, into one depository, may, without hesitation, be pronounced impracticable. Hence the necessity of an auxiliary which the public debt at once presents.

This part of the fund will be always ready to come in aid of the specie. It will more and more command a ready sale; and can therefore expeditiously be turned into coin if an exigency of the Bank should at any time require it. This quality of prompt convertibility into coin, renders it an equivalent for that necessary agent of Bank circulation; and distinguishes it from a fund in land of which the sale would generally be far less compendious and at great disadvantage. The quarter yearly receipts of interest will also be an actual addition to the specie fund during the intervals between them and the half yearly dividends of profits. The objection to combining land with specie, resulting from their not being generally in possession of the same persons, does not apply to the debt, which will always be found in considerable quantity among the monied and trading people.

The debt composing part of the capital, besides its collateral effect in enabling the Bank to extend its operations, and consequently to enlarge its profits, will produce a direct annual revenue of six per centum from the Government, which will enter into the half yearly dividends received by the Stockholders.

When the present price of the public debt is considered, and the effect which its conversion into Bank Stock, incorporated with a specie fund, would in all probability have to accelerate its rise to the proper point, it will easily be discovered, that the operation presents in its outset a very considerable advantage to those who may become subscribers; and from the influence, which that rise would have on the general mass of the Debt, a proportional benefit to all the public creditors, and, in a sense, which has been more than once adverted to, to the community at large.

There is an important fact, which exemplifies the fitness of the public Debt, for a bank fund, and which may serve to remove doubts in some minds on this point. It is this, that the Bank of England in its first erection rested wholly on that foundation. The subscribers to a Loan to Government of one million two hundred thousand pounds sterling were incorporated as a Bank; of which the Debt created by the Loan, and the interest upon it, were the sole fund. The subsequent augmentations of its capital, which now amounts to between eleven and twelve millions of pounds sterling, have been of the same nature.

IV. C. 2. Why is the bank not allowed to lend more than its capital?

The confining of the right of the Bank to contract debts to the amount of its capital is an important precaution, which is not to be found in the constitution of the Bank of North America, and which, while the fund consists wholly of coin, would be a restriction attended with inconveniencies, but would be free from any if the composition of it should be such as is now proposed. The restriction exists in the establishment of the Bank of England, and as a source of security is worthy of imitation. The consequence of exceeding the limit there is, that each Stockholder is liable to the excess, in proportion to his interest in the Bank. When it is considered, that the Directors owe their appointments to the choice of the Stockholders, a responsibility of this kind, on the part of the latter, does not appear unreasonable. But, on the other hand, it may be deemed a hardship upon those, who may have dissented from the choice. And there are many among us, whom it might perhaps discourage from becoming concerned in the institution. These reasons have induced the placing of the responsibility upon the Directors, by whom the limit prescribed should be transgressed.

IV. C. 3. Why are loans to the U.S. government, states governments, and foreign governments restricted?

The interdiction of loans on account of the United States, or of any particular State, beyond the moderate sum specified, or of any foreign power, will serve as a barrier to executive incroachments; and to combinations inauspicious to the safety or contrary to the policy of the Union.

IV. C. 4. Why are the bank's interest rates limited?

The limitation of the rate of interest is dictated by the consideration, that different rates prevail in different parts of the Union; and as the operations of the Bank may extend through the whole, some rule seems to be necessary. There is room for a question, whether the limitation ought not rather to be to five than to six per cent, as proposed. It may with safety be taken for granted, that the former rate would yield an ample dividend; perhaps as much as the latter, by the extension which it would give to business. The natural effect of low interest is to increase trade and industry; because undertakings of every kind can be prosecuted with greater advantage. This is a truth generally admitted; but it is requisite to have analised the subject, in all its relations, to be able to form a just conception of the extent of that effect. Such an analysis cannot but satisfy an intelligent mind, that the difference of one per cent, in the rate at which money may be had, is often capable of making an essential change for the better in the situation of any country or place.

Every thing, therefore, which tends to lower the rate of interest is peculiarly worthy of the cares of Legislators. And though laws which violently sink the legal rate of interest greatly below the market level are not to be commended, because they are not calculated to answer their aim, yet whatever has a tendency to effect a reduction, without violence to the natural course of things, ought to be attended to and pursued. Banks are among the means most proper to accomplish this end; and the moderation of the rate at which their discounts are made, is a material ingredient towards it; with which their own interest, viewed on an enlarged and permanent scale, does not appear to clash.

But as the most obvious ideas are apt to have greater force, than those which depend on complex and remote combinations, there would be danger, that the persons whose funds must constitute the Stock of the Bank would be diffident of the sufficiency of the profits to be expected, if the rate of loans and discounts were to be placed below the point to which they have been accustomed; and might on this account be indisposed to embarking in the plan. There is, it is true, one reflection, which in regard to men actively engaged in trade ought to be a security against this danger; it is this, that the accommodations which they might derive in the way of their business, at a low rate, would more than indemnify them for any difference in the dividend, supposing even that some diminution of it were to be the consequence. But upon the whole, the hazard of contrary reasoning among the mass of monied men is a powerful argument against the experiment. The institutions of the kind already existing add to the difficulty of making it. Maturer reflection and a large capital may of themselves lead to the desired end.

IV. C. 5. Why should the U.S. purchase $2 million of the bank's stock?

The last thing, which will require any explanatory remark, is the authority proposed to be given to the President to subscribe to the amount of two millions of Dollars on account of the public. The main design of this is to enlarge the specie fund of the Bank, and to enable it to give a more early extension to its operations. Though it is proposed to borrow with one hand what is lent with the other, yet the disbursement of what is borrowed will be progressive, and Bank notes may be thrown into circulation, instead of the gold and silver. Besides, there is to be an annual reimbursement of a part of the sum borrowed, which will finally operate as an actual investment of so much specie. In addition to the inducements to this measure, which results from the general interest of the Government, to enlarge the sphere of the utility of the Bank, there is this more particular consideration, to wit, that as far as the dividend on the Stock shall exceed the interest paid on the loan, there is a positive profit.

V. A FINAL WORD ON THE BANK OF NORTH AMERICA

The Secretary begs leave to conclude, with this general observation, that if the Bank of North America shall come forward with any propositions, which have for object the ingrafting upon that institution the characteristics, which shall appear to the Legislature necessary to the due extent and safety of a National Bank, there are, in his judgment, weighty inducements to giving every reasonable facility to the measure. Not only the pretensions of that institution, from its original relation to the Government of the United States, and from the services it has rendered, are such as to claim a disposition favourable to it, if those who are interested in it are willing on their part to place it on a footing satisfactory to the Government, and equal to the purposes of a Bank of the United States; but its cooperation would materially accelerate the accomplishment of the great object, and the collision, which might otherwise arise, might, in a variety of ways, prove equally disagreeable and injurious. The incorporation or union here contemplated, may be effected in different modes, under the auspices of an Act of the United States, if it shall be desired by the Bank of North America, upon terms, which shall appear expedient to the Government.

All which is humbly submitted
Alexander Hamilton,
Secy of the Treasury

APPENDIX 3

Report on Manufactures

Full title: *Report on the Subject of Manufactures*

https://founders.archives.gov/documents/Hamilton/01-10-02-0001-0007
(modern editorial notes not included)

[Philadelphia, December 5, 1791
Communicated on December 5, 1791]

I. INTRODUCTION

The Secretary of the Treasury in obedience to the order of ye House of Representatives, of the 15th day of January 1790, has applied his attention, at as early a period as his other duties would permit, to the subject of Manufactures; and particularly to the means of promoting such as will tend to render the United States, independent on foreign nations, for military and other essential supplies. And he there [upon] respectfully submits the following Report.

The expediency of encouraging manufactures in the United States, which was not long since deemed very questionable, appears at this time to be pretty generally admitted. The embarrassments, which have obstructed the progress of our external trade, have led to serious reflections on the necessity of enlarging the sphere of our domestic commerce: the restrictive regulations, which in foreign markets abrige the vent of the increasing surplus of our Agricultural produce, serve to beget an earnest desire, that a more extensive demand for that surplus may be created at home: And the complete success, which has rewarded manufacturing enterprise, in some valuable branches, conspiring with the promising symptoms, which attend some less mature essays, in others, justify a hope, that the obstacles to the growth of this species of industry are less formidable than they were apprehended to be; and that it is not difficult to find, in its further extension; a full indemnification for any external disadvantages, which are or may be experienced, as well as an accession of resources, favourable to national independence and safety.

II. ARGUMENTS AGAINST MANUFACTURING

II. A. First argument

II. A. 1. Others say: Agriculture is the most productive use of resources.

There still are, nevertheless, respectable patrons of opinions, unfriendly to the encouragement of manufactures. The following are, substantially, the arguments, by which these opinions are defended.

"In every country (say those who entertain them) Agriculture is the most beneficial and productive object of human industry. This position, generally, if not universally true, applies with peculiar emphasis to the United States, on account of their immense tracts of fertile territory, uninhabited and unimproved. Nothing can afford so advantageous an employment for capital and labour, as the conversion of this extensive wilderness into cultivated farms. Nothing equally with this, can contribute to the population, strength and real riches of the country."

"To endeavor by the extraordinary patronage of Government, to accelerate the growth of manufactures, is in fact, to endeavor, by force and art, to transfer the natural current of industry, from a more, to a less beneficial channel. Whatever has such a tendency must necessarily be unwise. Indeed it can hardly ever be wise in a government, to attempt to give a direction to the industry of its citizens. This under the quicksighted guidance of private interest, will, if left to itself, infallibly find its own way to the most profitable employment: and 'tis by such employment, that the public prosperity will be most effectually promoted. To leave industry to itself, therefore, is, in almost every case, the soundest as well as the simplest policy."

"This policy is not only recommended to the United States, by considerations which affect all nations, it is, in a manner, dictated to them by the imperious force of a very peculiar situation. The smallness of their population compared with their territory—the constant allurements to emigration from the settled to the unsettled parts of the country—the facility, with which the less independent condition of an artisan can be exchanged for the more independent condition of a farmer, these and similar causes conspire to produce, and for a length of time must continue to occasion, a scarcity of hands for manufacturing occupation, and dearness of labor generally. To these disadvantages for the prosecution of manufactures, a deficiency of pecuniary capital being added, the prospect of a successful competition with the manufactures of Europe must be regarded as little less than desperate. Extensive manufactures can only be the offspring of a redundant, at least of a full population. Till the latter shall characterise the situation of this country, 'tis vain to hope for the former."

"If contrary to the natural course of things, an unseasonable and premature spring can be given to certain fabrics, by heavy duties, prohibitions, bounties, or by other forced expedients; this will only be to sacrifice the interests of the community to those of particular classes. Besides the misdirection of labour, a virtual monopoly will be given to the persons employed on such fabrics; and an enhancement of price, the inevitable consequence of every monopoly, must be defrayed at the expence of the other parts of the society. It is far preferable, that those persons should be engaged in the cultivation of the earth, and that we should procure, in exchange for its productions, the commodities, with which foreigners are able to supply us in greater perfection, and upon better terms."

This mode of reasoning is founded upon facts and principles, which have certainly respectable pretensions. If it had governed the conduct of nations, more generally than it has done, there is room to suppose, that it might have carried them faster to prosperity and greatness, than they have attained, by the pursuit of maxims too widely opposite. Most general theories, however, admit of numerous exceptions, and there are few, if any, of the political kind, which do not blend a considerable portion of error, with the truths they inculcate.

In order to an accurate judgement how far that which has been just stated ought to be deemed liable to a similar imputation, it is necessary to advert carefully to the considerations, which plead in favour of manufactures, and which appear to recommend the special and positive encouragement of them; in certain cases, and under certain reasonable limitations.

II. A. 2. Hamilton's response.
II.

II. A. 2. a. Agriculture need not be the only industry.

It ought readily to be conceded, that the cultivation of the earth—as the primary and most certain source of national supply—as the immediate and chief source of subsistence to man—as the principal source of those materials which constitute the nutriment of other kinds of labor—as including a state most favourable to the freedom and independence of the human mind—one, perhaps, most conducive to the multiplication of the human species—has intrinsically a strong claim to pre-eminence over every other kind of industry.

II. A. 2. b. What are the profits of agriculture vs. manufacturing?

But, that it has a title to any thing like an exclusive predilection, in any country, ought to be admitted with great caution. That it is even more productive than every other branch of Industry requires more evidence, than has yet been given in support of the position. That its real interests, precious and important as without the help of exaggeration, they truly are, will be advanced, rather than injured by the due encouragement of manufactures, may, it is believed, be satisfactorily demonstrated. And it is also believed that the expediency of such encouragement in a general view may be shewn to be recommended by the most cogent and persuasive motives of national policy.

It has been maintained, that Agriculture is, not only, the most productive, but the only productive species of industry. The reality of this suggestion in either aspect, has, however, not been verified by any accurate detail of facts and calculations; and the general arguments, which are adduced to prove it, are rather subtil and paradoxical, than solid or convincing.

Those which maintain its exclusive productiveness are to this effect.

Labour, bestowed upon the cultivation of land produces enough, not only to replace all the necessary expences incurred in the business, and to maintain the persons who are employed in it, but to afford together with the ordinary profit on the stock or capital of the Farmer, a nett surplus, or rent for the landlord or proprietor of the soil. But the labor of Artificers does nothing more, than replace the Stock which employs them (or which furnishes materials tools and wages) and yield the ordinary profit upon that Stock. It yields nothing equivalent to the rent of land. Neither does it add any thing to the total value of the whole annual produce of the land and labour of the country. The additional value given to those parts of the produce of land, which are wrought into manufactures, is counterbalanced by the value of those other parts of that produce, which are consumed by the manufacturers. It can therefore only be by saving, or parsimony not by the positive productiveness of their labour, that the classes of Artificers can in any degree augment the revenue of the Society.

To this it has been answered—

I   "That inasmuch as it is acknowleged, that manufacturing labour reproduces a value equal to that which is expended or consumed in carrying it on, and continues in existence the original Stock or capital employed—it ought on that account alone, to escape being considered as wholly unproductive: That though it should be admitted, as alleged, that the consumption of the produce of the soil, by the classes of Artificers or Manufacturers, is exactly equal to the value added by their labour to the materials upon which it is exerted; yet it would not thence follow, that it added nothing to the Revenue of the Society, or to the aggregate value of the annual produce of its land and labour. If the consumption for any given period amounted to a given sum and the increased value of the produce manufactured, in the same period, to a like sum, the total amount of the consumption and production during that period, would be equal to the two sums, and consequently double the value of the agricultural produce consumed. And though the increment of value produced by the classes of Artificers should at no time exceed the value of the produce of the land consumed by them, yet there would be at every moment, in consequence of their labour, a greater value of goods in the market than would exist independent of it."

II—"That the position, that Artificers can augment the revenue of a Society, only by parsimony, is true, in no other sense, than in one, which is equally applicable to Husbandmen or Cultivators. It may be alike affirmed of all these classes, that the fund acquired by their labor and destined for their support is not, in an ordinary way, more than equal to it. And hence it will follow, that augmentations of the wealth or capital of the community (except in the instances of some extraordinary dexterity or skill) can only proceed, with respect to any of them, from the savings of the more thrifty and parsimonious."

III—"That the annual produce of the land and labour of a country can only be encreased, in two ways—by some improvement in the productive powers of the useful labour, which actually exists within it, or by some increase in the quantity of such labour: That with regard to the first, the labour of Artificers being capable of greater subdivision and simplicity of operation, than that of Cultivators, it is susceptible, in a proportionably greater degree, of improvement in its productive powers, whether to be derived from an accession of Skill, or from the application of ingenious machinery; in which particular, therefore, the labour employed in the culture of land can pretend to no advantage over that engaged in manufactures: That with regard to an augmentation of the quantity of useful labour, this, excluding adventitious circumstances, must depend essentially upon an increase of capital, which again must depend upon the savings made out of the revenues of those, who furnish or manage that, which is at any time employed, whether in Agriculture, or in Manufactures, or in any other way."

But while the exclusive productiveness of Agricultural labour has been thus denied and refuted, the superiority of its productiveness has been conceded without hesitation. As this concession involves a point of considerable magnitude, in relation to maxims of public administration, the grounds on which it rests are worthy of a distinct and particular examination.

One of the arguments made use of, in support of the idea may be pronounced both quaint and superficial. It amounts to this—That in the productions of the soil, nature co-operates with man; and that the effect of their joint labour must be greater than that of the labour of man alone.

This however, is far from being a necessary inference. It is very conceivable, that the labor of man alone laid out upon a work, requiring great skill and art to bring it to perfection, may be more productive, in value, than the labour of nature and man combined, when directed towards more simple operations and objects: And when it is recollected to what an extent the Agency of nature, in the application of the mechanical powers, is made auxiliary to the prosecution of manufactures, the suggestion, which has been noticed, loses even the appearance of plausibility.

It might also be observed, with a contrary view, that the labour employed in Agriculture is in a great measure periodical and occasional, depending on seasons, liable to various and long intermissions; while that occupied in many manufactures is constant and regular, extending through the year, embracing in some instances night as well as day. It is also probable, that there are among the cultivators of land more examples of remissness, than among artificers. The farmer, from the peculiar fertility of his land, or some other favorable circumstance, may frequently obtain a livelihood, even with a considerable degree of carelessness in the mode of cultivation; but the artisan can with difficulty effect the same object, without exerting himself pretty equally with all those, who are engaged in the same pursuit. And if it may likewise be assumed as a fact, that manufactures open a wider field to exertions of ingenuity than agriculture, it would not be a strained conjecture, that the labour employed in the former, being at once more constant, more uniform and more ingenious, than that which is employed in the latter, will be found at the same time more productive.

But it is not meant to lay stress on observations of this nature—they ought only to serve as a counterbalance to those of a similar complexion. Circumstances so vague and general, as well as so abstract, can afford little instruction in a matter of this kind.

Another, and that which seems to be the principal argument offered for the superior productiveness of Agricultural labour, turns upon the allegation, that labour employed in manufactures yields nothing equivalent to the rent of land; or to that nett surplus, as it is called, which accrues to the proprietor of the soil.

But this distinction, important as it has been deemed, appears rather verbal than substantial.

It is easily discernible, that what in the first instance is divided into two parts under the denominations of the ordinary profit of the Stock of the farmer and rent to the landlord, is in the second instance united under the general appellation of the ordinary profit on the Stock of the Undertaker; and that this formal or verbal distribution constitutes the whole difference in the two cases. It seems to have been overlooked, that the land is itself a Stock or capital, advanced or lent by its owner to the occupier or tenant, and that the rent he receives is only the ordinary profit of a certain Stock in land, not managed by the proprietor himself, but by another to whom he lends or lets it, and who on his part advances a second capital to stock & improve the land, upon which he also receives the usual profit. The rent of the landlord and the profit of the farmer are therefore nothing more than the ordinary profits of two capitals belonging to two different persons, and united in the cultivation of a farm: As in the other case, the surplus which arises upon any manufactory, after replacing the expences of carrying it on, answers to the ordinary profits of one or more capitals engaged in the prosecution of such manufactory. It is said one or more capitals; because in fact, the same thing which is contemplated, in the case of the farm, sometimes happens in that of a manufactory. There is one, who furnishes a part of the capital, or lends a part of the money, by which it is carried on, and another, who carries it on, with the addition of his own capital.

Out of the surplus, which remains, after defraying expences, an interest is paid to the money lender for the portion of the capital furnished by him, which exactly agrees with the rent paid to the landlord; and the residue of that surplus constitutes the profit of the undertaker or manufacturer, and agrees with what is denominated the ordinary profits on the Stock of the farmer. Both together make the ordinary profits of two capitals [employed in a manufactory; as in the other case the rent of the landlord and the revenue of the farmer compose the ordinary profits of two Capitals] employed in the cultivation of a farm.

The rent therefore accruing to the proprietor of the land, far from being a criterion of exclusive productiveness, as has been argued, is no criterion even of superior productiveness. The question must still be, whether the surplus, after defraying expences, of a given capital, employed in the purchase and improvement of a piece of land, is greater or less, than that of a like capital employed in the prosecution of a manufactory: or whether the whole value produced from a given capital and a given quantity of labour, employed in one way, be greater or less, than the whole value produced from an equal capital and an equal quantity of labour employed in the other way: or rather, perhaps whether the business of Agriculture or that of Manufactures will yield the greatest product, according to a compound ratio of the quantity of the Capital and the quantity of labour, which are employed in the one or in the other.

The solution of either of these questions is not easy; it involves numerous and complicated details, depending on an accurate knowlege of the objects to be compared. It is not known that the comparison has ever yet been made upon sufficient data properly ascertained and analised. To be able to make it on the present occasion with satisfactory precision would demand more previous enquiry and investigation, than there has been hitherto either leisure or opportunity to accomplish.

Some essays however have been made towards acquiring the requisite information; which have rather served to throw doubt upon, than to confirm the Hypothesis, under examination: But it ought to be acknowledged, that they have been too little diversified, and are too imperfect, to authorise a definitive conclusion either way; leading rather to probable conjecture than to certain deduction. They render it probable, that there are various branches of manufactures, in which a given Capital will yield a greater total product, and a considerably greater nett product, than an equal capital invested in the purchase and improvement of lands; and that there are also some branches, in which both the gross and the nett produce will exceed that of Agricultural industry; according to a compound ratio of capital and labour: But it is on this last point, that there appears to be the greatest room for doubt. It is far less difficult to infer generally, that the nett produce of Capital engaged in manufacturing enterprises is greater than that of Capital engaged in Agriculture.

In stating these results, the purchase and improvement of lands, under previous cultivation are alone contemplated. The comparison is more in favour of Agriculture, when it is made with reference to the settlement of new and waste lands; but an argument drawn from so temporary a circumstance could have no weight in determining the general question concerning the permanent relative productiveness of the two species of industry. How far it ought to influence the policy of the United States, on the score of particular situation, will be adverted to in another place.

The foregoing suggestions are not designed to inculcate an opinion that manufacturing industry is more productive than that of Agriculture. They are intended rather to shew that the reverse of this proposition is not ascertained; that the general arguments which are brought to establish it are not satisfactory; and consequently that a supposition of the superior productiveness of Tillage ought to be no obstacle to listening to any substantial inducements to the encouragement of manufactures, which may be otherwise perceived to exist, through an apprehension, that they may have a tendency to divert labour from a more to a less profitable employment.

It is extremely probable, that on a full and accurate devellopment of the matter, on the ground of fact and calculation, it would be discovered that there is no material difference between the aggregate productiveness of the one, and of the other kind of industry; and that the propriety of the encouragements, which may in any case be proposed to be given to either ought to be determined upon considerations irrelative to any comparison of that nature.

II   But without contending for the superior productiveness of Manufacturing Industry, it may conduce to a better judgment of the policy, which ought to be pursued respecting its encouragement, to contemplate the subject, under some additional aspects, tending not only to confirm the idea, that this kind of industry has been improperly represented as unproductive in itself; but [to] evince in addition that the establishment and diffusion of manufactures have the effect of rendering the total mass of useful and productive labor in a community, greater than it would otherwise be. In prosecuting this discussion, it may be necessary briefly to resume and review some of the topics, which have been already touched.

To affirm, that the labour of the Manufacturer is unproductive, because he consumes as much of the produce of land, as he adds value to the raw materials which he manufactures, is not better founded, than it would be to affirm, that the labour of the farmer, which furnishes materials to the manufacturer, is unproductive, because he consumes an equal value of manufactured articles. Each furnishes a certain portion of the produce of his labor to the other, and each destroys a correspondent portion of the produce of the labour of the other. In the mean time, the maintenance of two Citizens, instead of one, is going on; the State has two members instead of one; and they together consume twice the value of what is produced from the land.

If instead of a farmer and artificer, there were a farmer only, he would be under the necessity of devoting a part of his labour to the fabrication of cloathing and other articles, which he would procure of the artificer, in the case of there being such a person; and of course he would be able to devote less labor to the cultivation of his farm; and would draw from it a proportionably less product. The whole quantity of production, in this state of things, in provisions, raw materials and manufactures, would certainly not exceed in value the amount of what would be produced in provisions and raw materials only, if there were an artificer as well as a farmer.

Again—if there were both an artificer and a farmer, the latter would be left at liberty to pursue exclusively the cultivation of his farm. A greater quantity of provisions and raw materials would of course be produced—equal at least—as has been already observed, to the whole amount of the provisions, raw materials and manufactures, which would exist on a contrary supposition. The artificer, at the same time would be going on in the production of manufactured commodities; to an amount sufficient not only to repay the farmer, in those commodities, for the provisions and materials which were procured from him, but to furnish the Artificer himself with a supply of similar commodities for his own use. Thus then, there would be two quantities or values in existence, instead of one; and the revenue and consumption would be double in one case, what it would be in the other.

If in place of both these suppositions, there were supposed to be two farmers, and no artificer, each of whom applied a part of his labour to the culture of land, and another part to the fabrication of Manufactures—in this case, the portion of the labour of both bestowed upon land would produce the same quantity of provisions and raw materials only, as would be produced by the intire sum of the labour of one applied in the same manner, and the portion of the labour of both bestowed upon manufactures, would produce the same quantity of manufactures only, as would be produced by the intire sum of the labour of one applied in the same manner. Hence the produce of the labour of the two farmers would not be greater than the produce of the labour of the farmer and artificer; and hence, it results, that the labour of the artificer is as possitively productive as that of the farmer, and, as positively, augments the revenue of the Society.

The labour of the Artificer replaces to the farmer that portion of his labour, with which he provides the materials of exchange with the Artificer, and which he would otherwise have been compelled to apply to manufactures: and while the Artificer thus enables the farmer to enlarge his stock of Agricultural industry, a portion of which he purchases for his own use, he also supplies himself with the manufactured articles of which he stands in need.

He does still more—Besides this equivalent which he gives for the portion of Agricultural labour consumed by him, and this supply of manufactured commodities for his own consumption—he furnishes still a surplus, which compensates for the use of the Capital advanced either by himself or some other person, for carrying on the business. This is the ordinary profit of the Stock employed in the manufactory, and is, in every sense, as effective an addition to the income of the Society, as the rent of land.

The produce of the labour of the Artificer consequently, may be regarded as composed of three parts; one by which the provisions for his subsistence and the materials for his work are purchased of the farmer, one by which he supplies himself with manufactured necessaries, and a third which constitutes the profit on the Stock employed. The two last portions seem to have been overlooked in the system, which represents manufacturing industry as barren and unproductive.

In the course of the preceding illustrations, the products of equal quantities of the labour of the farmer and artificer have been treated as if equal to each other. But this is not to be understood as intending to assert any such precise equality. It is merely a manner of expression adopted for the sake of simplicity and perspicuity. Whether the value of the produce of the labour of the farmer be somewhat more or less, than that of the artificer, is not material to the main scope of the argument, which hitherto has only aimed at shewing, that the one, as well as the other, occasions a possitive augmentation of the total produce and revenue of the Society.

II. A. 2. c. Manufacturing makes a community more productive in 7 ways.

It is now proper to proceed a step further, and to enumerate the principal circumstances, from which it may be inferred—That manufacturing establishments not only occasion a possitive augmentation of the Produce and Revenue of the Society, but that they contribute essentially to rendering them greater than they could possibly be, without such establishments. These circumstances are—

1. The division of Labour.
2. An extension of the use of Machinery.
3. Additional employment to classes of the community not ordinarily engaged in the business.
4. The promoting of emigration from foreign Countries.
5. The furnishing greater scope for the diversity of talents and dispositions which discriminate men from each other.
6. The affording a more ample and various field for enterprize.
7. The creating in some instances a new, and securing in all, a more certain and steady demand for the surplus produce of the soil. Each of these circumstances has a considerable influence upon the total mass of industrious effort in a community. Together, they add to it a degree of energy and effect, which are not easily conceived. Some comments upon each of them, in the order in which they have been stated, may serve to explain their importance.

II. A. 2. c. i. First benefit: Manufacturing allows division of labor.

I.   As to the Division of Labour.

It has justly been observed, that there is scarcely any thing of greater moment in the œconomy of a nation, than the proper division of labour. The seperation of occupations causes each to be carried to a much greater perfection, than it could possible acquire, if they were blended. This arises principally from three circumstances.

1st—The greater skill and dexterity naturally resulting from a constant and undivided application to a single object. It is evident, that these properties must increase, in proportion to the separation and simplification of objects and the steadiness of the attention devoted to each; and must be less, in proportion to the complication of objects, and the number among which the attention is distracted.

2nd. The œconomy of time—by avoiding the loss of it, incident to a frequent transition from one operation to another of a different nature. This depends on various circumstances—the transition itself—the orderly disposition of the impliments, machines and materials employed in the operation to be relinquished—the preparatory steps to the commencement of a new one—the interruption of the impulse, which the mind of the workman acquires, from being engaged in a particular operation—the distractions hesitations and reluctances, which attend the passage from one kind of business to another.

3rd. An extension of the use of Machinery. A man occupied on a single object will have it more in his power, and will be more naturally led to exert his imagination in devising methods to facilitate and abrige labour, than if he were perplexed by a variety of independent and dissimilar operations. Besides this, the fabrication of Machines, in numerous instances, becoming itself a distinct trade, the Artist who follows it, has all the advantages which have been enumerated, for improvement in his particular art; and in both ways the invention and application of machinery are extended.

And from these causes united, the mere separation of the occupation of the cultivator, from that of the Artificer, has the effect of augmenting the productive powers of labour, and with them, the total mass of the produce or revenue of a Country. In this single view of the subject, therefore, the utility of Artificers or Manufacturers, towards promoting an increase of productive industry, is apparent.

II. A. 2. c. ii. Second benefit: Manufacturing allows use of machinery.

II. As to an extension of the use of Machinery a point which though partly anticipated requires to be placed in one or two additional lights.

The employment of Machinery forms an item of great importance in the general mass of national industry. 'Tis an artificial force brought in aid of the natural force of man; and, to all the purposes of labour, is an increase of hands; an accession of strength, unincumbered too by the expence of maintaining the laborer. May it not therefore be fairly inferred, that those occupations, which give greatest scope to the use of this auxiliary, contribute most to the general Stock of industrious effort, and, in consequence, to the general product of industry?

It shall be taken for granted, and the truth of the position referred to observation, that manufacturing pursuits are susceptible in a greater degree of the application of machinery, than those of Agriculture. If so all the difference is lost to a community, which, instead of manufacturing for itself, procures the fabrics requisite to its supply from other Countries. The substitution of foreign for domestic manufactures is a transfer to foreign nations of the advantages accruing from the employment of Machinery, in the modes in which it is capable of being employed, with most utility and to the greatest extent.

The Cotton Mill invented in England, within the last twenty years, is a signal illustration of the general proposition, which has been just advanced. In consequence of it, all the different processes for spining Cotton are performed by means of Machines, which are put in motion by water, and attended chiefly by women and Children; [and by a smaller] number of [persons, in the whole, than are] requisite in the ordinary mode of spinning. And it is an advantage of great moment that the operations of this mill continue with convenience, during the night, as well as through the day. The prodigious affect of such a Machine is easily conceived. To this invention is to be attributed essentially the immense progress, which has been so suddenly made in Great Britain in the various fabrics of Cotton.

II. A. 2. c. iii. Third benefit: Manufacturing allows people to work who otherwise might not be employed.

III. As to the additional employment of classes of the community, not ordinarily engaged in the particular business.

This is not among the least valuable of the means, by which manufacturing institutions contribute to augment the general stock of industry and production. In places where those institutions prevail, besides the persons regularly engaged in them, they afford occasional and extra employment to industrious individuals and families, who are willing to devote the leisure resulting from the intermissions of their ordinary pursuits to collateral labours, as a resource of multiplying their acquisitions or [their] enjoyments. The husbandman himself experiences a new source of profit and support from the encreased industry of his wife and daughters; invited and stimulated by the demands of the neighboring manufactories.

Besides this advantage of occasional employment to classes having different occupations, there is another of a nature allied to it [and] of a similar tendency. This is—the employment of persons who would otherwise be idle (and in many cases a burthen on the community), either from the byass of temper, habit, infirmity of body, or some other cause, indisposing, or disqualifying them for the toils of the Country. It is worthy of particular remark, that, in general, women and Children are rendered more useful and the latter more early useful by manufacturing establishments, than they would otherwise be. Of the number of persons employed in the Cotton Manufactories of Great Britain, it is computed that 4/7 nearly are women and children; of whom the greatest proportion are children and many of them of a very tender age.

And thus it appears to be one of the attributes of manufactures, and one of no small consequence, to give occasion to the exertion of a greater quantity of Industry, even by the same number of persons, where they happen to prevail, than would exist, if there were no such establishments.

II. A. 2. c. iv. Fourth benefit: Manufacturing encourages immigration by those who don't want to farm, but might want to work in a factory.

IV. As to the promoting of emigration from foreign Countries. Men reluctantly quit one course of occupation and livelihood for another, unless invited to it by very apparent and proximate advantages. Many, who would go from one country to another, if they had a prospect of continuing with more benefit the callings, to which they have been educated, will often not be tempted to change their situation, by the hope of doing better, in some other way. Manufacturers, who listening to the powerful invitations of a better price for their fabrics, or their labour, of greater cheapness of provisions and raw materials, of an exemption from the chief part of the taxes burthens and restraints, which they endure in the old world, of greater personal independence and consequence, under the operation of a more equal government, and of what is far more precious than mere religious toleration—a perfect equality of religious privileges; would probably flock from Europe to the United States to pursue their own trades or professions, if they were once made sensible of the advantages they would enjoy, and were inspired with an assurance of encouragement and employment, will, with difficulty, be induced to transplant themselves, with a view to becoming Cultivators of Land.

If it be true then, that it is the interest of the United States to open every possible [avenue to] emigration from abroad, it affords a weighty argument for the encouragement of manufactures; which for the reasons just assigned, will have the strongest tendency to multiply the inducements to it.

Here is perceived an important resource, not only for extending the population, and with it the useful and productive labour of the country, but likewise for the prosecution of manufactures, without deducting from the number of hands, which might otherwise be drawn to tillage; and even for the indemnification of Agriculture for such as might happen to be diverted from it. Many, whom Manufacturing views would induce to emigrate, would afterwards yield to the temptations, which the particular situation of this Country holds out to Agricultural pursuits. And while Agriculture would in other respects derive many signal and unmingled advantages, from the growth of manufactures, it is a problem whether it would gain or lose, as to the article of the number of persons employed in carrying it on.

II. A. 2. c. v. Fifth benefit: Manufacturing lets more people use their talents to the fullest.

V.   As to the furnishing greater scope for the diversity of talents and dispositions, which discriminate men from each other.

This is a much more powerful mean of augmenting the fund of national Industry than may at first sight appear. It is a just observation, that minds of the strongest and most active powers for their proper objects fall below mediocrity and labour without effect, if confined to uncongenial pursuits. And it is thence to be inferred, that the results of human exertion may be immensely increased by diversifying its objects. When all the different kinds of industry obtain in a community, each individual can find his proper element, and can call into activity the whole vigour of his nature. And the community is benefitted by the services of its respective members, in the manner, in which each can serve it with most effect.

If there be anything in a remark often to be met with—namely that there is, in the genius of the people of this country, a peculiar aptitude for mechanic improvements, it would operate as a forcible reason for giving opportunities to the exercise of that species of talent, by the propagation of manufactures.

II. A. 2. c. vi. Sixth benefit: Manufacturing gives more opportunity for ingenuity and invention.

VI.   As to the affording a more ample and various field for enterprise.

This also is of greater consequence in the general scale of national exertion, than might perhaps on a superficial view be supposed, and has effects not altogether dissimilar from those of the circumstance last noticed. To cherish and stimulate the activity of the human mind, by multiplying the objects of enterprise, is not among the least considerable of the expedients, by which the wealth of a nation may be promoted. Even things in themselves not positively advantageous, sometimes become so, by their tendency to provoke exertion. Every new scene, which is opened to the busy nature of man to rouse and exert itself, is the addition of a new energy to the general stock of effort.

The spirit of enterprise, useful and prolific as it is, must necessarily be contracted or expanded in proportion to the simplicity or variety of the occupations and productions, which are to be found in a Society. It must be less in a nation of mere cultivators, than in a nation of cultivators and merchants; less in a nation of cultivators and merchants, than in a nation of cultivators, artificers and merchants.

II. A. 2. c. vii. Seventh benefit: Manufacturing creates a steadier demand for agricultural produce.

VII. As to the creating, in some instances, a new, and securing in all a more certain and steady demand, for the surplus produce of the soil.

This is among the most important of the circumstances which have been indicated. It is a principal mean, by which the establishment of manufactures contributes to an augmentation of the produce or revenue of a country, and has an immediate and direct relation to the prosperity of Agriculture.

It is evident, that the exertions of the husbandman will be steady or fluctuating, vigorous or feeble, in proportion to the steadiness or fluctuation, adequateness, or inadequateness of the markets on which he must depend, for the vent of the surplus, which may be produced by his labour; and that such surplus in the ordinary course of things will be greater or less in the same proportion.

For the purpose of this vent, a domestic market is greatly to be preferred to a foreign one; because it is in the nature of things, far more to be relied upon.

It is a primary object of the policy of nations, to be able to supply themselves with subsistence from their own soils; and manufacturing nations, as far as circumstances permit, endeavor to procure, from the same source, the raw materials necessary for their own fabrics. This disposition, urged by the spirit of monopoly, is sometimes even carried to an injudicious extreme. It seems not always to be recollected, that nations, who have neither mines nor manufactures, can only obtain the manufactured articles, of which they stand in need, by an exchange of the products of their soils; and that, if those who can best furnish them with such articles are unwilling to give a due course to this exchange, they must of necessity make every possible effort to manufacture for themselves, the effect of which is that the manufacturing nations abrige the natural advantages of their situation, through an unwillingness to permit the Agricultural countries to enjoy the advantages of theirs, and sacrifice the interests of a mutually beneficial intercourse to the vain project of selling every thing and buying nothing.

But it is also a consequence of the policy, which has been noted, that the foreign demand for the products of Agricultural Countries, is, in a great degree, rather casual and occasional, than certain or constant. To what extent injurious interruptions of the demand for some of the staple commodities of the United States, may have been experienced, from that cause, must be referred to the judgment of those who are engaged in carrying on the commerce of the country; but it may be safely assumed, that such interruptions are at times very inconveniently felt, and that cases not unfrequently occur, in which markets are so confined and restricted, as to render the demand very unequal to the supply.

Independently likewise of the artificial impediments, which are created by the policy in question, there are natural causes tending to render the external demand for the surplus of Agricultural nations a precarious reliance. The differences of seasons, in the countries, which are the consumers make immense differences in the produce of their own soils, in different years; and consequently in the degrees of their necessity for foreign supply. Plentiful harvests with them, especially if similar ones occur at the same time in the countries, which are the furnishers, occasion of course a glut in the markets of the latter.

Considering how fast and how much the progress of new settlements in the United States must increase the surplus produce of the soil, and weighing seriously the tendency of the system, which prevails among most of the commercial nations of Europe; whatever dependence may be placed on the force of natural circumstances to counteract the effects of an artificial policy; there appear strong reasons to regard the foreign demand for that surplus as too uncertain a reliance, and to desire a substitute for it, in an extensive domestic market.

To secure such a market, there is no other expedient, than to promote manufacturing establishments. Manufacturers who constitute the most numerous class, after the Cultivators of land, are for that reason the principal consumers of the surplus of their labour.

This idea of an extensive domestic market for the surplus produce of the soil is of the first consequence. It is of all things, that which most effectually conduces to a flourishing state of Agriculture. If the effect of manufactories should be to detach a portion of the hands, which would otherwise be engaged in Tillage, it might possibly cause a smaller quantity of lands to be under cultivation but by their tendency to procure a more certain demand for the surplus produce of the soil, they would, at the same time, cause the lands which were in cultivation to be better improved and more productive. And while, by their influence, the condition of each individual farmer would be meliorated, the total mass of Agricultural production would probably be increased. For this must evidently depend as much, if not more, upon the degree of improvement; than upon the number of acres under culture.

It merits particular observation, that the multiplication of manufactories not only furnishes a Market for those articles, which have been accustomed to be produced in abundance, in a country; but it likewise creates a demand for such as were either unknown or produced in inconsiderable quantities. The bowels as well as the surface of the earth are ransacked for articles which were before neglected. Animals, Plants and Minerals acquire an utility and value, which were before unexplored.

The foregoing considerations seem sufficient to establish, as general propositions, That it is the interest of nations to diversify the industrious pursuits of the individuals, who compose them—That the establishment of manufactures is calculated not only to increase the general stock of useful and productive labour; but even to improve the state of Agriculture in particular; certainly to advance the interests of those who are engaged in it. There are other views, that will be hereafter taken of the subject, which, it is conceived, will serve to confirm these inferences.

III   Previously to a further discussion of the objections to the encouragement of manufactures which have been stated, it will be of use to see what can be said, in reference to the particular situation of the United States, against the conclusions appearing to result from what has been already offered.

II. B. Second argument against manufacturing

II. B. 1. Others say: Manufacturing isn't suitable for states with large amounts of unsettled land.

It may be observed, and the idea is of no inconsiderable weight, that however true it might be, that a State, which possessing large tracts of vacant and fertile territory, was at the same time secluded from foreign commerce, would find its interest and the interest of Agriculture, in diverting a part of its population from Tillage to Manufactures; yet it will not follow, that the same is true of a State, which having such vacant and fertile territory, has at the same time ample opportunity of procuring from abroad, on good terms, all the fabrics of which it stands in need, for the supply of its inhabitants. The power of doing this at least secures the great advantage of a division of labour; leaving the farmer free to pursue exclusively the culture of his land, and enabling him to procure with its products the manufactured supplies requisite either to his wants or to his enjoyments. And though it should be true, that in settled countries, the diversification of Industry is conducive to an increase in the productive powers of labour, and to an augmentation of revenue and capital; yet it is scarcely conceivable that there can be any [thing] of so solid and permanent advantage to an uncultivated and unpeopled country as to convert its wastes into cultivated and inhabited districts. If the Revenue, in the mean time, should be less, the Capital, in the event, must be greater.

II. B. 2. Hamilton's response

To these observations, the following appears to be a satisfactory answer—

II. B. 2. a. We cannot dispose of all our agricultural produce, because we cannot freely trade abroad.

1. If the system of perfect liberty to industry and commerce were the prevailing system of nations—the arguments which dissuade a country in the predicament of the United States, from the zealous pursuits of manufactures would doubtless have great force. It will not be affirmed, that they might not be permitted, with few exceptions, to serve as a rule of national conduct. In such a state of things, each country would have the full benefit of its peculiar advantages to compensate for its deficiencies or disadvantages. If one nation were in condition to supply manufactured articles on better terms than another, that other might find an abundant indemnification in a superior capacity to furnish the produce of the soil. And a free exchange, mutually beneficial, of the commodities which each was able to supply, on the best terms, might be carried on between them, supporting in full vigour the industry of each. And though the circumstances which have been mentioned and others, which will be unfolded hereafter render it probable, that nations merely Agricultural would not enjoy the same degree of opulence, in proportion to their numbers, as those which united manufactures with agriculture; yet the progressive improvement of the lands of the former might, in the end, atone for an inferior degree of opulence in the mean time: and in a case in which opposite considerations are

pretty equally balanced, the option ought perhaps always to be, in favour of leaving Industry to its own direction.

But the system which has been mentioned, is far from characterising the general policy of Nations. [The prevalent one has been regulated by an opposite spirit.]

The consequence of it is, that the United States are to a certain extent in the situation of a country precluded from foreign Commerce. They can indeed, without difficulty obtain from abroad the manufactured supplies, of which they are in want; but they experience numerous and very injurious impediments to the emission and vent of their own commodities. Nor is this the case in reference to a single foreign nation only. The regulations of several countries, with which we have the most extensive intercourse, throw serious obstructions in the way of the principal staples of the United States.

In such a position of things, the United States cannot exchange with Europe on equal terms; and the want of reciprocity would render them the victim of a system, which should induce them to confine their views to Agriculture and refrain from Manufactures. A constant and encreasing necessity, on their part, for the commodities of Europe, and only a partial and occasional demand for their own, in return, could not but expose them to a state of impoverishment, compared with the opulence to which their political and natural advantages authorise them to aspire.

Remarks of this kind are not made in the spirit of complaint. 'Tis for the nations, whose regulations are alluded to, to judge for themselves, whether, by aiming at too much they do not lose more than they gain. 'Tis for the United States to consider by what means they can render themselves least dependent, on the combinations, right or wrong of foreign policy.

It is no small consolation, that already the measures which have embarrassed our Trade, have accelerated internal improvements, which upon the whole have bettered our affairs. To diversify and extend these improvements is the surest and safest method of indemnifying ourselves for any inconveniences, which those or similar measures have a tendency to beget. If Europe will not take from us the products of our soil, upon terms consistent with our interest, the natural remedy is to contract as fast as possible our wants of her.

II. B. 2. b. It's possible that manufacturing will not divert people from settling empty lands in the U.S.

2. The conversion of their waste into cultivated lands is certainly a point of great moment in the political calculations of the United States. But the degree in which this may possibly be retarded by the encouragement of manufactories does not appear to countervail the powerful inducements to affording that encouragement.

An observation made in another place is of a nature to have great influence upon this question. If it cannot be denied, that the interests even of Agriculture may be advanced more by having such of the lands of a state as are occupied under good cultivation, than by having a greater quantity occupied under a much inferior cultivation, and if Manufactories, for the reasons assigned, must be admitted to have a tendency to promote a more steady and vigorous cultivation of the lands occupied than would happen without them—it will follow, that they are capable of indemnifying a country for a diminution of the progress of new settlements; and may serve to increase both the capital [value] and the income of its lands, even though they should abrige the number of acres under Tillage.

But it does, by no means, follow, that the progress of new settlements would be retarded by the extension of Manufactures. The desire of being an independent proprietor of land is founded on such strong principles in the human breast, that where the opportunity of becoming so is as great as it is in the United States, the proportion will be small of those, whose situations would otherwise lead to it, who would be diverted from it towards Manufactures. And it is highly probable, as already intimated, that the accessions of foreigners, who originally drawn over by manufacturing views would afterwards abandon them for Agricultural, would be more than equivalent for those of our own Citizens, who might happen to be detached from them.

II. C. Third argument against manufacturing

II. C. 1. Others say: Manufacturing will grow on its own, without government encouragement.

The remaining objections to a particular encouragement of manufactures in the United States now require to be examined.

One of these turns on the proposition, that Industry, if left to itself, will naturally find its way to the most useful and profitable employment: whence it is inferred, that manufactures without the aid of government will grow up as soon and as fast, as the natural state of things and the interest of the community may require.

II. C. 2. Hamilton's response: Four reasons the growth of industry might be delayed

Against the solidity of this hypothesis, in the full latitude of the terms, very cogent reasons may be offered. These have relation to—the strong influence of habit and the spirit of imitation—the fear of want of success in untried enterprises—the intrinsic difficulties incident to first essays towards a competition with those who have previously attained to perfection in the business to be attempted—the bounties premiums and other artificial encouragements, with which foreign nations second the exertions of their own Citizens in the branches, in which they are to be rivalled.

II. C. 2. a. People might not switch to manufacturing because they are creatures of habit.

Experience teaches, that men are often so much governed by what they are accustomed to see and practice, that the simplest and most obvious improvements, in the [most] ordinary occupations, are adopted with hesitation, reluctance and by slow gradations. The spontaneous transition to new pursuits, in a community long habituated to different ones, may be expected to be attended with proportionably greater difficulty. When former occupations ceased to yield a profit adequate to the subsistence of their followers, or when there was an absolute deficiency of employment in them, owing to the superabundance of hands, changes would ensue; but these changes would be likely to be more tardy than might consist with the interest either of individuals or of the Society. In many cases they would not happen, while a bare support could be ensured by an adherence to ancient courses; though a resort to a more profitable employment might be practicable. To produce the desireable changes, as early as may be expedient, may therefore require the incitement and patronage of government.

II. C. 2. b. People might not switch to manufacturing because they fear failure.

The apprehension of failing in new attempts is perhaps a more serious impediment. There are dispositions apt to be attracted by the mere novelty of an undertaking—but these are not always those best calculated to give it success. To this, it is of importance that the confidence of cautious sagacious capitalists both citizens and foreigners, should be excited. And to inspire this description of persons with confidence, it is essential, that they should be made to see in any project, which is new, and for that reason alone, if, for no other, precarious, the prospect of such a degree of countenance and support from government, as may be capable of overcoming the obstacles, inseperable from first experiments.

II. C. 2. c. People might not take up manufacturing because they are daunted by competition with countries where manufacturing has been going on for a long time.

The superiority antecedently enjoyed by nations, who have preoccupied and perfected a branch of industry, constitutes a more formidable obstacle, than either of those, which have been mentioned, to the introduction of the same branch into a country, in which it did not before exist. To maintain between the recent establishments of one country and the long matured establishments of another country, a competition upon equal terms, both as to quality and price, is in most cases impracticable. The disparity in the one, or in the other, or in both, must necessarily be so considerable as to forbid a successful rivalship, without the extraordinary aid and protection of government.

II. C. 2. d. People might be discouraged because other countries subsidize manufacturing enterprises, which allows their products to be sold more cheaply abroad.

But the greatest obstacle of all to the successful prosecution of a new branch of industry in a country, in which it was before unknown, consists, as far as the instances apply, in the bounties premiums and other aids which are granted, in a variety of cases, by the nations, in which the establishments to be imitated are previously introduced. It is well known (and particular examples in the course of this report will be cited) that certain nations grant bounties on the exportation of particular commodities, to enable their own workmen to undersell and supplant all competitors, in the countries to which those commodities are sent. Hence the undertakers of a new manufacture have to contend not only with the natural disadvantages of a new undertaking, but with the gratuities and remunerations which other governments bestow. To be enabled to contend with success, it is evident, that the interference and aid of their own government are indispensible.

Combinations by those engaged in a particular branch of business in one country, to frustrate the first efforts to introduce it into another, by temporary sacrifices, recompensed perhaps by extraordinary indemnifications of the government of such country, are believed to have existed, and are not to be regarded as destitute of probability. The existence or assurance of aid from the government of the country, in which the business is to be introduced, may be essential to fortify adventurers against the dread of such combinations, to defeat their effects, if formed and to prevent their being formed, by demonstrating that they must in the end prove fruitless.

II. C. 2. e. Summary of reasons manufacturing will not increase without government support.

Whatever room there may be for an expectation that the industry of a people, under the direction of private interest, will upon equal terms find out the most beneficial employment for itself, there is none for a reliance, that it will struggle against the force of unequal terms, or will of itself surmount all the adventitious barriers to a successful competition, which may have been erected either by the advantages naturally acquired from practice and previous possession of the ground, or by those which may have sprung from positive regulations and an artificial policy. This general reflection might alone suffice as an answer to the objection under examination; exclusively of the weighty considerations which have been particularly urged.

II. D. Fourth objection to manufacturing

II. D. 1. Others say: The U.S. doesn't have the workers and capital needed to establish large manufacturing enterprises.

The objections to the pursuit of manufactures in the United States, which next present themselves to discussion, represent an impracticability of success, arising from three causes—scarcity of hands—dearness of labour—want of capital.

The two first circumstances are to a certain extent real, and, within due limits, ought to be admitted as obstacles to the success of manufacturing enterprize in the United States. But there are various considerations, which lessen their force, and tend to afford an assurance that they are not sufficient to prevent the advantageous prosecution of many very useful and extensive manufactories.

II. D. 2. Hamilton's response

II. D. 2. a. In some places in the U.S., the population is already dense enough for manufacturing to be carried on.

With regard to scarcity of hands, the fact itself must be applied with no small qualification to certain parts of the United States. There are large districts, which may be considered as pretty fully peopled; and which notwithstanding a continual drain for distant settlement, are thickly interspersed with flourishing and increasing towns. If these districts have not already reached the point, at which the complaint of scarcity of hands ceases, they are not remote from it, and are approaching fast towards it: And having perhaps fewer attractions to agriculture, than some other parts of the Union, they exhibit a proportionably stronger tendency towards other kinds of industry. In these districts, may be discerned, no inconsiderable maturity for manufacturing establishments.

But there are circumstances, which have been already noticed with another view, that materially diminish every where the effect of a scarcity of hands. These circumstances are—the great use which can be made of women and children; on which point a very pregnant and instructive fact has been mentioned—the vast extension given by late improvements to the employment of Machines, which substituting the Agency of fire and water, has prodigiously lessened the necessity for manual labor—the employment of persons ordinarily engaged in other occupations, during the seasons, or hours of leisure; which, besides giving occasion to the exertion of a greater quantity of labour by the same number of persons, and thereby encreasing the general stock of labour, as has been elsewhere remarked, may also be taken into the calculation, as a resource for obviating the scarcity of hands—lastly the attraction of foreign emigrants. Whoever inspects, with a careful eye, the composition of our towns will be made sensible to what an extent this resource may be relied upon. This exhibits a large proportion of ingenious and valuable workmen, in different arts and trades, who, by expatriating from Europe, have improved their own condition, and added to the industry and wealth of the United States. It is a natural inference from the experience, we have already had, that as soon as the United States shall present the countenance of a serious prosecution of Manufactures—as soon as foreign artists shall be made sensible that the state of things here affords a moral certainty of employment and encouragement—competent numbers of European workmen will transplant themselves, effectually to ensure the success of the design. How indeed can it otherwise happen considering the various and powerful inducements, which the situation of this country offers; addressing themselves to so many strong passions and feelings, to so many general and particular interests?

It may be affirmed therefore, in respect to hands for carrying on manufactures, that we shall in a great measure trade upon a foreign Stock; reserving our own, for the cultivation of our lands and the manning of our Ships; as far as character and circumstances [shall] incline. It is not unworthy of remark, that the objection to the success of manufactures, deduced from the scarcity of hands, is alike applicable to Trade and Navigation; and yet these are perceived to flourish, without any sensible impediment from that cause.

II. D. 2. b. Laborers' wages are not much higher than in some parts of Europe, and the use of machinery can lower expenses.

As to the dearness of labour (another of the obstacles alledged) this has relation principally to two circumstances, one that which has been just discussed, or the scarcity of hands, the other, the greatness of profits.

As far as it is a consequence of the scarcity of hands, it is mitigated by all the considerations which have been adduced as lessening that deficiency.

It is certain too, that the disparity in this respect, between some of the most manufacturing parts of Europe and a large proportion of the United States, is not nearly so great as is commonly imagined. It is also much less in regard to Artificers and manufacturers than in regard to country labourers; and while a careful comparison shews, that there is, in this particular, much exaggeration; it is also evident that the effect of the degree of disparity, which does truly exist, is diminished in proportion to the use which can be made of machinery.

To illustrate this last idea—Let it be supposed, that the difference of price, in two Countries, of a given quantity of manual labour requisite to the fabrication of a given article is as 10; and that some mechanic power is introduced into both countries, which performing half the necessary labour, leaves only half to be done by hand, it is evident, that the difference in the cost of the fabrication of the article in question, in the two countries, as far as it is connected with the price of labour, will be reduced from 10. to 5, in consequence of the introduction of that power.

This circumstance is worthy of the most particular attention. It diminishes immensely one of the objections most strenuously urged, against the success of manufactures in the United States.

To procure all such machines as are known in any part of Europe, can only require a proper provision and due pains. The knowledge of several of the most important of them is already possessed. The preparation of them here, is in most cases, practicable on nearly equal terms. As far as they depend on Water, some superiority of advantages may be claimed, from the uncommon variety and greater cheapness of situations adapted to Mill seats, with which different parts of the United States abound.

So far as the dearness of labour may be a consequence of the greatness of profits in any branch of business, it is no obstacle to its success. The Undertaker can afford to pay the price.

II. D. 2. c. Some other expenses of manufacturers are lower in the U.S., offsetting the higher wages of laborers.

There are grounds to conclude that undertakers of Manufactures in this Country can at this time afford to pay higher wages to the workmen they may employ than are paid to similar workmen in Europe. The prices of foreign fabrics, in the markets of the United States, which will for a long time regulate the prices of the domestic ones, may be considered as compounded of the following ingredients—The first cost of materials, including the Taxes, if any, which are paid upon them where they are made: the expence of grounds, buildings machinery and tools: the wages of the persons employed in the manufactory: the profits on the capital or Stock employed: the commissions of Agents to purchase them where they are made; the expence of transportation to the United States [including insurance and other incidental charges;] the taxes or duties, if any [and fees of office] which are paid on their exportation: the taxes or duties [and fees of office] which are paid on their importation.

As to the first of these items, the cost of materials, the advantage upon the whole, is at present on the side of the United States, and the difference, in their favor, must increase, in proportion as a certain and extensive domestic demand shall induce the proprietors of land to devote more of their attention to the production of those materials. It ought not to escape observation, in a comparison on this point, that some of the principal manufacturing Countries of Europe are much more dependent on foreign supply for the materials of their manufactures, than would be the United States, who are capable of supplying themselves, with a greater abundance, as well as a greater variety of the requisite materials.

As to the second item, the expence of grounds buildings machinery and tools, an equality at least may be assumed; since advantages in some particulars will counterbalance temporary disadvantages in others.

As to the third item, or the article of wages, the comparison certainly turns against the United States, though as before observed not in so great a degree as is commonly supposed.

The fourth item is alike applicable to the foreign and to the domestic manufacture. It is indeed more properly a result than a particular, to be compared.

But with respect to all the remaining items, they are alone applicable to the foreign manufacture, and in the strictest sense extraordinaries; constituting a sum of extra charge on the foreign fabric, which cannot be estimated, at less than [from 15 to 30] ₽ Cent. on the cost of it at the manufactory.

This sum of extra charge may confidently be regarded as more than a Counterpoise for the real difference in the price of labour; and is a satisfactory proof that manufactures may prosper in defiance of it in the United States. To the general allegation, connected with the circumstances of scarcity of hands and dearness of labour, that extensive manufactures can only grow out of a redundant or full population, it will be sufficient, to answer generally, that the fact has been otherwise—That the situation alleged to be an essential condition of success, has not been that of several nations, at periods when they had already attained to maturity in a variety of manufactures.

The supposed want of Capital for the prosecution of manufactures in the United States is the most indefinite of the objections which are usually opposed to it.

II. D. 2. d. How can the amount of capital in a country be increased?

It is very difficult to pronounce any thing precise concerning the real extent of the monied capital of a Country, and still more concerning the proportion which it bears to the objects that invite the employment of Capital. It is not less difficult to pronounce how far the effect of any given quantity of money, as capital, or in other words, as a medium for circulating the industry and property of a nation, may be encreased by the very circumstance of the additional motion, which is given to it by new objects of employment. That effect, like the momentum of descending bodies, may not improperly be represented, as in a compound ratio to mass and velocity. It seems pretty certain, that a given sum of money, in a situation, in which the quick impulses of commercial activity were little felt, would appear inadequate to the circulation of as great a quantity of industry and property, as in one, in which their full influence was experienced.

It is not obvious, why the same objection might not as well be made to external commerce as to manufactures; since it is manifest that our immense tracts of land occupied and unoccupied are capable of giving employment to more capital than is actually bestowed upon them. It is certain, that the United States offer a vast field for the advantageous employment of Capital; but it does not follow, that there will not be found, in one way or another, a sufficient fund for the successful prosecution of any species of industry which is likely to prove truly beneficial.

The following considerations are of a nature to remove all inquietude on the score of want of Capital.

II. D. 2. d. i. The introduction of banks will increase capital.

The introduction of Banks, as has been shewn on another occasion has a powerful tendency to extend the active Capital of a Country. Experience of the Utility of these Institutions is multiplying them in the United States. It is probable that they will be established wherever they can exist with advantage; and wherever, they can be supported, if administered with prudence, they will add new energies to all pecuniary operations.

II. D. 2. d. ii. Some foreigners will probably be willing to invest capital in the U.S.

The aid of foreign Capital may safely, and, with considerable latitude be taken into calculation. Its instrumentality has been long experienced in our external commerce; and it has begun to be felt in various other modes. Not only our funds, but our Agriculture and other internal improvements have been animated by it. It has already in a few instances extended even to our manufactures.

It is a well known fact, that there are parts of Europe, which have more Capital, than profitable domestic objects of employment. Hence, among other proofs, the large loans continually furnished to foreign states. And it is equally certain that the capital of other parts may find more profitable employment in the United States, than at home. And notwithstanding there are weighty inducements to prefer the employment of capital at home even at less profit, to an investment of it abroad, though with greater gain, yet these inducements are overruled either by a deficiency of employment or by a very material difference in profit. Both these Causes operate to produce a transfer of foreign capital to the United States. 'Tis certain, that various objects in this country hold out advantages, which are with difficulty to be equalled elsewhere; and under the increasingly favorable impressions, which are entertained of our government, the attractions will become more and More strong. These impressions will prove a rich mine of prosperity to the Country, if they are confirmed and strengthened by the progress of our affairs. And to secure this advantage, little more is now necessary, than to foster industry, and cultivate order and tranquility, at home and abroad.

It is not impossible, that there may be persons disposed to look with a jealous eye on the introduction of foreign Capital, as if it were an instrument to deprive our own citizens of the profits of our own industry: But perhaps there never could be a more unreasonable jealousy. Instead of being viewed as a rival, it ought to be Considered as a most valuable auxiliary; conducing to put in Motion a greater Quantity of productive labour, and a greater portion of useful enterprise than could exist without it. It is at least evident, that in a Country situated like the United States, with an infinite fund of resources yet to be unfolded, every farthing of foreign capital, which is laid out in internal ameliorations, and in industrious establishments of a permanent nature, is a precious acquisition.

And whatever be the objects which originally attract foreign Capital, when once introduced, it may be directed towards any purpose of beneficial exertion, which is desired. And to detain it among us, there can be no expedient so effectual as to enlarge the sphere, within which it may be usefully employed: Though induced merely with views to speculations in the funds, it may afterwards be rendered subservient to the Interests of Agriculture, Commerce & Manufactures.

But the attraction of foreign Capital for the direct purpose of Manufactures ought not to be deemed a chimerial expectation. There are already examples of it, as remarked in another place. And the examples, if the disposition be cultivated can hardly fail to multiply. There are also instances of another kind, which serve to strengthen the expectation. Enterprises for improving the Public Communications, by cutting canals, opening the obstructions in Rivers and erecting bridges, have received very material aid from the same source.

When the Manufacturing Capitalist of Europe shall advert to the many important advantages, which have been intimated, in the Course of this report, he cannot but perceive very powerful inducements to a transfer of himself and his Capital to the United States. Among the reflections, which a most interesting peculiarity of situation is calculated to suggest, it cannot escape his observation, as a circumstance of Moment in the calculation, that the progressive population and improvement of the United States, insure a continually increasing domestic demand for the fabrics which he shall produce, not to be affected by any external casualties or vicissitudes.

But while there are Circumstances sufficiently strong to authorise a considerable degree of reliance on the aid of foreign Capital towards the attainment of the object in view, it is satisfactory to have good grounds of assurance, that there are domestic resources of themselves adequate to it. It happens, that there is a species of Capital actually existing within the United States, which relieves from all inquietude on the score of want of Capital—This is the funded Debt.

II. D. 2. d. iii. The public debt, when funded, is a species of capital.

The effect of a funded debt, as a species of Capital, has been Noticed upon a former Occasion; but a more particular elucidation of the point seems to be required by the stress which is here laid upon it. This shall accordingly be attempted.

Public Funds answer the purpose of Capital, from the estimation in which they are usually held by Monied men; and consequently from the Ease and dispatch with which they can be turned into money. This capacity of prompt convertibility into money causes a transfer of stock to be in a great number of Cases equivalent to a payment in coin. And where it does not happen to suit the party who is to receive, to accept a transfer of Stock, the party who is to pay, is never at a loss to find elsewhere a purchaser of his Stock, who will furnish him in lieu of it, with the Coin of which he stands in need. Hence in a sound and settled state of the public funds, a man possessed of a sum in them can embrace any scheme of business, which offers, with as much confidence as if he were possessed of an equal sum in Coin.

II. D. 2. d. iii. (1). Public bonds do not destroy other forms of capital.

This operation of public funds as capital is too obvious to be denied; but it is objected to the Idea of their operating as an augmentation of the Capital of the community, that they serve to occasion the destruction of some other capital to an equal amount.

The Capital which alone they can be supposed to destroy must consist of—The annual revenue, which is applied to the payment of

Interest on the debt, and to the gradual redemption of the principal—The amount of the Coin, which is employed in circulating the funds, or, in other words, in effecting the different alienations which they undergo.

But the following appears to be the true and accurate view of this matter.

1st. As to the point of the Annual Revenue requisite for Payment of interest and redemption of principal.

As a determinate proportion will tend to perspicuity in the reasoning, let it be supposed that the annual revenue to be applied, corresponding with the modification of the 6 per Cent stock of the United States, is in the ratio of eight upon the hundred, that is in the first instance six on Account of interest, and two on account of Principal.

Thus far it is evident, that the Capital destroyed to the capital created, would bear no greater proportion, than 8 to 100. There would be withdrawn from the total mass of other capitals a sum of eight dollars to be paid to the public creditor; while he would be possessed of a sum of One Hundred dollars, ready to be applied to any purpose, to be embarked in any enterprize, which might appear to him eligible. Here then the Augmentation of Capital, or the excess of that which is produced, beyond that which is destroyed is equal to Ninety two dollars. To this conclusion, it may be objected, that the sum of Eight dollars is to be withdrawn annually, until the whole hundred is extinguished, and it may be inferred, that in process of time a capital will be destroyed equal to that which is at first created.

But it is nevertheless true, that during the whole of the interval, between the creation of the Capital of 100 dollars, and its reduction to a sum not greater than that of the annual revenue appropriated to its redemption—there will be a greater active capital in existence than if no debt had been Contracted. The sum drawn from other Capitals in any one year will not exceed eight dollars; but there will be at every instant of time during the whole period, in question a sum corresponding with so much of the principal, as remains unredeemed, in the hands of some person, or other, employed, or ready to be employed in some profitable undertaking. There will therefore constantly be more capital, in capacity to be employed, than capital taken from employment. The excess for the first year has been stated to be Ninety two dollars; it will diminish yearly, but there always will be an excess, until the principal of the debt is brought to a level with the redeeming annuity, that is, in the case which has been assumed by way of example, to eight dollars. The reality of this excess becomes palpable, if it be supposed, as often happens, that the citizen of a foreign Country imports into the United States 100 dollars for the purchase of an equal sum of public debt. Here is an absolute augmentation of the mass of Circulating Coin to the extent of 100 dollars. At the end of a year the foreigner is presumed to draw back eight dollars on account of his Principal and Interest, but he still leaves, Ninety two of his original Deposit in circulation, as he in like manner leaves Eighty four at the end of the second year, drawing back then also the annuity of Eight Dollars: And thus the Matter proceeds; The capital left in circulation diminishing each year, and coming nearer to the level of the annuity drawnback. There are however some differences in the ultimate operation of the part of the debt, which is purchased by foreigners, and that which remains in the hands of citizens. But the general effect in each case, though in different degrees, is to add to the active capital of the Country.

Hitherto the reasoning has proceeded on a concession of the position, that there is a destruction of some other capital, to the extent of the annuity appropriated to the payment of the Interest and the redemption of the principal of the deb⟨t⟩ but in this, too much has been conceded. There is at most a temp⟨orary⟩ transfer of some other capital, to the amount of the Annuity, from those who pay to the Creditor who receives; which he again restor⟨es⟩ to the circulation to resume the offices of a capital. This he does ei⟨ther⟩ immediately by employing the money in some branch of Industry, or mediately by lending it to some other person, who does so employ ⟨it⟩ or by spending it on his own maintenance. In either sup⟨position⟩ there is no destruction of capital, there is nothing more ⟨than a⟩ suspension of its motion for a time; that is, while it is ⟨passing⟩ from the hands of those who pay into the Public coffers, & thence ⟨through⟩ the public Creditor into some other Channel of circulation. ⟨When⟩ the payments of interest are periodical and quick and made by instrumentality of Banks the diversion or suspension of capita⟨l⟩ may almost be denominated momentary. Hence the deduction on this Account is far less, than it at first sight appears to be.

There is evidently, as far as regards the annuity no destruction nor transfer of any other Capital, than that por⟨tion⟩ of the income of each individual, which goes to make up the Annuity. The land which furnishes the Farmer with the s⟨um⟩ which he is to contribute remains the same; and the like m⟨ay⟩ be observed of other Capitals. Indeed as far as the Tax, w⟨hich⟩ is the object of contribution (as frequently happens, when it doe⟨s⟩ not oppress, by its weight) may have been a Motive to greate⟨r⟩ exertion in any occupation; it may even serve to encrease the contributory Capital: This idea is not without importanc⟨e⟩ in the general view of the subject.

It remains to see, what further deduction ought to be mad⟨e⟩ from the capital which is created, by the existence of the Debt; on account of the coin, which is employed in its circulation. This is susceptible of much less precise calculation, than the Article which has been just discussed. It is impossible to say what proportion of coin is necessary to carry on the alienations which any species of property usually undergoes. The quantity indeed varies according to circumstances. But it may still without hesitation be pronounced, from the quickness of the rotation, or rather of the transitions, that the medium of circulation always bears but a small proportion to the amount of the property circulated. And it is thence satisfactorily deducible, that the coin employed in the Negociations of the funds and which serves to give them activity, as capital, is incomparably less than the sum of the debt negotiated for the purposes of business.

It ought not, however, to be omitted, that the negotiation of the funds becomes itself a distinct business; which employs, and by employing diverts a portion of the circulating coin from other pursuits. But making due allowance for this circumstance there is no reason to conclude, that the effect of the diversion of coin in the whole operation bears any considerable proportion to the amount of the Capital to which it gives activity. The sum of the debt in circulation is continually at the Command, of any useful enterprise—the coin itself which circulates it, is never more than momentarily suspended from its ordinary functions. It experiences an incessant and rapid flux and reflux to and from the Channels of industry to those of speculations in the funds.

There are strong circumstances in confirmation of this Theory. The force of Monied Capital which has been displayed in Great Britain, and the height to which every species of industry has grown up under it, defy a solution from the quantity of coin which that kingdom has ever possessed. Accordingly it has been Coeval with its funding system, the prevailing opinion of the men of business, and of the generality of the most sagacious theorists of that country, that the operation of the public funds as capital has contributed to the effect in question. Among ourselves appearances thus far favour the same Conclusion. Industry in general seems to have been reanimated. There are symptoms indicating an extension of our Commerce. Our navigation has certainly of late had a Considerable spring, and there appears to be in many parts of the Union a command of capital, which till lately, since the revolution at least, was unknown. But it is at the same time to be acknowledged, that other circumstances have concurred, (and in a great degree) in producing the present state of things, and that the appearances are not yet sufficiently decisive, to be intirely relied upon.

In the question under discussion, it is important to distinguish between an absolute increase of Capital, or an accession of real wealth, and an artificial increase of Capital, as an engine of business, or as an instrument of industry and Commerce. In the first sense, a funded debt has no pretensions to being deemed an increase of Capital; in the last, it has pretensions which are not easy to be controverted. Of a similar nature is bank credit and in an inferior degree, every species of private credit.

But though a funded debt is not in the first instance, an absolute increase of Capital, or an augmentation of real wealth; yet by serving as a New power in the operation of industry, it has within certain bounds a tendency to increase the real wealth of a Community, in like manner as money borrowed by a thrifty farmer, to be laid out in the improvement of his farm may, in the end, add to his Stock of real riches.

There are respectable individuals, who from a just aversion to an accumulation of Public debt, are unwilling to concede to it any kind of utility, who can discern no good to alleviate the ill with which they suppose it pregnant; who cannot be persuaded that it ought in any sense to be viewed as an increase of capital lest it should be inferred, that the more debt the more capital, the greater the burthens the greater the blessings of the community.

But it interests the public Councils to estimate every object as it truly is; to appreciate how far the good in any measure is compensated by the ill; or the ill by the good, Either of them is seldom unmixed.

II. D. 2. d. iv. Although the funded debt can function as capital, it is not a good thing to accumulate debt.

Neither will it follow, that an accumulation of debt is desireable, because a certain degree of it operates as capital. There may be a plethora in the political, as in the Natural body; There may be a state of things in which any such artificial capital is unnecessary. The debt too may be swelled to such a size, as that the greatest part of it may cease to be useful as a Capital, serving only to pamper the dissipation of idle and dissolute individuals: as that the sums required to pay the Interest upon it may become oppressive, and beyond the means, which a government can employ, consistently with its tranquility, to raise them; as that the resources of taxation, to face the debt, may have been strained too far to admit of extensions adequate to exigencies, which regard the public safety.

Where this critical point is, cannot be pronounced, but it is impossible to believe, that there is not such a point.

And as the vicissitudes of Nations beget a perpetual tendency to the accumulation of debt, there ought to be in every government a perpetual, anxious and unceasing effort to reduce that, which at any time exists, as fast as shall be practicable consistently with integrity and good faith.

Reasonings on a subject comprehending ideas so abstract and complex, so little reducible to precise calculation as those which enter into the question just discussed, are always attended with a danger of running into fallacies. Due allowance ought therefore to be made for this possibility. But as far as the Nature of the subject admits of it, there appears to be satisfactory ground for a belief, that the public funds operate as a resource of capital to the Citizens of the United States, and, if they are a resource at all, it is an extensive one.

II. E. Fifth argument against manufacturing

II. E. 1. Others say: manufacturing can't work here.

II. E. 2. Hamilton's response: Numerous examples show manufacturing is already working.

To all the arguments which are brought to evince the impracticability of success in manufacturing establishments in the United States, it might have been a sufficient answer to have referred to the experience of what has been already done. It is certain that several important branches have grown up and flourished with a rapidity which surprises: affording an encouraging assurance of success in future attempts: of these it may not be improper to enumerate the most considerable.

II. E. 2. a. Skins

I of Skins.

Tanned and tawed leather dressed skins, shoes,boots and Slippers, harness and sadlery of all kinds. Portmanteau's and trunks, leather breeches, gloves, muffs and tippets, parchment and Glue.

II. E. 2. b. Iron

II of Iron

Barr and Sheet Iron, Steel, Nail-rods & Nails, implem⟨ents⟩ of husbandry, Stoves, pots and other household utensils, the steel and Iron work of carriages and for Shipbuildin⟨g,⟩ Anchors, scale beams and Weights & Various tools of Artificers, arms of different kinds; though the manufacture of these last has of late diminished for want of demand.

II. E. 2. c. Wood

III of Wood

Ships, Cabinet Wares and Turnery, Wool and Cotton ca⟨rds⟩ and other Machinery for manufactures and husband⟨ry,⟩ Mathematical instruments, Coopers wares of every kind.

II. E. 2. d. Flax and hemp

IV of flax & Hemp

Cables, sail-cloth, Cordage, twine and packthread.

II. E. 2. e. Bricks, tiles, pottery

V   Bricks and coarse tiles & Potters Wares.

II. E. 2. f. Alcohol

VI Ardent Spirits, and malt liquors.

II. E. 2. g. Paper products

VII   Writing and printing Paper, sheathing and wrapping Paper, pasteboards, fillers or press papers, paper hangings.

II. E. 2. h. Hats and shoes

VIII   Hats of furr and Wool and of mixtures of both, Womens Stuff and Silk shoes.

II. E. 2. i. Sugar

IX Refined Sugars.

II. E. 2. j. Oils and soaps

X   Oils of Animals and seeds; Soap, Spermaceti and Tallow Candles.

II. E. 2. k. Copper and brass wares

XI   Copper and brass wares, particularly utensils for distillers, Sugar refiners and brewers, And—Irons and other Articles for household Use, philosophical apparatus

II. E. 2. l. Tin wares

XII   Tin Wares, for most purposes of Ordinary use.

II. E. 2. m. Carriages

XIII Carriages of all kinds

II. E. 2. n. Snuff and tobacco

XIV Snuff, chewing & smoking Tobacco.

II. E. 2. o. Starch and hair powder

XV Starch and Hairpowder.

II. E. 2. p. Lampblack and paint

XVI Lampblack and other painters colours,

II. E. 2. q. Gunpowder

XVII Gunpowder

II. E. 2. r. Household manufactures

Besides manufactories of these articles which are carried on as regular Trades, and have attained to a considerable degree of maturity, there is a vast scene of household manufacturing, which contributes more largely to the supply of the Community, than could be imagined; without having made it an object of particular enquiry. This observation is the pleasing result of the investigation, to which the subject of the report has led, and is applicable as well to the Southern as to the middle and Northern States; great quantities of coarse cloths, coatings, serges, and flannels, linsey Woolseys, hosiery of Wool, cotton & thread, coarse fustians, jeans and Muslins, check⟨ed⟩ and striped cotton and linen goods, bed ticks, Coverlets and Counterpanes, Tow linens, coarse shirtings, sheetings, toweling and table linen, and various mixtures of wool and cotton, and of Cotton & flax are made in the household way, and in many instances to an extent not only sufficient for the supply of the families in which they are made, but for sale, and (even in some cases) for exportation. It is computed in a number of districts that $\frac{2}{3}\frac{3}{4}$ and even 4/5 of all the clothing of the Inhabitants are made by themselves. The importance of so great a progress, as appears to have been made in family Manufactures, within a few years, both in a moral and political view, renders the fact highly interesting.

Neither does the above enumeration comprehend all the articles, that are manufactured as regular Trades. Many others occur, which are equally well established, but which not being of equal importance have been omitted. And there are many attempts still in their Infancy, which though attended with very favorable appearances, could not have been properly comprized in an enumeration of manufactories, already established. There are other articles also of great importance, which tho' strictly speaking manufactures are omitted, as being immediately connected with husbandry: such are flour, pot & pearl ash, Pitch, tar, turpentine and the like.

II. F. Sixth argument against manufacturing

II. F. 1. Others say: Manufacturing gives unfair advantages to particular classes.

There remains to be noticed an objection to the encouragement of manufactures, of a nature different from those which question the probability of success. This is derived from its supposed tendency to give a monopoly of advantages to particula(r) classes at the expence of the rest of the community, who, it is affirmed, would be able to procure the requisite supplies of manufactured articles on better terms from foreigners, than from our own Citizens, and who it is alledged, are reduced to a necessity of paying an enhanced price for whatever they want, by every measure, which obstructs the free competition of foreign commoditi(es.)

It is not an unreasonable supposition, that measures, which serve to abridge the free competition of foreign Articles, have a tendency to occasion an enhancement of prices and it is not to be denied that such is the effect in a number of Cases; but the fact does not uniformly correspond with the theory. A reduction of prices has in several instances immediately succeeded the establishment of a domestic manufacture. Whether it be that foreign Manufacturers endeavour to suppla(nt) by underselling our own, or whatever else be the cause, the effect has been such as is stated, and the reverse of what mig(ht) have been expected.

II. F. 2. Hamilton's response: Eventually manufacturing makes prices cheaper, allowing more people able to afford more goods.

But though it were true, that the immedi(ate) and certain effect of regulations controuling the competition of foreign with domestic fabrics was an increase of price, it is universally true, that the contrary is the ultimate effect with every successful manufacture. When a domestic manufacture has attained to perfection, and has engaged in the prosecution of it a competent number of Persons, it invariably becomes cheaper. Being free from the heavy charges, which attend the importation of foreign commodities, it can be afforded, and accordingly seldom or never fails to be sold Cheaper, in process of time, than was the foreign Article for which it is a substitute. The internal competition, which takes place, soon does away every thing like Monopoly, and by degrees reduces the price of the Article to the minimum of a reasonable profit on the Capital employed. This accords with the reason of the thing and with experience.

Whence it follows, that it is the interest of a community with a view to eventual and permanent oeconomy, to encourage the growth of manufactures. In a national view, a temporary enhancement of price must always be well compensated by a permanent reduction of it.

It is a reflection, which may with propriety be indulged here, that this eventual diminution of the prices of manufactured Articles; which is the result of internal manufacturing establishments, has a direct and very important tendency to benefit agriculture. It enables the farmer, to procure with a smaller quantity of his labour, the manufactured produce of which he stan⟨ds⟩ in need, and consequently increases the value of his income and property.

III. ARGUMENTS IN FAVOR OF MANUFACTURING

III. A. Manufacturing will give us a better trading position.

The objections which are commonly made to the expediency of encouraging, and to the probability of succeeding in manufacturing pursuits, in the United states, having now been discussed; the Considerations which have appeared in the Course of the discussion, recommending that species of industry to the patronage of the Government, will be materially strengthened by a few general and some particular topics, which have been naturally reserved for subsequent Notice.

III. A. 1. A country's trading position is better if it can offer manufactured goods as well as agricultural produce.

I   There seems to be a moral certainty, that the trade of a country which is both manufacturing and Agricultural will be more lucrative and prosperous, than that of a Country, which is, merely Agricultural.

One reason for this is found in that general effort of nations (which has been already mentioned) to procure from their own soils, the articles of prime necessity requisite to their own consumption and use; and which serves to render their demand for a foreign supply of such articles in a great degree occasional and contingent. Hence, while the necessities of nations exclusively devoted to Agriculture, for the fabrics of manufacturing st⟨ates⟩ are constant and regular, the wants of the latter for the products of the former, are liable to very considerable fluctuations and interruptions. The great inequalities resulting from difference of seasons, have been elsewhere remarked: This uniformity of deman⟨d⟩ on one side, and unsteadiness of it, on the other, must necessarily ha⟨ve⟩ a tendency to cause the general course of the exchange of commodit⟨ies⟩ between the parties to turn to the disadvantage of the merely agricultural States. Peculiarity of situation, a climate and soil ada⟨pted⟩ to the production of peculiar commodities, may, sometimes, contradi⟨ct⟩ the rule; but there is every reason to believe that it will be fou⟨nd⟩ in the Main, a just one.

III. A. 2. A country is more attractive to traders if it has a diverse selection of goods.

Another circumstance which gives a superiority of commercial advantages to states, that manufact⟨ure⟩ as well as cultivate, consists in the more numerous attractions, which a more diversified market offers to foreign Customers, and greater scope, which it affords to mercantile enterprise. It is ⟨a⟩ position of indisputable truth in Commerce, depending too on very obvious reasons, that the greatest resort will ever be to those mar⟨ts⟩ where commodities, while equally abundant, are most various. Each difference of kind holds out an additional inducement. And it is a position not less clear, that the field of enterprise must be enlarged to the Merchants of a Country, in proportion ⟨to⟩ the variety as well as the abundance of commodities which they find at home for exportation to foreign Markets.

III. A. 3. A country that has a diverse selection of goods is less likely to be harmed if demand for any one item is stagnant.

A third circumstance, perhaps not inferior to either of the other two, conferring the superiority which has been stated has relation to the stagnations of demand for certain commodities which at some time or other interfere more or less with the sale of all. The Nation which can bring to Market, but few articles is likely to be more quickly and sensibly affected by such stagnations, than one, which is always possessed of a great variety of commodities. The former frequently finds too great a proportion of its stock of materials, for sale or exchange, lying on hand—or is obliged to make injurious sacrifices to supply its wants of foreign articles, which are Numerous and urgent, in proportion to the smallness of the number of its own. The latter commonly finds itself indemnified, by the high prices of some articles, for the low prices of others—and the Prompt and advantageous sale of those articles which are in demand enables its merchant the better to wait for a favorable change, in respect to those which are not. There is ground to believe, that a difference of situation, in this particular, has immensely different effec⟨ts⟩ upon the wealth and prosperity of Nations.

III. A. 4. Conclusion: Manufacturing helps improve trade and bring more wealth into a country.

From these circumstances collectively, two important inferences are to be drawn, one, that there is always a higher probability of a favorable balance of Trade, in regard to countries in which manufactures founded on the basis of a thriving Agriculture flourish, than in regard to those, which are confined wholly or almost wholly to Agriculture; the other (which is also a consequence of the first) that countries of the former description are likely to possess more pecuniary wealth, or money, than those of the latter.

Facts appear to correspond with this conclusion. The importations of manufactured supplies seem invariably to drain the merely Agricultural people of their wealth. Let the situation of the manufacturing countries of Europe be compared in this particular, with that of Countries which only cultivate, and the disparity will be striking. Other causes, it is true, help to Account for this disparity between some of them; and among these causes, the relative state of Agriculture; but between others of them, the most prominent circumstance of dissimilitude arises from the Comparative state of Manufactures. In corroboration of the same idea, it ought not to escape remark, that the West India Islands, the soils of which are the most fertile, and the Nation, which in the greatest degree supplies the rest of the world, with the precious metals, exchange to a loss with almost every other Country.

As far as experience at home may guide, it will lead to the same conclusion. Previous to the revolution, the quantity of coin, possessed by the colonies, which now compose the United states, appeared, to be inadequate to their circulation; and their debt to Great-Britain was progressive. Since the Revolution, the States, in which manufactures have most increased, have recovered fastest from the injuries of the late War, and abound most in pecuniary resources.

It ought to be admitted, however in this as in the preceding case, that causes irrelative to the state of manufactures account, in a degree, for the Phœnomena remarked. The continual progress of new settlements has a natural tendency to occasion an unfavorable balance of Trade; though it indemnifies for the inconvenience, by that increase of the national capital which flows from the conversion of waste into improved lands: And the different degrees of external commerce, which are carried on by the different States, may make material differences in the comparative state of their wealth. The first circumstance has reference to the deficien⟨cy⟩ of coin and the increase of debt previous to the revolution; the last to the advantages which the most manufacturing states appear to have enjoyed, over the others, since the termination of the late War.

But the uniform appearance of an abundance of specie, as the concomitant of a flourishing state of manufacture⟨s⟩ and of the reverse, where they do not prevail, afford a strong presumption of their favourable operation upon the wealth of a Country.

III. B. Manufacturing will make a nation better able to defend itself.

Not only the wealth; but the independence and security of a Country, appear to be materially connected with the prosperity of manufactures. Every nation, with a view to those great objects, ought to endeavour to possess within itself all the essentials of national supply. These comprise the means of Subsistence habitation clothing and defence.

The possession of these is necessary to the perfection of the body politic, to the safety as well as to the welfare of the society; the want of either, is the want of an important organ of political life and Motion; and in the various crises which await a state, it must severely feel the effects of any such deficiency. The extreme embarrassments of the United States during the late War, from an incapacity of supplying themselves, are still matter of keen recollection: A future war might be expected again to exemplify the mischiefs and dangers of a situation, to which that incapacity is still in too great a degree applicable, unless changed by timely and vigorous exertion. To effect this change as fast as shall be prudent, merits all the attention and all the Zeal of our Public Councils; 'tis the next great work to be accomplished.

The want of a Navy to protect our external commerce, as long as it shall Continue, must render it a peculiarly precarious reliance, for the supply of essential articles, and must serve to strengthen prodigiously the arguments in favour of manufactures.

III. C. Manufacturing has some more specific advantages.

To these general Considerations are added some of a more particular nature.

III. C. 1. We lose money by shipping bulky agricultural products to Europe, and paying for imports of manufactured goods.

Our distance from Europe, the great fountain of manufactured supply, subjects us in the existing state of things, to inconvenience and loss in two Ways.

The bulkiness of those commodities which are the chief productions of the soil, necessarily imposes very heavy charges on their transportation, to distant markets. These charges, in the Cases, in which the nations, to whom our products are sent, maintain a Competition in the supply of their own markets, principally fall upon us, and form material deductions from the primitive value of the articles furnished. The charges on manufactured supplies, brought from Europe are greatly enhanced by the same circumstance of distance. These charges, again, in the cases in which our own industry maintains no competition, in our own markets, also principally fall upon us; and are an additional cause of extraordinary deduction from the primitive value of our own products; these bei⟨ng⟩ the materials of exchange for the foreign fabrics, which we consume.

III. C. 2. Our frontier settlements need lots of coarse manufactured goods, which are expensive to import.

The equality and moderation of individual prope⟨rty⟩ and the growing settlements of new districts, occasion in this country an unusual demand for coarse manufactures; The charges of which being greater in proportion to their greater bulk augment the disadvantage, which has been just described.

As in most countries domestic supplie⟨s⟩ maintain a very considerable competition with such foreign productions of the soil, as are imported for sale; if the extensive establishment of Manufactories in the United states does not create a similar competition in respect to manufactured articles, it appears to be clearly deducible, from the Considerations which have been mentioned, that they must sustain a double loss in their exchanges with foreign Nations; strongly conducive to an unfavorable balance of Trade, and very prejudicial to their Interests.

These disadvantages press with no small weight, on the landed interest of the Country. In seasons of peace, they cause a serious deduction from the intrinsic value of the products of the soil. In the time of a War, which shou'd either involve ourselves, or another nation, possessing a Considerable share of our carrying trade, the charges on the transportation of our commodities, bulky as most of them are, could hardly fail to prove a grievous burthen to the farmer; while obliged to depend in so great degree as he now does, upon foreign markets for the vent of the surplus of his labour.

As far as the prosperity of the Fisheries of the United states is impeded by the want of an adequate market, there arises another special reason for desiring the extension of manufactures. Besides the fish, which in many places, would be likely to make a part of the subsistence of the persons employed; it is known that the oils, bones and skins of marine animals, are of extensive use in various manufactures. Hence the prospect of an additional demand for the produce of the Fisheries.

III. C. 3. North and South can both benefit from manufacturing.

One more point of view only remains in which to Consider the expediency of encouraging manufactures in the United states.

It is not uncommon to meet with an opin⟨ion⟩ that though the promoting of manufactures may be the interest of a part of the Union, it is contrary to that of another part. The Northern & southern regions are sometimes represented as having adverse interests in this respect. Those are called Manufacturing, these Agricultural states; and a species of opposition is imagined to subsist between the Manufacturing a⟨nd⟩ Agricultural interests.

This idea of an opposition between those two interests is the common error of the early periods of every country, but experience gradually dissipates it. Indeed they are perceived so often to succour and to befriend each other, that they come at length to be considered as one: a supposition which has been frequently abused and is not universally true. Particular encouragements of particular manufactures may be of a Nature to sacrifice the interests of landholders to those of manufacturers; But it is nevertheless a maxim well established by experience, and generally acknowledged, where there has been sufficient experience, that the aggregate prosperity of manufactures, and the aggregate prosperity of Agriculture are intimately connected. In the Course of the discussion which has had place, various weighty considerations have been adduced operating in support of that maxim. Perhaps the superior steadiness of the demand of a domestic market for the surplus produce of the soil, is alone a convincing argument of its truth.

Ideas of a contrariety of interests between the Northern and southern regions of the Union, are in the Main as unfounded as they are mischievous. The diversity of Circumstances on which such contrariety is usually predicated, authorises a directly contrary conclusion. Mutual wants constitute one of the strongest links of political connection, and the extent of the⟨se⟩ bears a natural proportion to the diversity in the means of mutual supply.

Suggestions of an opposite complexion are ever to be deplored, as unfriendly to the steady pursuit of one great common cause, and to the perfect harmony of all the parts.

In proportion as the mind is accustomed to trace the intimate connexion of interest, which subsists between all the parts of a Society united under the same government—the infinite variety of channels which serve to Circulate the prosper⟨ity⟩ of each to and through the rest—in that proportion will it be little apt to be disturbed by solicitudes and Apprehensions which originate in local discriminations. It is a truth as important as it is agreeable, and one to which it is not easy to imagine exceptions, that every thing tending to establish substantial and permanent order, in the affairs of a Country, to increase the total mass of industry and opulence, is ultimately beneficial to every part of it. On the Credit of this great truth, an acquiescence may safely be accorded, from every quarter, to all institutions & arrangements, which promise a confirmation of public order, and an augmentation of National Resource.

But there are more particular considerations which serve to fortify the idea, that the encouragement of manufactures is the interest of all parts of the Union. If the Northern and middle states should be the principal scenes of such establishments, they would immediately benefit the more southern, by creating a demand for productions; some of which they have in common with the other states, and others of which are either peculiar to them, or more abundant, or of better quality, than elsewhere. These productions, principally are Timber, flax, Hemp, Cotton, Wool, raw silk, Indigo, iron, lead, furs, hides, skins and coals. Of these articles Cotton & Indigo are peculiar to the southern states; as are hitherto Lead & Coal. Flax and Hemp are or may be raised in greater abundance there, than in the More Northern states; and the Wool of Virginia is said to be of better quality than that of any other state: a Circumstance rendered the more probable by the reflection that Virginia embraces the same latitudes with the finest Wool Countries of Europe. The Climate of the south is also better adapted to the production of silk.

The extensive cultivation of Cotton can perhaps hardly be expected, but from the previous establishment of domestic Manufactories of the Article; and the surest encouragement and vent, for the others, would result from similar establishments in respect to them.

III. D. Summary: Why we should encourage manufacturing now.

If then, it satifactorily appears, that it is the Interest of the United states, generally, to encourage manufactures, it merits particular attention, that there are circumstances, which Render the present a critical moment for entering with Zeal upon the important business. The effort cannot fail to be materially seconded by a considerable and encreasing influx of money, in consequence of foreign speculations in the funds—and by the disorders, which exist in different parts of Europe.

The first circumstance not only facilita⟨tes⟩ the execution of manufacturing enterprises; but it indicates them as a necessary mean to turn the thing itself to advantage, and to prevent its being eventually an evil. If useful employment be not found for the Money of foreigners brought to the country to be invested in purchase⟨s⟩ of the public debt, it will quickly be reexported to defray the expence of an extraordinary consumption of foreign luxuries; and distressing drains of our specie may hereafter be experienced to pay the interest and redeem the principal of the purchased debt.

This useful employment too ought to be of a Nature to produce solid and permanent improvements. If the money merely serves to give a temporary spring to foreign commerce; as it cannot procure new and lasting outlets for the products of the Country; there will be no real or durable advantage gained. As far as it shall find its way in Agricultural ameliorations, in opening canals, and in similar improvements, it will be productive of substantial utility. But there is reason to doubt, whether in such channels it is likely to find sufficient employment, and still more whether many of those who possess it, would be as readily attracted to objects of this nature, as to manufacturing pursuits; which bear greater analogy to those to which they are accustomed, and to the spirit generated by them.

To open the one field, as well as the other, will at least secure a better prospect of useful employment, for whatever accession of money, there has been or may be.

There is at the present juncture a certain fermentation of mind, a certain activity of speculation and enterprise which if properly directed may be made subservient to useful purposes; but which if left entirely to itself, may be attended with pernicious effects.

The disturbed state of Europe, inclining its citizens to emigration, the requisite workmen, will be more easily acquired, than at another time; and the effect of multiplying the opportunities of employment to those who emigrate, may be an increase of the number and extent of valuable acquisitions to the population arts and industry of the

Country. To find pleasure in the calamities of other nations, would be criminal; but to benefit ourselves, by opening an asylum to those who suffer, in consequence of them, is as justifiable as it is pol⟨itic.⟩

IV. POLICIES USED BY OTHER COUNTRIES TO ENCOURAGE MANUFACTURES.

A full view having now been taken of the inducements to the promotion of Manufactures in the United states, accompanied with an examination of the principal objections which are commonly urged in opposition, it is proper in the next place, to consider the means, by which it may be effected, as introductory to a Specification of the objects which in the present state of things appear the most fit to be encouraged, and of the particular measures which it may be adviseable to adopt, in respect to each.

In order to a better judgment of the Means proper to be resorted to by the United states, it will be of use to Advert to those which have been employed with success in other Countries. The principal of these are.

IV. A. First means: Discourage certain imports.

I   Protecting duties—or duties on those foreign articles which are the rivals of the domestic ones, intended to be encouraged.

Duties of this Nature evidently amount to a virtual bounty on the domestic fabrics since by enhancing the charges on foreign Articles, they enable the National Manufacturers to undersell all their foreign Competitors. The propriety of this species of encouragement need not be dwelt upon; as it is not only a clear result from the numerous topics which have been suggested, but is sanctioned by the laws of the United states in a variety of instances; it has the additional recommendat⟨ion⟩ of being a resource of revenue. Indeed all the duties imposed on imported articles, though with an exclusive view to Revenue, have the effect in Contemplation, and except where they fall on raw materials wear a beneficent aspect towards the manufactures of the Country.

IV. B. Second means: Prohibit certain imports.

II.   Prohibitions of rival articles or duties equivalent to prohibitions.

This is another and an efficacious mean of encouraging national manufactures, but in general it is only fit to be employed when a manufacture, has made such a progress and is in so many hands as to insure a due competition, and an adequate supply on reasonable terms. Of duties equivalent to prohibitions, there are examples in the Laws of the United States, and there are other Cases to which the principle may be advantageously extended, but they are not numero⟨us.⟩

Considering a monopoly of the domestic market to its own manufacturers as the reigning policy of manufacturing Nations, a similar policy on the part of the United states in every proper instance, is dictated, it might almost be said, by the principles of distributive justice; certainly by the duty of endeavouring to secure to their own Citizens a reciprocity of advantages.

IV. C. Third means: Prohibit certain exports.

III   Prohibitions of the exportation of the materials of manufactures.

The desire of securing a cheap and plentiful supply for the national workmen, and, where the article is either peculiar to the Country, or of peculiar quality there, the jealousy of enabling foreign workmen to rival those of the nation, with its ow⟨n⟩ Materials, are the leading motives to this species of regulation. ⟨It⟩ ought not to be affirmed, that it is in no instance proper, but it is certainly one which ought to be adopted with great circumspect⟨ion⟩ and only in very plain Cases. It is seen at once, that its immedi⟨ate⟩ operation, is to abridge the demand and keep down the price of the produce of some other branch of industry, generally speaking, of Agriculture, to the prejudice of those, who carry it on; and tho⟨ough⟩ if it be really essential to the prosperity of any very important nati⟨onal⟩ Manufacture, it may happen that those who are injured in the first instance, may be eventually indemnified, by the superior ⟨steadiness⟩ of an extensive domestic market, depending on that prosperity: yet in a matter, in which there is so much room for nice and difficult combinations, in which such opposite considerations combat each other, prudence seems to dictate, that the expedient in question, ought to be indulged with a sparing hand.

IV. D. Fourth means: Offer bounties to producers of certain goods.

IV Pecuniary bounties

This has been found one of the most efficacious means of encouraging manufactures, and it is in some views, the best. Though it has not yet been practiced upon by the Government of the United states (unless the allowance on the exportation of dried and pickled Fish and salted meat could be considered as a bounty) and though it is less favored by public opinion than some other modes.

Its advantages, are these—

1   It is a species of encouragement more positive and direct than any other, and for that very reason, has a more immediate tendency to

stimulate and uphold new enterprises, increasing the chances of profit, and diminishing the risks of loss, in the first attempts.

2. It avoids the inconvenience of a temporary augmentation of price, which is incident to some other modes, or it produces it to a less degree; either by making no addition to the charges on the rival foreign article, as in the Case of protecting duties, or by making a smaller addition. The first happens when the fund for the bounty is derived from a different object (which may or may not increase the price of some other article, according to the nature of that object) the second, when the fund is derived from the same or a similar object of foreign manufacture. One per cent duty on the foreign article converted into a bounty on the domestic, will have an equal effect with a duty of two per Cent, exclusive of such bounty; and the price of the foreign commodity is liable to be raised, in the one Case, in the proportion of 1 ₱ Cent; in the other, in that of two ₱ Cent. Indeed the bounty when drawn from another source is calculated to promote a reduction of price, because without laying any new charge on the foreign article, it serves to introduce a competition with it, and to increase the total quantity of the article in the Market.

3 Bounties have not like high protecting duties, a tendency to produce scarcity. An increase of price is not always the immediate, though, where the progress of a domestic Manufacture does not counteract a rise, it is commonly the ultimate effect of an additional duty. In the interval, between the laying of the duty and a proportional increase of price, it may discourage importation, by interfering with the profits to be expected from the sale of the article.

4. Bounties are sometimes not only the best, but the only proper expedient, for uniting the encouragement of a new object of agriculture, with that of a new object of manufacture. It is the Interest of the farmer to have the production of the raw material promoted, by counteracting the interference of the foreig⟨n⟩ material of the same kind. It is the interest of the manufactu⟨rer⟩ to have the material abundant and cheap. If prior to the domes⟨tic⟩ production of the Material, in sufficient quantity, to supply the manufacturer on good terms; a duty be laid upon the importation of it from abroad, with a view to promote the raising of it at home, the Interests both of the Farmer and Manufacturer will be disserved. By either destroying the requisite supply, or raising the price of the article, beyond what can be afforded to be given for it, by the Conductor of an infant manufacture, it is abandoned or fails; an⟨d⟩ there being no domestic manufactories to create a demand for t⟨he⟩ raw material, which is raised by the farmer, it is in vain, that

the Competition of the like foreign article may have been destroy⟨ed.⟩

It cannot escape notice, that a duty upon the importation of ⟨an⟩ article can no otherwise aid the domestic production of it, than giving the latter greater advantages in the home market. It ca⟨n⟩ have no influence upon the advantageous sale of the article produced, in foreign markets; no tendency, there⟨fore⟩ to promote its exportation.

The true way to conciliate these two interests, is to lay a duty on foreign manufactures of the material, the growth of which is desired to be encouraged, and to apply the produce of that duty by way of bounty, either upon the production of the material itself or upon its manufacture at home or upon both. In this disposition of the thing, the Manufacturer commences his enterprise under every advantage, which is attainable, as to quantity or price, of the raw material: And the Farmer if the bounty be immediately to him, is enabled by it to enter into a successful competition with the foreign material; if the bounty be to the manufacturer on so much of the domestic material as he consumes, the operation is nearly the same; he has a motive of interest to prefer the domestic Commodity, if of equal quality, even at a higher price than the foreign, so long as the difference of price is any thing short of the bounty which is allowed upon the article.

Except the simple and ordinary kinds of household Manufactures, or those for which there are very commanding local advantages, pecuniary bounties are in most cases indispensable to the introduction of a new branch. A stimulus and a support not less powerful and direct is generally speaking essential to the overcoming of the obstacles which arise from the Competitions of superior skill and maturity elsewhere. Bounties are especially essential, in regard to articles, upon which those foreigners, who have been accustomed to supply a Country, are in the practice of granting them.

The continuance of bounties on manufactures long established must almost always be of questionable policy: Because a presumption would arise in every such Case, that there were natural and inherent impediments to success. But in new undertakings, they are as justifiable, as they are oftentimes necessary.

There is a degree of prejudice against bounties from an appearance of giving away the public money, without an immediate consideration, and from a supposition, that they serve to enrich particular classes, at the expence of the Community.

But neither of these sources of dislike will bear a serious examination. There is no purpose, to which public money can be more beneficially applied, than to the acquisition of a new and useful branch of industry; no Consideration more valuable than a permanent addition to the general stock of productive labour.

As to the second source of objection, it equally lies against other modes of encouragement, which are admitted to be eligible. As often as a duty upon a foreign article makes an addition to its price, it causes an extra expence to the Community, for the benefit of the domestic manufacturer. A bounty does no more: But it is the Interest of the society in each case, to submit to a temporary expence, which is more than compensated, by an increase of industry and Wealth, by an augmentation of resources and independence; & by the circumstance of eventual cheapness, which has been noticed in another place.

It would deserve attention, however, in the employment of this species of encouragement in the United states, as a reason for moderating the degree of it in the instances, in which it might be deemed eligible, that the great distance of this country from Europe imposes very heavy charges on all the fabrics which are brought from thence, amounting from [15 to 30] ₽ Cent on their value, according to their bulk.

IV. D. 1. Are bounties allowed, according to the Constitution?

A Question has been made concerning the Constitutional right of the Government of the United States to apply this species of encouragement, but there is certainly no good foundation for such a question. The National Legislature has express authority "To lay and Collect taxes, duties, imposts and excises, to pay the debts and provide for the Common defence and general welfare" with no other qualifications than that "all duties, imposts and excises, shall be uniform throughout the United states, that no capitation or other direct tax shall be laid unless in proportion to numbers ascertained by a census or enumeration taken on the principles prescribed in the Constitution, and that "no tax or duty shall be laid on articles exported from any state." These three qualifications excepted, the power to raise money is plenary, and indefinite; and the objects to which it may be appropriated are no less comprehensive, than the payment of the public debts and the providing for the common defence and "general Welfare." The terms "general Welfare" were doubtless intended to signify more than was expressed or imported in those which Preceded; otherwise numerous exigencies incident to the affairs of a Nation would have been left without a provision. The phrase is as comprehensive as any that could have been used; because it was not fit that the constitutional authority of the Union, to appropriate its revenues shou'd have been restricted within narrower limits than the "General Welfare" and because this necessarily embraces a vast variety of particulars, which are susceptible neither of specification nor of definition.

It is therefore of necessity left to the discretion of the National Legislature, to pronounce, upon the objects, which concern the general Welfare, and for which under that description, an appropriation of money is requisite and proper. And there seems to be no room for a doubt that whatever concerns the general Interests of learning of Agriculture of Manufactures and of Commerce are within the sphere of the national Councils as far as regards an application of Money.

The only qualification of the generallity of the Phrase in question, which seems to be admissible, is this—That the object to which an appropriation of money is to be made be General and not local; its operation extending in fact, or by possibility, throughout the Union, and not being confined to a particular spot.

No objection ought to arise to this construction from a supposition that it would imply a power to do whatever else should appear to Congress conducive to the General Welfare. A power to appropriate money with this latitude which is granted too in express terms would not carry a power to do any other thing, not authorised in the constitution, either expressly or by fair implication.

IV. E. Fifth means: Pay premiums to those who produce superior quality.

V. Premiums

These are of a Nature allied to bounties, though distinguishable from them, in some important features.

Bounties are applicable to the whole quantity of an article produced, or manufactured, or exported, and involve a correspondent expence. Premiums serve to reward some particular excellence or superiority, some extraordinary exertion or skill, and are dispensed on⟨ly⟩ in a small number of cases. But their effect is to stimulate gener⟨al⟩ effort. Contrived so as to be both honorary and lucrative, they address themselves to different passions; touching the chords as well of emulation as of Interest. They are accordingly a very economical mean of exciting the enterprise of a Whole Community.

There are various Societies in different countries, whose object is the dispensation of Premiums for the encouragemen⟨t⟩ of Agriculture Arts manufactures and Commerce; and though they are for the most part voluntary associations, with comparatively slender funds, their utility has been immense. Much has been done by this mean in great Britain: Scotland in particular owes materially to it a prodigious amelioration of Condition. From a similar establishment in the United states, supplied and supported by the Government of the Union, vast benefits might reasonably be expected. Some further ideas on this head, shall accordingly be submitted, in the conclusion of this report.

IV. F. Sixth means: Exempt raw materials from import duties.

VI   The Exemption of the Materials of manufactures from duty.

The policy of that Exemption as a general rule, particularly in reference to new Establishments, is obvious. It can hardly ever be adviseable to add the obstructions of fiscal burthens to the difficulties which naturally embarrass a new manufacture; and where it is matured and in condition to become an object of revenue, it is generally speaking better that the fabric, than the Material should be the subject of Taxation. Ideas of proportion between the quantum of the tax and the value of the article, can be more easily adjusted, in the former, than in the latter case. An argument for exemptions of this kind in the United States, is to be derived from the practice, as far as their necessities have permitted, of those nations whom we are to meet as competitors in our own and in foreign Markets.

There are however exceptions to it; of which some examples will be given under the next head.

The Laws of the Union afford instances of the observance of the policy here recommended, but it will probably be found adviseable to extend it to some other Cases. Of a nature, bearing some affinity to that policy is the regulation which exempts from duty the tools and implements, as well as the books, cloths and household furniture of foreign artists, who come to reside in the United states; an advantage already secured to them by the Laws of the Union, and which, it is, in every view, proper to Continue.

IV. G. Seventh means: Remove import duties on goods used for manufacturing.

VII   Drawbacks of the duties which are imposed on the Materials of Manufactures.

It has already been observed as a general rule that duties on those materials, ought with certain exceptions to be foreborne. Of these exceptions, three cases occur, which may serve as examples— one—where the material is itself, an object of general or extensive consumption, and a fit and productive source of revenue: Another, where a manufacture of a simpler kind [the competition of which with a like domestic article is desired to be restrained,] partakes of the Nature of a raw material, from being capable, by a further process to be converted into a manufacture of a different kind, the introduction or growth of which is desired to be encouraged; a third where the Material itself is a production of the Country, and in sufficient abundance to furnish cheap and plentiful supply to the national Manufacturer.

Under the first description comes the article of Molasses. It is not only a fair object of revenue; but being a sweet, it is just that the consumers of it should pay a duty as well as the Consumer⟨s⟩ of sugar.

Cottons and linens in their White state fall under the second description. A duty upon such as are imported is proper to promote the domestic Manufacture of similar articles in the same state. A drawback of that duty is proper to encourage the printing and staining at home of those which are brought from abroad: When the first of these manufac⟨tures⟩ has attained sufficient maturity in a Country, to furnish a full supply for ⟨the⟩ second, the utility of the drawback ceases.

The article of Hemp either now does or may be expected soon to exemplify the third Case, in the United states.

Where duties on the materials of manufactures are not laid for the purpose of preventing a competition with some domestic production, the same reasons which recommend, as a general rule, the exemption of those materials from duties, would recommend as a like General rule, the allowance of draw backs, in favor of the manufacturer. Accordingly such drawbacks are familiar in countries which systematically pursue the business of manufactures; which furnishes an argument for the observance of a similar policy in the United states; and the Idea has been adopted by the laws of the Union in the instances of salt and Molasses. It is believed that it will be found advantageous to extend it to some other Articles.

IV. H. Eighth means: Encourage inventions.

VIII   The encouragement of new inventions and discoveries, at home, and of the introduction into the United States of such as may have been made in other countries; particularly those, which relate to machinery.

This is among the most useful and unexceptionable of the aids, which can be given to manufactures. The usual means of that encouragement are pecuniary rewards, and, for a time, exclusive privileges. The first must be employed, according to the occasion, and the utility of the invention, or discovery: For the last, so far as respects "authors and inventors" provision has been made by Law. But it is desireable in regard to improvements and secrets of extraordinary value, to be able to extend the same benefit to Introducers, as well as Authors and Inventors; a policy which has been practiced with advantage in other countries. Here, however, as in some other cases, there is cause to regret, that the competency of the authority of the National Government to the good, which might be done, is not without a question. Many aids might be given to industry; many internal improvements of primary magnitude might be promoted, by an authority operating throughout the Union, which cannot be effected, as well, if at all, by an authority confined within the limits of a single state.

But if the legislature of the Union cannot do all the good, that might be wished, it is at least desirable, that all may be done, which is practicable. Means for promoting the introduction of foreign improvements, though less efficaciously than might be accomplished with more adequate authority, will form a part of the plan intended to be submitted in the close of this report.

It is customary with manufacturing nations to prohibit, under severe penalties, the exportation of implements and machines, which they have either invented or improved. There are already objects for a similar regulation in the United States; and others may be expected to occur from time to time. The adoption of it seems to be dictated by the principle of reciprocity. Greater liberality, in such respects, might better comport with the general spirit of the country; but a selfish and exclusive policy in other quarters will not always permit the free indulgence of a spirit, which would place us upon an unequal footing. As far as prohibitions tend to prevent foreign competitors from deriving the benefit of the improvements made at home, they tend to increase the advantages of those by whom they may have been introduced; and operate as an encouragement to exertion.

IV. I. Ninth means: Impose quality inspection.

IX   Judicious regulations for the inspection of manufactured commodities.

This is not among the least important of the means, by which the prosperity of manufactures may be promoted. It is indeed in many cases one of the most essential. Contributing to prevent frauds upon consumers at home and exporters to foreign countries—to improve the quality & preserve the character of the national manufactures, it cannot fail to aid the expeditious and advantageous Sale of them, and to serve as a guard against successful competition from other quarters. The reputation of the flour and lumber of some states, and of the Pot ash of others has been established by an attention to this point. And the like good name might be procured for those articles, wheresoever produced, by a judicious and uniform system of Inspection; throughout the ports of the United States. A like system might also be extended with advantage to other commodities.

IV. J. Tenth means: Stimulate better circulation of money.

X   The facilitating of pecuniary remittances from place to place is a point of considerable moment to trade in general, and to manufactures in particular; by rendering more easy the purchase of raw materials and provisions and the payment for manufactured supplies. A general circulation of Bank paper, which is to be expected from the institution lately established will be a most valuable mean to this end. But much good would also accrue from some additional provisions respecting inland bills of exchange. If those drawn in one state payable in another were made negotiable, everywhere, and interest and damages allowed in case of protest, it would greatly promote negotiations between the Citizens of different states, by rendering them more secure; and, with it the convenience and advantage of the Merchants and manufacturers of each.

IV. K. Eleventh means: Improve transportation infrastructure.

XI   The facilitating of the transportation of commodities.
Improvements favoring this object intimately concern all the domestic interests of a community; but they may without impropriety be mentioned as having an important relation to manufactures. There is perhaps scarcely any thing, which has been better calculated to assist the manufactures of Great Britain, than the ameliorations of the public roads of that Kingdom, and the great progress which has been of late made in opening canals. Of the former, the United States stand much in need; and for the latter they present uncommon facilities.

The symptoms of attention to the improvement of inland Navigation, which have lately appeared in some quarters, must fill with pleasure every breast warmed with a true Zeal for the prosperity of the Country. These examples, it is to be hoped, will stimulate the exertions of the Government and the Citizens of every state. There can certainly be no object, more worthy of the cares of the local administrations; and it were to be wished, that there was no doubt of the power of the national Government to lend its direct aid, on a comprehensive plan.

This is one of those improvements, which could be prosecuted with more efficacy by the whole, than by any part or parts of the Union. There are cases in which the general interest will be in danger to be sacrificed to the collission of some supposed local interests. Jealousies, in matters of this kind, are as apt to exist, as they are apt to be erroneous.

The following remarks are sufficiently judicious and pertinent to deserve a literal quotation. "Good roads, canals, and navigable rivers, by diminishing the expence of carriage, put the remote parts of a country more nearly upon a level with those in the neighborhood of the town. They are upon that account the greatest of all improvements. They encourage the cultivation of the remote, which must always be the most extensive circle of the country. They are advantageous to the Town by breaking down the monopoly of the country in its neighborhood. They are advantageous even to that part of the Country. Though they introduce some rival commodities into the old Market, they open many new markets to its produce. Monopoly besides is a great enemy to good management, which can never be universally established, but in consequence of that free and universal competition, which forces every body to have recourse to it for the sake of self defence. It is not more than Fifty years ago that some of the countries in the neighborhood of London petitioned the Parliament, against the extension of the turnpike roads, into the remoter counties. Those remoter counties, they pretended, from the cheapness of Labor, would be able to sell their grass and corn cheaper in the London Market, than themselves, and they would thereby reduce their rents and ruin their cultivation. Their rents however have risen and their cultivation has been improved, since that time."

Specimens of a spirit, similar to that which governed the counties here spoken of present themselves too frequently to the eye of an impartial observer, and render it a wish of patriotism, that the body in this Country, in whose councils a local or partial spirit is least likely to predominate, were at liberty to pursue and promote the general interest, in those instances, in which there might be danger of the interference of such a spirit.

V. WE SHOULD NOT IMPOSE TAXES THAT DISCOURAGE MANUFACTURING.

The foregoing are the principal of the means, by which the growth of manufactures is ordinarily promoted. It is, however, not merely necessary, that the measures of government, which have a direct view to manufactures, should be calculated to assist and protect them, but that those which only collaterally affect them, in the general course of the administration, should be gaurded from any peculiar tendency to injure them.

There are certain species of taxes, which are apt to be oppressive to different parts of the community, and among other ill effects have a very unfriendly aspect towards manufactures. All Poll or Capitation taxes are of this nature. They either proceed, according to a fixed rate, which operates unequally, and injuriously to the industrious poor; or they vest a discretion in certain officers, to make estimates and assessments which are necessarily vague, conjectural and liable to abuse. They ought therefore to be abstained from, in all but cases of distressing emergency.

All such taxes (including all taxes on occupations) which proceed according to the amount of capital supposed to be employed in a business, or of profits supposed to be made in it are unavoidably hurtful to industry. It is in vain, that the evil may be endeavoured to be mitigated by leaving it, in the first instance, in the option of the party to be taxed, to declare the amount of his capital or profits.

Men engaged in any trade of business have commonly weighty reasons to avoid disclosures, which would expose, with any thing like accuracy, the real state of their affairs. They most frequently find it better to risk oppression, than to avail themselves of so inconvenient a refuge. And the consequence is, that they often suffer oppression.

When the disclosure too, if made, is not definitive, but controulable by the discretion, or in other words, by the passions & prejudices of the revenue officers, it is not only an ineffectual protection, but the possibility of its being so is an additional reason for not resorting to it.

Allowing to the public officers the most equitable dispositions; yet where they are to exercise a discretion, without certain data, they cannot fail to be often misled by appearances. The quantity of business, which seems to be going on, is, in a vast number of cases, a very deceitful criterion of the profits which are made; yet it is perhaps the best they can have, and it is the one, on which they will most naturally rely. A business therefore which may rather require aid, from the government, than be in a capacity to be contributory to it, may find itself crushed by the mistaken conjectures of the Assessors of taxes.

Arbitrary taxes, under which denomination are comprised all those, that leave the quantum of the tax to be raised on each person, to the discretion of certain officers, are as contrary to the genius of liberty as to the maxims of industry. In this light, they have been viewed by the most judicious observers on government; who have bestowed upon them the severest epithets of reprobation; as constituting one of the worst features usually to be met with in the practice of despotic governments.

It is certain at least, that such taxes are particularly inimical to the success of manufacturing industry, and ought carefully to be avoided by a government, which desires to promote it

VI. WHAT MANUFACTURING SHOULD THE GOVERNMENT ENCOURAGE?

VI. A. Factors to consider

The great copiousness of the subject of this Report has insensibly led to a more lengthy preliminary discussion, than was originally contemplated, or intended. It appeared proper to investigate principles, to consider objections, and to endeavour to establish the utility of the thing proposed to be encouraged; previous to a specification of the objects which might occur, as meriting or requiring encouragement, and of the measures, which might be proper, in respect to each. The first purpose having been fulfilled, it remains to pursue the second. In the selection of objects, five circumstances seem intitled to particular attention; the capacity of the Country to furnish the raw material—the degree in which the nature of the manufacture admits of a substitute for manual labour in machinery—the facility of execution—the extensiveness of the uses, to which the article can be applied—its subserviency to other interests, particularly the great one of national defence. There are however objects, to which these circumstances are little applicable, which for some special reasons, may have a claim to encouragement.

VI. B. Specific manufactures to encourage

A designation of the principal raw material of which each manufacture is composed will serve to introduce the remarks upon it. As, in the first place—

VI. B. 1. Iron

Iron

The manufactures of this article are entitled to preeminent rank. None are more essential in their kinds, nor so extensive in their uses. They constitute in whole or in part the implements or the materials or both of almost every useful occupation. Their instrumentality is everywhere conspicuous.

It is fortunate for the United States that they have peculiar advantages for deriving the full benefit of this most valuable material, and they have every motive to improve it, with systematic care. It is to be found in various parts of the United States, in great abundance and of almost every quality; and fuel the chief instrument in manufacturing it, is both cheap and plenty. This particularly applies to Charcoal; but there are productive coal mines already in operation, and strong indications, that the material is to be found in abundance, in a variety of other places.

The inquiries to which the subject of this report has led have been answered with proofs that manufactories of Iron, though generally understood to be extensive, are far more so than is commonly supposed. The kinds, in which the greatest progress has been made, have been mentioned in another place, and need not be repeated; but there is little doubt that every other kind, with due cultivation, will rapidly succeed. It is worthy of remark that several of the particular trades, of which it is the basis, are capable of being carried on without the aid of large capitals.

Iron works have very greatly increased in the United States and are prosecuted, with much more advantage than formerly. The average price before the revolution was about Sixty four Dollars ⅌. Ton—at present it is about Eighty; a rise which is chiefly to be attributed to the increase of manufactures of the material.

The still further extension and multiplication of such manufactures will have the double effect of promoting the extraction of the Metal itself, and of converting it to a greater number of profitable purposes.

Those manufactures too unite in a greater degree, than almost any others, the several requisities, which have been mentioned, as proper to be consulted in the selection of objects.

The only further encouragement of manufactories of this article, the propriety of which may be considered as unquestionable, seems to be an increase of the duties on foreign rival commodities.

Steel is a branch, which has already made a considerable progress, and it is ascertained that some new enterprizes, on a more extensive scale, have been lately set on foot. The facility of carrying it to an extent, which will supply all internal demands, and furnish a considerable surplus for exportation cannot be doubted. The duty upon the importation of this article, which is at present seventy five cents ⅌ Cwt., may it is conceived be safely and advantageously extended to 100 Cents. It is desireable, by decisive arrangements, to second the efforts, which are making in so very valuable a branch.

The United States already in a great measure supply themselves with Nails & Spikes. They are able, and ought certainly, to do it intirely. The first and most laborious operation, in this manufacture is performed by water mills; and of the persons afterwards employed a great proportion are boys, whose early habits of industry are of importance to the community, to the present support of their families, and to their own future comfort. It is not less curious than true, that in certain parts of the country, the making of Nails is an occasional family manufacture.

The expendiency of an additional duty on these articles is indicated by an important fact. About one million 800,000 pounds of them were imported into the United States in the course of a year ending the 30th. of September 1790. A duty of two Cents ℔ lb would, it is presumeable, speedily put an end to so considerable an importation. And it is in every view proper that an end should be put to it.

The manufacture of these articles, like that of some others, suffers from the carelessness and dishonesty of a part of those who carry it on. An inspection in certain cases might tend to correct the evil. It will deserve consideration whether a regulation of this sort cannot be applied, without inconvenience, to the exportation of the articles either to foreign countries, or from one state to another.

The implements of husbandry are made in several States in great abundance. In many places it is done by the common blacksmiths. And there is no doubt that an ample supply for the whole country can with great ease be procured among ourselves.

Various kinds of edged tools for the use of Mechanics are also made; and a considerable quantity of hollow wares; though the business of castings has not yet attained the perfection which might be wished. It is however improving, and as there are respectable capitals in good hands, embarked in the prosecution of those branches of iron manufactories, which are yet in their infancy, they may all be contemplated as objects not difficult to be acquired.

To ensure the end, it seems equally safe and prudent to extend the duty ad valorem upon all manufactures of Iron, or of which iron is the article of chief value, to ten per Cent.

Fire arms and other military weapons may it is conceived, be placed without inconvenience in the class of articles rated at 15 ℔. Cent. There are already manufactories of these articles, which only require the stimulus of a certain demand to render them adequate to the supply of the United States.

It would also be a material aid to manufactories of this nature, as well as a mean of public security, if provision should be made for an annual purchase of military weapons, of home manufacture to a certain determinate extent, in order to the formation of Arsenals; and to replace from time to time such as should be withdrawn for use, so as always to have in store the quantity of each kind, which should be deemed a competent supply.

But it may hereafter deserve legislative consideration, whether manufactories of all the necessary weapons of war ought not to be established, on account of the Government itself. Such establishments are agreeable to the usual practice of Nations and that practice seems founded on sufficient reason.

There appears to be an improvidence, in leaving these essential instruments of national defence to the casual speculations of individual adventure; a resource which can less be relied upon, in this case than in most others; the articles in question not being objects of ordinary and indispensable private consumption or use. As a general rule, manufactories on the immediate account of Government are to be avoided; but this seems to be one of the few exceptions, which that rule admits, depending on very special reasons.

Manufactures of Steel, generally, or of which steel is the article of chief value, may with advantage be placed in the class of goods rated at 7½ per Cent. As manufactures of this kind have not yet made any considerable progress, it is a reason for not rating them as high as those of iron; but as this material is the basis of them, and as their extension is not less practicable, than important, it is desireable to promote it by a somewhat higher duty than the present.

A question arises, how far it might be expedient to permit the importation of iron in pigs and bars free from duty. It would certainly be favourable to manufactures of the article; but the doubt is whether it might not interfere with its production.

Two circumstances, however, abate if they do not remove apprehension, on this score; one is, the considerable increase of price, which has been already remarked, and which renders it probable, that the free admission of foreign iron would not be inconsistent with an adequate profit to the proprietors of Iron Works; the other is, the augmentation of demand, which would be likely to attend the increase of manufactures of the article, in consequence of the additional encouragements proposed to be given. But caution nevertheless in a matter of this kind is most adviseable. The measure suggested ought perhaps rather to be contemplated, subject to the lights of further experience, than immediately adopted.

VI. B. 2. Copper

Copper

The manufactures of which this article is susceptible are also of great extent and utility. Under this description, those of brass, of which it is the principal ingreedient, are intended to be included.

The material is a natural production of the Country. Mines of Copper have actually been wrought, and with profit to the undertakers, though it is not known, that any are now in this condition. And nothing is easier, than the introduction of it, from other countries, on moderate terms, and in great plenty.

Coppersmiths and brass founders, particularly the former, are numerous in the United States; some of whom carry on business to a respectable extent.

To multiply and extend manufactories of the materials in question is worthy of attention and effort. In order to this, it is desireable to facilitate a plentiful supply of the materials. And a proper mean to this end is to place them in the class of free articles. Copper in plates and brass are already in this predicament, but copper in pigs and bars is not—neither is lapis calaminaris, which together with copper and charcoal, constitute the component ingredients of brass. The exemption from duty, by parity of reason, ought to embrace all such of these articles, as are objects of importation. An additional duty, on brass wares, will tend to the general end in view. These now stand at 5 ⅌. Cent, while those of tin, pewter and copper are rated at 7½. There appears to be a propriety in every view in placing brass wares upon the same level with them; and it merits consideration whether the duty upon all of them ought not to be raised to 10 ⅌. Cent.

VI. B. 3. Lead

Lead

There are numerous proofs, that this material abounds in the United States, and requires little to unfold it to an extent, more than equal to every domestic occasion. A prolific mine of it has long been open in the South Western parts of Virginia, and under a public administration, during the late war, yielded a considerable supply for military use. This is now in the hands of individuals, who not only carry it on with spirit; but have established manufactories of it, at Richmond, in the same State.

The duties, already laid upon the importation of this article, either in its unmanufactured, or manufactured state, ensure it a decisive advantage in the home market—which amounts to considerable encouragement. If the duty on pewter wares should be raised it would afford a further encouragement. Nothing else occurs as proper to be added.

VI. B. 4. Coal

Fossil Coal

This, as an important instrument of manufactures, may without impropriety be mentioned among the subjects of this Report.

A copious supply of it would be of great consequence to the iron branch: As an article of household fuel also it is an interesting production; the utility of which must increase in proportion to the decrease of wood, by the progress of settlement and cultivation. And its importance to navigation, as an immense article of transportation coastwise, is signally exemplified in Great Britain.

It is known, that there are several coal mines in Virginia, now worked; and appearances of their existence are familiar in a number of places.

The expediency of a bounty on all the species of coal of home production, and of premiums, on the opening of new mines, under certain qualifications, appears to be worthy of particular examination. The great importance of the article will amply justify a reasonable expence in this way, if it shall appear to be necessary to and shall be thought it likely to answer the end.

VI. B. 5. Wood

Wood

Several manufactures of this article flourish in the United States. Ships are no where built in greater perfection, and cabinet wares, generally, are made little if at all inferior to those of Europe. Their extent is such as to have admitted of considerable exportation.

An exemption from duty of the several kinds of wood ordinarily used in these manufactures seems to be all, that is requisite, by way of encouragement. It is recommended by the consideration of a similar policy being pursued in other countries, and by the expediency of giving equal advantages to our own workmen in wood. The abundance of Timber proper for ship building in the United States does not appear to be any objection to it. The increasing scarcity and the growing importance of that article, in the European countries, admonish the United States to commence, and systematically to pursue, measures for the preservation of their stock. Whatever may promote the regular establishment of Magazines of Ship Timber is in various views desireable.

VI. B. 6. Skins

Skins

There are scarcely any manufactories of greater importance, than of this article. Their direct and very happy influence upon Agriculture, by promoting the raising of Cattle of different kinds, is a very material recommendation.

It is pleasing too, to observe the extensive progress they have made in their principal branches; which are so far matured as almost to defy foreign competition. Tanneries in particular are not only carried on as a regular business, in numerous instances and in various parts of the Country; but they constitute in some places a valuable item of incidental family manufactures.

Representations however have been made, importing the expediency of further encouragement to the Leather-Branch in two ways—one by increasing the duty on the manufactures of it, which are imported—the other by prohibiting the exportation of bark. In support of the latter it is alleged that the price of bark, chiefly in consequence of large exportations, has risen within a few years from [about three Dollars to four dollars and a half per cord.]

These suggestions are submitted rather as intimations, which merit consideration, than as matters, the propriety of which is manifest. It is not clear, that an increase of duty is necessary: and in regard to the prohibition desired, there is no evidence of any considerable exportation hitherto; and it is most probable, that whatever augmentation of price may have taken place, is to be attributed to an extension of the home demand from the increase of manufactures, and to a decrease of the supply in consequence of the progress of Settlement; rather than to the quantities which have been exported.

It is mentioned however, as an additional reason for the prohibition, that one species of the bark usually exported is in some sort peculiar to the country, and the material of a very valuable dye, of great use in some other manufactures, in which the United States have begun a competition.

There may also be this argument in favor of an increase of duty. The object is of importance enough to claim decisive encouragement and the progress, which has been made, leaves no room to apprehend any inconvenience on the score of supply from such an increase.

It would be of benefit to this branch, if glue which is now rated at 5 perCent, were made the object of an excluding duty. It is already made in large quantities at various tanneries; and like paper, is an entire œconomy of materials, which if not manufactured would be left to perish. It may be placed with advantage in the class of articles paying 15 perCent.

VI. B. 7. Grain

Grain

Manufactures of the several species of this article have a title to peculiar favor; not only because they are most of them immediately connected with the subsistence of the citizens; but because they enlarge the demand for the most precious products of the soil.

Though flour may with propriety be noticed as a manufacture of Grain, it were useless to do it, but for the purpose of submitting the expediency of a general system of inspection, throughout the ports of the United states; which, if established upon proper principles, would be likely to improve the quality of our flour every where, and to raise its reputation in foreign markets. There are however considerations which stand in the way of such an arrangement.

Ardent spirits and malt liquors are, next to flour, the two principal manufactures of Grain. The first has made a very extensive, the last a considerable progress in the United States. In respect to both, an exclusive possession of the home market ought to be secured to the domestic manufacturers; as fast as circumstances will admit. Nothing is more practicable & nothing more desireable.

The existing laws of the United States have done much towards attaining this valuable object; but some additions to the present duties, on foreign distilled spirits, and foreign malt liquors, and perhaps an abatement of those on home made spirits, would more effectually secure it; and there does not occur any very weighty objection to either.

An augmentation of the duties on imported spirits would favour, as well the distillation of Spirits from molasses, as that from Grain. And to secure to the nation the benefit of the manufacture, even of foreign materials, is always of great, though perhaps of secondary importance.

A strong impression prevails in the minds of those concerned in distilleries (including too the most candid and enlightened) that greater differences in the rates of duty on foreign and domestic spirits are necessary, completely to secure the successful manufacture of the latter; and there are facts which entitle this impression to attention.

It is known, that the price of molasses for some years past, has been successively rising in the West India Markets, owing partly to a competition, which did not formerly exist, and partly to an extension of demand in this country; and it is evident, that the late disturbances in those Islands, from which we draw our principal supply, must so far interfere with the production of the article, as to occasion a material enhancement of price. The destruction and devastation attendant on the insurrection in Hispaniola, in particular, must not only contribute very much to that effect, but may be expected to give it some duration. These circumstances, and the duty of three cents per Gallon on molasses, may render it difficult for the distillers of that material to maintain with adequate profit a competition, with the rum brought from the West Indies, the quality of which is so considerably superior.

The consumption of Geneva or Gin in this country is extensive. It is not long since distilleries of it have grown up among us, to any importance. They are now becoming of consequence, but being still in their infancy, they require protection.

It is represented, that the price of some of the materials is greater here, than in Holland, from which place large quantities are brought, the price of labour considerably greater, the capitals engaged in the business there much larger, than those which are employed here, the rate of profits, at which the Undertakers can afford to carry it on, much less—the prejudices, in favor of imported Gin, strong. These circumstances are alleged to outweigh the charges, which attend the bringing of the Article, from Europe to the United states and the present difference of duty, so as to obstruct the prosecution of the manufacture, with due advantage.

Experiment could perhaps alone decide with certainty the justness of the suggestions, which are made; but in relation to branches of manufacture so important, it would seem inexpedient to hazard an unfavourable issue, and better to err on the side of too great, than of too small a difference, in the particular in question.

It is therefore submitted, that an addition of two cents per Gallon be made to the duty on imported spirits of the first class of proof, with a proportionable increase on those of higher proof; and that a deduction of one cent per Gallon be made from the duty on spirits distilled within the United states, beginning with the first class of proof, and a proportionable deduction from the duty on those of higher proof.

It is ascertained, that by far the greatest part of the malt liquors consumed in the United States are the produce of domestic breweries.

It is desireable, and, in all likelihood, attainable, that the whole consumption should be supplied by ourselves.

The malt liquors, made at home, though inferior to the best are equal to a great part of those, which have been usually imported. The progress already made is an earnest of what may be accomplished. The growing competition is an assurance of improvement. This will be accelerated by measures, tending to invite a greater capital into this channel of employment.

To render the encouragement to domestic breweries decisive, it may be adviseable to substitute to the present rates of duty eight cents per gallon generally; and it will deserve to be considered as a gaurd against evasions, whether there ought not to be a prohibition of their importation, except in casks of considerable capacity. It is to be hoped, that such a duty would banish from the market, foreign malt liquors of inferior quality; and that the best kind only would continue to be imported till it should be supplanted, by the efforts of equal skill or care at home.

Till that period, the importation so qualified would be an useful stimulous to improvement: And in the mean time, the payment of the increased price, for the enjoyment of a luxury, in order to the encouragement of a most useful branch of domestic industry, could not reasonably be deemed a hardship.

As a further aid to the manufactures of grain, though upon a smaller scale, the articles of Starch, hair powder and wafers, may with great propriety be placed among those, which are rated at 15 perCent. No manufactures are more simple, nor more completely within the reach of a full supply, from domestic sources, and it is a policy, as common as it is obvious, to make them the objects either of prohibitory duties, or of express prohibition.

VI. B. 8. Flax and hemp

Flax and Hemp

Manufactures of these articles have so much affinity to each other, and they are so often blended, that they may with advantage be considered in conjunction. The importance of the linnin branch to agriculture—its precious effects upon household industry—the ease, with which the materials can be produced at home to any requisite extent—the great advances, which have been already made, in the coarser fabricks of them, especially in the family way, constitute claims, of peculiar force, to the patronage of government.

This patronage may be afforded in various ways; by promoting the growth of the materials; by increasing the impediments to an advantageous competition of rival foreign articles; by direct bounties or premiums upon the home manufacture.

First.   As to promoting the growth of the materials.

In respect to hemp, something has been already done by the high duty upon foreign hemp. If the facilities for domestic production were not unusually great, the policy of the duty, on the foreign raw material, would be highly questionable, as interfering with the growth of manufactures of it. But making the proper allowances for those facilities, and with an eye to the future and natural progress, of the country, the measure does not appear, upon the whole, exceptionable. A strong wish naturally suggests itself, that some method could be devised of affording a more direct encouragement to the growth both of flax and hemp; such as would be effectual, and at the same time not attended with too great inconveniences. To this end, bounties and premiums offer themselves to consideration; but no modification of them has yet occurred, which would not either hazard too much expence, or operate unequally in reference to the circumstances of different parts of the Union; and which would not be attended with very great difficulties in the execution.

Secondly—

As to encreasing the impediments to an advantageous competition of rival foreign articles.

To this purpose, an augmentation of the duties on importation is the obvious expedient; which, in regard to certain articles, appears to be recommended by sufficient reasons.

The principal of these articles is Sail cloth; one intimately connected with navigation and defence; and of which a flourishing manufactory is established at Boston and very promising ones at several other places.

It is presumed to be both safe and adviseable to place this in the class of articles rated at 10 Per cent. A strong reason for it results from the consideration that a bounty of two pence sterling per ell is allowed, in Great Britain, upon the exportation of the sail cloth manufactured in that Kingdom.

It would likewise appear to be good policy to raise the duty to 7½ perCent on the following articles. Drillings, Osnaburghs, Ticklenburghs, Dowlas, Canvas, Brown Rolls, Bagging, and upon all other linnens the first cost of which at the place of exportation does not exceed 35 cents per yard. A bounty of 12½ ℔ Cent, upon an average on the exportation of such or similar linnens from Great-Britain encourages the manufacture of them in that country and increases the obstacles to a successful competition in the countries to which they are sent.

The quantities of tow and other household linnens manufactured in different parts of the United States and the expectations, which are derived from some late experiments, of being able to extend the use of labour-saving machines, in the coarser fabrics of linnen, obviate the danger of inconvenience, from an increase of the duty upon such articles, and authorize a hope of speedy and complete success to the endeavours, which may be used for procuring an internal supply.

Thirdly. As to direct bounties, or premiums upon the manufactured articles.

To afford more effectual encouragement to the manufacture, and at the same time to promote the cheapness of the article for the benefit of navigation, it will be of great use to allow a bounty of two Cents ℔ yard on all Sail Cloth, which is made in the United States from materials of their own growth. This would also assist the Culture of those materials. An encouragement of this kind if adopted ought to be established for a moderate term of years, to invite to new undertakings and to an extension of the old. This is an article of importance enough to warrant the employment of extraordinary means in its favor.

VI. B. 9. Cotton

Cotton

There is something in the texture of this material, which adapts it in a peculiar degree to the application of Machines. The signal Utility of the mill for spinning of cotton, not long since invented in England, has been noticed in another place; but there are other machines scarcely inferior in utility which, in the different manufactories of this article are employed either exclusively, or with more than ordinary effect. This very important circumstance recommends the fabricks of cotton, in a more particular manner, to a country in which a defect of hands constitutes the greatest obstacle to success.

The variety and extent of the uses to which the manufactures of this article are applicable is another powerful argument in their favor.

And the faculty of the United States to produce the raw material in abundance, & of a quality, which though alledged to be inferior to some that is produced in other quarters, is nevertheles capable of being used with advantage, in many fabrics, and is probably susceptible of being carried, by a more experienced culture, to much greater perfection—suggests an additional and a very cogent inducement to the vigorous pursuit of the cotton branch, in its several subdivisions.

How much has been already done has been stated in a preceding part of this report.

In addition to this, it may be announced, that a society is forming with a capital which is expected to be extended to at least half a million of dollars; on behalf of which measures are already in train for prosecuting on a large scale, the making and printing of cotton goods.

These circumstances conspire to indicate the expediency of removing any obstructions, which may happen to exist, to the advantageous prosecution of the manufactories in question, and of adding such encouragements, as may appear necessary and proper.

The present duty of three cents ℔ lb. on the foreign raw material, is undoubtedly a very serious impediment to the progress of those manufactories.

The injurious tendency of similar duties either prior to the establishment, or in the infancy of the domestic manufacture of the article, as it regards the manufacture, and their worse than inutility, in relation to the home production of the material itself, have been anticipated particularly in discussing the subject of pecuniary bounties.

Cotton has not the same pretensions, with hemp, to form an exception to the general rule.

Not being, like hemp an universal production of the Country it affords less assurance of an adequate internal supply; but the chief objection arises from the doubts; which are entertained concerning the quality of the national cotton. It is alledged, that the fibre of it is considerably shorter and weaker, than that of some other places; and it has been observed as a general rule, that the nearer the place of growth to the Equator, the better the quality of the cotton. That which comes from Cayenne, Surrinam and Demarara is said to be preferable, even at a material difference of price, to the Cotton of the Islands.

While a hope may reasonably be indulged, that with due care and attention the national cotton may be made to approach nearer than it now does to that of regions, somewhat more favored by climate; and while facts authorize an opinion, that very great use may be made of it, and that it is a resource which gives greater security to the cotton fabrics of this country, than can be enjoyed by any which depends wholly on external supply it will certainly be wise, in every view, to let our infant manufactures have the full benefit of the best materials on the cheapest terms.

It is obvious that the necessity of having such materials is proportioned to the unskilfulness and inexperience of the workmen employed, who if inexpert, will not fail to commit great waste, where the materials they are to work with are of an indifferent kind.

To secure to the national manufactures so essential an advantage, a repeal of the present duty on imported cotton is indispensible.

A substitute for this, far more encouraging to domestic production, will be to grant a bounty on the national cotton, when wrought at a home manufactory; to which a bounty on the exportation of it may be added. Either or both would do much more towards promoting the growth of the article, than the merely nominal encouragement, which it is proposed to abolish. The first would also have a direct influence in encouraging the manufacture.

The bounty which has been mentioned as existing in Great Britain, upon the exportation of coarse linnens not exceeding a certain value, applies also to certain discriptions of cotton goods of similar value.

This furnishes an additional argument for allowing to the national manufacturers the species of encouragement just suggested, and indeed for adding some other aid.

One cent per yard, not less than of a given width, on all goods of cotton, or of cotton and linnen mixed, which are manufactured in the United States; with the addition of one cent ℔ lb weight of the material; if made of national cotton; would amount to an aid of considerable importance, both to the production and to the manufacture of that valuable article. And it is conceived, that the expence would be well justified by the magnitude of the object.

The printing and staining of cotton goods is known to be a distinct business from the fabrication of them. It is one easily accomplished and which, as it adds materially to the value of the article in its white state, and prepares it for a variety of new uses, is of importance to be promoted.

As imported cottons, equally with those which are made at home, may be the objects of this manufacture, it will merit consideration, whether the whole, or a part of the duty, on the white goods, ought not to be allowed to be drawn back in favor of those, who print or stain them. This measure would certainly operate as a powerful encouragement to the business; and though it may in a degree counteract the original fabrication of the articles it would probably more than compensate for this disadvantage, in the rapid growth of a collateral branch, which is of a nature sooner to attain to maturity. When a sufficient progress shall have been made, the drawback may be abrogated; and by that time the domestic supply of the articles to be printed or stained will have been extended.

If the duty of 7½ ℔. Cent on certain kinds of cotton goods were extended to all goods of cotton, or of which it is the principal material, it would probably more than counterbalance the effect of the drawback proposed, in relation to the fabrication of the article. And no material objection occurs to such an extension. The duty then considering all the circumstances which attend goods of this description could not be deemed inconveniently high; and it may be inferred from various causes that the prices of them would still continue moderate.

Manufactories of cotton goods, not long since established at Beverly, in Massachusetts, and at Providence in the state of Rhode Island and conducted with a perseverence corresponding with the patriotic motives which began them, seem to have overcome the first obstacles to success; producing corduroys, velverets, fustians, jeans, and other similar articles of a quality, which will bear a comparison with the like articles brought from Manchester. The one at Providence has the merit of being the first in introducing [into the United States] the celebrated cotton mill; which not only furnishes materials for that manufactory itself, but for the supply of private families for household manufacture.

Other manufactories of the same material; as regular businesses, have also been begun at different places in the state of Connecticut, but all upon a smaller scale, than those above mentioned. Some essays are also making in the printing and staining of cotton goods. There are several small establishments of this kind already on foot

VI. B. 10. Wool

Wool.

In a country, the climate of which partakes of so considerable a proportion of winter, as that of a great part of the United States, the woolen branch cannot be regarded, as inferior to any, which relates to the cloathing of the inhabitants.

Household manufactures of this material are carried on, in different parts of the United States, to a very interesting extent; but there is only one branch, which, as a regular business, can be said to have acquired maturity. This is the making of hats.

Hats of wool, and of wool mixed with furr, are made in large quantities, in different States; & nothing seems wanting, but an adequate supply of materials, to render the manufacture commensurate with the demand.

A promising essay, towards the fabrication of cloths, cassimires and other woolen goods, is likewise going on at Hartford in Connecticut.

Specimens of the different kinds which are made, in the possession of the Secretary, evince that these fabrics have attained a very considerable degree of perfection. Their quality certainly surpasses anything, that could have been looked for, in so short a time, and under so great disadvantages; and conspires with the scantiness of the means, which have been at the command of the directors, to form the eulogium of that public spirit, perseverance and judgment, which have been able to accomplish so much.

To cherish and bring to maturity this precious embryo must engage the most ardent wishes—and proportionable regret, as far as the means of doing it may appear difficult or uncertain.

Measures, which should tend to promote an abundant supply of wool, of good quality, would probably afford the most efficacious aid, that present circumstances permit.

To encourage the raising and improving the breed of sheep, at home, would certainly be the most desireable expedient, for that purpose; but it may not be alone sufficient, especially as it is yet a problem, whether our wool be capable of such a degree of improvement, as to render it fit for the finer fabrics.

Premiums would probably be found the best means of promoting the domestic, and bounties the foreign supply. The first may be within the compass of the institution hereafter to be submitted—The last would require a specific legislative provision. If any bounties are granted they ought of course to be adjusted with an eye to quality, as well as quantity.

A fund for the purpose may be derived from the addition of 2½ per Cent, to the present rate of duty, on Carpets and Carpeting; an increase, to which the nature of the Articles suggests no objection, and which may at the same time furnish a motive the more to the fabrication of them at home; towards which some beginnings have been made.

VI. B. 11. Silk

Silk.

The production of this Article is attended with great facility in most parts of the United States, Some pleasing essays are making in Connecticut, as well towards that, as towards the Manufacture of what is produced. Stockings, Handkerchiefs Ribbons & Buttons are made though as yet but in small quantities.

A Manufactory of Lace upon a scale not very extensive has been long memorable at Ipswich in the State of Massachusetts.

An exemption of the material from the duty, which it now pays on importation, and premiums upon the production, to be dispensed under the direction of the Institution before alluded to, seem to be the only species of encouragement adviseable at so early a stage of the thing.

VI. B. 12. Glass

Glass

The Materials for making Glass are found every where. In the United States there is no deficiency of them. The sands and Stones called Tarso, which include flinty and chrystalline substances generally, and the Salts of various plants, particularly of the Sea Weed Kali or Kelp constitute the essential ingredients. An extraordinary abundance of Fuel is a particular advantage enjoyed by this Country for such manufactures. They, however, require large Capitals and involve much manual labour.

Different manufactories of Glass are now on foot in the United States. The present duty of 12½ per Cent on all imported articles of glass amount to a considerable encouragement to those Manufactories. If any thing in addition is judged eligible, the most proper would appear to be a direct bounty, on Window Glass and black Bottles.

The first recommends itself as an object of general convenience; the last adds to that character, the circumstance of being an important item in breweries. A Complaint is made of great deficiency in this respect.

VI. B. 13. Gunpowder

Gun Powder

No small progress has been of late made in the manufacture of this very important article: It may indeed be considered as already established; but its high importance renders its further extension very desireable.

The encouragements, which it already enjoys, are a duty of 10 per Cent on the foreign rival article, and an exemption of Salt petre one of the principal ingredients of which it is composed, from duty. A like exemption of Sulphur, another chief ingredient, would appear to be equally proper. No quantity of this Article has yet been produced, from internal sources. The use made of it in finishing the bottoms of Ships, is an additional inducement to placing it in the class of free goods. Regulations for the careful inspection of the article would have a favourable tendency.

VI. B. 14. Paper

Paper

Manufactories of paper are among those which are Arrived at the greatest maturity in the United States, and are most adequate to national supply. That of paper hangings is a branch, in which respectable progress has been made.

Nothing material seems wanting to the further success of this valuable branch which is already protected by a competent duty on similar imported Articles.

In the enumeration of the several kinds, made subject to that duty, Sheathing and Cartridge paper have been omitted. These, being the most simple manufactures of the sort, and necessary to military supply, as well as Ship building, recommend themselves equally with those of other descriptions, to encouragement, and appear to be as fully within the compass of domestic exertions.

VI. B. 15. Printed books

Printed books

The great number of presses disseminated throughout the Union, seem to afford an assurance, that there is no need of being indebted to foreign Countries for the printing of the Books, which are used in the United States. A duty of ten per Cent instead of five, which is now charged upon the Article, would have a tendency to aid the business internally.

It occurs, as an objection to this, that it may have an unfavourable aspect towards literature, by raising the prices of Books in universal use in private families Schools and other Seminaries of learning. But the difference it is conceived would be without effect.

As to Books which usually fill the Libraries of the wealthier classes and of professional Men, such an Augmentation of prices, as might be occasioned by an additional duty of five per Cent would be too little felt to be an impediment to the acquisition.

And with regard to books which may be specially imported for the use of particular seminaries of learning, and of public libraries, a total exemption from duty would be adviseable, which would go far towards obviating the objection just mentioned. They are now subject to a duty of 5 ₱ Cent.

As to the books in most general family use, the constancy and universality of the demand would insure exertions to furnish them at home and the means are compleatly adequate. It may also be expected ultimately, in this as in other cases, that the extension of the domestic manufacture would conduce to the cheapness of the article.

It ought not to pass unremarked, that to encourage the printing of books is to encourage the manufacture of paper.

VI. B. 16. Sugars and chocolate

Refined Sugars and Chocolate.

Are among the number of extensive and prosperous domestic manufactures.

Drawbacks of the duties upon the materials, of which they are respectively made, in cases of exportation, would have a beneficial influence upon the manufacture, and would conform to a precedent, which has been already furnished, in the instance of molasses, on the exportation of distilled spirits.

Cocoa the raw material now pays a duty of one cent ⅌ lb., while chocolate which is a prevailing and very simple manufacture, is comprised in the mass of articles rated at no more than five ⅌ Cent.

There would appear to be a propriety in encouraging the manufacture, by a somewhat higher duty, on its foreign rival, than is paid on the raw material. Two cents ⅌ lb. on imported chocolate would, it is presumed, be without inconvenience.

VII. OBJECTIONS TO THE USE OF BOUNTIES

The foregoing heads comprise the most important of the several kinds of manufactures, which have occurred as requiring, and, at the same time, as most proper for public encouragement; and such measures for affording it, as have appeared best calculated to answer the end, have been suggested.

The observations, which have accompanied this delineation of objects, supercede the necessity of many supplementary remarks. One or two however may not be altogether superfluous.

Bounties are in various instances proposed as one species of encouragement.

It is a familiar objection to them, that they are difficult to be managed and liable to frauds. But neither that difficulty nor this danger seems sufficiently great to countervail the advantages of which they are productive, when rightly applied. And it is presumed to have been shewn, that they are in some cases, particularly in the infancy of new enterprises indispensable.

It will however be necessary to guard, with extraordinary circumspection, the manner of dispensing them. The requisite precautions have been thought of; but to enter into the detail would swell this report, already voluminous, to a size too inconvenient.

If the principle shall not be deemed inadmissible the means of avoiding an abuse of it will not be likely to present insurmountable obstacles. There are useful guides from practice in other quarters.

It shall therefore only be remarked here, in relation to this point, that any bounty, which may be applied to the manufacture of an article, cannot with safety extend beyond those manufactories, at which the making of the article is a regular trade.

It would be impossible to annex adequate precautions to a benefit of that nature, if extended to every private family, in which the manufacture was incidentally carried on, and its being a merely incidental occupation which engages a portion of time that would otherwise be lost, it can be advantageously carried on, without so special an aid.

The possibility of a diminution of the revenue may also present itself, as an objection to the arrangements, which have been submitted.

But there is no truth, which may be more firmly relied upon, than that the interests of the revennue are promoted, by whatever promotes an increase of National industry and wealth.

In proportion to the degree of these, is the capacity of every country to contribute to the public Treasury; and where the capacity to pay is increased, or even is not decreased, the only consequence of measures, which diminish any particular resource is a change of the object. If by encouraging the manufacture of an article at home, the revenue, which has been wont to accrue from its importation, should be lessened, an indemnification can easily be found, either out of the manufacture itself, or from some other object, which may be deemed more convenient.

The measures however, which have been submitted, taken aggregately, will for a long time to come rather augment than decrease the public revenue.

There is little room to hope, that the progress of manufactures, will so equally keep pace with the progress of population, as to prevent, even, a gradual augmentation of the product of the duties on imported articles.

As, nevertheless, an abolition in some instances, and a reduction in others of duties, which have been pledged for the public debt, is proposed, it is essential, that it should be accompanied with a competent substitute. In order to this, it is requisite, that all the additional duties which shall be laid, be appropriated in the first instance, to replace all defalcations, which may proceed from any such abolition or diminution. It is evident, at first glance, that they will not only be adequate to this, but will yield a considerable surplus.

This surplus will serve.

First. To constitute a fund for paying the bounties which shall have been decreed.

VIII. CONGRESS SHOULD SET ASIDE A SUM FOR A BOARD TO PROMOTE THE ARTS, AGRICULTURE, MANUFACTURING, AND TRADE

Secondly. To constitute a fund for the operations of a Board, to be established, for promoting Arts, Agriculture, Manufactures and Commerce. Of this institution, different intimations have been given, in the course of this report. An outline of a plan for it shall now be submitted.

Let a certain annual sum, be set apart, and placed under the management of Commissioners, not less than three, to consist of certain Officers of the Government and their Successors in Office.

Let these Commissioners be empowered to apply the fund confided to them—to defray the expences of the emigration of Artists, and Manufacturers in particular branches of extraordinary importance—to induce the prosecution and introduction of useful discoveries, inventions and improvements, by proportionate rewards, judiciously held out and applied—to encourage by premiums both honorable and lucrative the exertions of individuals, And of classes, in relation to the several objects, they are charged with promoting—and to afford such other aids to those objects, as may be generally designated by law.

The Commissioners to render [to the Legislature] an annual account of their transactions and disbursments; and all such sums as shall not have been applied to the purposes of their trust, at the end of every three years, to revert to the Treasury. It may also be enjoined upon them, not to draw out the money, but for the purpose of some specific disbursment.

It may moreover be of use, to authorize them to receive voluntary contributions; making it their duty to apply them to the particular objects for which they may have been made, if any shall have been designated by the donors.

There is reason to believe, that the progress of particular manufactures has been much retarded by the want of skilful workmen. And it often happens that the capitals employed are not equal to the purposes of bringing from abroad workmen of a superior kind. Here, in cases worthy of it, the auxiliary agency of Government would in all probability be useful. There are also valuable workmen, in every branch, who are prevented from emigrating solely by the want of means. Occasional aids to such persons properly administered might be a source of valuable acquisitions to the country.

The propriety of stimulating by rewards, the invention and introduction of useful improvements, is admitted without difficulty. But the success of attempts in this way must evidently depend much on the manner of conducting them. It is probable, that the placing of the dispensation of those rewards under some proper discretionary direction, where they may be accompanied by collateral expedients, will serve to give them the surest efficacy. It seems impracticable to apportion, by general rules, specific compensations for discoveries of unknown and disproportionate utility.

The great use which may be made of a fund of this nature to procure and import foreign improvements is particularly obvious. Among these, the article of machines would form a most important item.

The operation and utility of premiums have been adverted to; together with the advantages which have resulted from their dispensation, under the direction of certain public and private societies. Of this some experience has been had in the instance of the Pennsylvania society, [for the Promotion of Manufactures and useful Arts;] but the funds of that association have been too contracted to produce more than a very small portion of the good to which the principles of it would have led. It may confidently be affirmed that there is scarcely any thing, which has been devised, better calculated to excite a general spirit of improvement than the institutions of this nature. They are truly invaluable.

IX. CONCLUSION: WHY SHOULD THE GOVERNMENT BE ENCOURAGING MANUFACTURES?

In countries where there is great private wealth much may be effected by the voluntary contributions of patriotic individuals, but in a community situated like that of the United States, the public purse must supply the deficiency of private resource. In what can it be so useful as in prompting and improving the efforts of industry?

All which is humbly submitted
[Alexander Hamilton
Secy of the Treasury]

APPENDIX 4

A Selection of Primary Sources Related to the Panic of 1792

On the Panic of 1792, see §7.2. The excerpts are copied from Founders Online, omitting the modern editorial notes.

1. HAMILTON TO WILLIAM SETON, 1/18/1792

William Seton was cashier of the Bank of New York, which Hamilton had helped establish in 1784. In mid-January 1792, different sets of promoters in New York proposed the "Million Bank", the "State Bank", and the "Merchants Bank of New York". A few days later, the promoters agreed to consolidate into a single bank. The proponents of the "Million Bank" and the "State Bank" had ties to William Duer (see no. 5).

> I have learnt with infinite pain the circumstance of a new Bank having started up in your City. Its effects cannot but be in every view pernicious. These extravagant sallies of speculation do injury to the Government and to the whole system of public Credit, by disgusting all sober Citizens and giving a wild air to every thing. It is impossible but that three great banks in one City must raise such a mass of artificial Credit, as must endanger every one of them & do harm in every view.
>
> I sincerely hope That the Bank of New York will listen to no coalition with this newly engendered Monster. A better alliance, I am strongly persuaded, will be brought about for it, & the joint force of two solid institutions will without effort or violence remove the excrescence, which has just appeared, and which I consider as a dangerous tumour in your political and commercial œconomy.

I express myself in these strong terms to you confidentially; not that I have any objection to my opinion being known as to the nature & tendency of the thing.

https://founders.archives.gov/documents/Hamilton/01-10-02-0113

2. WILLIAM SETON TO HAMILTON, 1/22/1792

Your kind favor of the 18. I recd last night. I had no doubt you would condemn the numerous carrying ons here in the Strongest terms. The folly & madness that rages at present is a disgrace to us. There is no say where it will end—but it is the strongest proof that could be given, how necessary & usefull a coallition between the Bank of the U S. & this Institution [the Bank of New York] would be in the plan proposed. It is the only thing that can destroy this combination of Speculators. Be assured this Bank will never listen to a Coallition with these madmen. They have aimed too deep a strike at our existence to be forgot or forgiven; for had not the rapidity with which they wanted to carry on their plan defeated their own intentions there is no saying what the immediate consequences might have been to us—for in less than two hours we were called upon for upwards of 500 000 Dollars.

https://founders.archives.gov/documents/Hamilton/01-10-02-0119

3. HAMILTON TO WILLIAM SETON, 2/10/1792

I sincerely hope the Petitioners for a New Bank may be frustrated; but I fear more than I hope. General Schuyler will do every thing in his power against them. Every day unfolds the mischievous tendency of this mad scheme. The enemies to Banks & Credit are in a fair way of having their utmost malignity gratified. ...

The state of things however requires unusual circumspection. Every existing bank ought within prudent limits to abrige its operations. The superstructure of Credit is now too vast for the foundation. It must be gradually brought within more reasonable dimensions or it will tumble.

https://founders.archives.gov/documents/Hamilton/01-11-02-0027

4. JAMES TILLARY TO HAMILTON, 3/6/1792

Tillary was a New York City physician and politician.

> The Bank Mania rages violently in this City, & it is made an engine to help the Governors re-election. Judge Yates' sudden & unexpected resignation, or rather declination—Judge Jays sudden & unexpected acceptation—The obstinacy of Gov Clinton—The interference of Burr, & the tergiversation of the Chancellor, confound divide & distract the City. If the Conflict was to terminate in the Triumph or defeat of either of the Candidates, it would be of less consequence, but I either see, or fancy I see, the Malignant spirit of Antifederalism hovering over our land & ready to seize the first favorable opportunity of making a Stand.
>
> https://founders.archives.gov/documents/Hamilton/01-11-02-0083

5. WILLIAM DUER TO HAMILTON, 3/12/1792

Duer was on the Board of Treasury under the Articles of Confederation (1787-1788), and was on Hamilton's staff at the Treasury Department for a few months in late 1789 and early 1790. In March, Duer learned that the Treasury Department was about to bring suit against him for a deficiency of $200,000 in his accounts as a member of the Board.

> I find by a Letter from Colo. Wadsworth that News has arrived there of my hav[in]g skipt Payment. The Fact is that I have been compelled to do it, with Respect to a certain Description of Notes, which were issued by my agent during my absence from this City—the Circumstances are too long and too Painful to detail: you shall know them on my Arrival in Phila. for which Place I will certainly set off to morrow. Colo. Wadsworth writes me that Unless I arrive this day a Suit will Certainly be brought against me. For Heavens sake, Use for once your Influence to defer this till my Arrival—when it will not be Necessary. My Public Transactions are not blended with my private affairs. Every Farthing will be Immediately accounted for. Of this I pledge my Honor. If a Suit should be brought on the Part of the Public, under my present distrest Circumstances, My Ruin is complete. I despatch this by Express in order that this Step may not be taken—if it is I am sure that those who persue this Measure will in a short Time lament the Consequence.
>
> https://founders.archives.gov/documents/Hamilton/01-11-02-0099

6. HAMILTON TO WILLIAM DUER, 3/14/1792

> Your letter of the 11th.1 got to hand this day. I am affected beyond measure at its contents; especially as it was too late to have any influence upon the event you were apprehensive of—Mr. Woolcott's instructions [to bring suit against Duer for the deficiency in his accounts with the Treasury] having gone off yesterday.
>
> I trust however the alternative which they present to the Attorney ... and the discretion he will use in managing the affair will enable you to avoid any pernicious éclat; if your affairs are otherwise retrievable.
>
> Be this as it may—Act with fortitude and honor. If you cannot reasonably hope for a favourable extrication do not plunge deeper. Have the courage to make a full stop. Take all the care you can in the first place of Institutions of public Utility and in the next of all fair Creditors.
>
> God bless you and take care of you and your family. I have experienced all the bitterness of soul, on your account, which a warm attachment can inspire. I will not now pain you with any wise remarks, though if you recover the present stroke, I shall take great liberties with you. Assure yourself in good and bad fortune of my sincere friendship and affection.
>
> https://founders.archives.gov/documents/Hamilton/01-11-02-0108

7. ROBERT TROUP TO HAMILTON, 3/19/1792

Troup, a lawyer in New York, had been Hamilton's friend since their college days.

> I now am forced to write to you by an event which has called into action all my feelings & overwhelmed me with grief, the bitterness of which can only be conceived by an heart like yours. Before I enter upon this painful subject I must inform you that before Genl Schuyler went to Philadelphia I had totally withdrawn myself from all engagements with the friends of the new bank [the "Million Bank"] & had left the thing to its fate. After mature reflection upon the subject I saw that it would be productive of real evil—and it was manifest to me that there was mingled with the motives of some of the leaders of the association a large portion of personal enmity to you & of rooted

hatred of the government. ... If no other cause existed to prove the ruinous tendency of the establishment of another bank the present convulsion in this City furnishes the dearest evidence of it. This convulsion is immediately owing to the event above alluded to—Our friend Duer's failure. This poor man is in a state of almost complete insanity; and his situation is a source of inexpressible grief to all his friends. On Saturday night his friends met at his house & staid with him till near 12 o'Clock when we broke up in confusion without being able to agree upon a single measure. An effort was made on Sunday to collect another meeting at my house which was effected. All we could do was to draw up a notification & sign it—by which we said that from the magnitude & variety of Duer's operations he would not be able to make any specific propositions to his creditors till next saturday when we requested a meeting of the creditors. I find this has composed the public mind which had been much irritated and threatned to break forth into acts of violence. What will be the result God only knows. The truth is that the notes unpaid amount to about half a million of dollars & Duer has not a farthing of money or a particle of stock to pay them with. All the property he has in the World is some land in the Province of Maine upon which there is a heavy encumbrance of purchase Money due. You will ask what has become of his money & Stock. His answer is & he calls God to witness the truth of it that every iota of money & stocks has been applied by him to the satisfaction of engagements personally made with him upon a confidence in his honor and friendship. Such is the state of things. We all see the absolute necessity of supporting his character & extricating him if possible from his embarrassments. For this purpose we are endeavoring to open a loan upon his land—for nothing but money will satisfy the voracious appetites of his note holders. If we fail in this attempt & there is nothing offered but land I fear his reputation will be eternally blasted & that his person will be endangered. Widows, orphans, merchants mechanicks &c are all concerned in the notes. And in the large number are some low & turbulent spirits. We shall also attempt the loan in Philadelphia. If your friends in Philadelphia view the subject in the light we do here, they will suppose that Duer's total bankruptcy will affect the public interest by bringing the funding system into odium. I am strongly impressed with the mischiefs that will result from it myself and I am striving day & night to put Matters upon the best footing I can. My heart bleeds for Duer and My purse shall flow for him as far as prudence will warrant. This letter is for your own eye only. Communicate Duer's situation to our friends & give us your advice by the earliest opportunity. I am exceedingly thankful for your last letter & shall ever regard it as the most unequivocal testimony of your friendship.

The Moment Jay came forward I abandoned all ideas of Burr & have constantly been doing every thing in my power to promote Jay's election. If we can carry it the state will be blessed. He is one of the worthiest of men—& independent of his character I owe him obligations which my heart tells me I never can discharge. With regard to Burr's election I have a secret to tell you which I cannot communicate till I see you. I have reason to suspect that we have both been abused. No good can result from any explanations at present; and therefore I shall be quiet. This hint is most confidentially communicated.

https://founders.archives.gov/documents/Hamilton/01-11-02-0123

8. WILLIAM SETON TO HAMILTON, 3/21/1792

Your very kind favor of the 19 I recd yesterday & this day as it contained matters of the utmost importance to this Institution laid it before our board. You may be assured that so far from restricting our operations so as not to offend any accomodation in the present distress, we have gone as far & perhaps farther than prudence would have dictated. It is true no new Loans have very lately been made, but the reductions required of the old, have been very trifling compard to the Security the Bank had a right to have in this time of suspention & distrust—had it not been for the great drain of Specie we have had, & the dread that it might be followd, by a further one from the captiousness of our dealers & the hint of opposition—no doubt we should have gone on loaning with the same confidence as we did but in this failure of our friend Duer so many were tainted it is next to impossible to say whom can be counted on again in advance.

The Interview that our directors have already had with that of the Branch [of the Bank of the U.S.]; & the improved genl intention of both, drive away all idea of any apprehension of our being distressed by that Institution. With certainy the two

Directions are perfectly disposed to assist each other in case of Emergency & I trust such confidential Communication will be kept up as to occasion a mutual accomodation. It is what I have pressed & pointed out from the first,—the prosperity of both depends upon it. I delivered your Letter to the Collector & have requested him to furnish us between this & Friday with a list of the Names of & Sums that the Merchants have to pay for duties between this and the last of April. The Board will do any thing to Accomodate their payments.

We are now in a much better situation than we were—our balance of actual Specie exceeds the balance due to our depositors not taking in the money due the Public, & the Treasurer of the State of New York ...

We have now about 100,000 Dollars National Notes, & they are increasing daily. By the deposits of the Collector & from our receiving them of those who have no other manner to pay us & each other—the State of Credit is so deranged, and the evil resulting from the Creating of this Mass of artificial credit supported only by usurious Loans is so universal that there is no forming a judgment of the evil situation of individuals. If Duer is not able to satisfy his Creditors by what he is to say to them on Saturday, the day appointed for their Convention—the Consequence will be awfull & I shall tremble for him. Stocks rose a little yesterday in consequence of the Intelligence of the Treasurer having entered the Market at Phila.—but today they are down again. Perhaps a purchase for the public if consistent with policy might be of good Consequence here, & one or two hundred thousand Dollars of the Balance we owe the Public thrown into Circulation in this way would not injure us as it would pass from hand to hand & merely fill up the vacuum of drooping Credit without draining us of Specie.

https://founders.archives.gov/documents/Hamilton/01-11-02-0131

9. ROBERT TROUP TO HAMILTON, 3/24/1792

Things here are in a calamitous state. My heart is nearly broken with the distresses of our friend Duer. Read the enclosed & judge what my feelings must be from your own. Great pains have been taken to excite the public rage agt. him & his friends. Among others I have been marked out as an object of resentment—for being one of his Lawyers. It is true I am so—but I have done nothing but what a sincere friend & an honest man ought to do. But no consideration will influence me to desert him in the present hour of his deep distress. I shall however take care to engage in nothing that will be unbecoming the respect every mans owes himself.

B. L——n [Brockholst Livingston] & some others are triumphing over this unfortunate Mans distress and they are preying upon the vitals of public credit by every artifice & combination that can be devised to depress stocks. I am obliged to abandon these men as devoid of every sentiment which humanity inspires—and at a future time you will shudder at the tale of perfidy which I shall unfold to you.

Indeed my dear friend I am frantic with the pangs I feel for the public welfare and for the honor & happiness of our friend. I hope for a favorable change but at present shadows clouds & darkness rest upon the prospect of it. No Man's affairs could be more complex & deranged—& few men's more extensive. I have no connexion with him but what is dictated by friendship & benevolence.

https://founders.archives.gov/documents/Hamilton/01-26-02-0002-0323

10. NICHOLAS LOW TO HAMILTON, 3/25/1792

Low, a New York City merchant, was one of the directors of the Society for Establishing Useful Manufactures, of which Hamilton was also a member.

You will I am sure do every Thing in your power that can be warranted by the principles of Prudence & Discretion to contribute to the Support of publick & private Credit in this alarming State of it. ... [W]hatever Projects may have been formed by some Individuals among ourselves heretofore for draining the vaults [of specie] no Man who shall be detected in them hereafter will be permitted to live in this City. ... I am in hopes that we have seen nearly the end of bankruptcies in consequence of the shock created by Duers stoppage.

https://founders.archives.gov/documents/Hamilton/01-26-02-0002-0325

11. WILLIAM SETON TO HAMILTON, 4/9/1792

[E]very thing still is going down Hill. The extent of the evil, or the amount of Contracts &ca, it is impossible to form a judgement of but I understand from everybody that this week will be the most distressing period of any. ...[S]o many failures are daily happening that I fear many of our old Loans are in jeopardy.

https://founders.archives.gov/documents/Hamilton/01-11-02-0208

12. WILLIAM SETON TO HAMILTON, 4/11/1792

I find upon enquiry from those who are most conversant in the nature and extent of the Stock Contracts, that Monday the 15th of this month is the day which will probably produce the greatest distress, of course the day on which relief will be the most essential. What is called here the Company, of which Mr Macomb is the ostensible person, have on that day to take Stock or pay differences on half a Million. If they do not comply, then all other Contracts are a float, & the sacrifices must be very great. If they only pay the differences & dont take the Stock, this may be calculated at the rates that the distress will cause the price of Stock to be at, which will go near to ruin them, so that it is of infinite consequence to the Community that the Company should not be too much oppressed if they mean to comply with their Engagements, or that the Public should have immediately relief, if they do not mean to comply. Therefore if it was possible that I could go into the Market for you in force that day, and that it was known I should do so, it would in all probability save the City from utter ruin. Perhaps such a day may never occur again. I take the liberty of mentioning this to you, as your answer can reach me on Saturday which would be time enough. [Alexander Macomb defaulted on payments on 4/12/1792.]

https://founders.archives.gov/documents/Hamilton/01-11-02-0216

13. HAMILTON TO WILLIAM SETON, 4/12/1792

Seton (of the Bank of New York) was acting on behalf of the Treasury Department in purchasing stock with money from the Sinking Fund.

I have your letters of the 10th1 & 11th and more to my distress than surprise I learn by other letters a confirmation of what you apprehended namely Mr. Macombs failure. This misfortune has I fear a long tail to it.

The inclosed you will perceive [for purchase of stock with Sinking Fund money] gives you additional latitude. The terms as heretofore, for six ℔ Cents 20/ three per Cents 12/ & deferred 12/6.

You must judge of the best mode & manner of applying the sum. The operations here not being extensive, I have found it best to eke out my aid. I doubt whether this will answer with you. My reason was to keep up men's spirits by *appearing often* though not much at one time.

https://founders.archives.gov/documents/Hamilton/01-11-02-0227

14. HAMILTON TO WILLIAM SHORT, 4/16/1792

Short was the American chargé d'affaires in Paris. Hamilton regularly sent him updates on American finances.

Sir,

The fluctuation of the price of the Stocks in the United States is a circumstance that cannot have failed to attract your attention nor to excite a temporary feeling in the minds of foreigners. Tho' I doubt not it will be well explained by the Agents of those Citizens of other Countries who have vested their Monies in our funds, I think it necessary that some ideas should be communicated to you on which you can found a true opinion either for your own satisfaction or that of persons interested in our National Welfare, with whom you may have occasion to confer.

The moderate size of the domestic debt of the United States appears to have created the most intemperate ideas of speculation in the minds of a very few persons, whose natural ardor has been encreased by great success in some of the early stages of the melioration of the market value of the Stock. To combinations of private Capitals thus acquired or increased, Sums of specie, obtained as well at the most extravagant rates of premium as at common interest, were added, and to these were joined purchases of stock on credits for various terms so as to create a delusive confidence, that the concentration of so much Stock in a few hands would secure a very high Market rate. This expectation was increased by comparing the Market values of the several species of our funds with those of the same species of Stock in Great Britain, the United Netherlands and other parts of Europe, without due allowance for the deductions which should have been made on account of the great difference in the value of Money and the objections arising from our Distance from those European Money holders, whose capitals they expected to attract and other relative circumstances. At the time when many heavy engagements thus formed were becoming due, some contentions among the dealers in and proprietors of the debt took place, and counter combinations were formed to render the crisis of payment and speculation as inconvenient and disadvantageous as possible. By these means, those eventual contracts, it was probably hoped, could be more cheaply complied with, and moreover that a reduced Market would afford further opportunities of beneficial speculation. The extreme indiscretion of the first mentioned speculations and the distress, which, it was manifest, they must produce, excited perhaps and animated the movements of the other party and brought on a scene of private distress for money both Artificial and real which probably has not been equalled in this Country. It happened in the Winter Season when the influx of Cash articles of trade, as returns from abroad, is nearly suspended, and when quantities of specie were sent from the Sea ports to the interior Country for the purchase of produce, to supply the demand for the Spring exportation.

The Banks, who can always perceive the approach of these things, were influenced to limit their operations, and particularly the Bank of the United States, which was then preparing for the opening of its Branches, or offices of discounts and deposit in Boston, New york, Baltimore and Charleston.

The United States, you would presume, could not be insensible of so fit a moment to make purchases of the public Stock, and the Treasurer was accordingly authorized to buy; but tho' the appearances of private distress for money were so great he could not obtain for several days the sum of fifty thousand Dollars, at the highest rates at which the public purchases had before been made. The holders who were free from engagements were averse to selling—the principal persons, who were under engagements, they could not comply with, were obliged or disposed to place their effects in the hands of their Creditors, who did not chuse to add to their own disappointments of great profits actual losses, by unseasonable sales of the Bankrupts property.

The Stock in the Market therefore was really made scarce. A quarters interest has just been paid. Some of the cautious monied people have begun to purchase. The specie is returning from the Country and the heaviest private engagements having now fallen due, the declension of Stock may be considered as arrested. There is little doubt that the difficulty for money among the dealers in the debt will be at no time so great as it has been, after the present week, and that changes of a favorable complexion are to be confidently expected. At first moderate perhaps, afterwards such as will carry the funds up to their due value.

Should you be of opinion that the State of things in France will render some intimation of these events useful there, you will be good enough to communicate them to Mr Morris our Minister at that Court.

I have the honor to be with great consideration   Sir   Your most obedt Servant

Alexander Hamilton

https://founders.archives.gov/documents/Hamilton/01-11-02-0235

15. HENRY REMSEN TO THOMAS JEFFERSON, 4/11/1792

Remsen served as Jefferson's chief clerk at the State Department for two years, resigning his post sometime between mid-March 1792, when he went on leave due to the death of his father, and early April of that year, when this letter was written in New York.

The difficulties among those who dealt in stocks, or endorsed notes (some from friendly and others from interested motives) for dealers in stocks, have been daily encreasing; and from the connection there was between the dealers, and the dependance of one on another, no time can be fixed for their determination. On the contrary, facts hourly occurring warrant the expectation, that those difficulties will continue to encrease, and only end in the bankruptcy of 9/10ths. of them. Mr. McComb, with a fortune of £60,000 he brought with him to this City a few years ago and which he had considerably augmented since, and with a valuable ship and cargo just arrived from India, has not been able to fulfil his engagements, and has of course failed. Many others in independent situations have experienced the like fate, and I can safely add that ¼ of the citizens are affected by these failures. ...

https://founders.archives.gov/documents/Jefferson/01-23-02-0352

16. HENRY REMSEN TO THOMAS JEFFERSON, 4/23/1792

Dear Sir

I had the honor of receiving your favour of the 14th. on the 15th.; but a desire to communicate such intelligence as might be relied on, respecting the calamitous event which has happened here, and the proceedings of the mob, induced me to delay it until now.

A very intelligent person who is interested in the funds of the U.S., but who has not meddled with them for a twelvemonth past, and can therefore be supposed to speak without biass, attributes the whole of this business to Mr. Duer. Astonished at the rapid rise of the funds, he took such pains to ascertain it's cause, as to discover enough to convince him that it was without foundation, and originated in the spirit of monopoly. In this enquiry, he found that Duer had formerly, and at very enhanced prices, contracted to receive from different people and about at the same time, a number of the New York bank shares, exceeding considerably the number in existence. When the time for delivery arrived the shares were not to be had; and the consequence was, that those which did exist rose almost immediately 40 pr. Cent, and Duer received the difference of price. His success with respect to this plan, gave birth probably to the other for monopolizing the stocks of the U.S., and which has ended in his disgrace and the ruin of many of his fellow citizens. At first he purchased this kind of stock on his own account and on credit, and pledged it to the endorsers of his notes as security: but it continuing to rise, they associated themselves with him in business to appearance so very profitable, and formed themselves into a company, known among the stock dealers by the name of the 6 pr. Cent company. Their purchases and dealings however were extended to all kinds of stock. It is believed, and with reason that Duer alone knew the true state of their funds, and that the others (W. Livingston, Macomb, Whippo &c.) conceived themselves perfectly safe till very lately. Besides the monopoly by the company, Duer was engaged in a monopoly of Stocks on his own acct.; and finding no other people to endorse his notes whose credit was sufficient, he engaged John Pintard (formerly interpreter of the french language for your Departmt.) to procure money for him at an usurious interest, and allowed him £1000 pr. annm. for his services. Pintard employed the lower kind of brokers to effect it, and was extremely successful in raising money, principally among the middling and poorer classes of people. It was the practice of these brokers, who are little better than robbers, to go into every house where they thought there was money, and also to ascertain which of the small traders kept running accounts with the bank (for many of them did, and do still) and to ask them whether they had any money to put out on good interest, offering 1, 2 or 3 pr. Cent pr. Month as they found it necessary. To those who hesitated they offered a greater interest—and there are instances where they have applied 4 or 5 times in vain, and succeeded in the 5th. or 6th. application, by encreasing their offers. The lenders then received notes signed by Duer and endorsed by Pintard, with the assurance that they were perfectly safe, as he received a transfer of stock more than sufficient to cover every note he endorsed. This went on some months, and probably some notes were renewed several times, the interest being discounted or added to the principal on the renewal. But it is to be observed, that as money grew scarcer the interest was raised from 1, 2 and 3, to 4, 5 and 6 pr. Cent per month.—Several procuresses, and other people of the same character became creditors of Duer in this way.

The high prices given by the Company, and by Duer, for stocks from the commencement of their late rise, which was I believe in November or December last, occasioned a great influx from every part of the continent. This market concentrated 9/10th. of the quantity that was held merely for speculation at one time. A part of it was bought directly by the company or Duer for cash, and the cash carried away; but a very considerable and perhaps the greatest part by merchants, or men who possessed money or credit. These gave for it 22/, 23/ or 24/ cash, and sold it to the company or Duer on credit, some payable for when delivered, and others payable for at a future day and deliverable immediately, for 25/, 26/ and 27/. There are others who bought for 22/ and sold for 23/; these sold for 24/, the third purchaser sold for 25/, the fourth for 26/, the fifth for 27/ or 28/, the last purchaser being the company. All these dealings were on credit. The company failing and the stock falling in value, much lower than the first price of 22/, every one of those persons lose, some their whole fortunes, others the greater part of it. It would be impossible to relate the particulars of this ruinous business. The sum of it is, that the wealthy people who engaged in it have lost by the company, and the less wealthy by Duer, thro' the agency of Pintard. It has totally annihilated all confidence between man and man, and checked in a most surprising degree merchandizing and fair trade.

It appears that the Company intended to raise 6 pr. Cents to 30/, and 3 pr. Cents and deferred to 20/ each; and that they would privately sell a part of their own stock to raise money, in order to effect their object by exaltg. the public value of it, and thereby induce people to buy.

It might be supposed that this business was quite important enough to engage the whole time and attention of one man, but the fact proves the contrary. Duer's projecting spirit could not brook confinement to a single object however important. After settling a plan of operations with Pintard for the part he was to act in the department assigned him, and furnishing him with blanks for notes ready signed, to be filled up as occasions required, and after fixing principles whereon the agent of the 6 pr. Cent company was to govern himself, Duer in conjunction with W. Livingston purchased a large ship, and sent her with many thousand dolls. to India. Of one man alone they got 80,000 dollars, on giving their note for 100,000 payable on the ship's return. He also bought a large tract of territory in one of the Eastern States, and contracted for many parcels of land in N. Jersey, in the vicinity of the spot contemplated for the establishment of the manufactory. He was already largely interested in lands on the Ohio; and had the contract for supplying our army with rations, and the frenchmen on the Scioto also with rations.

It is said here that the U.S. will experience some loss on account of his not having taken up the drafts of his agent, who was stationed at fort Pitt to pay for the provisions destined for our troops; Genl. St. Clair having been obliged to endorse them, which makes it the duty of the U.S. to pay them.

Before McComb engaged in speculation, he was in high repute and of extensive credit: His landed estate alone was computed to be worth £60,000: But just before he declared himself a bankrupt and while he was tottering, he has been guilty of many vile, unprincipled acts, such as delaying the declaration of his bankruptcy until after the sailing of the packet, that advices of his situation might not go by her to England, receiving stock to a great amount on the 2d. of April, and assuring upon his honour those who delivered it, that he was able to and would pay for it on the 13th.—remitting this very stock, and all other that he possessed by the packet to England to comply with a contract there—selling bills under such assurances of their being honored, as could not be disputed, to the amount of 80,000 £ Stlg., when he knew his failure to be inevitable; and also conveying beyond the reach of his creditors all his property here, whether real or personal. He is now in gaol with Duer—Whippo and Pintard have secreted themselves—and W. Livingston has retired to his country seat amidst his tenants. Among the less notorious dealers and defaulters, the fulfilment of Contracts has ceased, and they appear to be entirely dissolved and disregarded. Things in general however wear a better aspect than they did a few days since, and the stocks are getting up slowly to par.

Three or four days after the sailing of the English packet, a pilot boat, similar in construction and size to the Virginia built boats that ply in the Chesapeake, was dispatched for England. Many think she will never get there, being too small to escape should the weather prove tempestuous. It is conjectured that the holders of Macomb's sterling bills sent her off with the hope of her reaching England before the packet. Others suppose that Macomb himself sent her, dreading that some intimation of his approaching fate had been sent by the packet, while a few think that she conveys dispatches from the Secretary of the Treasury for our bankers in Holland. The first two appear to me to be probable; but the real object remains a secret to all except those who sent her. A gentleman wished to send a letter by her, but the Captn. refused to take it, and said £1000 should not tempt him to carry it.

The collection of people about the gaol has consisted chiefly of boys and servants, who went from a motive of curiosity rather than the design of doing mischief. They assembled in consequence of handbills dispersed thro' the city, by some unknown person, exciting the citizens to inflict punishment on the authors of their wrongs, since they could obtain no redress. It is said some attempts were really made by a few individuals to enter the gaol. The magistracy thought it necessary to have a guard of constables and watchmen in it every night. On one or two nights the crowd stoned the gaol, and broke some windows and lamps; but it is a question whether this disorderly behaviour did not proceed from resentment against the constables &c., who in several instances treated the persons who were quiet spectators with great rudeness, for not retiring to their homes. For the two past nights there has been no collection of people at the gaol. During the two nights of the greatest disorder, no lives were lost nor limbs broken, neither were the militia called out, or a gun fired.—The public mind is however so far from acquiescing in the series of calamitous events with which it has been aflicted, day after day, that but little address would be necessary to raise a mob that all the force of the city could not withstand. In every place Duer and his associates are execrated, and it is a remark in every person's mouth, that were they torn to pieces, or hung without undergoing any form of trial, it would be only a necessary example and a just punishment. I do not apprehend any thing serious while they remain in confinement, since their creditors seem bent more on recovering a part of the property which is concealed, than on inflicting punishment personally; but it will be dangerous for either of them to appear again in public, unless they previously surrender their property.

Suffer me here, Sir, to obtrude an idea which may suggest some advantages to the Government and it's citizens. However well meant the law for reducing the public debt was, there have been disadvantages resulting from the manner of purchasing on the part of the U.S., that more than balance, in my mind, the advantages from the reduction that has been made. On the development of Duer's and the company's plans they were evident. The 6 pr. cent stock fell to 18/9, and the other kinds in proportion. Had Government then purchased to the extent of it's ready money, or it's resources, privately, instead of coming forward with fixed prices, they would with the same money have got more stock than they have done. The money thrown into circulation would have been the same and have afforded equal relief, and it would in addition, by reducing in a greater quantity the stock kept for speculation, have rendered the residue of a more stable value. It strikes me that money is rather scarce in this country; barely sufficient for a circulating medium. If then in this rage for speculation the matter of speculation, that is the stocks, can be reduced in quantity, the more advantageous it would be for the community. In the last public purchase but a small proportion that was offered could be taken—in fact it commenced and ended in a moment—for all had their papers ready and handed them in at the same time. The consequence was, that what was refused fell almost as low as it was before. Besides many supposing the treasury of the U.S. to be an inexhaustible mine, and arguing from precedt. bought on credit; and thus what was intended as a relief, did in a certain degree operate as an evil. Had the Government a sum in it's coffers sufficient to pay off the whole, or only half of it's debts at once, perhaps it would be true policy to purchase publicly. To any objection to private purchases, may [be] opposed the irredeemibility of the 6 pr. Cents; for few can believe that the continuance of the debt will prove a blessing. Nay the merchants, who it was supposed would feel none of the duties imposed on the articles of their trade for paying the interest, further than as far as their own consumption went, complain, and say that commerce is scarcely worth pursuing on this very account, and that they are stretched almost to a violation of our commercial laws.

I hope you will excuse me for thus offering my opinion without asking, or even without being warranted by any circumstance, except the favorable opinion you have been pleased to express of me.—Indeed, Sir, I feel much obliged by your friendly and delicate conduct while I had the honor of being employed in your Office; and I assure you nothing but the most pressing necessity could have induced me to a change. I knew, and I have since experienced, that no person but myself could do justice to my mother, and my young brothers and sisters, in attending to the concerns of my deceased parent. I am under the most grateful and lasting acknowledgments for the certificate you favored me with, which is more full than I expected; and I regard it as a testimonial to be of use whenever I should have occasion to exhibit it.

I shall not venture, Sir, to trouble you with any reflections on the pamphlet I sent you, further than to observe, that whoever has read it of my acquaintance, have ascribed it to party spirit, and envy—to disappointed ambition perhaps—but none have to what the author asserts his design to be, in publishing it, the public good. To one who has given up the peaceful enjoyment of domestic happiness, and devoted the best part of his life to the public, to uninterrupted labour and incessant cares, it would be a cruel sensation did he suppose the pamphlet above mentioned spoke the public voice, but as he must know it does not, that it is only intended to serve a political movement, and the purpose of party, he must have the approbation not only of his own conscience, but the approbation of all those who are honest and good men. You know so much of pamphleteers in Europe, Sir, and of their capability to blacken the best of men and measures, that I persuade myself you consign the one in question to the forgetfulness he deserves. I have heard it conjectured that Mr. Ames was the author, but Mr. King disbelieves it, or pretends to do so.

I cannot yet judge whether Govr. Clinton or Mr. Jay will be elected. Their advocates are respectively very zealous and sanguine. The great sale of land to Macomb has lessened Govr. Clinton's interest among the farmers in the upper part of the state, where he was formerly very popular; but in this city and indeed in the whole southern district of which this city is only a small part, he will have a decided majority of votes. Mr. Jay has gone on the Eastern circuit, and will not return before the election is over.—I have the honor to be with great respect and attachment, Dr. Sir Your obliged & obedt. Servt.

Henry Remsen

P.S. I must not omit to mention a rumour of Mr. King and Mr. Lawrence the one a Senator and the other a Representative from this State in the legislature of the U.S., being among the unfortunates in speculation. The latter very deeply.

https://founders.archives.gov/documents/Jefferson/01-23-02-0397

APPENDIX 5

Important Writings by Hamilton Related to His Financial Programs and to the Threads of the Gordian Knot

The excerpts are copied from Founders Online, omitting modern editorial notes.

1. 1779 OR 1780: "LETTER ON CURRENCY"

Written to an unknown recipient between December 1779 and March 1780, from the army's winter headquarters at Morristown, New Jersey. Includes discussion of money in circulation, a bank, trade, debt, manufacturing, barter, need for a foreign loan, depreciation of currency, paper money, speculators, taxes, the wealthy, and monopolies.

See main text §3.3.2 and Sylla and Cowen, *Alexander Hamilton on Finance, Credit, and Debt,* Chapter 1. They list the possible recipients as Robert Morris (see §3.3.3, 3.4, and 3.10.1), Philip Schuyler (New York State senator, 1780-1784, and Hamilton's father-in-law), and John Sullivan (Revolutionary War hero and delegate to the Continental Congress in 1780-1781).

> A great source of error in disquisitions of this nature is the judging of events by abstract calculations, which though geometrically true are false as they relate to the concerns of beings governed more by passion and prejudice than by an enlightened sense of their interests. A degree of illusion mixes itself in all the affairs of society. The opinion of objects has more influence than their real nature. The quantity of money in circulation is certainly a chief cause of its decline; but we find it is depreciated more than five times as much as it ought to be by this rule. The excess is derived from opinion, a want of confidence. In like

manner we deceive ourselves when we suppose the value will increase in proportion as the quantity is lessened.

https://founders.archives.gov/documents/Hamilton/01-02-02-0559-0002

2. 1780, 9/3: LETTER TO CONGRESSMAN JAMES DUANE

Written in response to a query from Duane. Includes discussion of the centrifugal tendency of the states, circulation of money, debt, frontiers, revenue, weakness of the Articles of Confederation, military funding, the need for a convention of states to consider a new confederacy, trade, banks, paper money, foreign debt, taxes, specie, and a mint.

See main text §3.3.2 and Sylla and Cowen, *Alexander Hamilton on Finance, Credit, and Debt,* Chapter 2.

> The fundamental defect is a want of power in Congress. It is hardly worth while to show in what this consists, as it seems to be universally acknowleged, or to point out how it has happened, as the only question is how to remedy it. It may however be said that it has originated from three causes—an excess of the spirit of liberty which has made the particular states show a jealousy of all power not in their own hands; ... a diffidence in Congress of their own powers, by which they have been timid and indecisive in their resolutions, constantly making concessions to the states, till they have scarcely left themselves the shadow of power; a want of sufficient means at their disposal to answer the public exigencies and of vigor to draw forth those means ...

https://founders.archives.gov/documents/Hamilton/01-02-02-0838

3. 1781, 4/30: LETTER TO ROBERT MORRIS, SUPERINTENDENT OF FINANCES

Written just after Hamilton resigned as Washington's aide-de-camp. Includes discussion of the foreign debt, extinguishing the debt, money in circulation, revenue (taxes), agriculture vs. manufacturing and trade, banks, why good credit is essential, specie, paper money, barter, stable currency, and what happens if we lose the war.

See main text §3.3.3 and Sylla and Cowen, *Alexander Hamilton on Finance, Credit, and Debt,* Chapter 3.

> A national debt if it is not excessive will be to us a national blessing; it will be powerfull cement of our union. It will also create a necessity for keeping up taxation to a degree which without being oppressive, will be a spur to industry; remote as we are from Europe and shall be from danger, it were otherwise to be feard our popular maxims would incline us to too great parsimony and indulgence. We labour less now

> than any civilized nation of Europe, and a habit of labour in the people is as essential to the health and vigor of their minds and bodies as it is conducive to the welfare of the State. We ought not to Suffer our self-love to deceive us in a comparrison, upon these points.
>
> https://founders.archives.gov/documents/Hamilton/01-02-02-1167

4. 1781-1782: "THE CONTINENTALIST," 6 ESSAYS

Published in *The New-York Packet, and the American Advertiser* on 7/12/1781, 7/19/1781, 8/9/1781, 8/30/1781, 4/18/1782, and 7/4/1782. Includes discussion of the centrifugal impetus of states, revenue (land sales, capitation tax), regulation of trade, extinguishing the debt, French loans, and banks.

See main text §3.3.4 and Sylla and Cowen, *Alexander Hamilton on Finance, Credit, and Debt,* Chapter 4.

> History is full of examples, where in contests for liberty, a jealousy of power has either defeated the attempts to recover or preserve it in the first instance, or has afterwards subverted it by clogging government with too great precautions for its felicity, or by leaving too wide a door for sedition and popular licenciousness. In a government framed for durable liberty, not less regard must be paid to giving the magistrate a proper degree of authority, to make and execute the laws with rigour, than to guarding against encroachments upon the rights of the community. As too much power leads to despotism, too little leads to anarchy, and both eventually to the ruin of the people.
>
> https://founders.archives.gov/documents/Hamilton/01-02-02-1179 (with links to the other five essays)

5. 1787-1788: FEDERALIST PAPERS, 51 ESSAYS

See main text §3.9. Two samples:

No. 1, 10/27/1787, on the centrifugal tendency of the United States.

> Among the most formidable of the obstacles which the new Constitution will have to encounter may readily be distinguished the obvious interest of a certain class of men in every State to resist all changes which may hazard a diminution of the power, emolument, and consequence of the offices they hold under the State establishments; and the perverted ambition of another class of men, who will either hope to aggrandize themselves by the confusions of their country, or will flatter themselves with fairer prospects of elevation from the subdivision of the empire into several partial confederacies than from its union under one government.
>
> https://avalon.law.yale.edu/18th_century/fed01.asp

No. 11, on the benefits to commerce of a stronger central government.

> In a state so insignificant our commerce would be a prey to the wanton intermeddlings of all nations at war with each other; who, having nothing to fear from us, would with little scruple or remorse, supply their wants by depredations on our property as often as it fell in their way. The rights of neutrality will only be respected when they are defended by an adequate power. A nation, despicable by its weakness, forfeits even the privilege of being neutral.

https://avalon.law.yale.edu/18th_century/fed11.asp

6. 1790, 1/9: FIRST REPORT ON PUBLIC CREDIT

See Chapter 3 and Appendix 1; also Sylla and Cowen, *Alexander Hamilton on Finance, Credit, and Debt,* Chapter 7, and Holloway, *Hamilton versus Jefferson*, Chapter 2.

7. 1790, 5/28: TO PRESIDENT GEORGE WASHINGTON

Regarding back pay for the army. Includes discussion of debt and discrimination.

> A regulation therefore having a retrospective operation, and prescribing, with regard to past transactions, new and unknown requisites, by which the admission of Claims is to be guided, is an infraction of the rights of Individuals, acquired under preexisting Laws, and a contravention of the public faith, pledged by the course of public proceedings. It has consequently a tendency not less unfriendly to public credit, than to the security of property. ... It is perhaps always better, that partial evils should be submitted to, than that principles should be violated. In the infancy of our present government, peculiar strictness and circumspection are called for by the too numerous instances of relaxations, which in other quarters & on other occasions, have discredited our Public measures.

https://www.founders.archives.gov/documents/Hamilton/01-06-02-0313

8. 1790, 9/15: TO PRESIDENT GEORGE WASHINGTON.

Founders Online title: "Enclosure: Answers to Questions proposed by the President of the United States to the Secretary of the Treasury." Includes discussion of the frontier, neutrality in foreign relations, and the centrifugal tendency of the United States.

> We are but just recovering from the effects of a long arduous and exhausting war. The people but just begin to realise the sweets of repose. We are vulnerable both by water and land without either fleet or army. We have a considerable debt in proportion to the resources which the state of things permits the government to command. Measures have been recently entered upon for the restoration of credit, which a war could hardly fail to disconcert, and which if disturbed would be fatal to the means of prosecuting it. Our national government is in its infancy. The habits and dispositions of our people are ill suited to those liberal contributions to the treasury, which a war would necessarily exact. There are causes which render war in this country more expensive, and consequently more difficult to be carried on than in any other. There is a general disinclination to it in all classes. The theories of the speculative and the feelings of all are opposed to it. The support of public opinion (perhaps more essential to our government than to any other) could only be looked for in a war evidently resulting from necessity. These are general reasons against going into war.

https://founders.archives.gov/documents/Washington/05-06-02-0212-0002

9. 1790, 12/14: REPORT ON A NATIONAL BANK

See Chapter 5 and Appendix 2, as well as Sylla and Cowen, *Alexander Hamilton on Finance, Credit, and Debt*, Chapter 10, and and Holloway, *Hamilton versus Jefferson*, Chapter 4.

10. 1791, 1/28: REPORT ON THE ESTABLISHMENT OF A MINT

See Sylla and Cowen, *Alexander Hamilton on Finance, Credit, and Debt*, Chapter 11.

> The unequal values allowed in different parts of the Union to coins of the same intrinsic worth; the defective species of them, which embarrass the circulation of some of the States; and the dissimularity in their several Monies of account, are inconveniencies, which if not to be ascribed to the want of a National Coinage, will at least be most effectually remedied by the establishment of one; a measure that will at the same time give additional security against impositions, by counterfeit as well as by base currencies.

https://founders.archives.gov/documents/Hamilton/01-07-02-0334-0004

11. 1791, 2/23: REPORT ON THE CONSTITUTIONALITY OF A NATIONAL BANK

See main text §5.4; Sylla and Cowen, *Alexander Hamilton on Finance, Credit, and Debt*, Chapter 12; and Holloway, *Hamilton versus Jefferson*, Chapter 5.

https://founders.archives.gov/documents/Hamilton/01-08-02-0060-0003

12. 1791, 12/5: REPORT ON THE SUBJECT OF MANUFACTURES

See Chapter 6 and Appendix 3, as well as Sylla and Cowen, *Alexander Hamilton on Finance, Credit, and Debt*, Chapter 14, and Holloway, *Hamilton versus Jefferson*, Chapter 7.

13. 1792, 1/23: REPORT ON THE PUBLIC DEBT AND LOANS

To the House of Representatives. Includes discussion of the debt (domestic, unsubscribed, amounts payable to foreign military, extinguishment, sinking fund), assumption, and sale of land to raise revenue to pay off the debt.

> The purchases of the debt already made have left a sum of interest in the Treasury, which will be increased by future purchases—certain sums payable to the United States in their own securities, will, when received, have a similar effect. And there is ground to calculate on a saving upon the operations, which are in execution with regard to the foreign debt. The sale of the Western Lands, when provision shall be made for it, may be expected to produce a material addition to such a fund. It is therefore submitted, that it be adopted as a principle, that all interest which shall have ceased to be payable; by any of the means above specified, shall be set apart and appropriated in the most firm and inviolable manner, as a fund for sinking the public debt, by purchase or payment...

https://founders.archives.gov/documents/Hamilton/01-10-02-0124-0001

14. 1792, 4/16: TO WILLIAM SHORT

Hamilton gives Short, the American chargé d'affaires in Paris, a concise explanation of the Panic of 1792.
See §7.2 and Appendix 4, no. 14.

15. 1792, MAY TO AUGUST: "THE VINDICATION," 4 ESSAYS.

See main text §3.10.2 and §4.4.4-4.4.5. No. 1 includes discussion of the centrifugal tendency of the United States, including Jefferson's actions.

> There is yet another class of opponents to the Government & its administration, who are of too much consequence not to be mentioned, a sect of political Doctors—a kind of Popes in Government—standards of political orthodoxy who brand with heresy all opinions but their own—men of sublimated imaginations and weak judgments pretenders to profound knowlege, yet ignorant of the most useful of all sciences, the science of human nature—men who dignify themselves with the appellation of Philosophers, yet are destitute of the first elements of true philosophy—Lovers of paradoxes, men who maintain expressly that Religion is not necessary to Society, and very nearly that Government itself is a nuisance, that Priests and Clergymen of all descriptions are worse than useless.
>
> https://founders.archives.gov/documents/Hamilton/01-11-02-0376

No. 2 includes discussion of debt, attacks on the funding system, and American credit in Europe.

> When we hear the epithets "vile matter" "corrupt mass" bestowed upon the public Debt and the owners of it indiscriminately maligned as the harpies and vultures of the community, there is ground to suspect that those who hold the language though they may not dare to avow it contemplate a more summary process for getting rid of debts than that of paying them. Indeed Charity itself cannot avoid concluding from the language and conduct of some men (and some of them of no inconsiderable importance) that in their vocabularies creditor and enemy are synonimous terms and that they have a laudable antipathy against every man to whom they owe money either as individuals or as members of the Society.
>
> https://founders.archives.gov/documents/Hamilton/01-11-02-0377-0002

No.3 includes a discussion of why the debt must be paid.

> The principle which shall be assumed here is this—that the established rules of morality and justice are applicable to nations as well as to Individuals; that the former as well as the latter are bound to keep their promises, to fulfil their engagements, to respect the rights of property which others have acquired under contracts with them. Without this, there is an end of all distinct ideas of right or wrong justice or injustice in relation to Society or Government. There can be no such thing as rights—no such thing as property or liberty. All the boasted advantages of a constitution of Government vanish in air. Every thing must float on the variable and vague opinions of the Governing party of whomsoever composed.
>
> https://founders.archives.gov/documents/Hamilton/01-11-02-0378

No. 4 includes a discussion of various types of discrimination and types of debt: old emissions of Continental money, loan office debt, and payments to the army.

> A leading character of every part of the Debt is, that it was in its origin made alienable. It was payable to the holder, either in capacity of Assignee or bearer; far the greatest part of the latter description. The Contract therefore was, in its very essence, a contract between the Government and the actual holder.

https://founders.archives.gov/documents/Hamilton/01-11-02-0379

16. 1792, 5/26: TO EDWARD CARRINGTON

Carrington was supervisor of the revenue for the District of Virginia and Hamilton's long-time friend. This letter includes a discussion of the centrifugal tendency of the United States, particularly the opposition of Madison and Jefferson to funding the debt and to the national bank, and their support of discrimination.

See main text §5.4.

> Whatever were the original merits of the funding system, after having been so solemnly adopted, & after so great a transfer of property under it, what would become of the Government should it be reversed? What of the National Reputation? Upon what system of morality can so atrocious a doctrine be maintained? In me, I confess it excites indignation & horror!
>
> What are we to think of those maxims of Government by which the power of a Legislature is denied to bind the Nation by a Contract in an affair of property for twenty four years? For this is precisely the case of the debt. What are to become of all the legal rights of property, of all charters to corporations, nay, of all grants to a man his heirs & assigns for ever, if this doctrine be true? What is the term for which a government is in capacity to contract?

https://founders.archives.gov/documents/Hamilton/01-11-02-0349

17. 1792, 8/18: TO PRESIDENT GEORGE WASHINGTON

Hamilton's answer to complaints Jefferson submitted to Washington. Includes discussion of extinguishing the debt, discrimination, assumption, revenue, the centrifugal tendency of the United States, speculation, the national bank, the accusation that Hamilton is a monarchist, and investment in agriculture, manufacturing, and trade.

See main text §4.2.2.1 and §4.3.

> The Antifœderal Champions alluded to may be taught to abate their exultation by being told that the great body of the fœderalists, or rather the great body of the people are of opinion that none of their predictions have been fulfilled—That the beneficial effects of the Government have exceeded expectation and are witnessed by the general prosperity of the Nation.

https://founders.archives.gov/documents/Hamilton/01-12-02-0184-0002

18. 1792, 9/5: CIVIS

Published in the *National Gazette*, Philadelphia. A summary of the government's actions regarding the debt. Includes discussion of extinguishing the debt, payment of arrears of interest, the Bank of the U.S., and the excise tax on alcohol.

See main text §4.1.4.

> Congress met under the present government on the first of April, 1789. To put it in motion they had a vast and very arduous work before them. This was of course a primary object; a provision for the debt a secondary one. It was natural then that the first session should have been exhausted in organizing the government, and that a systematic provision for the debt should be postponed, as in fact it was, to the second session. A temporary and partial provision of revenue only was accordingly made, by very moderate duties of impost, far short of an adequate fund for the support of government, and the payment of the interest on the debt, to take effect on the first of August, 1789; which was as early as the law could be promulgated throughout the union, and the subordinate executive arrangements made for carrying it into execution. ...

https://founders.archives.gov/documents/Hamilton/01-12-02-0247

19. 1792, 9/11: FACT, NO. 1

Published in the *National Gazette*. Includes a discussion of Hamilton's statements on extinguishing debt, circulation of money, taxing rather than taking out a loan to defend the frontier, and paper money.

See main text §4.3.

> A certain description of men are for getting out of debt; yet are against all taxes for raising money to pay it off; they are amongst the foremost for carrying on war, and yet will have neither loans nor taxes. They are alike opposed to what creates debt, and to what avoids it.

https://founders.archives.gov/documents/Hamilton/01-12-02-0274

20. 1793, 2/13-2/14: REPORT RELATIVE TO THE LOANS NEGOTIATED UNDER ACTS OF 8/4/1790 AND 8/12/1790

Presented to the House of Representatives as a response to the Giles Resolutions. Includes discussion of payments of America's foreign debts and why funds for that are not kept separate from funds for the domestic debt; funds for Indian wars on the frontier; possible problems getting future loans in Europe due to French Revolution; and government dealings with banks.

See main text §7.3.

> Even in a time of complete peace, in a country, where a small extent of monied capital forbids a reliance upon large pecuniary aids to be suddenly obtained, a prudent administrator of the finances could not feel entirely at ease, with a less sum at all times in the command of the treasury, than 500.000 dollars, for meeting current demands and extra-exigencies, which, in the affairs of a nation, are every moment to be expected. But, with a war actually on hand, and a possibility of its extension to a more serious length, he would be inexcusable in leaving himself with a less sum at command; unless from an impracticability of doing otherwise. It would be always his duty to combine two considerations—the chance of extra-calls for money, and a possibility of some failure in the receipts which were expected. Derangements of various kinds may happen in the commercial circle, capable of interrupting, for a time, the punctual course of payments to the Treasury. It is necessary, to a certain extent, to be prepared for such casualties.
>
> https://founders.archives.gov/documents/Hamilton/01-14-02-0013-0001

21. 1793, 2/19: REPORT ON STATE OF TREASURY AT BEGINNING OF EACH QUARTER, 1791-1792

Presented to the House of Representatives as a response to the Giles Resolutions. Includes discussion of banks, the Panic of 1792, the Sinking Fund, and payment of the quarterly interest on domestic debt.

> The payment of interest upon a public debt, at thirteen different places, is an operation as difficult and complicated as it is new. In carrying it into execution, it is of necessity to lodge for some time previous to the expiration of each quarter, at several of the loan offices, drafts of the Treasurer for the sums estimated to be necessary at those offices, with blanks for the direction, and with liberty to the respective officers to dispose of them upon different places, as a demand accrues. This arrangement has an eye to two purposes; to avoid large previous

accumulations at particular points; to facilitate the placing of the requisite sums, where they are wanted, without the transportation of specie.

https://founders.archives.gov/documents/Hamilton/01-14-02-0032-0001

22. 1795, 1/16: SECOND REPORT ON PUBLIC CREDIT

Full title: "Report on a Plan for the Further Support of Public Credit." Submitted to the House of Representatives and the Senate. Includes discussion of American credit and finances, including all sources of revenue since 1789; review of provisions for funding the debt and paying interest; provisions for extinguishing the domestic debt in 23 years and paying off the foreign debt; sale of western land; current revenue and debt; unsubscribed debt; and committing revenue inviolably to pay off debt rather than voting annually to fund it.

See main text §2.5.3 and §7.1, and Sylla and Cowen, *Alexander Hamilton on Finance, Credit, and Debt,* Chapter 16.

> Credit is an intire thing. Every part of it has the nicest sympathy with every other part. Wound one limb, and the whole Tree shrinks and decays. The security of each Creditor is inseperable from the security of all Creditors. The boundary between foreigner and Citizen, would not be deemed a sufficient barrier against extending the precedent of an invasion of the rights of the former to the latter. The most judicious and cautious would be most apt to reason thus, and would only look for stronger shades of apparent necessity or expediency to govern the extension. And in affairs of Credit, the opinion of the Judicious and cautious, may be expected to prevail. Hence the Government, by sequestering the property of foreign Citizens in the public funds at the commencement of a war, would impair at least if not destroy that Credit, which is the best resource in war. 'Tis in vain to attempt to disparage Credit, by objecting to it its abuses. What is there not liable to abuse or misuse?

Introductory note: https://founders.archives.gov/documents/Hamilton/01-18-02-0052-0001.
Text: https://founders.archives.gov/documents/Hamilton/01-18-02-0052-0002

23. 1795, JULY: A DEFENCE OF THE FUNDING SYSTEM

Unpublished manuscript. Includes discussion of the debt, discrimination, assumption, extinguishing the debt, the Sinking Fund, the centrifugal tendency of the United States, revenue, American credit, the frontier, the Whiskey Rebellion, speculation, land sales, stock ownership by foreigners, circulation of money, and government bonds as active capital.

See main text §2.2.3.1, §3.4., and §3.10.2, and Sylla and Cowen, *Alexander Hamilton on Finance, Credit, and Debt,* Chapter 17.

> It is easy to perceive that such a heretogenous mass of opinions not merely speculative but actuated by different interests and passions could not fail to produce much embarrassment to the person who was to devise the plan of a provision for the public debt—if he had been provident enough to sound the ground and probe the state of opinions.
>
> It was proper for him to endeavour to unite two ingredients in his plan, intrinsic goodness [and] a reasonable probability of success.
>
> It may be thought that the first was his only concern—that he ought to have devised such a plan as appeared to him absolutely the best leaving its adoption or rejection to the chance of events and to the responsibility of those whose province it was to decide.
>
> But would not this have been to refine too much? If a plan had been offered too remote from the prevailing opinions—incapable of conciliating a sufficient number to constitute a majority—what would have been the consequences? The Minister would have been defeated in his first experiment. Before he had established any reputation for a knowlege of the business of his department, he might be sure that the blame of his ill-success would have fallen on his want of skill not upon the ignorance or perverseness of those who had rejected his plan.
>
> https://founders.archives.gov/documents/Hamilton/01-19-02-0001

24. 1801, 3/21: ADDRESS TO THE ELECTORS OF NEW YORK STATE

Includes discussion of the centrifugal tendency of the United States, the Federalists vs. Antifederalists in New York State, the Quasi-War with France, revenue, debt, the funding system (including discrimination, assumption, and extinguishment), the frontier, military expenses, the Jay Treaty, the Sedition law, Indian hostilities, the Whiskey Rebellion, and Fries's Rebellion,

See main text §4.1.5, opening of Chapter 8, and §8.5.5.

> In regard to these sects, which compose the pith and essence of the antifederal party, we believe it to be true, that the contest between us is indeed a war of principles—a war between tyranny and liberty, but not between monarchy and republicanism. It is a contest between the tyranny of jacobinism, which confounds and levels every thing, and the mild reign of rational liberty, which rests on the basis of an efficient and well balanced government, and through the medium of stable laws, shelters and protects, the life, the reputation, the prosperity, the civil and religious rights of every member of the community.
>
> https://founders.archives.gov/documents/Hamilton/01-25-02-0197

25. 1801-1802: THE EXAMINATION, 18 ESSAYS

Published in the *New-York Evening Post* from 12/17/1801 to 4/8/1802. An extensive critique of Jefferson.

See main text §4.3 and opening of Chapter 8.

No. 1, 12/17/1801: Introduction.

> The Message of the President, by whatever motives it may have been dictated, is a performance which ought to alarm all who are anxious for the safety of our Government, for the respectability and welfare of our nation. It makes, or aims at making, a most prodigal sacrifice of constitutional energy, of sound principle, and of public interest, to the popularity of one man.
>
> https://founders.archives.gov/documents/Hamilton/01-25-02-0264-0002

No. 4, 12/26/1801: Includes discussion of domestic and foreign debt, the funding plan, why funds must be pledged to extinguish the debt, and the excise tax on liquor.

> To a government, the character of which has not yet been established by time, the example of sudden and questionable innovations, may be expected to be in the highest degree detrimental. Prudent men every where are apt to take the alarm at great changes not manifestly beneficial and proper; a disposition which has been much increased by the terrible events of the present revolutionary æra. Yet, disregarding these salutary and obvious reflections, the President has ventured, in the very infancy of his administration, upon the bold and unjustifiable step of recommending to the legislative body, a renunciation of the whole internal revenue of the country; though the nation is at this moment encumbered with a considerable public debt; and though that very revenue, is, by the existing laws, an established fund for its discharge.
>
> https://founders.archives.gov/documents/Hamilton/01-25-02-0269

No. 9, 1/18/1802: Includes discussion of citizenship and naturalization, the centrifugal tendency of the United States, and the federal government's proper functions.

> [T]o the care of the Federal Government are confided directly, those great general interests on which all particular interests materially depend: our safety in respect to foreign nations; our tranquility in respect to each other; the foreign and mutual commerce of the states; the establishment and regulation of the money of the country; the management of our national finances; indirectly, the security of liberty by the guarantee of a republican form of government to each state; the security of property by the interdiction of laws violating the obligation of contracts &

> issuing the emissions of paper money under state authority; (from both of which causes the right of property had experienced serious injury); the prosperity of agriculture and manufactures as intimately connected with that of commerce, and as depending in a variety of ways upon the agency of the general Government: In a word, it is the province of the general Government to manage the greatest number of those concerns in which its provident activity and exertion are of most importance to the people; and we have only to compare the state of our country antecedent to its establishment, with what it has been since, to be convinced that the most operative causes of public prosperity depend upon that general Government. It is not meant, by what has been said, to insinuate that the state Governments are not extremely useful in their proper spheres; but the object is to guard against the mischiefs of exaggerating their importance in derogation from that of the general Government. Every attempt to do this is, remotely, a stab at the Union of these states; a blow to our collective existence as one people—and to all the blessings which are interwoven with that sacred fraternity.
>
> https://founders.archives.gov/documents/Hamilton/01-25-02-0286

No. 18, 4/8/1802: Includes discussion of what was achieved under Federalist presidents, debt, revenue, the funding system, the frontier, the Barbary pirates, and extinguishing the debt.

> Upon this anticipation the assumption of the state debts, and other apparently bold measures of the government were avowedly predicated, in opposition to the feeble & contracted views of the little politicians, who now triumph in the success of their arts, and enjoy the benefits of a policy, which they had neither the wi[s]dom to plan nor the spirit to adopt—idly imagining that the cunning of a demagogue and the talents of a statesman are synonymous. Consummate in the paltry science of courting and winning popular favor, they falsely infer that they have the capacity to govern, and they will be the last to discover their error. But let them be assured that the people will not long continue the dupes of their pernicious sorceries.
>
> https://founders.archives.gov/documents/Hamilton/01-25-02-0316

APPENDIX 6

Select Bibliography

This list includes the scholarly works I found most helpful.

Brookhiser, Richard. *Alexander Hamilton, American.* Simon & Schuster, 1999.

Cowen, David Jack. *The Origins and Economic Impact of the First Bank of the United States.* Garland Publishing, 2000.

Federici, Michael P. *The Political Philosophy of Alexander Hamilton.* Johns Hopkins University, 2012.

Ferguson, E. James. *The Power of the Purse: A History of American Public Finance, 1776-1790.* For the Omohundro Institute of Early American History and Culture by the University of North Carolina Press, 1961.

Gordon, John Steele. *An Empire of Wealth, The Epic History of American Economic Power.* Harper Collins, 2004.

Gordon, John Steele. *Hamilton's Blessing: The Extraordinary Life and Times of Our National Debt.* Walker and Company, 1997.

Holloway, Carson. "Debating Alexander Hamilton's Case for American Manufacturing Greatness." Law and Liberty, 8/2/2017.

> https://lawliberty.org/forum/debating-alexander-hamiltons-case-for-american-manufacturing-greatness/

Holloway, Carson. *Hamilton versus Jefferson in the Washington Administration: Completing the Founding or Betraying the Founding?* Cambridge University Press, 2015.

Holloway, Carson. "The Myth of Hamiltonian Big Government." The Daily Signal, 4/23/2015.

> https://www.dailysignal.com/2015/04/23/the-myth-of-hamiltonian-big-government/

Irwin, Douglas A. "The Aftermath of Hamilton's 'Report on Manufactures'." National Bureau of Economic Research, Working Paper 9943. August 2003.

McDonald, Forrest. *Alexander Hamilton: A Biography.* W.W. Norton, 1979.

Nelson, John R., Jr. *Liberty and Property: Political Economy and Policymaking in the New Nation, 1789-1812.* Johns Hopkins University, 1987.

Newton, Michael. *Alexander Hamilton: The Formative Years.* Eleftheria Publishing, 2015.

Newton, Michael. *Angry Mobs and Founding Fathers: The Fight for Control of the American Revolution.* Eleftheria Publishing, 2011.

Newton, Michael. *Discovering Hamilton: New Discoveries in the Lives of Alexander Hamilton, His Family, Friends, and Colleagues, From Various Archives Around the World.* Eleftheria Publishing, 2019.

Parenti, Christian. *Radical Hamilton: Economic Lessons from a Misunderstood Founder.* Verso, 2020.

Pisasale, Gene. *Alexander Hamilton, Architect of the American Financial System.* Gene Pisasale / Historic Insights, 2017.

Rappleye, Charles. *Robert Morris: Financier of the American Revolution.* Simon & Schuster, 2010.

Sambasivam, Richard. "What Do Bond Prices Tell Us About the Early Republic?" Journal of the American Revolution, 8/25/2016.

https://allthingsliberty.com/2016/08/bond-prices-tell-us-early-republic/

Sylla, Richard. *Alexander Hamilton, The Illustrated Biography.* Sterling, 2016.

Sylla, Richard, and David J. Cowen. *Alexander Hamilton on Finance, Credit, and Debt.* Columbia University, 2018.

Sylla, Richard, Robert E. Wright, and David J. Cowen. "Alexander Hamilton, Central Banker: Crisis Management during the U.S. Financial Panic of 1792." *Business History Review* (Harvard College), v. 83, no. 1 (Spring 2009), pp. 61-86.

https://www.jstor.org/stable/40538573

Taylor, George Rogers. "American Economic Growth Before 1840: An Exploratory Essay." *Journal of Economic History* v. 24, no. 4 (December 1964), pp. 427-444.

Wolfe, Peter. *Alexander Hamilton: His Early Financial and Economic Thinking.* Opus, 2016.

Wright, Robert F., and David J. Cowen. *Financial Founding Fathers: The Men Who Made America Rich.* University of Chicago, 2006.

Wright, Robert F. *The First Wall Street: Chestnut Street, Philadelphia and the Birth of American Finance.* University of Chicago, 2005.

Wright, Robert E. *Hamilton Unbound.* Contributions in Economics and Economic History, No. 228. Greenwood Press, 2002.

Wright, Robert E. *One Nation Under Debt: Hamilton, Jefferson, and the History of What We Owe.* McGraw-Hill Education, 2008.

About the Author

At age 7, I won my first writing award: a three-foot-long fire truck with an ear-splitting siren. I've been addicted to writing ever since. As an independent researcher, freelance writer, and lecturer, I indulge my curiosity and share my delight in art and history. This is my fifth volume on Alexander Hamilton; the others are *Alexander Hamilton: A Brief Biography, Alexander Hamilton: A Friend to America* (2 volumes), and *Alexander Hamilton and the Reynolds Affair*. On art history, I've recently published *Innovators in Sculpture* and *Innovators in Painting*, as well as *Getting More Enjoyment from Sculpture You Love*. Sam Roberts of the *New York Times* called my *Outdoor Monuments of Manhattan: A Historical Guide* (New York University Press, 2007) "a perfect walking-tour accompaniment to help New Yorkers and visitors find, identify and better appreciate statues famous and obscure." For an up-to-date list of my books and essays, visit DianneDuranteWriter.com/ books-essays.

www.ingramcontent.com/pod-product-compliance
Lightning Source LLC
Chambersburg PA
CBHW071852290426
44110CB00013B/1119